The SCHOOL of FEMININITY

MARY WOLLSTONECRAFT
(Mrs. William Godwin)

The SCHOOL of FEMININITY

*A Book For and About Women As They
Are Interpreted Through Feminine
Writers of Yesterday and Today*

By MARGARET LAWRENCE

ILLUSTRATED

KENNIKAT PRESS, INC./PORT WASHINGTON, N. Y.

THE SCHOOL OF FEMININITY

Copyright 1936 by Frederick A. Stokes Company
Reissued in 1966 by Kennikat Press

Library of Congress Catalog Card No: 66-25924

Analysed in the ESSAY & GENERAL LITERATURE INDEX

CONTENTS

ILLUSTRATIONS

FOREWORD

The School of Femininity is not an all-inclusive résumé of the writing of women. Neither is it an academic nor exclusive study of only the very finest aspects of the writing done by women.

It is a pattern of thought, vaguely resembling a theory, and has been traced through the writing of those women in which it is to be found in great part or in small part since the beginning of the feminist revolt.

The pattern is followed through the writing of certain selected women using English in the fiction form during the nineteenth and twentieth centuries. There is one exception in the inclusion of Mary Wollstonecraft, who did not write fiction but prose essays. This inclusion is justified on the ground of the impact of her ideas upon all women since her time.

There are many popular writers among women who have not been brought into this study. No slight is intended. The selection has been based entirely upon the appearance of the feminist pattern in the work of the women presented.

The writers of the nineteenth century have been treated with fuller detail. In their cases the evidence is all in. In the cases of the twentieth-century writers it is not all in. Most of them are still writing. Some of them have only begun to write. Nearly all of them will continue in the general course of events to write for some time. The material, therefore, of all the contemporary writers classes itself as tentative evidence, and has to be handled tentatively. For this reason the modern pattern of feminism in *The School of Femininity* has been restricted in most cases to what may be called a "key book." From these "key books" the contribution of the author to *The School of Femininity* has been appraised.

The pattern of thought is this—that women for the first time in history upon a large scale are saying their particular say about themselves, about men, and about life as it treats them separately and together with men. In *The Twentieth-Century School of Femininity* the writers have been listed in groups. The grouping is in no sense arbitrary. There are writers who are blends of the various groups, and there are other writers who, by reason of continued development, elude any final placing of them in a group. The classification has been used merely to facilitate the isolation of a contributing idea or set of ideas in a general school of feminine writing.

MARGARET LAWRENCE.

PART I

THE NINETEENTH-CENTURY SCHOOL OF FEMININITY

~~~~~~

The SCHOOL *of* FEMININITY

~~~~~~

CHAPTER I

WE WRITE AS WOMEN

SAPPHO WROTE HER BEAUTIFUL lyrics, and then there was a long silence. It was a silence broken here and there by the letters women wrote, and the diaries they kept, but they were personal, and so we do not have them to show as the writing of women. The little songs that were made to sing to children, the little phrases made to say to a lover, all these were of the very fabric of a woman's expression of herself, but they could not be kept as literature. They were too fleeting. They were like prayers, something a woman would not think of putting down to show. But there must have been many of them.

There is a legend from Tudor days which tells why it was that women attempted no formal intellectual composition. It tells us that Margaret More, the young daughter of Sir Thomas More, wanted to help in the great work of Erasmus, her father's friend. Erasmus was making a new Latin translation of the New Testament, and Margaret, who was, as Erasmus himself said, "an elegant Latinist," decided she would make the concordance. One day her father found her in tears over the work. He took the manuscript gently from her, and explained to her that such was not a woman's work. It would take, he said, too much of her energy to sustain the enterprise to the end. Sir Thomas did not use the words we would use now in describing the difference between the nervous equipment of men and women, yet he made it very clear to Margaret that there was a

3

difference. He was kind, and said he was proud of her desire to do the task, but to allow her to do it would be a mistake. It would consume her, he explained, and leave no residue either of emotion, or thought, and that would be very sad for her happiness as a woman. Women, he taught her, must save all their energies for the race. With his fine clear perception of things he turned her imagination softly away from scholarship, and directed it upon one whom he called "yon tall stripling," and Margaret, who adored her father, believed him to be right, and obeyed him.

Women in general were like Margaret More, and accepted a man's version of their womanhood.

Until the feminist revolt.

The feminist revolt began suddenly at the end of the eighteenth century. Yet it was not a sudden or separated tide of emotion in women. It was part of a gradual change of consciousness brought about by the development of skepticism. Which makes it difficult to isolate the movement as a study in itself.

When the French people began to question, and to upset ordained customs about class and the distribution of power, they said nothing about the particularized injustices of women. However, when one accepted social idea gets questioned, so do others. "Who decreed fixed class inequalities?" "Who, then, laid down the habit of assuming that women could never be the equals of men?"

It was a rhetorical question. The answer was that history showed no women who looked as if they were the equals of men. Women had designed no buildings, and no bridges. They had sailed no ships. They had written neither books nor music. They had never sculptured images for the churches to which they went to pray, nor made pictures for their homes. Not one word of prophecy had ever been uttered by a woman, and there were very few saints among them. There was no fertility in women, except as the earth was fertile, taking the seed that was put into it, and reproducing it in its kind. So, men general-

ized, from Buddha to the lowest male slave, from princes to
the humblest soldiers, about women. And women let it be at
that until the end of the eighteenth century.

Suddenly it was all irritating to women. It is not easy to
explain the sudden arrival of the irritation. But, as one century
turned into a new century, women began to feel inferior about
not having done what men had done in the world. They forgot
that there was nothing, after all, to feel inferior about. There
had been great buildings and highways in Babylon. There had
been art and religion. Maybe there was music and literature.
But what was left of Babylon? Nothing except a memory.
There was very little left of Greece, and still less of Egypt.
That is—of their cultures. But the race had survived. What
were theories of government? Or of religion? Things that the
race played with. Things that disappeared with time like
buildings and roads. But the race went on, and to have kept
it going on through wars, through the sicknesses that follow
wars, and through all the accidents of living which make it
hard for little children to grow up, this had been real work,
and lasting work, and eternally creative work. It had been the
work of women. And nothing else had mattered so very much.

But it began to matter to women that they had taken no part
in the other things. Because it was the other things that men
counted as achievements. They took the survival of the race
for granted. They were not in the main respectful towards
the racial function of women. They paid women only one respect, and that was to keep them out of the wars, and to some
extent out of economics. But that extent was lessening. And
it was upon this lessening extent that the feminist movement
gathered its force. If girls were to be turned out of their homes
to earn their own way, then they would have to push themselves into the places of education and opportunity. Earning
a living took preparation. When girls opened the books which
their brothers studied they found they could also learn them,
and sometimes with more ease than their brothers exhibited.
What then was to prevent them from doing everything men

did in the world, and eventually getting some political recognition? They began to think that maybe the only reason they had not built buildings, and put bridges up, and made songs and stories, was that they had never thought very much about trying. They thought next about the unsaid thoughts of women all down through the centuries. There was so little they had to go upon. The women who were in the histories were the women whom men had cause to remember.

They were the Queens and the Courtesans.

Cleopatra, with her amorous stride, and her drooped eyelids; immutable Greek Helen, with her shadow still lingering in the dreams of men; Mary Stuart, with her heart-shaped, heart-moving exquisite sad face; witty Nell Gwynn, with her exhilarating laughter. True there had been an Aspasia, giving counsel as well as pleasure to a Greek ruler; there had been Héloïse, the scholarly equal of her lover; there had been that inscrutable magnificent actress among the Tudors, playing with men, and using them well to her own advantage—Elizabeth.

There were great ladies always surrounding the men of history, the conduct of whose lives demanded an art so delicate there was no time for other arts. Surely these women must have thought, and sometimes have written their thoughts down for keeping. But no. The thoughts of women were something they hid carefully. Even Elizabeth's thoughts. It was better to draw out the thoughts of men. For thoughts never held men to women. Except their own masculine thoughts, such as were expressed with confidence to a grateful feminine audience. That was the art of the great lady. To provide beauty for men when they wanted beauty, and interest when they wanted interest, and even solitude when they wanted that. This was the technique of a woman in her salon. It was thought held in control and unexpressed. It brought men to the height of their powers.

It was all very well, perhaps, for the great lady in her salon, women, turning it over in their minds, concluded to themselves. Except that it was tinged with harlotry. Even intellectual harlotry. The woman must always please the man. For her kingdom might be lost by the untimely lift of an amused eyebrow. And then she would have nothing to show for all the infinite human art of it, and the patience, and even for the love.

But there were other women besides great ladies and harlots. There were the women of the middle class. It was these women who took to the idea of "rights." The great lady would never have toyed with the idea. She had too many compensating privileges. The harlot would never have bitten into the idea. She was too busy. It was the middle-class women also who took to the novel. The great lady would have written memoirs. For there was no need to create fiction when what went on in her salon was completely entertaining. The harlot would have written text books. She knew there was still a lot to be learned. Nevertheless, it was through the influence of the great lady, and also through the influence of the harlot, that "rights" came to have their vogue. In the salons of France skepticism got its grooming. Polished minds derided with pointed sallies the dug-in ideas of people, and met applause. Intellectual reputations were made under the clever social guidance of very feminine salonnières. And the ideas sponsored by these intellectuals spread from the socially impeccable folk who used them decoratively out to others who put them into practical application. The harlot fed the vanity of men, and pushed them to extremes, and collected from them in extremes. Between ideas and collections the French Revolution was precipitated. And from the French Revolution the feminist movement was produced.

Not that the revolutionary leaders in their progressive phases wanted to make the position of women in the state more powerful. The bad influence of women in higher places was too well known. Feminine vanity, feminine short-sightedness, and feminine acquisitiveness were things to be controlled. There had been only one Jeanne d'Arc, and there had been too many Pompadours.

But in England the revolutionary platform of liberty, equality and fraternity was interpreted by a woman to include women. This was Mary Wollstonecraft.

The skeptic's question, "Who said so?" raged in her blood. She dismissed all the waywardness of women with power when they did get it by the explanation that it was the result of having to scheme shamefully to get it. Having to wangle everything through the pleasuring of men was at the root of all wrong that might be in women. So she was convinced. And up against the comparatively few women who, by reason of superlatively endowed bodies and superlatively crafty minds, did get something out of men, she put the generations of ordinary women who got nothing. Sex, she was certain, was only a part of a woman's life, as it was of a man's; but civilization had brought it about that it had to be the lever of everything to her. When she had to use it constantly and calculatingly, it twisted her nature out of its normal. It was pitifully unnecessary, and it destroyed the honesty between men and women. The worst of it all to Mary Wollstonecraft was that it was in the women of the biggest intellectual capacity that the twist was most likely to be socially dangerous. "Give us freedom," she wrote flamingly in her *Vindication of the Rights of Women*. "Let us be direct," and then there would be no more female barnacles, and no more corroding of the feminine imagination.

It was the cry of a very young woman who thought that civilization could begin again. "Male and female created He them." She made it a cause, and the rich emotional appeal of her book made her famous throughout England, and fixed her ideas in the minds of other women. Thousands of women stirred in their dissatisfactions. Here was something they could pin their dissatisfaction upon. But how could they go about getting free? There was so little a middle-class woman could do. She could marry. If she did not marry, then she was just unfortunate. She could look after the children of other women. She could teach these children, or she could sew. But both teaching and sewing demanded definite inclinations and some amount of training. This was too bad. Because it was usually only after she had failed in due time to get herself married that a woman had to think of what she could do to support herself. Gradually women found they could write. Writing after all was not so different from talking. You just set down what you heard around you, and what you would say yourself. Novels were only a further development of the gossip of women. The art of it was in managing to transfer to paper the impression of reality. Women thought of the letters they had written to relatives describing the doings of their small communities—what he said to her, what she wished he had said instead—what she did to make herself secure in his affections—what it might have been that came between them—and how this woman or that one took charge of all the family. It was not so hard. It could be done bit by bit. And it might make money. For people liked to read about other people. Just as they liked to talk about them.

In the first of the English novels by women there are two currents. Varyingly the underfeeling of sexual resentment seeps through to the surface, though for the most part it is held in with creditable artistic restraint. It is creditable in that women were new to their writing, and, like all new writers of every age, they were using their own experience for their material, and personal experience is inevitably set down at the beginning with all its accompanying emotionalism. But in another way the restraint is not so creditable. It was habitual with women. It was their tradition and their motivation. Exemplary resignation. But here and there it breaks down in the writing, as often it must have broken down in individual cases of temperamental hysteria. This is to be seen in the studies of the various writers and in their various books. The same writer will let herself go in one book, and pull herself back in another; feeling herself along to a kind of middle emotional and artistic way. This remains true until to-day.

For it is only in a few of the modern women writers that the feminist movement is over. Only a few of them treat writing as art. With most of them it is still a most personal matter to write, as well as a way of making money. Which is not in any way condemning the women writers or their writing. It makes the reading of them still a business of feminist research and a journey of psychological discovery. And that is highly entertaining, as well as profoundly engrossing.

After all it is not such a long time since it began—only a century and a half. In a study of them taken as a body we may omit the odd woman who wrote before the time of Mary Wollstonecraft. This can be done safely for the simple reason that what they wrote has not lived, except to the historian diligently interested in obscure premature signs of a coming force.

From the time of Mary Wollstonecraft until to-day the writing of women has gathered itself into a mass of literary material, and is a vital provocative moving field of study. It may seem at first that it is an artificially exaggerated policy to separate the writing of the women of any time from the writing of the men of that same time. Women are influenced, it may be claimed justly, by the work of the men of their decade, or two decades, just as they are influenced by the current events of it, and the changing aspects of the economic and psychological world. That would be so, if the feminist movement were not still a factor in the thoughts of the women writers, and a factor that stands larger than any other factor of influence. It would also be finally true if the writing of women were not so distinctly feminine as it is, both in the psychological current of it, and in the technique. There is a peculiar feminine quality to nearly all of it, if not absolutely all, which makes it as safe as it ever can be safe to generalize. Taken altogether from the time of Mary Wollstonecraft and Miss Austen to the time of Pearl Buck and Edna Ferber, it represents a stream of feminine consciousness which we may study as the writing of *woman*. The individual writers of our time vary, as the Brontë sisters varied from Miss Austen, and as George Eliot varied from all the others. The variations are slight and subtle, but quite definite. The observer has to watch closely all the writings as they come freshly out of women to see all the modifications. She has to watch from the mental distance of some historical awareness, otherwise it is not possible to relate the writing of one woman to the writing of other women. The watcher has also to have some comprehension of the meaning of the discoveries of Freud in relation to the sexuality of women. There are times when, between what history discloses and what Freud suggests, one might improve upon Ecclesiastes, and lament, "Vanity of vanities; all is sex." But there are other times when one may realize that in the century and a half women have been writing they have set down enough of what drives them emotionally, and of what passes in their minds, to bring the race much closer to an understanding of itself, and perhaps a little nearer to easing the pain there is between men and women.

After women have put down all the pent-up sorrows of womanhood in a world made for men by men; and after they have satisfied themselves that they can hold whatever they want to get in that world, we shall be racially much further on, no matter what conclusions we may draw tentatively, or finally, about women and their work.

For the present we are in the middle of a period of commercial feminism which would have astonished Plato, who in the memory of the race was the first man to take the cause of women to mind. And what it would do to John Stuart Mill, who in the nineteenth century championed women, is an idea for idle cogitation.

If Plato could meet Mr. Mill in front of a news-stand in any big city in America, and if both of them were to flip over the pages of women's magazines, and read the advertising sections of them, what they might say commentatively to each other would be highly enlightening. The slogan of "equality" is tantalizing when set against all the sales pressure and the astute publicity directed towards the modern purchaser of most modern manufactures—the woman. It is a world from which Plato would retreat back into the shades. And Mill, we may be certain, would wish frantically for some modern incarnation of his good friend, Mrs. Taylor, to interpret for him. No woman, he would gather, or at least no proportionate representation of women, in the counsels of state government—yet practically the whole of business aimed at her sales resistance. No woman in the Church in a position of power—yet the most of the current publications modeled to suit her taste in feeling and in thought. Very little law-giving among women, but plenty of the payment of taxes. Only occasionally creative art. But lots of commercial presentations of what women like to look upon themselves as being—pretty girls on magazines—pretty girls with so little in their faces; nothing of suffering—nothing of inner poise—but admirable wearing of clothes. Still no building of bridges or cathedrals, but quite a lot of flying. Plato would marvel that after all it was not government, but rather the adventure of commerce which had attracted women. Why? Maybe he would remember Xantippe, who had resented Socrates sitting around asking philosophical questions. Were women always practical?

"'Decorate your finger nails. The institute of finger nail beauty has a new hibiscus shade.' Listen to this advertisement," Mill would say excitedly to Plato. "'Your husband's stenographer puts adorable shades on her finger nails—try it yourself—maybe he will stay at home if you make the home as bright as his office.'" "It is intimidation." But Plato would smile patiently, and remind him that it had been done by the courtesans of Greece quite some time ago, only the color then was called *pomegranate*. Still would Mill be upset about it. This was not what he had thought women would do with their freedom—to allow themselves to be scared into buying things. Plato would counsel him to look at it fatalistically. After all, women still had to hold the men. The body had an effective appeal. Page after page they would turn. Garments to make the figures of women svelte, liquids to make their mouths sweet, gossamer silk hose to give glamour to their legs. "Gossamer," Plato would repeat resignedly. "That is poetry. Yes, poetry used for commercial advertising, and advertising used to promote the sexual interests of women, and sex producing the feeling of poetry in the mind. An everlasting circle." While he was meditating upon this, Mill would discover that the fiction in the magazines was very excellent fiction. He would undertake to explain to Plato the use of fiction as an attractive way of keeping the data of romance. But Plato by this time would be preparing to disappear back into the mysterious place of death. He had learned enough. Mill would continue his reading. He was a sentimental man, and women had always interested him. He would like the way the modern woman was gathering romantic and practical facts concerning herself in the magazines. Over his shoulder two other gentlemen would be reading, but he would not be aware of them. They are alive gentlemen, and so not of his exact dimension in time and space. They—Herr Freud and Mr. Sinclair Lewis—being two modern men, who have followed Plato and Mr. Mill in taking a hand in the slow push of the feminist movement. Mill would read on. Stories; stories; very clever technical stories; mostly about love in the lives of modern women. How to combine love with a career in the world; how to keep a man happy without concentrating too hard upon him; how to evolve within the mind a fund of emotional insurance against emotional changes. Does marital security satisfy women—or do they want slightly dangerous romance? Should a woman have the baby she wants by the man she loves regardless of prevailing marriage customs? Mr. Lewis would nod in gratification. It was his story, *Ann Vickers*, that was holding the attention of Mr. Mill longest. Freud would look slightly bored. Fiction was such a circuitous way around. Why must women always have fiction? Could they never get away from their dreams? Well, why should they? Their dreams told everything there was to tell about them. And the new dreams of women were at least more honest dreams. As such it was an advance. "Right you are," Sinclair Lewis might very well say, having himself written the most powerfully honest book concerning women that has been written in our time.

CHAPTER II

MARY WOLLSTONECRAFT

Who Walked an Emotional Tight Rope

MARY WOLLSTONECRAFT MIGHT have been as docile as Margaret More if she had been born the child of a man like Sir Thomas More. But it happened that she was born the child of a man who strutted in all the pretensions of masculine superiority, without producing any of the results of it.

So Mary began to think very early that they were pretensions utterly unfounded upon fact.

The more she thought about it, the more indignant she became. She hated lies, and, out of indignation that was personal, and hatred that was intellectually related to a profound sense of justice, she generalized from a particular case to a whole field of biological law. It was natural. She was an ardent young person, and she did not like what she saw around her.

Her father was the head of his family. But she had to get out and earn her own living. There was no sense, therefore, in his taking it upon himself to tell her what she might, or might not, do. Economies had made the tribal rule an empty shadow. There was no wisdom in letting that shadow remain lingering around. It could be blown away. It would take, of course, quite some power to blow it away, but it could be done.

It was only a pretty idea, which pleased men.

The sinister effect of it, though, was hard to shake off. Mary raged at it. Girls were brought up in its power. So were boys. It made the girls economically inadequate to what was before them. It made boys unnecessarily conceited. Girls were given no education that would prepare them for earning their own

14

living. Boys were given more education often than they could
personally make use of.

Mary went on raging inwardly as she moved from one position to another. She was a governess. She knew she had not
had sufficient training. She held her positions well enough because of her quick adaptable mind, but she realized how thin a
front she was putting up. She was angry at being forced to be
part of the vicious scheme of things. It was like this. Girls
were being badly educated by women who themselves had been
badly educated. It was all wrong. It was unjust. So in her
anger she sat down and wrote her first book, *Thoughts on the
Education of Daughters*. It was the year 1786; Mary was
twenty-five, and the French Revolution was gathering in the
etheric waves. The text of her book was co-education.

A publisher in London, Joseph Johnson, saw a touch of some
kind of genius in Mary Wollstonecraft's thinking and writing.
He decided it would be a good wager to help her. He told her
that teaching was short-circuiting her, and he gave her enough
work editorially and in the writing of pamphlets to make it
possible for her to give up teaching and settle herself in London
as a woman of letters. Mary was an attractive young woman.
Her indignation had not made her bitter. It had merely given
her a personal eagerness which was charming. She was almost
instantly popular socially among the brilliant men who were
Johnson's friends and clients, as well as customers. Mary became more and more winning, and she began to have a little
more confidence in the pretensions of men. This was to have its
effect later on in her life.

Then the French Revolution burst upon an astonished world.
Edmund Burke in England published his opinions upon it. It
was a menace, he said. It was not just a concern of France. It
would spread, challenging established order. Particularly established property. Mary Wollstonecraft wrote an answer to
Burke. She was in sympathy with the Revolution, both in its
theory and in its fact. She knew about social differences and
what they do to the minds of people. She had been a governess

in a castle once. She did not wonder at the determined rage of the French middle class. Johnson published her answer to Burke in a pamphlet called *A Vindication of the Rights of Man.* It was virile writing. It was the inescapable subject of the time. It made Mary Wollstonecraft famous in England, and it led to her great book.

It—*The Vindication of the Rights of Women*—pushed her into history. It made her the trumpeter of femininity.

Women, she said, are the equals of men. Sex is only a part of their functioning, even as it is with men. To make life a sexual enterprise for women has been the sin of civilization against women. And also against the race. For the race, she was certain, could rise no higher than its women.

The book astonished England almost as much as the French Revolution did. Men made a joke of it. Women bridled at it. The woman must be a wanton. She must be a disgruntled old maid. She was neither, but that did not matter to the people who talked about her. She must be. How otherwise could she be saying it had ruined women to have to get everything through men.

It was an astonishing book. It was vehement; it was heavily argumentative; and it was ruthlessly persistent in its arguments. It was as if the writer had set up all the men of the world and conducted a debate with them about women. It was magnificent oratorical writing.

Women, she cried, have a right to an economic chance. We had built our theories about them upon another theory which had no actual existence. It was assumed that it was only the reproductiveness of women that mattered; and at the same time reproductiveness in them was not honored, or tended, or trained. She had put her finger upon a truth; and that is what gave her book its impetus into history. The industrial era was beginning. Women would be forced into competition with men, as the industries of the home gave way before the factory. They were not being prepared for it; they were being allowed to grow up thinking men would protect them. It was all wrong. It must be changed.

It had always been wrong anyway, she went on. Women would be the better and the stronger for taking their part in the world. And the sexual side of life would be better for not having so much attention forced upon it. That, of course, would remain to be seen; but Mary Wollstonecraft was very sure of it. She was young. She knew nothing about sexual laws, and still less about sexual lawlessness. She had only a vague instinct to guide her. There were no books to go by. There had been no research. There was only this racial habit of considering women as wives and mothers, or harlots. It could not be right. What about the women who had no chance to be wives and mothers, and no taste for being harlots? There were plenty of women like that. They must have their chance.

Mary herself had taken her chance, and she knew how difficult it was. It was an eager, active, good mind she had, but to get it into use took many, many times the effort it ought to have taken. Simply because she was a woman, and as such was working against the social current. It was social tragedy, she wrote, this anchoring down of the feminine mind to the sexual functioning. What Mary did not realize was that it was more than a social tragedy. It was an inevitable biological tragedy. But there was nobody to show her all the data for this. There was only custom, and custom was something that could be changed. As she thought.

Her book was not only a plea that it might be changed, but also a text book upon how the change might be accomplished.

It should start with the education of girls, she said. So much weight should not be placed upon the silly cultural adornments meant to attract the male. Indifferent artistic talent should be turned to practical outlets. It would be better, she said, to teach women the practice of medicine than to teach them to paint pictures. And sports, she wrote, were very important for the development of strong healthy women. Men, of course,

liked swooning, pale, helpless women, but what about the race?
Men should be educated to like healthy women, who would bear
healthy children. This, though it is commonplace to us to-day,
was startling in her time. All the essential strength of women
had been suppressed, she argued, for the indirect flattering of
the power of the male. It had held the race back. It was
power unevenly proportioned, and it overlooked the significance
of the female in the nurturing of the race. It was a magnificent
debate she put up. Nobody retorted to her that in the improvement of the stock it was the male who counted; that it
was the purity and the potency of the male seed which determined the vitality of the offspring. But if anybody had reminded her of this, she would in all likelihood have written an
extra chapter proving that the human race was not under the
same biological law as the animal race, and that therefore the
argument of the male importance of the stock was not a fixed
and fast argument.

More than the bodies of women, it was their minds that
concerned her. You could not send women out into the competitive world, she reasoned, and expect them to take care of
themselves, if you trained them mentally to fit into a harem.
This was the very point which gave the historic life to her book.
She had touched upon the central fallacy. The fallacy with
which even yet we have not dealt entirely. The equal education she demanded has come. The competitive world she foresaw has absorbed women; but the instinct of the harem is still
entrenched. Women have fought it with economic independence; men have set it aside because the setting aside of it
makes it much easier for them; and women, while they enjoy
independence, subconsciously resent the facility with which men
have accepted that independence. For economic independence
has not the slightest power to alter the biological law which is a
tragic law for women.

Mary Wollstonecraft was to learn this herself. It was almost
as if life set about trying her for what she had said.

There was a gentleman in Johnson's circle called Fuseli. He was a Swiss artist living in London. He had a wife. He also wanted to have Mary Wollstonecraft. But Mary had no flair for circumspectly conducted adultery. She was too ardent. More than that, it was all against her principles. It was too oriental. It was a small harem of two. She hated it. But the man attracted her. So she got out of his way. She went to France to see the Revolution. It would be less dangerous, she thought.

Life got her there. Or rather, a man got her. Gilbert Imlay was an American from the State of Kentucky and an adventurer. He had come over to France to see if he could interest the French government in a project to put the Spaniards completely out of the district of the lower Mississippi. Money and adventure and women by the way; that was life as Gilbert Imlay interpreted it for himself. He was debonair. He was full of *savoir-faire*. He was adroitly talkative. He knew all about how to love. He fascinated Mary Wollstonecraft. It was a tight rope, but she did not know that. Imlay was a dilettante in love, as well as an expert. Mary was very serious about it. She took the tight rope without the balancing stick of sophistication. And without the pliable sustaining slippers of fatalism.

Her passion for Imlay absorbed her. The French Revolution went on around her, but it was not nearly so engrossing as what was happening to her. Historians have cursed Imlay. If Mary had been alone she would have written vividly about what she saw taking place. The few letters she wrote to Johnson and other friends in England remain among the most valuable primary documents of the time. But there were very few of them. She pulled herself together for a time and wrote a study of the Revolution. It is heavy and routine in its presentation. She was laboring to remember she was a political writer, and this is what was expected of her. Her conclusions are most of them borne out by history. She could not help being wise politically. She had economic foresight. Even while she was in love. But the great work of the time was the volume of the letters she wrote to Imlay when he went on business trips away from her.

The Revolution to Imlay was a chance to make money. The Mississippi project fell through, but there were plenty of other projects for an energetic Kentuckian to get into. He rushed from town to town in France seeing about things. Mary was left. alone. She saw the French aristocrats go nonchalantly to their deaths. She heard the somber beating of the death drum as they passed. She felt the intensity of the middle-class people. She saw how the aristocrats' nonchalance bothered them. They wanted drama with death. Just as she wanted drama with the love she had for Imlay. She was getting it. She wrote letters to him. At first they were joyous, the letters of a happy, love-contained woman. She told him about taking the cat to bed with her for comfort, and what the women downstairs said about her advancing pregnancy. She told him how much she loved him, and how she missed him. She confided all her spells of sickness to him. They were the letters of a loving confident wife, even though there had not been any marriage. There could not be a marriage during the Revolution in France. Mary was English; Imlay was American. She was safe passing as an American; but any attempt at a civil marriage would disclose her English birth. England was now at war with revolutionary France. But what did it matter, anyway? They loved each other. Mary believed in the independence of women. So did Imlay. More than she did. Though she did not find that out until later. The letters changed. They became imploring. Imlay went away so often, and stayed away so long. He must make money, he said. It went on for three years. Mary told him about teaching her little girl to ask for her daddy. It was a long-drawn-out agony. Gradually it began to come over Mary that Imlay was not to be brought back by love, either of her or of the small daughter. Imlay was an accomplished side-stepper. He would not put himself on paper as being through. He said he was going to England. So Mary went back to England. It was no better there. Imlay had very soon to go to Norway. Mary went after him to Norway. It was pathetic. Had Mary been a great lady, it would not have been pathetic. She would have been amused. And if she had liked him well enough to try to keep him she would not have written him sad letters, but entertaining letters. She would have held him, if not permanently, at least for much longer than she did. But Mary was not a great lady. She was a sincere middle-class woman. She had determination in love as she had in her profession. She was true to her own emotions. She poured them into her letters, and they remain among the most poignant of the letters of women we have in our history. They were the very best of her writing. Imlay kept them, and later, when he needed money, sold them to Mary's husband, William Godwin. And Godwin, when he needed money, sold them to a publisher. Which is something for women to think about. Not that Mary would have minded. She was literary. She was also dead. So it would not have mattered to her that her heart was put on exhibition. She never knew that these letters of hers threw all the claims of her great book into a shadow. Equality! She was famous. Everything she wrote was published. But she could not hold her man. Not even with the child she had borne to him could she hold him. Not with tears, or signs of her fame, or the writing of letters. If Imlay had been fair it would have been different. Mary could have gathered her courage and faced the fact. That was the very center of her whole philosophy—truth between men and women. She did not know how much she was asking.

At last the inevitable third person told her that Imlay was two-timing her. Mary tried to drown herself. All the historians who have written about her marvel at a woman of her brilliance and success doing this. What was there to drown herself for? One wrong guess. Surely a brilliant woman would be permitted one wrong guess. But it was more than this. More too than the sickening realization of Imlay's consistent lying to her. One man; a lot of lies; bad judgment. No, it was far more than all these. It went back to her book and her creed. Truth between a man and a woman. Equality between men and women. No wonder she threw herself into the river. No wonder she cried when they saved her from the river.

But it was not long until she laughed. She had written during the very worst year of her life a book of travel letters from Norway. When it was published the very thoughtful Mr. William Godwin decided he was in love with its author. He persuaded her he was. He would be a father, he said, to her little girl. Only she must allow him the freedom of a small place of his own to which she must not come. Godwin abounded in ideas about what made men and women get tired of each other. They needed frequent absences. Mary must have smiled. She knew all about absences.

Godwin considered her an engaging companion. She was moody, of course, and given to bursts of wild indignation, as he used to explain indulgently to people. Godwin himself was a cold and well-collected person. He was good for Mary. He did not go in for gestures with love. She liked that. It was a change. Her flaming temperament pleased him. She was so real, and everything else was slightly unreal to Godwin. He enjoyed even her hatred of Imlay, not knowing quite enough about the psychology of sex to interpret that hatred correctly. He felt himself to be very worthy when Mary outlined the story of her life with the sinful Imlay. Godwin assures us in his memoirs about Mary that she told him all about it, and that during the last year of her life she worked upon a novel containing a villain who was Gilbert Imlay in person. Maybe it was. But that is only interesting inasmuch as it suggests that Mary was still in love with him.

Mary Wollstonecraft, as her contemporaries tell us, was a handsome woman with a most winning personality, and a great deal of sex appeal. Her picture painted by John Opie shows a pleasing woman with old-gold hair and golden-brown eyes. Her nose is short and straight, her chin is pointed, and her mouth is a mouth of love, with many temperamental planes in it, and a full lower lip. Her head is held with defiance. Its attitude is defensive. She has eagerness and ardor and vitality. But no reserves. It is not a baffling face. The features do not contradict one another. They are all straightforward and honest. She wears a soft white blouse open at the throat, and a little black velvet cap somewhat like the modern beret, pushed carelessly back to allow some freedom to the golden hair. The portrait tells as much about Mary Wollstonecraft as the letters to Imlay tell. We know why she bored the cavalier Imlay, and why she enchanted the pedantic Godwin. A man would always know where he was at with Mary Wollstonecraft. There was no elusiveness about her. She was like a sunny windy day. As invigorating. And as unmysterious.

This was the woman who gave the first impetus to the feminist movement, who took the cause of women between her full lips and never let it go. Not even when she was in love with Gilbert Imlay and tortured by his evasiveness. For her sorrow was as much for her cause as for herself. She had lived with him in freedom. It was equality, she said. Yet it was no equality. For when he wanted to go, and gave her every sign short of plain blunt matter-of-fact statement, which an intuitive woman or an experienced woman would have known, she begged him to stay. When he left she followed him with beseeching letters. She wanted him back. It was not for the support of her child. Mary Wollstonecraft had always been able to earn enough money to support several members of her family as well as her own self. It was for her own satisfaction she wanted him, and if Imlay had been less of an adventurer she would have held him by sheer perseverance in keeping after him. It is a pity we do not know Imlay's point of view. Even the heartiest of feminists among us may concede that conceivably the love of a rebel like Mary was likely to be totally without artistry. For artistry she would disdain as the technique of the great lady, or the trick of the harlot. To Mary's belief that was all done with. It was all to be fair and open and equal. We may smile to ourselves. Yet it did look as if Mary might be right. For the man that she got after her one sad failure was a much better man in the world's eyes than Imlay; and he agreed with her, and lived up to all her ideas. It looked as if the failure was Imlay's failure, and not hers. For Godwin was everything that Imlay was not. He was a man of some consequence in London, and there was nothing that could not be discussed fairly with him. Mary was grateful to him for his admiration of her, and responded to it with all the power she had in her for response.

Nevertheless, it is significant that during the last year of her life, and while she was carrying Godwin's child, she was focused upon the writing down in fiction of her tragedy with Imlay. Godwin did not mind. She was making a libertine out of Imlay. But also she was trying to get down something about a woman in love. It is a great pity it was never finished, for it would have been an interesting document whether or not it was a good novel.

Mary was then thirty-eight. Which is maturity for a woman. She was mellowed. Hard experience had made her not bitter but kindly. The letters she sent whimsically to Godwin in his retreat are sweet and womanly and touching. She cherished him with feminine tenderness. Godwin wrote afterwards about the cherishing tenderness of Mary. He remembered it more than the exciting brilliance of her.

She died in childbirth.

As she lay in the pain of it, and of the death that was upon her, she wrote to Godwin, hidden in his retreat, little reassuring notes, with no dramatization of herself or her experience in them, notes that are in every way the complete opposite of the letters she wrote to Imlay. They were the letters of a woman who was thinking, even in such agony, of the comforting of the man. So she died, in the old, old tradition of women, against which she had fought, expressing with her last literary gesture the care women have taken through the ages to put aside their own feelings. The pale child she was dying for was the Mary who later became Shelley's Mary, quiet and utterly devoted, with all her mother's fire burnt down in her to one all-consuming capacity for self-sacrifice, and her father's talent for recognizing genius pulled up in her to the practical sustaining of it.

Fuseli, who had loved Mary Wollstonecraft first, said, "Poor Mary." Nobody knows what Imlay said. Godwin was shaken completely out of his poise with grief. Later he saw to it that everything she had written was preserved for women, and for the new age in which they had both believed.

So it is that, because of his respect for her ideas, we have the record of Mary Wollstonecraft's life. Godwin possessed a meticulous regard for historical data. Mary Wollstonecraft, to his way of thinking, had written one of the greatest books that had ever been written. Therefore she was immortal, and everything that concerned her was the property of the race, and not just of him who had been her husband.

It is a really great tragedy that Mary Wollstonecraft should have died at thirty-nine, for she left the threads of her life untied. If she could have lived on until the serenity of age, she might have looked quietly back upon the years of her experience, and maybe have drawn its threads together so that we who followed her might be able to see the pattern of femininity that was woven by her. The threads needed drawing together, and Mary Wollstonecraft, being spiritually honest, would have been able to do it. As it is, we have ourselves to touch the broken threads, and feel their pattern imaginatively.

Her books were records of her inner life.

The Vindication of the Rights of Women is a collection of chaotic chapters written down in six weeks, so Godwin's memoir assures us. It is an impassioned importuning of both men and women for the remaking of a world. To men she said, "Passive and indolent women do not make the best wives." It was a startling announcement. Women themselves took it up, are saying it still, and working upon the assumption that men will come to believe it. To women she said it was better to govern oneself than to govern a man. That also was a startling announcement. Women thought it over. Well—maybe! It was not so practical, of course, things being as they were in the world that men had made for themselves. Over and over again she said that love as it was practised was not the supreme good of women; that confidence and peace of mind were far more to be sought, and they would be attained by taking part in the affairs of the world. Many young writers of our day have picked up that thread, and it has sent thousands of women into activity outside their homes.

But what she admitted in her letters to Gilbert Imlay, and also in the few sweet little notes to Godwin, was something quite different. Nothing else mattered very much to a woman but her relation to a man.

Maybe it should not have been so. But it was so.

All the writing of women in this which has been their age of self-discovery has moved backwards and forwards between these two moods of Mary Wollstonecraft. Godwin was an obedient tool of feminine destiny when he published her letters to Imlay in accompaniment of her great book. It does not matter what his motive may have been. Without them, *The Vindication* would have been a great book. But with them, it is, even as he thought, an immortal book. For it is a tragic piece of writing; a call to war in a war that can never be won.

It is a tragic figure she remains, this woman who led the feminist revolt. She was right in so many things. Industrial competition was upon women. They had to be roused to meet it. That is all *The Vindication* means, for all its rolling grandiose sentences, and the grip its author's fiery spirit managed to get into it in spite of her labored literary style. Women must get themselves ready and fit, and rid themselves of the notions of themselves that would handicap them in the fight. It is not literature. It is teaching. It is a kind of mental drilling for women. But what its author did not realize was that it was drilling them against the instinct of thousands upon thousands of years. Maybe it is too soon to be saying whether or not it has been worth trying, or if, when it has reached its complete trial, it will be right for the race. At the present it is an inevitable movement which has spread even to the Orient. All we can do is to watch the activity of women, particularly in their writing, for women will put down in fiction what they will not say from the platform, or in articles, or even in conversation among themselves. That is why it was such a pity Mary Wollstonecraft's own novel was never finished.

As literature it is her letters that count. They were torn from her. She was using the instinctive writing form of women. The strain of composition is nowhere evident in them. They are the real writing of a woman's spirit. As writing they are fine and pure. As a human document, they state, once and forever, that terrible distance there is between the mind of a woman and the mind of a man in love. This is true of her letters, whether they were the letters to the unworthy Imlay, or those to the very worthy Godwin. In their simplicity, in their pathetic phrasing, the spirit that was in Mary Wollstonecraft found its way to expression with sorrow, and then with compassion. "Everything is cold—cold as my expectations. You see I am hurt. I may perhaps be, some time or other, independent in every sense of the word. Ah, there is but one sense of it of consequence." This is taken from one of her last letters to Imlay. Again, "I cannot tear my affections from you. I think of you. God bless you. May you never know by experience what you have made me endure." These were the words of a woman whom Godwin said "was the greatest ornament her sex ever had to boast." His words, perhaps, are all we need to cherish for Mary's obituary. They were not words written in fresh harsh grief, but out of the memory of many years afterwards, when he had had time to think everything over, and to read the letters she had written to another man, and to look once more at the few little notes she had sent to him.

The relation of Godwin to Mary Wollstonecraft is profoundly interesting. He was utterly devoted to her. He constituted himself the answer and the justification of her creed. "I shall consider women in the grand light of human creatures who, in common with men, are placed on this earth to unfold their faculties." Godwin was proof that men could accept the creed. He could even set aside the overpowering male instinct about virginity and the love his wife had felt for another man. There is only one thing to bring up tentatively which lowers the light of Godwin. Mary was a famous woman; Godwin was vain. "This," he was saying to the world when he published her letters to Imlay, "is how Mary Wollstonecraft could love, but it was a love before the love of me, and she turned to me—I was the man who held her." He was also proving what a bad fellow his predecessor had been, and how fair he himself was, as well as being above jealousy and possessiveness. He was in addition linking himself forever with the immortality of Mary Wollstonecraft. Though none of this matters very much. He was useful in the destiny of the feminist movement.

When we examine the test of *The Vindication* closely, we can see very clearly a revolt that was as much an erotic revolt as it was economic. A whole section is devoted to putting the erotic relationship in its place. She knew nothing about it. All she knew was that it held women in what she considered was subjection to men. That was enough to know. It was therefore bad. She dismissed with an indignant book all the centuries of Oriental experience which taught that the erotic art was the art of women, and motherhood their satisfaction. She saw a race of free women meeting men on their own ground of attainment, working with them, playing games with them, and loving them if they cared to.

She had no conception of the possible effect of such freedom upon men. She could not know that the free woman and the independent woman, out of the very energy it takes to elbow her way in the world, loses some of her erotic attractiveness, unless she is superbly clever histrionically. She did not see far enough ahead to be able to weigh what might be gained in women against what might be lost in men. Nor the effect of that upon the race. That the male fulfilled himself in the admiration of the female, she knew. But she did not know that from his very male nature he could not be enraptured by a

female who could equal him in games or in business. If anyone had told her this was a sexual law, and not just a lazy habit
of male vanity, she could have said in all likelihood, "Well, that
is just too bad, but let the male change." It would have been
easy to say. But it was not so easy to live, as she found later
when she encountered herself the exceedingly male person called
Imlay. And if she really liked it when she did find it in living
with the not-so-male Godwin, she never said. Except that her
continued preoccupation with the failure of her experience
with Imlay during the year of her marriage to Godwin suggests
a lot. It was hardly the natural preoccupation of a woman
erotically satisfied.

The Vindication suffers from being written by a virgin who
knew nothing except by hearsay of the force she was trying to
upset. This was a pity. It throws her book out of line, brave
though it was, and powerful in its effect.

Economically Mary Wollstonecraft was sound. Politically
she was sound. Biologically she was so far off from the truth
that it pushes her ideas out of key. Wisely she pointed out the
deep gap between what was economically due to happen to
middle-class women, and the biological trend of their thinking.
She thought the gap was artificial, and could be closed. What
she could not foresee was that it would have to be bridged, and
that it might just be that a number of different designs of
bridges would have to be experimented with. The middle-class
woman of the nineteenth century in the main followed the
thesis laid down by Mary Wollstonecraft, and some of the
women of the twentieth century closed their eyes and jumped
the gap, and then had to jump back. For the modern woman
it is still a matter of jumping back and forth. Economic need
and biological urging. Professional ambition and erotic satisfaction. Sinclair Lewis, the newest recruit to the feminine
cause, shows it with terrible starkness in *Ann Vickers*. It demands the skill of a tight-rope walker from the circus, and the
endurance of a marathon swimmer, as well as the faith of the
revolutionist. Not to mention the fatalism of the explorer.

Every now and then a woman sits down beside the gap, and looks at it, and says it cannot be bridged. There is no equalizing of the biological law. Not while babies have to be born, as Sinclair Lewis points out, before women are forty. years old. That is the biological tragedy of women as it is called in Russia. It could not be expected that Mary Wollstonecraft should have known this. She knew the facts, but she did not know it was a law so unchanging and inexorable as to make the economic law seem childish. She thought biology could be dealt with to suit economics and a social theory. We know now that it will have to be economic and social theories that are dealt with to meet the requirements of biology.

Mary Wollstonecraft could have learned something from a conversation with Miss Austen. They were almost contemporaries. Miss Austen did not know so much about biology, but she knew a lot about instincts, and she respected them. She would have giggled over *The Vindication*. The biological law she translated politely with her own tongue in her cheek as a matrimonial game. What was the matter with it, she would have asked. It was never boring. It demanded skill. Even the skill of a tight-rope walker from the circus, and the endurance of the marathon swimmer. It needed some amount of faith. And it was just as well to bring fatalism to it, for truly you would not know for certain just what prize you might be taking home from the play. She would have said to Mary Wollstonecraft that the only gain she could see from the economic change for women would be a widening of the arena.

How much clearer Miss Austen's eyes were, time, as it has done with the feminist movement, is proving. Mary Wollstonecraft saw economic activity as something that would free women from having to please men. Miss Austen would have seen it as an opportunity to please more men with more thorough effectiveness, and a chance to select one that was right to the taste, after looking a number over. And what with the way the business woman adorns herself for business, and what with the whole adaptation of modern industry to the keying up of women as personable creatures, it does appear that maybe Miss Austen would have been right.

If the talk between them could have happened after Mary had lived with Imlay, she might have agreed a little with Miss Austen, though perhaps she would have put that experience down as only an initial bad guess about a man. Miss Austen would have giggled again. Perhaps she would have said nothing, but likely she would have made a note of it on a small scrap of paper, that in this game there were only two players, a man and a woman, and none of them altered so very much. Smiling to herself, she would have written it down, feeling sorry for Mary Wollstonecraft. As well she might. For we no longer read Mary. And we do read Miss Austen.

CHAPTER III

JANE AUSTEN

Who Rode a Flirtatious Merry-Go-Round

NOT EVEN TO-DAY IS THERE A
woman writer who has so deftly combined sophistication with
romance as Miss Austen did at the beginning of the nineteenth
century. Nor is there another woman writer down through
the years of women's writing who has been so elusive of herself
in her books. If she did set herself in the six novels, as they
tell us women always do when they write, it is very much as
if she did it with a light laugh, and said to her readers, "Find
me—if you can—I dare you." Her family helped to preserve
the hiding. With determined reticence they destroyed most
of her letters. It is as if they said soberly, "Here are the
novels, but we shall be damned if we let you have the personal
life of our eminent one." It was admirable. It saves Miss
Austen from all the new biographers who would, if they
could, get after her and show us all her abnormalities. It is
just too bad for them that her life gives them no hint. It lies
in its elusiveness and in its reserve secure from the psychological ghouls.

We do know that she was born into a family of scholars and
gentlefolk. The Austens were an old family compactly established in scholarship and gentle breeding for generations. The
sons were sent to Oxford. They entered the church or the
navy. The Leighs, from whom her mother came, were also of
fine blood and cultivation. Neither the Austens nor the Leighs
were aristocrats, but they were of the highest middle class.
Miss Austen's father was a rector who turned out polished intellectual sermons, and occasionally wrote a chaste literary essay.
Her mother was known to her family and the circle of her

friends as a wit. They tell us that she was unusually gifted as a writer of amusing letters. All of the children wrote naturally for the entertainment of one another. But none of them, so far as we know, burned with a desire for a career in letters. They were perfectly self-contained. And perfectly self-satisfied, probably. They had very little awareness of other planes of society, either above them or below them. They were not indignant about anything. They all had the feeling of comedy in living. They were sophisticates in a gentle way. In all likelihood they were also lightly skeptical, and in possession of the conservatism that goes with skepticism. They accepted family and class and a small community as a quite comfortable arrangement of existence. They had plenty of fun observing one another, and in noting the small variations from day to day in the characters of those in their immediate vicinity. The sailors went to their ships, but they came back, and girls could marry them. The young clergymen went up to Oxford, but they also came back, and girls could settle down with them. Estates were managed. Nobody was unduly rich. Nobody was distressingly poor. Nobody tried to climb out of one class into another. So there was no social strain. Sometimes one of the young men would fall into bad company when he was away from home, and spend more money than he had to spend. But there was always someone to fix his debts for him. Sometimes an odd flighty girl would take a trip with a young man, but there was always a family united behind her to make the young man come to line with her in honorable matrimony. Everyone went to church on Sunday mornings. But nobody went in for extravagant religious emotionalism. The business of life was to be comfortable and reasonably cultivated.

This was the background of Miss Austen. It is very nearly all we have to go on concerning her. Against this background there flits a personality that is the most evasive personality in all our literary history, except that of Shakespeare. It lights here, and it lifts there, never still long enough to study with precision and in detail. Miss Austen, a volatile histrionic being caught in that most baffling of all temperamental currents—the literary consciousness.

Contemporary comments upon her are so contradictory, one to the other, that they add to the confusion. One woman said that Miss Austen was a giddy person who liked to flirt with men, and who would rather dance than do anything else. She never answered a question seriously, this woman averred, but put the questioner on the defensive by a bit of flippant conversational fencing. Another woman said she was a prim sharp-tongued old maid. One relative said Miss Austen was a sweet lovable creature who never said an unkind thing to anyone. Another relative admitted that she had destroyed the famous lady's letters to her because they were of such an ill-nature that they would do her no amount of good. One record has it that she used to sit silently in social gatherings, gaining her copy by persistent observation. Another maintains that she was a most delightful person, socially affable, always in demand for parties, and particularly popular with young people. All of which indicated how inclined people are to see what they intend to see in others. But it also suggests the temperamental variability of the lady under discussion. She must have been a composite person with so many facets of expression that it was hard to put a label upon her.

The only portrait in existence is one that was sketched by her sister Cassandra. The eyes are large and dark. Their expression is slightly mocking. The eyebrows are arched teasingly. Her nose is almost Hebraic, with sensitively widened nostrils. Her mouth is small, with a thin upper lip, and a very definitely rounded lower lip. The shape of the face is nearly oval. Around her forehead there are little dark curls. She wears a white bonnet-like cap and a white dress with a square neck and short baby puffed sleeves. It is a very feminine picture, except for the brilliant intellectual eyes. It is a face of many contradictions. The arms have a lovely line. They tell us that she was tall, with a light well-formed figure, and that she moved quickly. Her coloring is brunette. There is no attitude struck

in the poise of the head. It is held naturally. Altogether it is
the portrait of an interesting young woman, who took notice
of everything that went on around her, who thought her own
thoughts, and took nothing too seriously. It is rather a patrician
face. It might have belonged to a great lady. And it is the
face of a woman whose mind was chaste. As well as ironical.

Miss Austen began to write consistently when she was twenty.
She began it to amuse her family. But as she proceeded it
would seem from the records that she kept it a secret from all
of them except her sister Cassandra. Though this is only a
tentatively held theory. We cannot be sure about anything
concerning Miss Austen which we build from contemporary
comments. They are too varied to be in any way reliable. It is
better to assume at the first merely this—that in twenty years
she wrote six novels and several fragments of novels. None of
them came out, we know, until six years before her death, but
all of them, we can be almost certain, were written long before
they were published. Which means that she put years of work
upon them. We cannot even be sure which of the finished
novels was completed first, but historical research workers believe now that it was *Northanger Abbey*.

Northanger Abbey is a burlesque of the novels which were
popular in Miss Austen's time. In these novels the heroine was
always beautiful, usually delicate and given to swooning ap-
p)priately in artistic settings, and often as not was badly treated
b/ her guardian. She was inevitably an orphan. She was always needing to be rescued, and the hero was a hero indeed.
You could hear the beat of his horse's hoofs, so often did he go
riding madly to come to the aid of the heroine. Miss Austen
read these novels, and she did a lot of thinking. Then she took
to writing.

It was as if she cocked her fine eyebrow and said, "Marvelous,
but this is the way it really is."

Her heroine was not beautiful, and was not an orphan, and
had lived seventeen years without any nobleman trying to se-
duce her in the keep of his castle. She was called Catherine;

her father was a clergyman, and she was one of a large family. She never languished over roses in the garden. She did not sing sad songs to her own accompaniment on the harp, but she could manage to listen to music without too much fatigue. She was an ordinary girl. But she had read plenty of novels; so she knew there must be a hero for her. She went to Bath, and while she waited for the hero to appear, she thought mostly about whether she would wear her sprigged muslin or her spotted muslin. The hero does appear, and what hero could resist the admiration Catherine hands to him? Naturally he falls in love with her. How could he help it? She provided him with a big opinion of himself. The story is carried on in the mood of burlesque. Miss Austen gave herself a thorough go at the popular conception of men and women and matrimony. This, she hints, is the way it usually happens, and the less a girl knows the better chance she has of making a man feel like a grand fellow. But she did not leave it sharp in its satire; she softened it with her own tolerance of people; the characters are mellowed by her artistry into accord with their surroundings. It is, for all its burlesque, human and real. She started in this book her immortal habit of creating a gallery for her heroines; the gallery which made her books famous; her extra people gathered in around the heroine, portraits of very familiar and very human beings.

Miss Austen considered that *Northanger Abbey* would have only an interest of time—that only while there was still a vogue for the high-colored romances of the time would people be able to get the points of her satire. She forgot about history, and about its taste for keeping what is amusing in its past in preference to what is noble. She overlooked the coming of a century which very definitely wanted to think of itself as a century of progress. What better sign of this progress could there be than the change in the position of women? Accordingly *Northanger Abbey* was preserved beyond its time—a shocking example of the shabby education of women. It was the symbol of the giddy merry-go-round they rode—sitting sedately on mock horses and lions and camels, round and round, spun from one central force, to the sound of pretty tunes—all to get a man to marry. The only drawback being that they could only get such men as themselves stepped up to take a ride on the merry-go-round.

The doings of women, and some of their thoughts, as they went round and round, is the theme of all her novels. The speed of the whirling platform varies in the individual books.

The most graceful of the books is *Pride and Prejudice*.

It opens like a play. It continues like a play. The story is told with conversations between the people in it, with a slight additional use of the letters they write to one another. It should be read aloud in order to get fully the fine light sound of the dialogue and the soft sparkle of its humor.

The taste of the book is given in the opening chapter. It is one of the cleverest pieces of tone-placing we possess in our literature. It is suave and short and masterly. There is not one unnecessary word in it. It introduces at once the theme and the people who will have to do with it. A new young man with an adequate fortune has arrived in a district, and at the breakfast table Mrs. Bennett, who has five daughters, tells her husband that he must call upon the young man in order to secure him for one of the girls. Mr. Bennett teases her lazily, debating whether or not he will call before any other father in the district calls. Mrs. Bennett fusses. As the story proceeds, Mr. Bennett goes on teasing, and his wife fussing, and between them they nearly lose two eligible young men for their two most attractive daughters, Jane and Elizabeth.

Mr. Bennett is an aloof person with a sardonic sense of humor. He had married a woman of no culture, and no social finesse, drawn in his youth by high animal spirits and prettiness. He is subconsciously ashamed of her, and of his own early bad judgment, so he defends himself by taking to the enjoyment of fools. He passes the time in reading and in making fun of his neighbors. The only person he likes very deeply is his daughter Elizabeth, who possesses many of his own characteristics. Elizabeth is fond of her father, but is subconsciously aware of something that is missing. So when she loves, it is a man who supplies in her mind the respect she has not been able to feel for her father. Miss Austen knew her feminine psychology. Elizabeth is the most fascinating of the Austen heroines. She is gay and arch and full of repartee, combining her mother's high spirits and her father's talent for observation with a way all of her own of making herself unforgettable. Her cousin, Mr. Collins, decides to marry her. His proposal to her is one of the most rollicking of Miss Austen's absurd bits of drama. Collins throughout the book is the clown; a pompous young clergyman without one grain of discernment in his tightly drawn brain. When Elizabeth refuses him, he interprets it as a piece of feminine technique—to tantalize the lover —and he proceeds to propose over again. Through the book he appears again and again; always at the tense moment Mr. Bennett receives a letter from Mr. Collins which brings him a laugh. In fact, as he explains, he would not lose Mr. Collins' correspondence for anything. It took the place in his life of the comic strip. Mr. Collins plods on, doing his clerical duty by his relatives in sober earnest. Truly they needed advice. For there were to be many troubles before Elizabeth could marry Darcy, the hero.

But all ended well. Miss Austen gave Elizabeth everything a woman's heart could ask. Darcy was not the conventionalized hero of the current romances. He had no dash. He was not particularly captivating. He was rather given to being unpleasant. He had a very high opinion of his own judgment, which was very reasonable, because it was a good judgment. Some of the critics have complained that he is only a shadow, and they explain it glibly by the spinsterhood of the author, and that she did not know men. Darcy is a shadow. He is a dream man; the man of the dream of the normal woman—a quiet, strong man of means, able to take control of the difficulties that would arise, and personable enough to rouse erotic interest. He was grave and dignified. He knew what he wanted. He loved Elizabeth before she loved him, which was the fulfilling of another dream in women—to have a man for whom a woman need not angle. He was also a one-woman man. He looked sardonically at the other woman, who was jealous of Elizabeth and determined herself to have Darcy. This was a man such as an intellectual woman like Miss Austen would herself desire. A man with the sense to look to his future comfort in the woman he chose to marry, who was not to be led off from his purpose by any of the wiles of silly women. He wanted a companion. Miss Austen rewards him with the loveliest of her heroines. In letting Elizabeth have Darcy, Miss Austen was being romantic, and neat in her romanticism. Elizabeth was open and true to herself throughout, and in the end she found love accompanied by comfort. She had a husband she could admire in all things, and a companion who appreciated her. She had both money and love.

Pride and Prejudice is technically the most perfect of the Austen novels. It is flawless in its craftsmanship. It is carried through from the beginning to the ending with an unflagging zest, and with meticulous regard for its form. It is simple portraiture, and yet it is at the same time most penetrating psychological disclosure. As the whirling platform speeds, we see into the power that makes it speed. But not with any *inside stuff* from the people themselves. They conduct themselves with matter-of-fact sedateness. They do not deal with their souls in public. Miss Austen did not know people who did. So there are none of them in her stories. What is to be gathered about motivation is to be gathered from casual conversations and habitual doings, just as it has to be gathered from life. In her books, and particularly in *Pride and Prejudice,* you have to come to your own conclusion about the inwardness of what takes place by listening to the conversations. There are plenty of signs for anyone who is on the alert for signs.

All through the book the reader is pulled by two amazingly balanced talents in the author, her sense of story-telling and her characterization. The action of the story is so smooth it gives the impression of floating. There is not one jerk in her timing. One event follows evenly upon the preceding event. The reader floats with the story. It hardly needs concentration, so natural is the pull of its unfolding. The characters fulfil themselves without a jar, and with complete naturalness. The reader feels before she is aware of it as if she were part of the circle itself. She lilts along with the gay melody of it. She gives herself to the whirl of the platform. She watches the gentlemen climbing on and jumping off. She smiles with gratification when the merry-go-round stops for a moment. Elizabeth has announced to her mother that she is marrying Mr. Darcy, and her mother says, "Dear me—fifty thousand pounds."

In *Sense and Sensibility* the speed is not so rapid. Miss Austen experimented with a slower tempo. She tried her hand with less attractive girls than Elizabeth. It is a study of two sisters—one who possesses a fund of good sense, and the other who has romantic sensibility, and it works itself out into quite an elaborated document upon how a girl should conduct herself when she is two-timed. Marianne, who has sensibility, falls into a decline, which was a malady that to-day would be diagnosed as a nervous breakdown. She is an exhibitionist. So everyone hears about her disappointment. The young man, according to her relatives, is a bad young man, and should be cut dead when met anywhere. He is a bad young man. He is one of the male flirts whom Miss Austen brings frequently into her stories, with a guileful tongue and convincing false ways with women. The other girl, Eleanor, has sense, but even that does not protect her from being taken in by another two-timing young man. Though it does protect her pride. She uses her head. She gets all the unflattering data. She makes herself consider it carefully. She confides in no one, but she allows the other lady involved to confide in her. An astute young lady, Eleanor! Somehow she manages to go on loving her young man. Subconsciously she seems to expect that he will disentangle himself. She waits until the end of the story, and puts in her time looking after Marianne, who is in a sad way indeed. While she is waiting for her lover to come to his senses, and while she is tending to her sister, Miss Austen brings in her gallery. Marianne weeps and Eleanor sketches, surrounded by a group of famous fools. There is a female Falstaff, a vigorous, vulgar old woman by the name of Mrs. Jennings, who is a meddler and a gossip, and takes it upon herself to lend a hand to getting every presentable young girl a husband. What she says about Marianne's lover would have been most upsetting to that young gentleman. But she says it most sagaciously to another gentleman, who has a pitying heart. She sees him as a consolation for Marianne. It works. Mrs. Jennings knew her men. She had married her own daughters most successfully by reason of that very knowledge. But what a trial Mrs. Jennings was to the reserved and ladylike Eleanor, and what a disappointment Eleanor was to Mrs. Jennings! Not a thing to do for the girl; not one slip of the tongue ever; a veritable clam of a girl. No drama in her, which was very unconsiderate of her elders, who looked to the young things for their amusement in life.

There is an impression of the jungle in *Sense and Sensibility*, which is not in any of the other Austen novels. The people show their claws. They prowl and they roar and sometimes they pounce. Eleanor and her sisters are badly treated by their stepbrother. Not because the stepbrother is cruel. Miss Austen was not making any bow to the prevailing taste for heroines that were put upon. It was merely over money. Greed haunts the whole story. Marianne's lover had been unfaithful because of money. The relatives of Eleanor's lover think of nothing else but money. Marriages are arranged and disarranged all on the basis of money. It dominates everything. It overshadows entirely the little fragment of romance that Miss Austen keeps going in the heart of Eleanor. Eleanor is just on the edge of being a prig. She will develop into the kind of a woman who likes to have something to have to forgive in her husband. We can see her moving that way. We can feel the underfeeling of boredom that the author had for her. A very worthy girl, and one estimably suited to marry a man of the type she did marry. But too repressed to be interesting. At the same time, Marianne is too unrepressed to be a pleasure to anyone but someone like Mrs. Jennings. But there is this to say—Marianne is one of the earliest presentations in the fiction of women of the neurotic. We remember both her and her sister because they belong to the portraiture of women which Miss Austen was bent upon doing.

Sense and Sensibility has a feeling of the economic insecurity of women which is not in any of the other novels. It must have been written when Miss Austen was worried about the financial future of herself and her sister Cassandra. We do know that there was a period of such worry in her life following the death of her father. Marianne and Eleanor have to leave their old home after the death of their father; their step-brother does not fulfil a promise he made to the father, and the young ladies are left in narrow circumstances. Another relative comes to their help. But Miss Austen drives it home that there is nothing these young gentlewomen can do for themselves, except to get married, and they are directed by their relatives to make the most of every chance they get to visit in big estates on account of the eligible gentlemen they may meet there. It has a sinister effect. The men are always respected for their incomes. It is not only the economic insecurity Miss Austen pushes forward in this story, but also the emotional insecurity. The happiness of women is shown to depend not upon their own making, but upon the emotional chivalry of men, and mostly there was not much of that. The author, of course, takes no position throughout the story regarding these facts. She merely lets the story tell itself. Everything ends well, but only by reasons of outside intervention. The young ladies themselves are helpless in the ordering of their lives.

Mansfield Park follows the same tempo as *Sense and Sensibility*. It starts out with the same theme of feminine dependence. Fanny, the heroine, was taken as a child into the

home of a wealthy uncle. Because she is poor and helpless, she
is somewhat shabbily treated by all her cousins except one.
That one is the second son of the family, and Fanny develops
an emotional fixation upon him. Fanny is a gentle creature, but
emotionally stubborn. She has a sad time of it. Cousin Edmund falls in love with another lady, and he makes Fanny
his confidante. The other lady, Mary Crawford, is worldly.
A marked habit of Miss Austen's was to make such women as
she brought into her stories from the world of society rather
heartless and calculating. It is the natural enough reaction of
a sheltered woman towards a woman who has taken her place
in a larger sphere; but she does it so persistently in all the six
novels that it looks something like emotional retaliation. The
strange part of *Mansfield Park* is that Miss Crawford, in spite
of the author, is the interesting woman of the story. She has
nonchalance and charm. Fanny is insipid and didactic beside
her. But she will never do for Edmund. He was to enter the
church, and Miss Crawford's ethical principles were always wavering. She had a brother Henry, and he enters the story, the
most fascinating of all Miss Austen's bad men. He enjoys seeing
ladies fall in love with him. After he has conquered all Fanny's
cousins he aims at her. He really does her a great service, for he
causes Cousin Edmund to see that she is an attractive young
woman. However, though Henry Crawford was much entertained by a lady who would not reciprocate, he never could
resist a lady who would. And to while away the time of
Fanny's resistance, he takes a jaunt with her married cousin.
Mary Crawford is not sufficiently shocked at adultery. She has
seen a lot of it, and is used to it. But her nonchalance shocks
Cousin Edmund. She will never do for him; so he puts her
out of his mind, and concentrates upon Fanny. The story
ends. In spite of herself Miss Austen made Henry and Mary
Crawford the attractive people of the story. Maybe people
like them had attracted her. Even though she could not advocate their immoral point of view. Henry sails through the
story, dapper, debonair, always entertaining, a man who was

not to be trusted, but was far more attractive as a person than the sober Edmund. Mary is almost a forecasting of the twentieth-century young woman. She liked the idea of Edmund's emotional nature—it was secure and would be faithful; but she was afraid it might be dull. She was a hedonist, and saw everything in relation to what it would give her. She did not intend to be hurt by men. So she cultivated a light hold upon life; nothing would disturb it. She did not permit herself to think highly of anyone; so she would never be disappointed. She was witty and quite self-contained, and well amused by everything that went on around her. She thought Fanny was pathetic. Her capacity for adoration would land her into suffering. Miss Crawford was independent. Was this what independence would do to women?

Not necessarily, Miss Austen declared, when she presented *Emma*. For Emma also was an heiress; but she was unspoiled, and in no way contaminated by the great world. She lived in a small community, and was the only young woman of wealth in the neighborhood. She ran the house for her father, who was a nervous elderly man, all taken up with his own ailments. She did not have enough to do. So she took to interfering in other people's affairs. She thought she would see to it that a young person called Harriet Smith, living in the village school for young ladies, got suitably married. She selected the young clergyman as being suitable. But the young clergyman interpreted Emma's interest in him as being personal, and was much humiliated when she refused him violently. He went away for a holiday, and returned with a wife; and from then on the story becomes a war between two women for the control of a community. The clergyman's wife is not going to allow Miss Emma Woodhouse, spinster, to rule the district. In the background stands Mr. George Knightely, who loves Emma, but has never declared himself. He is a great deal older than she is; he never flatters her; he usually tries to stop her impetuous doings, and often he has to tell her severely that she is more or less of a fool in her judgment of people. Into the story rides another of Miss Austen's young male flirts. He is Mr. Frank Churchill. He is secretly engaged to a young woman who is visiting in the neighborhood, one of those reserved and lovely young women who have no money of their own and are dependent. His aunt, whose heir he is, will never give her consent to an alliance with a penniless girl, so the engagement has to be secret. Again the question of the economic endowment comes darkly into Miss Austen's story. If money had not been so stressed, this engagement would not have been secret, and upon its being secret fell the cause of the sad part of the story. Mr. Churchill throws dust in the eyes of everyone by maintaining a flirtation with Emma. This of course is not so very serious in the end, because it makes Mr. Knightely jealous, and a little jealousy never hurts the best of men. Mr. Knightely was the best of men to the author. He is the spiritual companion of Mr. Darcy—a quiet, strong man, to whom a woman might turn in difficulty; who knew what he wanted, and was never drawn into any philandering for the sustaining of his male vanity. Meanwhile the war goes on between Emma and the clergyman's wife. The gallery in *Emma* is better than the gallery of any of the other books. The nervous old father comes into the story hesitatingly, never sure whether or not there should be parties, always recommending his guests to have a nice bowl of gruel instead of cakes and wine. There is an old maid in the village, garrulous and well-meaning, but running about everywhere talking endlessly about everything that is said and done. Miss Bates. She strikes terror into the heart of Emma. Is this what a spinster comes to at last? Then Harriet Smith, not as yet successfully married off, decides that inasmuch as Miss Emma Woodhouse has treated her as an equal, she might herself aspire to Mr. Knightely. Innocently she confides her hopes to Emma, and Emma fumes. At last she realizes. All the time she had taken it for granted that Mr. Knightely was hers; and perhaps she had lost him by flirting with Frank Churchill. But she had not. Mr. Knightely, though jealous, was not one to be put off his intentions. So the story ends

happily, with Mr. Knightely getting a suitable husband for
Harriet in the person of one of his tenants. Emma is sub-
dued. She respects superior judgment and superior action.
Frank Churchill's aunt dies, and he announces his engagement.
The clergyman's wife sits down and gnashes her teeth. Emma
Woodhouse has won. She is marrying the great man of the
community.

In *Emma* we see again that Miss Austen gives her heroine a
lover who has something of the father in him. Emma had
needed a father who was strong, and had not had it in her
sick elderly parent. Usually Miss Austen treated her love
scenes gingerly. She left the story when the declaration was
made, but in *Emma* she carries it on a little further, and the
relationship between Mr. Knightely and Emma is unfolded
delicately. The conversations between them while they are
trying to decide when to break the news to her father are tender
and sweet. The man is reserved and kind and considerate. The
girl is happily surrendering all her life to his keeping. The
comedy goes softly out, like the gradual lowering of a light,
and the romance is left.

Miss Austen hurried on to her last story, *Persuasion*. It is
short, and has a spiritual maturity far beyond all the other
books. It has an even tempo, melodic like a lovely waltz.
Emma had been quickly taken in march-time. But this last
story was different. It was not slow as *Sense and Sensibility*
was slow; it was not blurred in its rhythm as *Mansfield Park*
was; but it was carried on the time of dream music. Miss
Austen was dying when she wrote it, from a mysterious ailment
which was never apparently diagnosed, but seemed to have been
an actual burning-down of her vital forces. She had been a
strong woman. There was no infection in her blood stream, as
there was in the case of the Brontë sisters. The rest of her
family lived to old age. But she drooped early. For twenty
years she had lived two lives; one of which was that of a
normal woman, taking her part in her own community life, and
fulfilling all the duties which single women were called upon to

fulfil for the rest of the family. At the same time she had lived
an intensely inward life, creating six perfect novels, so living in
them, as she wrote and rewrote them, that they were created
rather than written. The books breathe with a life of their
own given them by a woman utterly devoted to making them
live. Not a jar comes into one of them; hardly a flaw enters
into any of them; not one touch of unreality or artificiality
spoils them. They are small worlds spinning of their own
volition. Truly it was creativeness that produced them.

And she had not had anybody to help her.

It was out of herself alone she had made them.

The heroine of *Persuasion* is Anne Eliot, who had been disappointed in love. The story opens with the heroine resigned
at twenty-eight to spinsterhood, with her mind feeding itself
on regrets, and her delicate bloom gone. She had let herself be
persuaded against her own inclination. For consideration of
money. The man she had loved had his way to make in the
navy. He had no inheritance. Neither had she. It was unwise, a mature and practical friend had advised her. So she
had broken her engagement. And had never been able to
love another man. Nothing else would ever matter to her; and
she had years and years of life to put in as best she might before
death would release her from the futility of living. The hero,
Captain Wentworth, returns from the sea, a successful com-
mander of one of His Majesty's ships. He intends to marry,
and Anne has to see him pay attention to another woman, and
to listen to him praised extravagantly by every woman he meets.
Still worse, she has to see the other woman regard him pos-
sessively. She has to go on. There are duties to her family.
Anne is the perfect spinster. She takes care of her sister's
children; she plays for the young people to dance; she sews by
herself. Then in the very nick of time another of Miss Austen's
bad men arrives. He has money; he will inherit a title; he is
looking for an elegant lady to wear the title. He is a gentleman who is shrewd about women by reason of a lot of experience. He does not like too young women; they are exacting.

He wants a lady who has had the edges of her disposition rounded off. He had an eye for his own comfort. So Anne was elected by this gentleman for the reception of his attentions. He knew that being loved would restore her bloom. He was quite confident about that. His confidence made his manner towards her fittingly proprietary. And it roused the ire of Captain Wentworth. Anne had been his. He had not minded her being a faded spinster; that was solacing to his vanity; but to be the chosen lady of a future baronet was different. Not that it would have happened. Anne was a one-man woman; she had turned down other chances. During a conversation with a mutual friend Anne has occasion, or takes it, to put into very moving words the emotional constancy of women. Captain Wentworth overhears it. By this time he has realized very thoroughly how second-rate his intended choice had been beside Anne. It is a romance, this last book of Miss Austen. Anne's passionate constancy brings her lover back to her. The words of Anne about the emotion of a woman are the nearest Miss Austen ever came to letting herself go. They are intensified words. It is the only passage in all her writing where the reader feels that the writer is momentarily choked by her own feeling.

Having written this book of subdued romance, in which there is hardly any gallery, but complete concentration upon the heroine herself, Miss Austen died.

The novels have been outlined in detail for three reasons. First, they remain to this day the greatest novels, considered artistically, written by a woman in English. Second, for their time they told an amazing amount about women, and accordingly are an intrinsic part of the feminist revolt, though, on account of the technical subtlety of the author, that element in their composition may easily be overlooked. Third, it is in the novels themselves that we search for the mind and the personality of Miss Austen.

Novelists sit down to do just one thing—to portray themselves. This has been psychologically proven so many times that it is almost unnecessary to state it as a premise for investigation. The self-portraiture may be deeply involved and circuitously achieved, but it is always a driving force behind the writing. It is true of men who write. But it is much truer of the women. That is, more directly true. The man, by his masculine nature, may expand himself into a creative field that is so far beyond the immediate self that the portraiture is almost lost. But the woman, by reason of the concentration upon herself which is the feminine endowment, never gets so very far away from herself. Usually, therefore, it is quite easy to detect the self-portraiture in the writing of women. But with Miss Austen it is not easy.

She began to write when as usual in her time she would have been getting married. Although she was born into a writing family, and although she took to writing naturally, there is no sign given us by her family of an early consciousness of literary vocation. She appears to have been a normal young woman with good health, and a generous appetite for parties and dancing. We could gather the taste for parties from the books themselves by the gusto with which the author describes them. She transfers the feeling of social affairs with an unmistakable flair for them. She liked the drama of them and the excitement. Her heroines rarely watch anxiously for letters; or hold upsetting sittings with themselves in their own rooms: they watch for parties; and they hold light parleys with their relatives over the teacups. Even when Marianne sheds her tears and bemoans the sad ending of her love affair, it is to the accompaniment of Mrs. Jennings entering her room with wine and nice jellies to comfort her. And when Anne resigns herself to her spinster fate, it is sitting at the piano she does it. When women let their heroines talk to their own souls, it is the writers' souls that are getting released. Miss Austen never permitted it in her heroines. So her soul eludes us, as her personal experience does also.

When the Austens took a united stand against publicity and made away with a great deal of the historical data, they really were gesturing magnificently to maintain their English reserve. It was a consistent middle-class action. With our clinically trained modern minds we would be inclined to think there was something serious they were hiding. Except for our knowledge, based upon clinical observation, that if there had been a sin, or an irregularity in Miss Austen's life, it would have come out in her novels. It did not. There is no sense of sin anywhere in her stories; but there is just enough pointed satire in them to make us think that what the family set out to hide might have been a touch of cattiness in their famous member. The novels are smoothed by many revisions, but the mind that could see so many absurdities in people, and get a kick out of them, could not have been a pretty, gentle, sweet mind. She probably made a lot of sharp remarks in her letters. They may have looked to the family not amusing, but just unpleasantly irritable. She had a right to be irritable. No woman could have worked for twenty years to perfect her art without sacrificing her nervous system to the strain. Besides the enduring mental creativeness there was the spinster's biological frustration. And that leads us into another field of speculation.

Can we draw from her stories what happened to a lively, attractive young woman at the end of the eighteenth century to turn her into a novelist? What set her burlesquing the popular conception of romance? What made her determined to portray women as they really were? What caused her to devote twenty years to the perfection of an art form? Why was she glad to die at forty? Her sister Cassandra admitted in a letter that Miss Austen died gladly.

All the novels are objective in appearance. Here is a woman, we may almost think, who successfully lost herself in portraying other people. There is no one character among her women who shadows herself through all the others, haunting the books as the creator of them. But when you take the heroines all together, you get a composite picture of womanhood, arch, high-spirited, clever womanhood, capable of moods of docility and neurotic waverings, capable also of being dull and sedate. If you add them together, the sum is a volatile expression of femininity, which for its amount of baffling surrender to varying moods would puzzle even the most thoroughly trained psychiatric clinician. When you look at this sum you are inclined to reverse your first judgment, and conclude that the work of Miss Austen is so completely and subtly subjective that it looks objective.

But why did Miss Austen have to set herself down in several women of great variability of temperament? For all their outer simplicity every one of Miss Austen's heroines is psychologically difficult. Which means that the author was a thousand times more difficult herself. Fanny in *Mansfield Park,* who is perhaps the simplest of them, is on the surface so gentle that everyone around her missed the resolute iron of her determination. Elizabeth in *Pride and Prejudice* is a deft-tongued young person who might easily appear to have equally deft emotions; instead of that she was almost sternly loyal. Emma is so enterprising it hides her childlike temperamental eagerness. Eleanor in *Sense and Sensibility* has such unfailing good sense that nobody around her would ever have accused her of extravagant feelings. Anne in *Persuasion* is so poised that no one could guess the tragedy underneath. None of these is a simple woman with simple emotions. They are also every one of them women of ability. Fanny was a keen student of literature. Elizabeth was a skilled conversationalist who could have shone in any of the great salons. Emma could have managed a business after a little training. Eleanor painted remarkably well, and Anne was a fine musician, as well as a person of general unusual culture.

The first book, *Northanger Abbey,* is a pressing satire on romance and the influence the ignorance of the lady has upon romance. The less a woman knows, Miss Austen says, the better can she flatter a man. Is that a cue?

Certainly it was another form of the Mary Wollstonecraft cry.

But Miss Austen does not make an issue of it. She made a

satirical story. And at the same time a human story. It might be amusing, but it was also pleasant. Out of the two elements of amusement and pleasantries Miss Austen built her stories. The men, that is, the hero men, the critics have assured us many times, are thinly done. These were in the main nineteenth-century critics, so they approved of a spinster's men being thin.

Miss Austen set out to write about woman and matrimony; which is a slightly different thing from writing about women and men. Matrimony is a state into which every woman was determined to get; or rather, into which all her relatives were determined to get her. It was a merry-go-round. Getting on it and getting men on it provided a lot of entertainment. The men of her stories should not be studied as men, but rather as symbols of masculinity such as would have to do with the ever-whirling merry-go-round. So, she portrays types. The male flirt appears frequently. He was a symbol of danger—a kind of golden apple that would take a woman's attention from her goal. He was particularly dangerous because from much practice he knew what pleased women. He was just more than a little feminine himself. He knew how phrases always caught the attention of women. Philanderers, according to Miss Austen, are always gifted with words. She must have met at least one of them, and perhaps have been taken in herself for a while. Because she pursues the type with vengeance throughout her books. And they always come to a bad end, usually marrying a shrew woman for motives of money, and being made an emotional prisoner by her. It may, of course, have only been a generic revenge she was taking, and not personal. For every woman, knowing that marital security is what is needed for her generic purpose, subconsciously despises the philandering male. He is not generally useful, attractive though he may momentarily be.

Against him Miss Austen sets the strong, truly masculine man. When a woman writes fiction, the men she uses will always line somewhere with her own experience. It must be.

Otherwise there is no emotional contact; and without emotional contact there is never any creative lifting. But the experience which is the writer's own is always disguised, and usually the disguise takes the form of a division of characteristics. For instance, in the modern writing of women the problem of the infidelity of men takes up a lot of story-telling time. Unless the woman is a scientific document writer, determined at the utter cost of romance to write down the truth, she will bring into her story two men; one will be the man she loves; she will make him faithful. That will be a fiction wish fulfilment. Then she will create another figure of probably lay masculinity to bear the sins of the other man. He will be unfaithful.

Miss Austen was not writing documents. The document writer of the period was Charlotte Brontë. Miss Austen was writing comedy romance. Therefore she would of necessity employ the most subtle disguise she could create. And as she had twenty years in which to secure her disguises, they are almost impenetrable. They were certainly impenetrable for her own time. But we know now much more than they knew then about women; and much more about fiction; and infinitely more about the labyrinthian turns of psychology in fiction.

To Elizabeth and to Emma, the most sprightly of her heroines, girls who are almost modern in their independence of mind, she gave her nicest men, Darcy and Knightely. Elizabeth and Emma are very much alike psychologically. Darcy and Knightely are almost identical figures. Both of these men had the sense to appreciate women with fire in them. Neither of them had to consider money; they were not *on the make*, and in need therefore of girls with money. Both of them were big enough themselves to enjoy a woman with a difficult temperament. Neither of them needed adoration; both of them preferred a deft-tongued companion who could give what Mr. Knightely called "a saucy look," and Mr. Darcy described as "an arch glance." When you return for another examination of Miss Austen's own portrait, you see eyes that were quite saucy, and eyebrows that arched provocatively.

We can reason with safety that the romances of Elizabeth and Emma were a deeply subconscious effort to create for the author a wish fulfilment. But we have to look for the lay figure bearing the faults of Darcy and Knightely in the other books, for Miss Austen was intensely creative, and did not put everything she had to say in one book, or even in two. In a definite sense the six finished books are one book; a composite picture of femininity in that time. Because she spent twenty years on them, and because of the reserved nature of her background, she spread the cause of her disappointment out among the six stories, and hit it deeply.

Two main propensities in the other men show—a hunger for flattery—a regard for money. Now we do know about Miss Austen that she worried about money. There was none for her to inherit. We can also assume with certainty that a mind like hers would far more likely have been inclined to tease men than to flatter them. Add to this her vengeance upon the man who pays momentary attention to a woman and then veers off without explaining to her. Maybe it could all have been objective observation; but in a woman observation is invariably subjective before it is objective; and personal before it is general. Remember also that Miss Austen in her time and in her circumstances could admit nothing about herself. Pride was all a woman had to protect her constancy. Pride would express itself in concealment, in sophistication. So we may conclude that in the early nineteenth century there was a young woman with a quick, clever tongue and no money who was disappointed that some man was put off by the cleverness and the lack of money, and after lingering for a little betook himself to a simple dull woman who had sufficient dowry, leaving the young woman to debate in herself whether it was principally her saucy tongue or her lack of money that had brought it upon her. Knowing, too, that she had many more moods than just one, that she could have played at being docile and dumb and pathetic, and coming gradually over the years to realize that after all it was money which counted. She may not tell us the color of a man's eyes, but she always sets down how much he had a year; she may not give an exact description of the appearance of her heroines, but she will be explicit about how much, and generally how little, they were likely to inherit.

Miss Austen made two famous comments about her writing. The first was a regret mentioned in a letter to her niece that she had begun so early. There were better things, she inferred, for a woman than writing, and writing when indulged in matured the brain too sharply. This goes back to her first book, *Northanger Abbey*, which leaves no possibility of evading the author's satirical belief that cleverness was an erotic handicap to women. The Austen family entertained itself by writing, and it must therefore have been known to everyone who visited the family how clever and sharp were the skits she wrote. The fragment, published only in recent years, of her very early work, *Love and Friendship*, is a hilarious piece of mockery. The mind of the young girl who wrote it was for its time a naughty mind, with no respect in it for the weakness of people. It would be an uncomfortable mind for a man to contemplate living with, unless he could afford from his own abundance of mentality to be amused, and at the same time pleased by a clever woman. Nobody taught young Jane Austen how to cover her cleverness with feminine allure, so a man would be likely to feel that she was seeing through him and laughing at him. That would be disconcerting to him.

The second comment was this—that her work was on a small ivory. They are the words of a very feminine person. The cleverness of Miss Austen was not what dominated her. Littleness always moves the emotion of the normal woman—the little baby—the little kitten—the little doll—and even the little flower. Miss Austen's work had to be on a small canvas. She was normal. So she reduced everything she wrote about to a small scale. Even her sentences are little. They are short and simple, modeled upon actual conversation. We hardly realize now what an innovation that was. But if we take a page of conversation from *Pride and Prejudice* and put it up beside a page of conversation from *Jane Eyre* by Charlotte Brontë, we will have the force of the creative invention it really was driven into us. *Jane Eyre* was the best seller of its year. The sentences are heavy and prolonged. The people talk to each other in essays. It is completely alien to us to-day. While *Pride and Prejudice*, which was not a best seller by any means, and only welcomed by a few very discerning literary critics, is in its technique as modern as the books of this year. Our short sentences are more staccato than hers. She ripples where we jerk. She is less nervous, and not in such a hurry.

They are healthier sentences than ours. There is a serenity of mind underlying all the satire of Miss Austen that is profoundly fatalistic. It is not a depressed fatalism, but rather natural and reconciled. This was life as she saw it for women. She makes fun of it, and at the same time she accepts it. It can be a pleasant life. It might also be a trying, restricted, helpless existence, but Miss Austen pulled her imagination back from that, when it edged towards it in *Sense and Sensibility*. And probably pulled herself back with supreme self-control. The supreme self-control of the artist. For Miss Austen herself as a woman had been disappointed. We can have no doubt about that. Every woman who does not get her man is disappointed; and getting a man in her time meant marrying him. But it was the disappointment of superiority of mind. She would have wanted a great deal. A mind as superior as hers was could be quiet in its erotic loneliness. The loss would be so deeply ingrained into her being that she might be superficially unaware of it. The artist, either male or female, has a curious self-containment which will tide the erotic nature over its loneliness. Miss Austen's fine work shows this self-containment. She forced herself to live out her creative life, giving herself to a world of her own making. It may be that the first writing of her stories allowed more of the personal restlessness to express itself, but in the twenty years she had time to take out any jarring personal phrase. She presented the novels smoothed out, and lightsome in their tone. They are happy; almost jaunty in their happiness. It was a miracle of technique—to take the matrimonial merry-go-round of middle-class women, in which she herself had been a failure, and make it a little planet by itself.

But suddenly she was tired. At forty. Her novels were getting recognition in high critical places. But she had come to the time when biology laughs at women who have evaded its laws. Six perfect novels; an extraordinarily talented woman. Erotically starved. The frustration she had valiantly fought off, and held out of her novels, got her finally. They called it a decline; it seems to have been a burning-out of her nervous forces. She gave up. Humor would not help then. It was of no avail to arch her satiric eyebrows. What in the end have women to do with humor? What will comedy do to preserve the race? Little ivories! But no little son. Did memory taunt her with the tall figure of the Darcy man? "I began to write too early," she had said to her niece. A dark man with quiet, strong ways, and great pride in him, and speech that was laconically to the point. Well, she had written amusing stories. Life was amusing. Women were amusing, and men never had the wit to look underneath the covering surfaces of femininity. Women, they said, had no humor. It was better not to have. She was glad to die. Racial futility must have struck Miss Austen at forty with terrific force. The more so as she was a woman of intellectual honesty. She was no high-brow, but she must have been amazingly clever. Otherwise she could never have handled her characters with such penetrating regard for their psychological motivation. There were no books on the subject to help her. Nobody discussed the psychology of women. It was sheer innovation from her. She took pricks at women. She exhibited their greediness and their complacent placidity. So many of them were stupid. "God, grant that I may have patience," she murmured when she was dying. It must have been something she had prayed often. But women were also pathetic, and brave sometimes. Men expected so little of them, and yet so much. It took the sweetness of the dove and the wiliness of the snake to serve them. And why should it be all left to women? The Darcy man knew what he wanted—it was brightness and a companionable mind. Would it ever come? "God, grant that I may have patience." It was the prayer of woman. Woman as she was at the beginning of the nineteenth century. She would need all her patience. The race and the need in a woman to be given to it. A man to be looked to. "As an equal," the ghost of Mary Wollstonecraft standing at her bed would have pronounced. "No, as a superior, still as a superior," Miss Austen would have answered. That would be the great difficulty—the higher women would develop, the more would they need from men for their erotic satisfaction—it was not to be found in equality. It would mean a lot of loneliness for some women. It would be a hard way, "gorgeous, heroic hard way," two dark spirits, the Brontë sisters, also gathered there, would add. They were neither dead then, nor dying—they were getting ready to be born; and even then it would not be so long until they were dead, so they could communicate with the dead and the dying. They would discuss with emphatic emotionalism the passionality of loneliness in women. It would be all right, they would say, if women had a magnificent image of a man to love. "Image," Mary Wollstonecraft would snort, "I never found them worth it." Miss Austen would arch her satiric eyebrows, and look at them with intellectual distaste. Charlotte Brontë would explain what yearning could do for the soul—women must yearn in order to possess their souls. And Emily Brontë, out of deep sympathy for the dying Miss Austen, might set aside her reserve sufficiently to assure her of the comfort of the grave; that after all it was the ultimate surrender for men—or for women— and that the law of the body was death, and the law of the spirit was silence. To find wisdom women must be silent. "Silent," Mary Wollstonecraft would explode, "that is just what women have been for far too long." Miss Austen would giggle. She would shrug her demure shoulders against the pillows, and lift her delicate hands in the last gesture of tolerant amusement, and say astutely, "I never met a silent woman." What could any of them answer to that? It would have been the last sardonic sophisticated say. Just as her books to-day have still the last say over all the women of her century.

CHAPTER IV

THE BRONTË SISTERS

Who Wrestled with Romance

THE BRONTËS WOULD HAVE excited an investigating psychiatrist. They were neurotic. But they did not know that. They took themselves to be geniuses.

They could hardly have avoided being neurotic. The mother died of cancer when they were all very small, and the father, after trying twice to get a stepmother for them, settled down to celibacy. Moroseness grew upon him. He spent most of his time in his study, preparing sermons and thinking about the sadness of living. A spinster aunt came to govern the household. She spent most of her time in her bedroom, ordering the meals from there, and having the children brought to her to be taught sewing and manners.

At first there were six children, five of them girls. But two of the girls died in childhood from tuberculosis. They were buried in the graveyard that was next door to their home. The four remaining children amused themselves by writing stories. Charlotte was the oldest of them, and the most energetic. Emily was a grave young person who never said very much. Branwell, the brother, was particularly sure of his genius. He had always a great deal to say. Anne, who was the youngest, was timid and frail. She usually followed the example of her two older sisters, but was not always sure whether to accept Charlotte's determined opinions or Emily's opposition to them. She never had an easy time.

The house and the graveyard were on the edge of the moors in the west riding of Yorkshire. The name of the village was Hawarth. It was a small community four miles away from a fair-sized town called Kneighley. Cars run now from Leeds and Halifax to Kneighley, and Hawarth is a place to which tourists go dutifully, but at the beginning of the nineteenth century it was a wild and inaccessible country. There was little besides the graveyard and the great moors for the children to see. Their father roused himself sufficiently to send them early to a resident school, but they had to be brought home again because of the tendency to tuberculosis which was in them all. It was a terrible forcing-house of genius. They had to be geniuses; there was nothing else for them to be. They had nobody to whom to compare themselves except the simple people of the village. So they were a world to themselves. It left them incapable of getting along with normal people when at last they did get away. They could not meet other people on equal terms.

The Reverend Patrick Brontë was an Irish peasant from the dark glens of Ulster. His name was originally Brunty. He was what the Irish call *the stranger child* in a large family of normal peasant children. He wanted to be more than a small farmer. He absorbed enough schooling to become a school-teacher in Ireland, and somehow managed to get to Cambridge, where he studied for orders in the Established Church of England. Then he changed his name to Brontë. The King of Spain had bestowed upon Lord Nelson the dukedom of Brontë, and there was nothing to prevent an ambitious young Irishman from taking the name. He was convinced that it had been his original family name. Had not many of the Spanish come to Ireland from time to time since the Armada? There was no great gap in his imagination between a Spanish duke and an Irish peasant.

All the change got him was a parsonage on the edge of the moors. He might just as well have remained in the brooding glens of Ulster. But the change to England did one thing; it gave his children a Cornish mother. Her family name was Branwell.

The Brontë history is a veritable trap for the commentator. Two years after Charlotte died the theories about them all began to be published, and it has kept up ever since. Each of the Brontës has her intellectual partisans, and the historian has to step warily. For all of the partisans can produce evidence which is convincing, and it is only in simple ignorance that the commentator can take the books and their authors for what they appear to be. Around the Brontë fame there lingers the sound of drunken laughter and drunken bragging. Branwell Brontë was the torment of his sisters before he died, and after he died he became the joker in their fame. He had a group of cronies who believed in his genius; and they remembered, so they said, that he had read to them sentences from a book he was writing. The sentences, they thought, sounded like Emily's sentences in her great fierce book of love, *Wuthering Heights.* It was easy to remember also that Charlotte had written her books with incredible speed; it was easy, in addition, to find confusing similarities in the writing. When Charlotte's fame was at its height the rest of them, except the father, were dead. She was alone in a house full of manuscripts. Charlotte herself was a problem. She slipped once or twice in the facts she gave. That made her technically a liar. Once technically established as a liar, it is hard to get accepted as a fundamentally truthful person. Charlotte had something to cover up. Maybe she had much more to cover up. So it went on. Emily was even a more problematic person. She was a mystic, which might mean anything. She hated to admit she wrote any of the work which she was said to have written. So it remains that about all we can be sure of is that they all had a microbe in their blood stream, and in addition were neurasthenic, and possibly a bit insane. Which makes their story provocative. Between them they wrote a number of books important in the history of the feminist movement. These books have held their place in literature because of their creative vitality, in spite of being completely out-moded emotionally, and in spite of faulty technique.

It is their place in the feminist movement that saves them spiritually from the laughter of Branwell's drunken ghost.

They have the marks of the feeling of women in them, the early feeling of indignant women.

They did not want to write as women. They sent their books out under the pen-names of Currer, Ellis, and Acton Bell, presumably three young men of letters. It was the pathetic nineteenth-century gesture of women. Even the great George Eliot could not keep away from it. The Brontës tried to write like men. They did everything they knew how to do in order to throw the color of masculinity into their writing. They were spiritually sincere, but on account of this desire to appear male, technically false. It makes their writing squint. They determined to write like rugged northern he-men. Yet it was a feminine emotionalism that drove them. So they struggled inwardly with the life they tried to get into their books. Branwell tittered in the background. Life was not to be struggled with, he said; it was to be dodged. He knew a dodge or two. He would put them wise. Anne and Charlotte shuddered and went on writing. Emily got up and put him to bed. And whether or not during the nights when she sat trying to get him sober she learned what she put into *Wuthering Heights* concerning the fierceness of men when they love, nobody will ever know for sure. Her sisters did not know then. For Emily Brontë was a woman who never showed her hand.

Branwell Brontë was brought into the Brontë writing-history almost immediately by the first biographer of Charlotte, Mrs. Gaskell. She was a ladylike nineteenth-century woman when it came to emotions. She had been fond of Charlotte. She had felt sorry for her. For Miss Brontë remained even through her fame a tragic figure, and would touch the heart of any mother. Mrs. Gaskell was certain of the genius of the work and its historical importance. Mrs. Gaskell was a profound feminist. Women to her were engulfed in the downtrodden masses. It was part of the program of elevation to be indignant at life. Charlotte was that. So Mrs. Gaskell took it upon herself as a literary and feminist duty to see that Charlotte was canonized. But there was one difficulty. Sin. There was a lot of sin in

Charlotte's most significant book, *Jane Eyre*. The hero, Mr. Rochester, made such a parade of mistresses as was never before made in English literature. More than that, there was Emily's great fierce book, *Wuthering Heights*. The love in it was not only devastatingly possessive; it was also unaware of the gulf that marriage vows were supposed to make between lovers when they were married to other people. That is how the situation looked to Mrs. Gaskell. She considered it carefully. These Brontë sisters were three unmarried ladies. They should not have known about men and the mistresses they had. They should not have let their heroines love men who tossed off bigamy like a drink, or who went mad with frustration over a woman married to another man. So, she brought Branwell up out of his sordid grave covered with drunken memories and a tainted delight in them. Branwell must have told his maiden sisters all about men. It was an alibi. Mrs. Gaskell must have been very satisfied about her own cleverness when she worked it out. She hoped, too, that it would fix the attention of all future historians of the Brontës, and keep them from investigating what Charlotte did when she was in Brussels. She did not worry so much about Emily. Emily was a mystic. Nobody at that time expected to understand mystics. More than that, Emily had carefully left no clues. That is, no clues as Mrs. Gaskell interpreted clues. Charlotte had. She was always breaking into French in her stories. She was always bringing in the foreigners she had met. Her favorite theme was a governess teaching in Brussels, always sorrowfully in love. It was enough to disturb a ladylike biographer. It was very fortunate that Branwell was there to take the load.

Mrs. Gaskell, for all that she accomplished one of the outstanding nineteenth-century biographies, did not know what she was writing about.

She saw Charlotte as she wanted to see her, a passionately tragic figure; the one child left to a strange old man, writing her heart out in memory of her two dead sisters, carrying on alone the tradition they had built together in love. It made a dramatic biography. But the truth was far more dramatic than she let the biography be.

The Brontë household was a household of terrible emotions. The writing that was done was secret writing. Emily was sullenly angry when Charlotte found her poems and insisted they should be put together with poems by Anne and herself and sent out for publication. That was their start.

It was the year 1845. Charlotte was twenty-nine years old. Emily was twenty-seven, and Anne was twenty-five. Branwell came in between Charlotte and Emily. He had returned home from his tutoring position, dismissed for dissipation and for making love to his employer's wife. It was a year of more than usual depression for the family. Mr. Brontë was going blind. The young women did not know what to do with themselves. Charlotte had outlined a plan of conducting a school at home. She had gone to Brussels to study French and German. She had made Emily go, too, for a while. But no children came to the school. It was a failure. Anne had come home from her position. She had been governess in the same family which had employed Branwell as tutor. She could not stay there. Branwell had disgraced them all. He spent his time in the public house of the village. Emily and Charlotte were on edge with each other. This was not new; but it was accentuated by a difference of opinion about how Branwell should be treated. It is just as well to emphasize here that these people, contained in a dreary house next door to a graveyard, were Irish and Cornish. Which means that they had Celtic implacability. They could sustain their hatreds. They differed only slightly in their emotional expression. Charlotte was a positive hater; she pursued her enemies with a stick. Emily was a negative hater. Her enemies stopped existing so far as she was concerned. They might as well be dead. Anne was a little of both on a much feebler scale, and she made an effort to be a good Christian. But they all had to hate something. That was part of their racial inheritance. Charlotte hated Branwell, and put all his shortcomings down in the letters she wrote to her intimate woman friend, Ellen Nussey. Emily had always disliked Charlotte. Charlotte was a fusser. When she began to treat Branwell badly, Emily started to hate her. When pity was not in a woman, that woman could just as well be dispensed with. That was Emily's view. Mild little Anne turned her hatred upon drink. The book she wrote later was a prohibitionist document. She was the first of the W.C.T.U. women.

It was a household of terrible emotion.

But the worst of the emotion was that which raged within Charlotte. The others knew nothing about it. But it was what, subconsciously, made her so bitter towards Branwell. Branwell by his own confession had fallen in love with a married woman, and had gloried in his emotion. He was a redheaded Celt; it made him seem like a heroic fellow, and very unusual. Charlotte looked at him sourly. Yes, he loved a woman and could not have her, so he took to dissipation on a big scale. Drink, drugs, and the let-down that follows. He set in to a prolonged orgy. Charlotte despised him. She knew what love was. She knew more than she said about love like Branwell's. She had fallen in love with a married man. But she had not taken to dissipation on a big scale. She had taken to work. She tried to found a school. Subconsciously she blamed the unattractive presence of Branwell for the failure of her school. Hating him helped her to stand the love that was tearing her heart out of her.

This is what Mrs. Gaskell had determined nobody should know about Charlotte. She hoped nobody would ever know it. She forgot about jealousy. She did not realize that the more famous Charlotte became the more active would become the jealousy of the other woman.

The Brussels story is not easy to get at. It is clear enough that Charlotte Brontë loved Monsieur Heger, to whose school she went first as a student, and later as a teacher. But it is not clear that Monsieur Heger loved her.

Whether he did, or did not, he was in a difficult position. His wife was a watchful woman, who had laid all her illusions away.

JANE AUSTEN

CHARLOTTE BRONTE
(Mrs. Arthur Bell Nicholls)

EMILY BRONTE

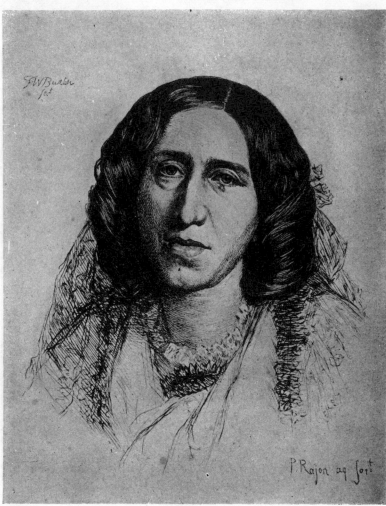

F.W.Burton

Photo, Frick Art Reference Library

GEORGE ELIOT

OLIVE SCHREINER

She believed in thinking the worst before it was the worst. It was a kind of marital insurance. Miss Brontë had no finesse in love. She shut her eyes and jumped emotionally. It was all very distressing to Monsieur Heger. Not to speak of its discomfort. Just how he stood emotionally himself, nobody knows. Charlotte wrote him letters that almost equaled the letters of Mary Wollstonecraft for pathos and ardor. When he answered them, it was in the handwriting of his wife, in the most careful of phrasing. Maybe he was a cautious man. Maybe he expected Charlotte to understand that this was finesse and the way an astute gentleman handled his wife's suspicions. Maybe he was a puzzled man, not knowing what he had done to rouse such passionate devotion. He is an enigma now. Perhaps he was then. Emily said that Charlotte overestimated him. She decided he could teach them nothing of much use, and went home, even though he put himself on record that he considered Emily's mentality superior to Charlotte's. Whatever the truth was about him, there was no mistaking Charlotte's passion for him. His wife decided that even a one-sided devotion was likely to be intoxicating to a man. There was no knowing the effect of its flattering persistence upon a susceptible male. Madame Heger was a Continental woman. If she could make Charlotte's devotion appear to be funny, it would be astute policy. And certainly it was. Charlotte was morbidly sensitive. The very respectable letters that came back in answer to hers did the trick. But not all at once. Madame Heger did not consider that she had heard the last of Charlotte. She had not either. In order to be forehanded she went through her husband's wastepaper basket, and she pasted together the fragments of four of Charlotte's broken-hearted letters. She locked them away in her jewel case, and left it and its contents to her daughter when she died. Many years later her daughter handed them to the British Museum. It was a posthumous revenge. All the sting was out of it. But it was the answer to the book which Charlotte wrote, *Villette*. Madame Heger walks in *Villette*, as sly a woman as ever ran a school for young women, and held on to a husband. She peeps through key-holes, and steams open letters. She searches bureau drawers. She pussyfoots it through the halls with felt on the soles of her shoes. You never knew when you would meet her suddenly in the dark. She kept a surveillance of her household that would have shamed a hotel detective. To keep a secret in her household you had to seal it in an air-tight container and bury it at midnight under a tree in the garden. Monsieur must have been a bland person indeed to stand it. But Charlotte paints him as a man of fascination, odd and clever and slightly brutal. The Brontë girls liked men to be men. They were Irish. They also liked men who were bound up hand and foot with tragedy. In that way they were Irish too.

But alas for her peace of mind, Charlotte was not fatalistic about it. She was tortured. She walked the streets of Brussels in the rain. Many times she would think she saw him coming. She wished she had gone home and stayed home when Emily had gone. She looked for him at every corner. She could not stay quiet. She had to keep going. Even in her room she paced the floor. One night in desperation she went into a Catholic church. The gentle face of the pitying eternal Mother touched her heart. She looked up and saw the suffering upon the eyelids of the Christ. There was understanding there. She went to the confession-box. Haltingly she told the kind old priest that she was a Protestant, but would he listen to her? He said he would. He told her it was more than a woman could bear. She must go home. Surgery, he said, was the only treatment. He said nothing to her about sin. He spoke only about pain. These things happened, he knew. Later on when Charlotte wrote *Villette* she forgot to be grateful for the sympathy and the wisdom. She included the whole system of Roman Catholicism in her hatred of Madame Heger. She went home. But the pain was no less. She walked the moors instead of the streets of Brussels. She still watched for him. She thought scornfully of herself, and of the priest who had pitied her. It would have been better if he had lashed her for her sin. Then she could have pitied herself. Charlotte was a puritan. She had no mercy. Not even upon herself.

She fell upon Emily's poems avidly. Writing was something to live for. They would publish everything they could get ready. Emily consented. There was nothing else to do. There was no opposing Charlotte. Print was like drink to her. After the poems came out she said they must all write a novel. She was raring to get her experiences in Brussels down. Maybe it would deliver her of her sin. Anne was enthusiastic. She said she was already at work upon a story. It was *Agnes Grey,* and it contained some of her own personal story as a governess. *Agnes Grey.* Charlotte thought about the gray streets of Brussels. But she must not tell too much. She began a story called *The Professor.* Emily looked at them writing in the sitting-room. It was as good an occupation as any. She talked it over with Branwell. Branwell said that together the two of them could write a novel that would make anything Charlotte would do pale and mediocre. What did she know about life, with her puritanical little fussy mind and her tight lips? Emily said they would try it. It would be good for Branwell, she thought, to put his mind on something else besides his tragedy. It might keep him from drinking. It would make him feel less of a failure. And for herself; well, she wrote anyway; the moods that came upon her as she pushed against the wind on the moors, and as she watched the snow drift against the gravestones, had to be gathered into phrases; for they came like music upon her.

Charlotte was afraid when she wrote *The Professor.* She was afraid of writing as a woman; she was afraid of committing herself too much. Maybe she was afraid of what her sister Emily would read into the story. Charlotte was always more sensitive to the opinions of Emily than she acknowledged. As a result of this fear, *The Professor* was lifeless. Its only point, so far as the feminist movement was concerned, is that it is the first appearance, so far as there is record, of the woman who insists on paying her own way after marriage. This was Charlotte's own cult. Not that it meant very much. It was only a flicker of resentful feeling. So far as her own inner history was concerned, *The Professor* contains a preliminary portrait of her enemy, Madame Heger. It is the only part of the book that has any life. Charlotte was at her emotional best when she let her hatreds run. Anne's story, *Agnes Grey*, was almost a companion to it in colorlessness. But it has honesty. It was written as a woman writes. It has no vitality, only pathos. Which was just about all that Anne herself had.

But it was quite different about Emily's great fierce book of love, *Wuthering Heights*.

Maurice Maeterlinck called it one of the very greatest love stories ever written in any language.

How could it have been written by a girl who had never known love? There is the mystic answer. Emily had lived before. This Brontë incarnation was only a period of pause; to think over, to remember, to gather together the meaning of previous experience.

It is psychologically a lazy explanation. Though inasmuch as it is a doctrine implicitly accepted for centuries by the Eastern half of the world, it is only the brave, foolish young West that would disturb it. And who can know?

Emily Brontë was a mystery. They said she had no lover. But nobody could be sure. She had been away from home for a while, teaching in a private family. She did not stay long. She left no record of what happened to her there. It is true that with the fame the Brontë family attained, no love affair of any of them had a chance of remaining concealed. There would always be somebody to recall something. But in Emily's case, love did not need to be an affair of meeting as lovers ordinarily meet. It would be a fusion of being which might take place at once from the most apparently superficial contact. She was a woman of intensity and the reserve that protects such intensity. She permitted no one to know anything about her.

The form of *Wuthering Heights* is ungainly. It shows the two writers plainly. It opens with a limp. The setting is given, and is played with in the manner of the literary dilettante of

the period. That was Branwell. Then suddenly the telling of
the story veers round to another person, an old woman who had
been a servant in the manor. Then it becomes rugged and
simple. That is Emily. It starts out to be a mystery story
bringing in ghosts; it turns out to be a terrible story of emotional frustration.

In bare outline the story concerns a group of people living in
a bleak manor house in the north of England. The master of
the house had returned from a journey bringing a little boy with
him of unknown parentage, dark, strange, vital little boy. He
is named Heathcliffe. There are two other children in the
house—a little girl called Catherine and a boy who is older. He
is the heir, and when he comes into his possessions he treats the
waif Heathcliffe as if he were the scum of the earth's population. Heathcliffe and Catherine love each other, but Catherine
has not sufficient courage to marry him in the face of her
brother's opinion of him. She marries a mild young man from
another manor house. Heathcliffe disappeared. But Catherine
knew the sin she was committing. She married the other man
with her teeth on edge. It was an affront to her nervous
system. Her mind was always with Heathcliffe. After a while
he returned, and in revenge married the sister of the man to
whom Catherine was married. It was an affront to his nervous
system. His mind was never away from Catherine. So the
disintegration set in. It killed Catherine. It twisted the moral
nature of Heathcliffe. Catherine haunted him, but there was
no peace in her spirit. She could not rest away from Heathcliffe. He was always aware of her when she came. Once he
paid the sexton to open her grave; he himself broke open her
coffin, and looked at her. He left the side of it open. When
his time came to die he left orders that the side of his coffin was
to be left open. He was to be beside Catherine in death.

It is an agonizing story. The susceptible reader cannot put
it down until the end. It leaves the imagination stunned. You
cannot examine its technique as you read any more than you
could study the technique of a storm at sea. You are swept

up in it. This was the work of a mind to whom death was a joke imposed upon a blind race; to whom the love of a man and a woman was a great and wonderful thing hardly guessed at by the blind fumbling about for the comforting of one another in their blindness. Souls, it would seem from its telling, come out from the original force together in twos. There is one mate. Catherine said, "I am Heathcliffe."

It is an idea that sentimental folk have taken up for themselves. It justifies to them the horror of finding another human being an absolute need; it softens down the insistence of sexual hunger.

But the writer of *Wuthering Heights* was no sentimentalist. It was a hard, strong mind that had the courage to set the idea not with beauty but with wild ugliness. It was a mind that could look without being very much surprised at sin. Heathcliffe became a man of no scruples or tenderness. He hated everyone who had kept him from Catherine, and the hatred included the second generation of the family. He made their lives a misery. To the mind writing that was nothing; nothing more than a diseased anatomy is to a surgeon; or a diseased imagination is to an alienist. It was an austere mind in very exact possession of the facts of frustration. It followed the sequence ruthlessly, and did not flinch.

Who was there among the Brontës with a mind like a surgeon? Not Branwell. Branwell was soft and maudlin. Even when he had added drugs to drink. He lay and wept; he wailed over his disappointments. He may have believed his lady was his soul mate; but when they told him to get out, he got out. He did not brood silently. He mooned. He beat against fate with his voice. Those who do that never take to writing for relief; they do not need to; they have their relief from the verbal self-dramatization.

Not Charlotte. She had a tempestuous temperament. She had thrown herself at Monsieur Heger. She enjoyed her own drama and its suffering. She did not tell it, but that was because she was ashamed of it. The shame was as much from the failure of response in the gentleman as from the fact of his marriage. Ardor was the outstanding emotional quality of Charlotte Brontë. In her late school-days she had gone almost homosexual in her devotion to Ellen Nussey. She wrote her letters that were nearly amorous. She wanted to live with her. She invited Ellen to the parsonage. Emily took Ellen for a walk on the moors and decided she was a harmless safety-valve for Charlotte, and afterwards ignored her. No, Charlotte was not a woman who could have any conception of a dammed-up force of feeling. Feeling swirled and whirlpooled in her. There was always somebody around to receive it.

Not Anne. She was a dutiful little person.

Not the old father. He would never have concealed a manuscript written in his virility. He was an imaginative swaggerer. He would have loved being literary. Emily would never have gotten away with taking his stuff.

There was only Emily who could have written it.

Inwardly the book shows the mind of a woman, for all its surgical quality. Heathcliffe is no man's drawing. He is the product of a woman's longing for a strong man, a great fierce man with the power in him to subdue her own strength. It would have taken such a man as Heathcliffe to conquer Emily Brontë. He has all the marks of an Irish hero from out of the old legends, a hero hemmed in by a narrow round of circumstances, but still a hero, who got control of the world he was in, and loved a woman all through his life. Fidelity in love is a characteristic of the stories of the early Irish. Love that goes on through the joke that death is would not be a preposterous idea to the Irish mind. Emily Brontë had all the signs of the Ulster mystic, and all the marks of the Ulster woman. And their taste in men. Wanting greatness.

She looked at Charlotte's volatile professor, and went home. She could learn nothing from a wee man like that. She looked at her father's curates, and took her dog for a walk instead. They were too mild for her. She loved the strong way of the wind on the moors.

Ellen Nussey said she was a magnetic person. You could feel her presence in a room. Her eyes were curiously lit up from within themselves. She was much better-looking than the other girls. She had dignity. When she did enter into conversation, her words were always kind. She had something strongly maternal about her. She was efficient in her movements. She had a light fine figure and a long stride. She was taller than the others. Charlotte was a very small creature with nervous quick movements. Her face was discontented. Anne was small and wistful, and might have been pretty if a little life could have gotten into her. Charlotte would never have been pretty. She had a burnt-up look. They were all brunettes. Branwell was the only ginger child, as the Irish name it, among them. Charlotte and Anne had the figures of children. Emily in other surroundings would have been a striking woman. Even Ellen Nussey saw that. Her hair was black and her eyes were the gray Celtic eyes that make so exotic an effect set against brunette coloring. Charlotte's eyes were also gray, but they were never exotic. They were short-sighted tired eyes. She was always working to make herself more informed. But she had vivacity. Emily was a still person. Anne was just shy. Emily's nose, according to Miss Nussey, was slightly aquiline, a nose of power. Charlotte's was short and straight. Nobody said anything about their voices, which is a pity. For the tone of a woman's voice is always one of the most interesting things about her. Branwell amused himself once by drawing the portraits of his sisters. Mr. Nicholls, who later married Charlotte, said it was a good portrait of his wife. So we are reasonably safe in assuming the other two are equally true to their models. Emily's mouth is full, with a short upper lip. Her chin is rounded. It must have been an oval face. Everything about Charlotte is sharp and pointed. Her lips are tightly held together and are thin. She sits precisely. Emily is leaning casually forward. The eyes are dreamy. It is the face of a woman of consequence. Anne's is a little girl's face, and is more like Emily's than Charlotte's. Both Emily and

Anne might have belonged to any period; but Charlotte is unmistakably the early nineteenth-century young woman with a
poker at her spine and a correctly adjusted shawl.

Emily's face is the only one among all the faces of the nineteenth-century women writers that might be modern. It is not
unlike the faces of the young women of to-day. There is a
peculiar resemblance in it somewhere to the face of Amelia
Earhart. A flyer's resolute face. Yes, she would have been
a woman to fly a ship over the world. A woman to whom death
would be a joke to be tackled at the time it came.

We cannot know historically whether or not she met the
man who was Heathcliffe. But he was her man. She did not
have the energy to get out and find him. She had a diseased
body. She knew it. She waited. As her body fell tissue by
tissue before the disease, her imagination rose to its power.
She forced it to. A great fierce man who would be cruel if he
did not get what he wanted; who would never be turned aside
from his purpose; whom no woman could dominate.

Out of it she evolved a hair-raising orgy of frustration. It
was sound psychiatry, which is the most amazing thing about
it, and the composition of a virgin living in a retreat in the
fourth decade of the nineteenth century, when the influence of
Freud had not been dreamed of. It could not, in any likelihood, have been the result of intense and acute observation. It
was an imaginative jump into a realm of knowledge that was
due later to be tapped by a scientific coterie of men in Vienna.
It is scientifically exact, but it is colored by the feminine imagination. It is a woman's virgin dream of love. It was not a
man's. It was not even an experienced woman's. It was virgin.
It was out of the very emotion that sent young women into
convents missing the man of their choice. It was out of the
very emotion that was to send many young women of a later
generation into a world of experience alien to them because
nothing very much mattered, missing the men of their choice.
Being virgin work it was not Branwell's. Though from Branwell she probably gathered the details of conversations. Emily

had an absorbing mind. She could see things, and hear them, through the medium of others. But the odd conversations of the local characters are only flourishes in the book; the gaunt story proceeds almost without them by itself, out of.a woman's picturing to herself of what love was. A dead woman rapped at the windows of Heathcliffe's house. He let her in. A male being rapped at the nature of Emily Brontë. She let him into her desire. She wrote a book in which death and life crossed each other, and mixed, and separated, and mixed again. It was her fate. She was already dying when she wrote the book. She was rousing herself to live before she died; and yet laughing at herself at the joke that death would play on her who had never lived. Maybe she believed as another still person of another age believed, da Vinci, that the spirit at death would mourn its parting from the experiencing body, and be lonely without it. Whatever it was, the book was a wild forlorn cry from a woman who was not made of the same substance quite as other women. There was a door out of her inexperience. She felt it at night. This was not the only world, she told herself. There was an-other very inner world, and outer, beyond actual experience. She forced herself to it. There were worlds upon worlds; planets moving in other orbits; maybe other races of men; one consecrated great plan. Often she stood by her window at night and watched the sky. A strange force would take her in its power. In the morning her eyes were different. Char-lotte began to grope towards some understanding of Emily. When she read her poems she was staggered. They were so strange. They were like echoes from unearthly music. What was Emily?

When Charlotte read *Wuthering Heights* she was staggered again. She knew that her own *Professor* was a silly tame story beside it. She sat down to begin another story; and some of the fire of *Wuthering Heights* transferred itself to the writing of *Jane Eyre*.

And *Jane Eyre* was the book of the year in England. Char-lotte Brontë had let loose all the pent-up hatreds of her nature.

She was no longer afraid. There had been hatred in her sister's book. But Charlotte's was a very concrete hatred and very personal. She went after the school that had killed her two older sisters. She made horrible images of the teachers and of the system. She took for her heroine a small plain-looking orphan girl who was designed by nature to be the butt of sadistic people. She wrote herself into little defenseless, tortured Jane Eyre. The hatred that forced the book out of her made its writing astoundingly vivid. It knocked its readers cold. The style was as tortured as the heroine. Charlotte liked being literary, and she never missed a chance to be literary; except when she was so angry she forgot. It was when she was raging angry that the book blazed with power; when she cooled off and got literary it was lame and pretentious; but fortunately for her ambitions the anger far outweighed the literature in it; so it went over. She was unquestionably influenced by Emily's Heathcliffe when she came to draw the hero, Mr. Rochester. Only, as she no doubt thought herself, she improved on him by giving her man a very Continental experience. He had had a group of mistresses, and liked nothing better than to brag about them; but when he was due, by reason of approaching middle age, to be touched by tender love, it was gentle, plain Jane to whom he turned. Not for him were the lovely ladies of title that were brought into the story. But he amused himself while he was trying to make up his mind what to do by philandering a bit; just enough to make Jane jealous. Jealousy made her lose her head. She came out flatly with her love of him. It was Charlotte's famous innovation. No woman had ever done such a thing in literature—certainly not in ladylike literature. It was a great triumph for Mr. Rochester. It gave him courage to plan his final sin. For all this time the bad man had been hiding in his attic a maniac wife, guarded by a gin-consuming nurse. Jane had sensed the mystery in the house. But that had added to her love. Mr. Rochester arranges a start into bigamy; but he is stopped at the altar. The facts have come out. Jane is horrified; but not nearly so horrified as when her darling makes her a proposition. Then she flees the country, as all good women fled in those days from sin. And she flees with only what she has on, and has many melodramatic accidents. But they are nothing compared to what happened to Rochester. His insane wife sets the house on fire, and jumps from the roof to her death. Rochester is paid by fate for his ways by having a burning brand hit him in the eyes; he is blinded for life. And little Jane comes radiantly back and marries him. Charlotte Brontë hugged herself; she had made a plain little woman come into her own; she had been most sophisticated and had not quailed before mistresses and sins and cases for the asylum. In fact she had treated them all with gusto. All London talked about the book. People got all mixed up about the identities of Currer, Ellis and Acton Bell. She thought it was necessary to go to London and straighten things out. But she was afraid to go by herself. So she took Anne. Emily was angry about the whole business. She was still angrier when Charlotte returned and explained that she had told the publisher they were three sisters. It was all a trap, Emily said. Publicity was vulgar. Besides being a nuisance. She must have had a moment of prevision. Publicity was certainly going to be both vulgar and a nuisance for the Brontë future. Not to mention what it was going to do to Brontë historians. That settled it for Emily. She would never write another novel.

But Charlotte had got going. This at last was living. The little plans for the school now seemed to be childish and forlorn. Here was literary fame. Emily looked at her and went off by herself to walk on the moors. But Anne was more impressed. She wanted to get in on the fame.

Emily puzzled Charlotte. There was no understanding the girl. What was she? She decided that she would put Emily into a book. That certainly was the way to deal with what bothered you. Anne was thinking too. But not about Emily. She took Emily for granted. She had been impressed by the sins in Charlotte's book. Sin paid. Not that Branwell ever made his pay. She decided to put Branwell into a book. She

patted her conscience by saying to herself that maybe it would
keep others from falling into a like sin. The father was coming
out in Anne. She wanted to preach. So she wrote *The Tenant
of Wildfell Hall.*

One day when Emily came in from the moors followed by her
dog, Keeper, Anne told her what she was doing. Emily looked
at her. She said quietly that she was surprised. It was bad
taste to use one's relatives for copy; it was cruelty to use the
weakness of another for professional material. It was also lazy.
What was the imagination for? Anne was hurt. She had not
meant any harm. Charlotte blazed at Emily. She should let
Anne alone. It was time that some woman had the courage
to write about what drink did to men and to the women tied
to them. Emily looked at her with disconcerting directness.
To make copy out of poor Branwell was wrong. They would
pay for it. She must have had another moment of prevision.
Branwell might very profitably have been left alone. But
Anne was firm. It was her duty. And Charlotte had encouraged her. Which was to be considered. For of the family
Charlotte was the successful author. Surely she should know
what would sell. What could Emily say to that? She could not
summon enough prevision to know that *Wuthering Heights*
would be read and reread when Charlotte's books were only
remembered as the books that somehow had got placed on the
school's supplementary-reading list because of some vague historical significance.

So the writing went on in that unhappy house. And so did
the germ. Branwell began to sink. Emily nursed him. His
father grieved over his only son. Charlotte hardened herself.
She knew that they had to stand it. But he had brought it on
himself. Anne thought to herself that it would not all be in
vain. People would know what drink did to men.

On the day of Branwell's funeral in September, Emily col-
lapsed. She never went out again on the moors. But she would
not stay in bed. She went about her usual household work.
She talked less than ever. Charlotte was frantic. She said she

was going to send for a London doctor. Emily said she would not see him if he did come. What would the use be? One morning in December she went to the cage where she kept a wild hawk she had tamed. Charlotte watched her and was frightened. Emily opened the door of the hawk's cage and told him to go free. He hesitated. She lifted him out and poised him on her hand, and sent him with a push out into the air. Emily was Irish; she was dying with a symbolic gesture. Charlotte was terrified. Emily turned; she put her hand to her throat; she struggled with her breath. She knew it had come, and she fought. She hated the publicity of death. Reserve was no armor against it. She struggled; she would not die. It was a horrible thing that would leave her helpless and open. She kept on her feet; she held on to the door until the germ had taken her last breath. It was a shocking pagan death.

It hurried the progress of the germ in little Anne. She sickened immediately. Charlotte called the doctor, only to learn that nothing could save Anne. She was already too far gone. Charlotte, however, tried to save her. She took her to Scarborough by the sea; but it was in vain. Anne died in May, and was buried in Scarborough. Charlotte returned to her father. She read Emily's last poems, among them that magnificent last psalm.

> *No coward soul is mine,*
> *No trembler in the world's storm-troubled sphere;*
> *I see heaven's glory shine,*
> *And faith shines equal, arming me from afar.*
>
> *O God within my breast,*
> *Almighty, ever-present Deity!*
> *Life—that in me has rest,*
> *As, undying Life—have power in thee!*
>
> *Vain are the thousand creeds*
> *That move men's hearts; unutterably vain;*

Worthless as withered weeds,
Or idlest froth amid the boundless main.

To waken doubt in one
Holding so fast by Thine infinity;
So surely anchored on
The steadfast rock of immortality.

With wide-embracing love
Thy spirit animates eternal years,
Pervades and broods above,
Changes, sustains, dissolves, creates and rears.

Though earth and man were gone,
And suns and universe ceased to be,
And Thou were left alone,
Every existence would exist in Thee.

There is not room for death,
Nor atom that his might could render void;
Thou—Thou art Being and Breath,
And what Thou art may never be destroyed.

Charlotte walked backward and forward in her lonely house.
She thought of Keeper, the dog, sitting in his sorrow on Emily's
grave. She thought about the wild hawk. What was Emily?

Charlotte tried to make Emily live in *Shirley*. But Charlotte
could only portray what she loved or what she hated. Emily
was beyond both love and hate. She had been spiritually
elusive, and humanly a most puzzling person. The pagan fierce
death; the religious faith of the last song. Which was Emily?
Animals and birds had known her instinctively, and were drawn
as by a magnet. Keeper never recovered from her death. His
dog heart was broken. Charlotte tried very hard with *Shirley*.
It was an interesting characterization she managed; but it was
not Emily.

The book rolls up in the end into feminist propaganda.
Charlotte saw her sister as one of the new women. She sets her

as she would have liked to have seen Emily, with wealth and friends. She did not realize that wealth would have meant nothing more to Emily than poverty. She creates conversations between Shirley and her intimate woman friend, Caroline Helstone, such as she imagined Emily would have conducted, had she ever cared to get into conversation. The conversations read like very learned essays on the freedom of women. Emily would have thought they were funny. Charlotte really had nothing to put into *Shirley*. The subject was beyond her emotional grip. Emily's temperamental aloofness had always tortured her sister. Her occasional sweetness had never been given to Charlotte. It had gone out to the weakness of Branwell and the pathos of Anne. Charlotte had utterly no comprehension of the mysticism of Emily; she had had no idea that the strangeness of her eyes had come out of a frustration which was a greater frustration than any of the frustrations in that house. Emily Brontë was a tragedy. She handled her tragedy well. She achieved calm. But she could only maintain it when she was alone on the moors. When she went into the world it was broken. So she took care not to go into the world. Emily had pushed herself so far down into the depths of her nature that she only existed in a dream. She needed a Teacher. She got quite far by herself, but she had missed the wisdom that would have made her able to preserve her poise in the world. That could only have come to her from a teacher whose training was far beyond any of the training of western religions. Emily would have understood the East. She could have sat at the feet of Lao-tse.

But all this was out of Charlotte's understanding. All she knew was that she missed the presence of Emily. It bothered her that she had not loved her enough. She took to lying about it. She assured everybody that Emily and she had been devoted to each other. In private she paced up and down with remorse. She had spent years of her life loving a man who had refused even to write to her. She had closed herself up in that love. And Emily had been dying all the time. Perhaps in great need of love. Charlotte hated the Hegers because they had taken her emotion for so long.

So she went for them in *Villette*. Emily had never liked them.

Sitting alone with an old father in that dismal house Charlotte got the Hegers out of her system. This time there was very little disguise. She herself lived in the small plain-looking shy English governess, Lucy Snow. The Heger *ménage* came to life in Madame Beck's school for young ladies. She dealt meticulously with Madame Beck's jealousies. Technically the story flags badly in places. Charlotte obviously got frightened at times and tried to cover herself up. She has to divide her love into two men, and little Lucy has to veer from one to the other without much reason for doing so. It makes it rather unconvincing. But the genuine emotion of the writer does get into scenes. With heart-breaking poignancy little Lucy struggled with her hopeless passion. That is very real. And the actual Monsieur Heger is very real and so is the pussyfooting Madame Beck. It is easy to understand why Charlotte should have been attracted to the man. He is fiery and uncertain with all the temperamental virility that the Brontë girls liked in men. It was easy to understand why she hated Madame. It was not only that she possessed Monsieur. She also possessed the bland and irritating self-containment which Charlotte always had lacked. She had the silent superiority that Emily had had, and in addition a completely worldly estimate of the motivation of other people.

The portrait of Madame Beck was so bitter that it floored Mrs. Gaskell when she came to do the biography. She went over to Brussels to look the woman up. Madame Heger felt it was her duty in the interest of history to show her Charlotte's letters. Mrs. Gaskell interpreted it as her duty to the feminine cause to ignore the letters. It would never do. She thought hers would remain the one absolute authoritative biography. She could be as wary as Madame Heger. She put so much outside controversial matter into her biography that it took all the attention. The school to which the Brontës had gone took action; Branwell's mistress sued her; Mr. Brontë considered having the booked banned; she had made him out to be a very eccentric person indeed, and hinted that the girls had all contracted the germ because they were starved in their childhood. Mrs. Gaskell was more astute than Victorian ladies were usually given credit for being. She really did outwit Madame Heger by making so much fuss about other matters that Brussels was left alone by the critics. If Charlotte had been wise she would have taken Mrs. Gaskell completely into her confidence; for then Mrs. Gaskell could have made even a neater job of it. Although it is just possible that she would never have undertaken to write the story of a woman who had loved a man in those circumstances. It was not nice. Brussels must have given her quite a jolt. For she had thought Charlotte was a nice woman. She had become acquainted with her two years before her death. Charlotte had visited her, and she had visited Hawarth. The tragedy of the family had caught her imagination. She knew it would make a gorgeous biography. Besides in her mind Charlotte was a literary pioneer and part of the feminist movement. She made a great heroine of her.

Charlotte Brontë did not exactly enjoy her fame.

It was compensation for the erotic wound. There is an historical rumor that the fame brought Monsieur Heger finally to her; that they met secretly in London. The Hegers admitted that Monsieur took a trip to London, and Charlotte during the years of her literary popularity was there several times every year. She was fêted. She met everybody of literary importance. But she was never able to be at ease among people. The cramped childhood told on her, and no amount of admiration could ever give her absolute self-confidence. She knew she was a small, badly-formed, plain-looking woman. Fame never alleviates that in a woman. She knew that she did not *take* with folk; she felt them looking at her interestedly, but still with appraisal. The least unfriendly criticism of her work brought

her instantly back to her sensitive youth, and crushed her
spirit. She never gained Emily's poise.

She got to need admiration; and her need of it led her to get
married. Her father's curate, Mr. Nicholls, had admired her
for a long time. He was a gentle Irishman, and had the racial
taste for sad people. Charlotte Brontë was a tragic figure to
him in spite of all her fame. Charlotte had never liked curates.
They were mild men. She had made them ridiculous in the
Shirley story, and Mr. Nicholls had recognized himself. But
that had not stopped him admiring her. He liked her literary
nerve, as much as he loved her personal lack of it. She accepted Mr. Nicholls.

Her father made just enough trouble about it to give it the
attraction of a cause to her. Mr. Brontë had enjoyed Charlotte's
fame. It had given him confidence again in the plan of existence. It justified his life. An operation had been performed
upon his eyes, and he was able again to take the pulpit and to
read all his daughter's books, and also to cherish her press notices.
He thought that Nicholls was decidedly forgetting his place to
aspire to the hand of Miss Brontë. In his opinion Charlotte
could have any man she wanted. So why fall back upon a
curate? Her health was much better. He no longer had to
worry when she got her feet wet or sat in a draft. The family
germ seemed to have been conquered by the fame.

Charlotte had decided to marry. She did not explain to her
father how ill at ease she still felt with the great men she met,
or that they only saw her as a queer little woman with an emotional talent for writing. After she was married she assured
everybody that she was very happy.

She seems to have been happy. Mr. Nicholls was devoted and
gentle. He was not the great fierce man of her temperamental
yearning. But maybe she knew by then that such men were
hard upon women, and demanded a lot of study. She would
have had no time for the study; her career was too important.
She would have had no energy either. She was too old, and in
addition she was tubercular. So she was well off with her gentle

curate, and probably she knew it. Maybe the historical rumor explains why she knew it. She was no longer yearning for Monsieur Heger.

She had only a few months of happiness. The germ crept up quietly all the time, and when she was pregnant in her thirty-ninth year it suddenly started to speed. The doctor who was called said it was hopeless. She died thinking she could not die she was so happy.

It was a mercy that she did die. If she had lived to hold a baby to her breast she would have been frightened about the hatreds she had put into publication. There was no taking them back.

She would have understood the need Madame Heger had felt to protect her family by whatever method would work. She would have understood the maternal emotion Emily had packed into her kindness to Branwell. She might even have felt some glimmering of the twisted psychology which leads people to be cruel to children. She would have known that literary cruelty and literary revenge did not correct it. She would have been ashamed of her books, and being Irish, she might have done something drastic.

It was better that she did not. For her three good books, *Jane Eyre, Shirley* and *Villette,* for all their awkward technique and their high-driven emotionalism, were valuable records. They were documents in the feminist movement. Mrs. Gaskell was right in her belief. Charlotte Brontë was a type. There were many middle-class women like her, unable to find the man who would have satisfied them, and with no real outlet for their energies.

She drove it home that women had feeling and passionality. She glorified feeling in women. Her characters were all subsidiary to that one main idea. She hated the romantic nonsense that men wrote about women. She also hated the picture Miss Austen drew of them. It was too matter-of-fact.

What she was really saying, though it is not clear that she knew it consciously, was that women needed a wider intellectual arena in order to find a more satisfying erotic life. They had to have a chance to explore. Love was far more important to them than to men; and yet they were hemmed in by the assumption men had that women were ordained by nature simply to respond to them.

She had been disillusioned personally, but that did not alter the truth of her work. Emily and Charlotte Brontë knew something more than Miss Austen knew, though they lacked her technical mastery. And at the same time Miss Austen knew something more than they knew—which was that after all the exploring, and all the illusion, it was best to take simply what was to be had, and never mind the longing for something else.

It was all an unending confusing circle.

It would have needed the wise fine mind of George Eliot to have explained the circle. Not that Charlotte Brontë would ever have listened to George Eliot. She would not have approved of her. George Eliot had done what Miss Brontë had not managed to do—to live openly with the man she loved, even though he did happen technically to be married to another woman. Her own bitterness had made Charlotte a puritan. It was the puritan in her that caused her to make such a to-do about passion. It was her puritanism that had led her to make a feminist cause out of little Jane Eyre telling Rochester she loved him. Miss Austen would have read that incident with distaste and some amusement. It was a gaucherie, and it was unnecessary. Mary Wollstonecraft would have cheered. It was her idea of equality. And why not? Miss Austen would have shrugged her beautifully molded shoulders. And Mary would have reminded her perhaps that if she had had the nerve to do it she might have got for herself the dark sardonic man she had obviously wanted. A shadow would have flitted over Miss Austen's bright eyes. And Emily Brontë would look at her strangely. She would be thinking it was all fate. Whether one was a fighting puritan like Charlotte, or a polite skeptic like Miss Austen, or an emotional rebel like Mary Wollstonecraft, it all came to the same thing in the end. There was between

men and women a bond that was peculiar to individuals, and a
fixation of emotional need. Sometimes you looked through life
and did not find it. Sometimes you found it and could not
have it. Sometimes when you did have it you also had great
sorrow. What did it matter? If only you recognized it and
were true to it. Maybe that was all that counted. She would
look towards George Eliot coming with pity in her deep-set
philosopher's eyes.

George Eliot was the only one among them who knew love in
its fulness. Having known it, she could set it to one side in
her writing. It was only a part of the need of the experiencing
spirit; life was a hard long way. It was not a business of getting
this, or holding onto that; nor was it a matter of saying one's
say. To understand; and not to judge. But she would never
be able to convince Charlotte Brontë of that. Not to judge?
What was the intellect for if not to judge? Women had in-
tellects and the right to use them in judgment. What sense
was there in suffering for its own sake? "Plenty," Emily would
at last answer her. "It is the law of the spirit finding its way
to God. Maybe in anguish like yours over Monsieur Heger, or
in remorse like Branwell's over himself. It may be in disappointment like Mary's because of Gilbert Imlay, or in temperamental restlessness like Miss Austen's; or in terrible loneliness
like mine. It is a law, and the wise submit to it." George
Eliot would agree, and add in her husky low voice, "We cannot
do anything else but submit, though there are various ways of
submitting." It would be just here that Miss Austen would
laugh lightly. "Variety." That is what had always taken her
fancy; the variety of ways in which women would arrive at the
same destiny. She would cock her arched eyebrow at George
Eliot and say to her, "Now you be careful not to get too inward
in your stories. It is a very tricky concern—the soul—especially the soul in women."

CHAPTER V

GEORGE ELIOT

Who Sat Like the Recording Angel and Wrote

QUEEN VICTORIA WAS AT THE zenith of her reign while George Eliot was at the zenith of her literary power. The Queen was persistently mourning the death of her admirable husband. The novelist was persistently addressing as husband a man to whom she was not legally married. Victoria lived in the shadow of a comfortable memory. George Eliot lived in the shadow of an uncomfortable erotic necessity. Both of them were very good women. Though the Queen, if she had been advised to honor George Eliot, certainly would not have seen fit to do so. And George Eliot would not have condemned her for that decision. She would have understood it. And she would not have expected the Queen to understand her. How could she? How could any woman whose children were growing up around her understand a woman who had broken the one code that protected women and children?

Young girls hid the copies of her books under their pillows when they heard the footsteps of their mothers. It is hard for us to realize now. But in their time the themes of George Eliot's books and their manner of treatment were discussed as we discussed *Grand Hotel*. They divided minds against minds. "It is not fit to be read by decent folk." So did the mid-Victorian woman decide concerning the pathetic story of Maggie Tulliver. Now the school children have to read it, and also think it is not fit to be read because it is so tediously moral. Which is something to think about.

Mary Ann Evans was a contemporary of the Queen. She was born in the same year, 1819, which was the year after Emily Brontë was born, and two years after Miss Austen died.

Her father was a land agent for an estate. Her grandfather had been a carpenter. Her mother came from yeoman stock, and was a solid, managing woman, who set much store by the substantial things of life. Mary Ann was the youngest of her three children. The father was an able, dependable man at his work, and very mild in his home, allowing his wife to rule the household as well as himself.

So there was no sense of sexual injustice planted in Mary Ann's girl mind. This is very important. She is the only one of the great first women writers of whom that can be said. And it made a marked difference in her point of view.

She was an emotional child. Nobody taught her that love was a most precious element, and therefore not to be squandered. People did not think at all about the minds or the emotions of children then. Nobody saw the little highly sensitized girl spending her first feelings in idolatry. Nobody told her it was asking for sorrow. Nobody explained to her that she was surrounding a mortal with her own imaginative wealth. Though they might have. For it was plain to be seen that she worshiped her brother. She followed him wherever he went like a small slave girl. He never realized the sensitivity of the love, nor anything about the nature of her which even the shading of a careless phrase could torture.

But she learned for herself. And by the time she went to school it was ideas that held her ardor. She took to them.

If a wise priest, or a devoted, magnetic teaching nun had been given the early training of her, she would have made a great *religieuse*. But it was not her fate, and all her life she looked for something to take complete possession of her, and never quite found it.

Religion as it was given to her was very much as it was given to Miss Austen. But the temperamental difference between the two was wide. Miss Austen took it as she found it. Mary Ann Evans was Celtic. The easy-going Anglicanism of her family was not enough for her. It did not possess a system of inner discipline. So she built one for herself. She had become afraid of her own emotionalism. So she set about to choke it. She had many duties. Her mother had died when she was in her early teens; her older sister had married; so Mary Ann took over the management of her father's house. She neglected nothing, not even the work of the dairy. She was herself an expert butter-maker. She added to these duties; she visited the sick and the poor. She did many good works. She refused to spend her time upon music. It upset her emotions. Color disturbed her too; so she wore only dark clothes. Beauty of line affected her senses; so she made her clothes like a nun's habit. She was trying in every way to still the rapture that would rise in her through any least light touch upon her sensuous nature. There were no mountains where she lived, and the sea with its great sound was far away. She kept her eyes away from the sailing clouds of the sky. She protected her skin from the play of the wind.

She drilled herself mercilessly. She read books that had to do with the setting aside of the self. But none of these books taught her that it was only with love that the self does get set successfully aside.

All the time she was longing to love, and needing to worship. But she could not know that. She was too young. Her mind was too good to let her love anyone who happened to be at hand. It was the Austen tragedy over again. Only without the emotional safety-valve which Miss Austen found so early in her satirical story-writing. It was the Brontë tragedy repeated without their racial safety-valve of hatred which was a relief to the need of love, there being always something handy to hate. Mary Ann Evans never, either in youth or in maturity, knew anything about hatred. So her suffering was the keener. It was suffering that came from emotions too compactly compressed.

Suddenly her scene changed.

Her father was aging, and it was time to retire. So he and Mary Ann moved to the town of Coventry.

It made a great difference. She found new friends to interest her, and to lift her attention away from herself. She got into an agnostic set, and she examined their ideas. They stimulated her. She had had enough of religion as she had been acquainted with it. Something had eluded her; so, much as she wanted to believe, she decided not to believe any longer. It was a young woman's decision. She did not know that she was taking the easiest way spiritually. England at the time was buzzing with religious debate. The Oxford Movement had begun, teaching the people that not since the sad revolt from Rome had there been real religion in England. The Evangelical side of the Church roused itself; Rome and anything that savored of Romanish practice was something that hid religion, they said, causing people to mistake the appeal to the senses for religion, and taking possession of the intellect through the emotions. Against both of them the agnostics set up their honest doubts. The whole business, they said, was a sham. At least they were positive; and Mary Ann Evans had come to a time in her inner experience when she had to be positive about something. She had been negative too long; her whole discipline of herself had been negative, and she got the full effect of it because of her extremely ardent temperament. Agnosticism was a cause; it called for martyrs; it demanded courage. She stopped going to church. She undertook to stand by her decision. Her father was aghast. He would have, he said, no unbelievers in his house. Mary Ann was adamant. She must be honest, she said. Something in her was satisfied. It was the more upsetting to her father inasmuch as by ordinary she was a quiet daughter such as a man would want to have in his house for his old age. She sat reading. She had no taste for life outside her home; she went sedately about her duties. She was in every way exemplary. Mary Ann went away on a visit to let him cool off, but during the visit her affection for her father got the better of her agnostic convictions, and her passion for martyrdom suspended itself for a while. Or maybe it merely veered conveniently. She could be a martyr by doing what she did not want to do; she could go to church to please her old father. It was well to endure some things for the sake of others. She compromised; and her father compromised. So long as she would attend church with him he did not mind what she chose to believe about it. Life went on as before.

Yet not quite as before.

Mary Ann had learned what it cost to go against the current. And she had pulled back. The cause had not been quite positive enough. Had it been a case of taking a stand for a belief she would in all likelihood have kept to her platform. Though maybe even belief would need to have included in her mind a personal sponsor. For all her intellectuality Mary Ann Evans was an intensely personal creature, needing love and encouragement along with her convictions.

The reaction was hard to bear. She had to give herself a lot of work. She began to translate from the German *Leben Jesu*, by Strauss, and, to be certain of the scholarship, she studied Hebrew. This was an indication of what was to come later. She had for a woman of her time a prodigious scholarship. But she never thought she knew enough for what she had undertaken. She added continually to her stores of information, and her mind was like a vault.

The translation and the study of Hebrew were exhausting work. Her health was never good, and it was broken when she finished the task. It took her two full years. When it was published it brought her no fame; for the translation was anonymous. But it did bring her in contact with a publisher who could appreciate an author with such admirable capacity for prolonged labor. This was to be important later. His name was Chapman, and he had plans in his head for the future.

Meanwhile the young woman was thankful she had put aside her convictions for her father. He was ailing. She nursed him devotedly. When he died she grieved. She was alone. Coventry was unbearable without him, and she was ill herself. So she went abroad for a while, and lived in Switzerland. But she did not have enough money to live there permanently. She had to find a way to earn her living, and she had realized at last that she had not lived at all.

The publisher Chapman was beginning to get his plans matured. He was taking over the management of the *Westminster Review*. Miss Evans, with her appetite for work, was his idea of what an associate editor should be. And he did not object to her being a woman. In fact it was quite otherwise. He knew that an unattached young woman of scholarship and a mania for improving her scholarship was an excellent bet. She would live for the magazine. She had nothing else to live for. She would do any amount of work and enjoy it. It was altogether likely too that she would wind her passionate nature around her employer. And that would be very good for his interests. It would clinch her devotion to her work. Miss Evans had unquestioned scholarship; she was no dilettante; she ate up work; she was pleasant, too, in a dignified way; he suspected in his man's way that she had passionate depths to her, and so far as he could see there was no lover in her life.

So it happened that Miss Evans went to London to work on the *Westminster Review*. She was thirty. Chapman arranged it that she would live in his house. That meant she would be always on the job. It also meant that she might begin to feel sorry for Chapman. For his wife did not understand him, and did not mind Miss Evans seeing that she did not.

It did not work out quite as Chapman anticipated.

Miss Evans certainly labored. It was certainly all she had to live for. But as a domestic arrangement it was not to her taste. She could feel sorry for a man whose wife did not understand him. That only demanded general human compassion. She had always had that. But she also had ardor which it would take more than the master of a harem to rouse, even a most skilled master. She was no dilettante in love; her emotions were as concentrated as her scholarship. The jealousy of Chapman's wife did not flatter her. There is some evidence that she considered Chapman as a lover. She was at that period academically interested in love. She saw that in the London

literary set nearly everything centered upon the relations between men and women. Religion there was not nearly so important as sex. Her objection to Chapman in relation to herself was that he was addicted to a variety of women. She had
no moral objection. It was just that she looked upon it as an
inability to concentrate. All through her life she had looked
upon the power to concentrate as the first essential. She could
not admire a man who was without it. She could not love without admiration.

All the literary men of London came to Chapman's house.
Marian, as she had begun to spell her name, took a liking to the
philosopher, Herbert Spencer. They used to talk together for
hours. Spencer studied her earnestly. She was a person. She
was not beautiful, but there was something about her that held
the attention. She was of medium height and of slight build,
yet in spite of actual slenderness gave an impression of weight
and heaviness. Which was due to her bone structure. It was
large. Her hair was chestnut brown, almost auburn. A touch
of ginger in her pigment. Her eyes were gray blue, and set
deeply in her head. They were not large, but were peculiarly
steady and luminous. Her mouth was sensual, and her hands
were large and finely formed. But the most striking feature
was her voice. It was contralto and its tones were husky and of
strangely moving quality. When she spoke it struck a chord in
the being of a man. It gave her completely away. It was the
voice of an *amoureuse*. Everyone who met her commented
upon its luxurious languor. Spencer regarded her speculatively.
She was a woman, he decided, who would affect some man so
deeply that he would never be able to get away from her. She
would absorb him. Once she was stirred she would develop a
talent for amour. He looked at her mouth; he listened to her
voice. He thought it was time he began to get out of her
way. He did not intend to be absorbed by any woman. Nobody knows for sure whether or not Miss Evans was involved
emotionally with Spencer. For all the passionality of her there
was a dignity of person to her that wasted no expression of feel-

ing where it was not likely to be respected. There was nothing avid about her, or even anxious. She was waiting.

She did not have to wait long. To Chapman's house there came a volatile little man who was ugly and fascinating. He, like Chapman, was a varietist, but only because it was the style in his set. His wife had run out on him. He overlooked it the first time. Ladies had rights. He was always an understanding fellow, and tolerant. But when she did it a second time he thought it was too much. He had three boys to bring up. He never missed a journalistic trick that would give him publicity and get the money. He went everywhere in London. He was the gay life of the literary parties. Once he had been an actor; so he knew the art of entertainment. He had touches of profundity, but chiefly it was a quick bright grasp of things he had—the perfect journalistic flair. When Miss Evans met him he was the author of the day. He had written a popular book on philosophy, and people were quoting him. It was George Henry Lewes. The dignified lady who was associate editor of the *Westminster Review* liked him. His volatility amused her. He gave her ideas. She could work on them. He had an ingratiating way with him which she found most enlivening. He never once said his wife did not understand him. He took her taste for other men as a matter of course. Marian Evans, who took nothing as a matter of course, fell in love with him. It may have started out as an affair; but it did not remain such. It became very quickly a companionship that fulfilled every phase of her nature. Lewes was ill and neglected and burdened with responsibilities. He was brave about it all. He could laugh at his own hard time. It stirred all the maternal cherishing kindness of her nature. More than that, it gave her a cause. She said she would live openly with him. Lewes breathed with relief. Nobody but himself had ever realized how much his mercurial temperament needed a strong, quiet, completely focused nature for its complement. He knew what his own temperament was. He felt it was histrionic. He could live convincingly with an idea for a while, but when he had reached the end of the idea he instinctively looked round for another. It had been the same with women. Miss Evans was a woman with whom he would never reach the end. His old ideas took new life when she got hold of them. He judged accurately in advance what a man's love would do for her. He wanted to see light deepen in her somber eyes. She was a person of grandeur, and it heartened his own slight temperamental shabbiness. He had never thought highly of volatility. It made him popular to be sure; but it was not what he wanted to be. Marian had never thought highly of her solidity. She knew her mind was ponderous and didactic. She could not help it. But it was not what she wanted to be. So they came to each other out of utter need. They stayed together for protection. Lewes was happy. He had always wanted a woman who could hold him in spite of his mercurial changeability.

Marian knew she could hold him. She would never, otherwise, have burned her social bridges. There could be no divorce. Lewes had condoned his wife's infidelities. Marian taught herself to believe that the marriage was automatically dissolved by the misconduct of Mrs. Lewes. She was sorry to have to proceed without the sanction of the law; but the law was a pace behind truth. It would change in time. She saw herself as a pioneer and a martyr. She was fulfilling the deepest note of her temperament. Only she did not quite know that she could not have had complete erotic fulfilment without martyrdom. It would have saved her much suffering if she had known it. It is probable that Lewes accepted her decision as a matter of course. Marian was a great woman. She could take a great brave step. He let it go at that. But there is no doubt that she went to him with almost religious solemnity. It was very much like entering an order. She was thirty-six. She loved the volatile little man with a mature woman's saved-up passion and a mother's yearning. His children needed a mother too. She was not breaking a home. She was making one. She was not stealing another woman's husband. She was salvaging what another woman had tossed away. All the complex emotionalism of her strange brooding nature was satisfied. It was heroic; it was concentrated; it was tragic. More than that, it was passionate. And they had an intellectual foundation to see them through. They would work together; they would make money for his children; they would be happy together. But she would not put her friends under any obligation to recognize her. So, before she took the final step she resigned her position.

It was all very sacramental. It was almost ceremonial.

They went to the Continent, and spent the first months of their union in Germany, where Lewes gathered the material for his biography of Goethe.

But before they returned the great event happened. Marian had begun her first story. She thought she would see if she could write fiction. She was not sure; but Lewes was absolutely sure. He said excitedly that she had it. She must write stories.

She had begun subconsciously because of her need to find some form of writing which would make money, and at the same time save her from having to push her literary wares in the open market.

She was afraid. It was one thing to have an inner conviction about what she had done; it was one thing to elope to the Continent; it was quite another thing to face the people who would look at her as if she were some sort of peculiar species; it was still another thing to walk as an equal among women who enjoyed the privilege of the law.

She had done what was not done. She could have managed a discreet case of adultery with Lewes. Nobody would have thought it unusual. For if they wanted to they could conveniently be not quite sure about it. There was no evading an open living together in sin. As Parnell, the Irish leader, said about the English, "Blessed are they who are not found out." Marian Lewes, as she was determined to call herself, law or no law, had seen to it that she was found out. Her brother had not answered her letter announcing her decision. Her friends had been carefully hesitant. When they did write to her they worded their letters so very carefully that they hurt even more than silence. They treated her as if she were temporarily insane. Humanly it was all very hard. But for fiction it was excellent. Not that it was much comfort.

She played with the idea for quite a while, promising Lewes to get consistently at it. He reminded her constantly. So there was no avoiding it. It had to be fiction. Lewes said it had to be. And she knew it had to be.

But it was a new form to her and she did not feel at home with it.

Her early critical work had been coldly, precisely, heavily intellectual. She had stifled all the natural emotional expression of her young years. But Lewes had brought it out of her again. She loved him ardently; she had sacrificed the world for her love of him. Love accompanied by tragedy will make a woman write emotionally if it is in her to write at all. She was afraid of emotionalism in writing, but Lewes encouraged her to let go. He knew that she had been plowed with it all. He treated her gently when he thought she needed that; he scolded her when she needed to be stirred; he set himself to make her work. He knew it would be her compensation. Finally she got her first story finished. Lewes read it and was moved. He kissed her, and said he would get it sold for her. He did. The editor of *Blackwood's Magazine* saw what it had in it. Who wrote it, he asked. Lewes said that was a secret. The author wished to remain anonymous. The editor concluded it must be some professional man who did not wish to let anyone know he wrote fiction lest it confuse them about his ability to carry on his profession normally. Lewes said nothing. That was as fitting an interpretation as any. But the story had to have some name attached to it. Marian was a woman without a legal name. There was no longer any Marian Evans, but neither was there any Marian Lewes except in her own imagination. What was she to do? What did the name matter? All she wanted was not to have to appear in public. She could not bear even the publication of a story. She shrank from the curiosity with which it would be read. She knew how people would read into its wording her own experience; she knew they would be looking ghoulishly for her vindication of herself. They would consider her story in relation to her personal conduct, and not in relation to its art. She could not face that. But it had to have some name. There is no record either in her letters or in her diary to indicate that she realized at the time what a momentous choice she was making. She looked at Lewes. He understood. Why not be "George" if she could not be Lewes? She smiled. With *George* they put *Eliot*. It did not mean anything at all except that it sounded like Evans. So *George Eliot* was the signature attached to the first of the *Scenes from Clerical Life*. The editor wrote that he wanted more stories from this author. She wrote two more for the series. They were sad little stories taken from life as she had seen it in her girlhood.

That was inevitable. In the months upon months of isolation when she had seen no one but Lewes, she had thought about her girlhood. She remembered it all vividly. Even the shadings of its emotionalism. She was oppressed by the difficulty of life. The three stories of *Clerical Life* had to do with people who were misunderstood. They were people who sorrowed in secret.

There must have been many people who had sorrows in secret because the stories were instantly popular. It was their humanity. They were not sentimental stories; yet they possessed that compassion for people which was to become the genius of George Eliot. It was as if a kind, comprehending mind was watching them. It was the secret way people thought of God; He watching, waiting, knowing it was how they handled their sorrows that counted. Or if it were not God, it was the way of the Recording Angel, seeing human actions in a far-off yet near review, letting the motivation temper judgment. Lewes was exuberant over the success of the stories. He made love to her, and said she must write more of them. To please him. The tender-hearted, volatile little man had been more upset than he had let her know concerning her sensitivity about public opinion. He wanted her to be able to laugh at society. He coaxed her into another story. He petted her through the first hard chapters.

It was *Adam Bede*. She let her mind wander among her early memories again. Adam was a portrait of her father. Dinah, the young Methodist preacher who was the heroine, is George Eliot herself during the period when she put everything aside except the mood of religion. Dinah was a Protestant *religieuse,* allowing herself no small feminine ways; stilling all her emotions in service to the sick and the forlorn.

She read it chapter by chapter to her faithful audience. He made suggestions; he lived in the story with her. He assured her that it was a great story. He told her that if he did not already love her he would love Dinah. He said she must not give too much of the front stage to Dinah's foil, Hetty Sorrel. The characters gained as she discussed them with Lewes. He laughed over the smart remarks of Mrs. Poyser, the farm wife who is one of George Eliot's most vivid characters. Lewes told her when she was off-color about men. But he could not tell her enough to make the men she drew live. She did not know men. She only knew types which had come under her studied observation. Lewes pulled her back when she got too tragic. He insisted upon her rustic dialogue, and with his sympathy the whole book took life with slow, careful, kind writing.

What did it matter, Lewes thought to himself, that people did not come to see her? She could create more amusing people than would come anyway. He began to be happy. He could see fame coming to his beloved "Polly." He had not hurt her life. Lewes was not altogether right about George Eliot. Created people were not enough for her. She had been hurt by society with a hurt from which she would never recover. But she was happy with him. It was one of the greatest loves of history. Not because of George Eliot's capacity for emotion; but because of the fine understanding of the quick-witted little man with whom she lived. Lewes was an extraordinary man. There is no other record in history of such devotion from a man to the work of a woman. And it has to be remembered always that Lewes was himself a writer and a successful writer. He was not a negative she-man, or in any way an intellectual gigolo. His devotion to the career of George Eliot turned out in the end to have been a piece of very shrewd guessing; but that was not its original motivation. There is no question of the sincerity of his determination that Marian should find in literary success compensation for her social suffering. What he did not know was that success is never compensation to a woman. George Eliot would have been happier as the quiet wife of a successful man. She started out to be such. She went to Germany and gave all her time and energy to helping him gather the material for his book. That was all she wanted from life. But society would not let her be his wife. She had to defend herself. But it is doubtful if she would even have done that if Lewes had not insisted upon it. It was good guessing in the end because the talent she had was such as brought to them far more money than his books would have brought. He did not know that at first. All he wanted was enough recognition for her to keep her at the writing. When she was writing she was not brooding over her isolation.

Adam Bede swept England off its feet. It touched people where they could feel. It was softly sweet as the countryside at noon; it was rugged too. There was no heaviness. It was a dear familiar story to most of its readers.

Lewes was wildly excited. He had always known, he said. George Eliot cried. She kept on crying. She could never write another story, she told him. She was finished; that was all that was in her. Lewes spent hours assuring her that she had only touched the surface of her genius. His book on Goethe had come out too, and had been well received; but its reception was nothing compared with the furor accorded *Adam Bede*. It was a very great man spiritually, and a very great lover, who could take the contrast as he took it. George Eliot must have known. She had always loved him dearly. She began to adore him.

Everybody was asking, "Who is George Eliot?" Lewes laughed. He wanted to say, "She is mine." But all he could say was, "George Eliot desires no personal publicity." However it had to be settled. An obscure gentleman began to hint to his acquaintances that he was George Eliot. George Eliot herself did not mind when the hint reached the newspapers. But Lewes minded. It made him furious. Someone was stealing from his Polly. He sat down to fight the thing out. He could not put the obscure gentleman in his place without giving the secret away. London smiled to itself. Ladies began to think that perhaps they should not let their daughters read the book. When they came to think of it, there was a seduction in it, and the author had not been very outraged about it. She had only been compassionate. It was just too bad that an immoral woman could write like that. It would undermine all moral teaching. Maybe not just directly. But what were you to say about the bad end of sinning when a woman who did not even have the consideration for other people of attempting to hide her sin wrote the best seller of the year? It was quite awkward. But the sales continued to go up.

The publisher suggested that another book be written. Lewes agreed. She would write another book. George Eliot looked helplessly at him. He threw her a playful kiss. It was a salute.

It was more than a salute. It was a kind of command. It set her at *The Mill on the Floss*.

The Mill on the Floss is one of the sweetest stories of childhood ever written, as well as one of the ablest. Long before there were departments of child psychology George Eliot sent Maggie Tulliver out into the world to make her plea for some understanding of childhood.

Maggie was herself. An ardent child who needed love more than she needed food and covering. Her need of it gave her a sensitivity that was almost unbearable. The sensitivity was bruised by her elders who saw her only as a troublesome youngster who could not conform to their rules. With sure strokes

George Eliot drew her picture. She was telling people what we now accept as something nobody would ever question—that the scars of childhood shape the maturity of the individual. But in her time it was a daring new suggestion. Some of the critics missed the point entirely. This is proved by their almost unanimous wish that she had not carried the story on to Maggie's maturity. The little girl story to them would have been perfect if it had been left at its sobbing youth. It would have been an artistic whole. But George Eliot was not primarily an artist, not even when she was writing most artistically. She was a thinker. She was a doctrinaire. She was a sibyl. She was a nineteenth-century appearance of the type of woman with whom the Greeks were familiar in their order of Delphic priestesses. Her mental processes were intuitive naturally. But she had trained them with exacting scholarship. She was not writing a sob story of childhood. She was following the pattern of a soul. She was noting the ultimate effect of the bruise of childhood. She was trying to tell that the child was the mother of the woman. But she was doing it with fiction. So she brought to her purpose all the art she could summon.

The theme of the story is repression, which is an old story to us now. But it was new then. Maggie was checked in the expression of her feelings. Her quick brain was checked too. Maggie disciplined herself exactly as Mary Ann Evans had disciplined herself. She read *The Imitation of Christ*. She thought she might attain peace of mind by severe processes of renunciation.

It is a book of tears. We read it to-day wondering at its power to affect us. It is hard for us to understand the Victorian application of the law of renunciation. We are practical. We cannot see what was gained. Neither could George Eliot.

With Maggie the characterization of women in fiction made an advance that was a leap. It was femininity struggling to live by its own pattern, and crushed by the decision of the world that it must live by another. We cannot overestimate what this single portrait of a girl meant in the feminist program. There had been no drawing of womanhood like it. Miss Austen's women conformed expertly, and got what they wanted by means of the conforming. Charlotte Brontë's women revolted dramatically, but it was a hysterical revolt, with all the writing emphasis placed upon the hysteria. Maggie was quite different. With a brain that was much better endowed than her brother's, she loved her brother with exaggerated devotion. She had to love. She had also to think. But the need to love far outweighed the need to think. The conflict within herself was painful. It is in the study of the pulling instincts and the tugging mentality that George Eliot accomplished her part of the feminist program. Conflict in Miss Austen's stories was merely sexual. She put it, of course, in the polite disguised language of her particular time, but it is very clear that what interested her was the war between men and women about their sexual need of each other which she called matrimony. She was concerned entirely with who captured whom, and how it was managed. Conflict in the Brontë stories was social; the women drawn both by Emily and Charlotte were women whom society had battered down, and the fight they put up was against society. With George Eliot the conflict contained these outer aspects of necessity for a story, but was chiefly focused upon its inner manifestation. In *Adam Bede* she had divided her study of womanhood into three women—Dinah, Hetty and Mrs. Poyser—but in *The Mill on the Floss* she took a big psychological step, and let it all be in one woman, Maggie Tulliver. It was more astounding to her time than we can have any idea of. We are used to novels by women which examine minutely their own purely feminine reactions to life. Maggie was something utterly new. There was sexual struggle; for she wanted Stephen. She captured him, but when she had, her own inner conflict came instantly to take him from her. There was social struggle. Maggie was a highly strung individualist; she was bound to wage war with her circumstances and *the pack*. But the theme does not concern these conflicts to any degree. It is all within Maggie herself. To put it simply, she is a spirit struggling between two forces: the passion of her feeling, and the effort to subdue that feeling by philosophy, which is thought held in control and applied impersonally. Miss Austen featured the schemes of women; the Brontë sisters featured the emotions of women; George Eliot set herself to getting down the quality of women as it came out of the fire of inner battle. On the whole this battle had little to do with men. It would have gone on actively had there been no men in the story. On the whole it had little to do with social circumstances. It would have gone on actively in a convent; or on an oasis in the desert. She was the first of the feminine psychiatric writers.

The next book was a short prose poem, *Silas Marner*.

Its theme is almost allegorical, and is familiar now to everyone who has gone through a course in English literature. Its style is classic in purity. The opening chapter is one of the most beautiful pieces of prose we have in English. Spiritually the story has an affinity with the Book of Job, and its treatment has a Biblical simplicity. Marner is a lonely weaver, sitting weaving, sitting thinking about fate, and disturbing the community in which he lives by his strangeness.

It was another facet of her mind. She was engrossed with the presence of fate. The soul as she saw it was a victim of fate. It did not know why it had to do as it did. The story came right out of her brooding over her own experience. Like Marner she was sitting by herself weaving, and wondering why it had all happened. She did not know why she had to need George Henry Lewes with a need so deep it threw everything else into the shade. She did not know why other people should feel they were under compulsion to punish her for what she had done. Nor did she know why they should be able to hurt her. Surely she was strong. And surely the need was strong. But so was the pain inflicted by those who had no right to inflict it. She knew it was a pattern weaving within herself. She was a philosopher writing fiction. She was a woman holding to philosophy for her own sustaining. More and more as the years passed, and the writing went on, was philosophy to be what interested her.

The Lewes household was now in comfort financially. The sons of Mr. Lewes came home from school. The older of them, Charles, was a fine musician. He played Beethoven to his stepmother for hours. She loved Beethoven as Lewes loved Goethe. Music had become a need for her. It gave her what she had not been able to find in the services of religion. It was something that was beyond the littleness of words. She knew the texts of the sonatas, and she received infinite pleasure in her stepson's reading of them.

Lewes busied himself with the details of her career. He had become an earnest man of business. He haggled with editors. He answered letters; he attended to the ordering of the household; he read all her reviews; such as were favorable he set apart for her attention; those that were not he destroyed. He would even have destroyed the issues of the papers that contained them if he could have. Nothing would be allowed to hurt her. He knew that the scar from the first years with him had remained. She had a morbid shrinking from criticism. He was wise enough to know that it could never be cured; there was no use, therefore, in trying to harden her. All he could do was to save her whenever he could from pain. Not that there was very much need to. George Eliot had become a literary personage. There was very little adverse criticism of her work. Her novels had been translated into French. She was respected as one of the very great of her age.

An editor of a new magazine, *The Cornhill*, offered ten thousand pounds for the serial rights of her next novel, whatever it might be, in advance. It was astounding for the time. It was the first occasion of so large a sum of money offered outright for fiction. George Eliot was appalled. Lewes was gratified. George Eliot said she could never write another novel. She was finished. Lewes teased her tolerantly. She had only just got going, he assured her. But she was not to be convinced. She was forty-two. In a little over five years she had written four books which had been consistent best sellers one after the other. She was tired. All her emotion was written out. She had had her say. Lewes was patient. It was only a moment of depression, he thought. Like moments came in between all her stories. He had always to tide her over her difficult times. At the beginning of each story and at the end she was frantic with nervousness. He was finding that more and more of his energy was demanded by her to carry her through the agony of creation. She wrote like a woman in labor. He had to treat her like a woman in labor. At the end of each ordeal he took her on a trip to the Continent, making all the arrangements, not even asking her where she would like to go. For after writing she would agree to anything he said in a daze of indifference. Generally he moved her after each trip to a new house. A new book he considered would be the better for being written in new surroundings, and after each book they had more money to spend upon their living. So the houses got bigger. So did the books.

For all her wavering uncertainties, George Eliot was taking her writing with prophetic seriousness. It was sacred. Yet she had to be driven to it. She would put off starting. She was not well enough to work, she would complain to him. Sometimes he believed her and took her on a little trip to the seaside. Sometimes he refused to listen to her, and closed her up in her study with paper and pens. He reminded her of the ten thousand pounds. It was a lot of money. The editor was depending upon her. She said she could not write a book worth ten thousand pounds. He explained to her that it was her name they were paying for. She said moodily that she had no name. He shook his head. Month after month; year after year. So it went on. Everything must stand still while he forced her to write. He got her the books she needed for reference. He went out and met interesting men, and came back and related to her what they had said about her books. He kept in touch with all the important people in London. He handed on to her the latest findings in science and philosophy. He commanded his son to play to her. He took her to the theater; he saw that her meals were served to her at the proper times; he made her take the necessary exercise. When she said she could not walk a step he ordered a carriage and took her for a drive. He was a faithful, loving, thoughtful little man. And he knew exactly how to handle her.

The book that cost the new editor ten thousand pounds was *Romola*. George Eliot said that when she began it she was a young woman, and when she finished it she was old. Lewes did not say what it did to him. She took two years to write it.

The ten thousand pounds must have overwhelmed her. George Eliot was always a dutiful woman, and Lewes had impressed upon her the advisability of giving the editor his money's worth. So she mobilized all her scholarship and added all his to it too.

It was her most ambitious undertaking.

Romola was a studious Florentine girl who came under the influence of the reforming priest, Savonarola. George Eliot's main purpose was to produce a portrait of Savonarola in fiction. She knew what she was attempting. She knew he was a psychologically twisted man with a peculiar consciousness about himself which we now label as paranoic. He considered himself to be appointed by God to smite the Florentines for their paganism. George Eliot, mindful of the ten thousand pounds always, thought that his personality should be set against an impressive study of the Florentines of the Renaissance. She did not think that people could understand him without also understanding Florence during the Renaissance. That might very well have been so. But unfortunately George Eliot herself had no emotional affinity with the Florentines. She could not make the street scenes of Florence take life. She could not even portray a Florentine woman.

Romola remains a woman of the nineteenth century in spite of her setting. She is a Maggie Tulliver with her passion completely subdued by the discipline of religion. She was cool and resigned, and much given to doing things that were right to do though they were very hard on her. Her inner destiny, as well as her outer, is dependent upon the effect which Savonarola produced upon Florence. So the story weaves slowly and heavily between the experience of Romola and the experience of the monk, and also in and out of incidental street scenes in Florence.

Romola is one book of George Eliot's upon which from the beginning until now there is confusing diversity of critical opinion.

Undoubtedly it was an intellectual achievement which is hardly equaled among historical novels. The Renaissance scholarship is meticulous; but the Renaissance spirit is not in it. No amount of scholarship could make a mind like George Eliot's able to interpret the rocking back and forth of the susceptible Florentines in one kind of an emotion or another. They were a people who responded like a harp to shrewd publicity. They had been under the sway of one of the masters of publicity of all history, Lorenzo the Magnificent. He was dead, but the glamour of his audacious personality still was over them. They were people who liked heroes. Savonarola was able to play for a while upon them. Lorenzo had taught them to adore beauty. All around them were quiet, lovely faces and perfect bodies. The finding of a Greek text was like the finding of a new continent. Phrases in Lorenzo's court were priceless treasures. To be sure, he robbed the people, but what did it matter if a few of the poor went a little more hungry than usual if only Florence could be adorned with art until it was like paradise. He gave them festivals and processions and wild constant excitement. It was more to them than bread. It was a city of lovers. Love was part of beauty—rich, full, pagan love full of laughter and episode. Lorenzo looked on in pleasure. Then Savonarola took to his pulpit and thundered at them. It was sin. Lorenzo laughed. He liked the monk's audacity, and maybe he understood what was ailing him. He never stopped him from preaching. Lorenzo had just died when the story of Romola opens. Savonarola was left to do what he liked with Florence. He played upon them accurately. He worked them up to a violent reaction. Into the bonfires they threw their pictures and their jewels and their sensuous fabrics. But it was not very long until they had veered again—they were all for throwing Savonarola himself into the bonfire. The whole city turned out to watch him burn. It was all beyond the power of George Eliot to depict; for they were an utterly pagan people without any compassion; excitable, lusty, sensitive, but not to suffering, only to beauty and their own amusement.

If she had isolated the study of her paranoic and the young woman he influenced, she could have accomplished a great study. But both of them are lost in the attempt she made to do a convincing portrait of the Florentines. Romola is a good portrait of a woman like herself. Savonarola himself is a good portrait. Religion was romance to him. It came to be the only romance to Romola. It was the first romance of George Eliot, and it was to be at the end the complete romance to her. She was struggling to get her feeling down. The drawing of Romola through her experience, the disciplining of her character into nunlike sweetness, is among the best of George Eliot's work. Romola is a philosopher woman, and the steps by which she becomes so are tenderly and sympathetically taken by the author. George Eliot knew what she was writing about. She knew too about Savonarola. She understood the emotion which drove him to command the sacrifice of artistic beauty. She herself had been like that in her youth. The only difference was that she was a woman. She would not take from children the toys and the ideas they needed to play with. She had tenderness for immaturity. Savonarola had none. He thought that spiritual maturity could be forced.

As pageantry the story fails; as character-drawing it succeeds. As a novel it fails to hold us now because the earnest effort to sustain the pageantry is at the expense of the inner studies. Savonarola and his student, Romola, move unconvincingly against the pageantry, quite as alien to the book as they were actually in the Florentine world.

Maybe George Eliot knew herself. She wrote no more for a while. Something had died down in her. She had to work incessantly with her writing. It no longer came spontaneously. She had passed the biological change of women. The change is clearly seen in the writing. Emotion had given place to intellectuality. Feeling had been taken up by thinking. Maggie had become Romola. It was a very great pity that Romola was set so ambitiously. For the analysis of a woman of her temperament was important. George Eliot herself was struggling to find a philosophy that was suited to women. Romola would have been much nearer to being the answer had the book been free of its determined pageantry. Ten thousand pounds had got in George Eliot's way, as it since has got in the way of many another writer.

Her next two books, *Felix Holt* and *Middlemarch*, were also books of ambition.

Felix Holt was a study of a political radical during the *hungry forties*. Critics have dutifully placed it in its correct chronological position in their analysis of her work, and are unanimously agreed that while for its time it was an admirable intellectual achievement, it is as a novel lifeless. George Eliot worked slavishly for meticulous accuracy. She read the files of the newspapers of the period. No book of the time escaped her. Her detail was flawless; her technique was flawless. But she was in a sphere in which her creative hands were tied. She was a woman, and she was trying to portray the emotion that dominated a young radical leader. She could not do it. Neither could she catch the despair of hungry people. She had never been hungry; she had never even been actually pinched for money.

Middlemarch is now published in two volumes. It was a literary experiment. She took a small English town for her canvas. She made use of interlocking stories. There is another woman in it who is a combination of Dinah, Romola and Maggie, having in her that curious ardor for martyrdom which was the fundamental emotion of the author's own nature. But this woman is not the center of the book. George Eliot had become a little weary of the woman that was herself. She was trying hard to get at what was in men. The interesting study in *Middlemarch* was a young doctor. To do him well she set herself to study as much medicine as a lay person may; she read scientifically; her facts were, as always, correct and in line with the latest medical development. The story is somber, for it leads the young doctor into the toils of a pretty woman who wants money and not devotion to a cause. Step by step he goes down. It was as if the recording angel were writing in pity.

Middlemarch shows the mature power of George Eliot at its height. Her mastery of character-building is in full swing. She takes artistic pleasure in the complex shuttle movement of her several stories. She keeps them all going with a magnificent fluidity simultaneously. It is technically the ablest of her books, and in some respects it has the most sublime expression of her deep understanding of human nature. It is utterly compassionate. She was at home in the setting. She was dealing with people whose emotions she could know; she had lived intimately among them. For Middlemarch was unquestionably Coventry. But she herself was not in it; she was looking on sympathetically without any uncomfortable emotion. It was the work of a serene old woman. She had gathered in all her own experience. She could watch other lives with knowledge and with that strange patience which comes with age. But she had not forgotten her own young ardor; she could remember the pangs. But she was far enough on to know that they all pass. It made a difference in her writing.

Lewes saw the difference. He exercised himself to prevent any stiffening of her artistry. Every Sunday there were receptions at the Priory, the house in which they had finally settled. George Eliot sat in dignity in a big chair by the fire. She always wore lace around her head like a mantilla. The callers were presented one by one to her by Lewes. The choicest of them were allowed to sit beside her for a while and chat. He never permitted any of them to bore her. He engineered the parties. He kept things moving. He watched her always out of the side of his eye. Often he would break suddenly off in a conversation with a guest and dodge through the crowd to her. He had known that there was something she wanted to say to him. He got rid of the people as soon as he saw tired lines coming around her eyes. There was always to-morrow's writing to think of. George Eliot was fastened to her writing. It was an implacable duty. She was locked in it, a captive. Lewes made the captivity as easy as he could. But he could never let her out of it. Why should he? He believed in her genius with one half of his mercurial nature; and with the other half he believed in the returns it had brought them. More than that, he still loved her; he was still thankful for the fame. He thought it made her happy. He thought it was what she had wanted most in life. Well, she had it. As for himself, it had all been enlivening. He had liked bargaining with editors; he had enjoyed writing astute letters to them; he entered into his management of her career with gusto. He had liked business details. He had of course liked writing just as well. He was a shrewd publicity man. He had had an amazingly swift comprehension of the public reactions. George Eliot had received all the benefit of it. Well, men were always slaves to women in one form or another. It was infinitely better to be the slave of a great woman than a little one. Marian had herself said so. It was more profitable too. He looked around the Priory. It was gratifying indeed. He did not mind being a second-string person. He had never taken his own ability very seriously. He set his hat on jauntily. He had to see another editor.

There were other people besides himself who knew that George Henry Lewes had a grasp of what the public would take. He was invited to become the editor of a new magazine—the *Fortnightly Review*. He took it on, and held it. He had organized the Eliot career thoroughly. He considered that he could now manage it with one hand. A magazine would be a bit of pleasant variety. It would also keep him in touch with all the ambitious, surging young minds. That was very necessary. He wanted to get all the bright young people he could to the Sunday receptions. Marian must not stiffen in her artistry. He was always pleased when he found how much the young people liked to come. He probably thought it was because of the maternal kindness of the great lady; though there is more than a probability it was because of the attractive little man who lived with her. Lewes was a personality with a zip to him. He put all his social talents into making the receptions a success. They became an event to those who were fortunate enough to be invited. Neither Lewes nor George Eliot ever mentioned the years ago when nobody would have accepted an invitation from them. Their union had been taken for granted when the fame became great.

But the fame had never made George Eliot feel intoxicated with it. She knew what her books had cost her; she knew what they had cost Lewes. She had ordered her philosophy into fiction; and Lewes had ordered the fiction into a thorough publicity. The older she grew the less power the result of their joint work had to affect her. She was still thinking.

Lewes had given her a Bible. She was reading it more and more. Her first martyrdom had been over the forms of religion. Her first book had been about the clergy. Kind men they were, as she presented them, usually insufficiently educated, struggling with an idea far too big for them, tormented by the human lots with which they found themselves incapable of dealing; tortured by the too much that was asked of them. Men, all of them, caught in an office too holy for them, and stumbling one way or another out of it. She had gone on from that trying to reach the mystery of divinity in her characters, Dinah, Maggie, Romola, Savonarola, Marner. Then she came to *Daniel Deronda*.

Daniel Deronda is a Jewish book. The story of an unworldly young man is crossed experimentally with the story of a worldly young woman, and though the story of Gwendolyn as she goes down to sorrow through her own selfishness is ably done, and her character is in some ways more perfectly achieved than any other of George Eliot's objective studies of women, it is at

the end only an incidental in the book. It is Deronda, and his
coming to the feet of a Jewish mystic, that is the real story. Religion was romance to George Eliot. Martyrdom was the way
of romance. The people who had preserved their laws and
their religion and their race through centuries of persecution
were to her the people of utmost romance. It was not just a
neurotic preoccupation with the suffering of the Jews, and a
glamorous view of their tantalizing, alien, persistently sustained
presence among Gentiles. She had learned Hebrew. She had
studied the Kaballah, the secret concealed teachings of the mystic Jews. She felt its wisdom; she was aware of its strange
foreknowledge. She read laws set down in veiled religious
language which many, many years later were to be discovered
as scientific truth. She caught hold of one abiding law—spiritual retribution. She looked back at the characters she had
drawn. That had underlain all the stories. She caught hold of
another fast rule—the lamb of trust slain at the Passover for
the saving of the people. She understood the Jews. She admired them, and she loved them. She knew what made the
Jewish merchants wary; she knew why the commercial Jew
swaggered. Against her Jewish mystic Ezra Cohen she set
another Ezra Cohen who was a pawnbroker. He was ruthless; he was a braggart; but he kept in his house the dying
old teacher, and considered it his racial duty and a particular
honor to his house. Around Ezra the mystic she wove a halo of
holiness; he was one of the princes of Israel. She put into his
mouth the teachings of the Kaballah. She made him fore-
shadow the return to Zion. Israel must be preserved, and assimilation defeated. In Deronda she drew the precursor of
Ludwig Lewisohn's Jewish heroes, lonely for their own spiritual
culture while living successfully in the midst of Gentile culture.

It has seemed an unreal story to most of the Gentile critics.
They could not understand what made her write it. They
missed the hunger for religion that is in all her books underneath
the compassionate humanity of her characterizations. Even the
Jews did not understand. They did not expect a Gentile to

have comprehension of their *secret spiritual city*. They did not particularly want any Gentile to comprehend. George Eliot was a Gentile. But she was a Celt, and the Celt is endowed with a peculiar ability to lose himself in something greater than himself. Judaism to George Eliot was great enough to take the surrender of herself to it. She was not Jewish. But there is just this to remember: The one character in her books which is like George Henry Lewes was Ladislaw in *Middlemarch,* a young Polish Jew. It makes the reader pause a moment to consider what the blood stream might have been in this engaging little man, who was both an actor and a literary man and a consummate player of publicity. It is just possible. If it were so, it is easy to explain *Daniel Deronda*. But it is just as easy to explain it by the concentration upon the history of the Old Testament, and the study of the Kaballah, and her own sense of martyrdom. Judaism was religiously akin to her. Religion was romance, and there could be no romance without suffering. *Daniel Deronda* was the consummation of the romance she had begun with *Scenes from Clerical Life*—the surrender of the soul to God through religion.

When she had written it George Eliot had finished her writing and her spiritual journey, though it was a few years before she died.

The little man died first. He was worn out. She was prostrated. "Here I and sorrow sit," she wrote in her loneliness. Her life was over, she said to herself. It really was over, though there was an epilogue.

Among the young people whom Lewes had brought to the Priory was a young man called John Cross. He had nothing much to do with himself except to spend his income. He appears to have been a case of the Œdipus complex. He tended his mother as carefully as George Henry Lewes tended George Eliot. His mother died within a few days of Lewes. He had nobody left to absorb him. George Eliot had nobody to turn to. She was sixty. Two of Mr. Lewes' sons had died before him, and Charles, the remaining son, was married and engrossed with

his family. It came about through these circumstances that
George Eliot married John Cross. He was twenty years
younger. He had to have another mother. George Eliot had
to have someone to help her. More than that, she had to have
legal marriage. The epilogue proved conclusively the secret
sorrowing of the twenty-five years of her illegal union, which
no amount of fame could assuage.

Marriage had taken on in her imagination heroic proportions because for all these years she had lived bravely without it.
What she did not realize was that because of its endurance and
her fame, her union with Lewes was accepted as marriage by
the onlookers. Her marriage to John Cross gave most of them
a jolt. She showed in this action her dependence upon Lewes'
sense of publicity. It was one of the worst things she could
have done. It brought the whole problem up again for discussion. It made her look like an elderly vampire. After managing to persuade Victorian England to accept her, she proved
by what she did that she had no idea that they had rationalized
themselves into accepting her. It was strange that she did not
know. She had had deep penetration into human psychology.
Illegality to get by at all must be of very romantic color. The
romance was broken in the imagination of people when George
Eliot walked off in the next year with a rich young man. But
there is this to add—it did bring at last a letter of recognition
from her brother. She was now a respectable married woman,
and as such could be recognized.

But even the defense of legality could not keep her alive.
The little man who was responsible for her was dead. John
Cross, though he tried hard, could not take his place. She died
seven months after her wedding, from the kidney complaint
which she had fought off for many years. John Cross laid her
beside Mr. Lewes. It was where she belonged. Her brother
came to the funeral, and was chief mourner along with John
Cross and Charles Lewes.

Mr. Cross took up the cause of her immortality much as
William Godwin had taken up that of Mary Wollstonecraft.

He wrote her biography, including in it her letters. So we have
everything to go on with in a study of George Eliot.

It has been the critical custom to say complacently that the
content of George Eliot's mind was masculine. It has been
allowed to pass because we are not really very sure at this
period about what quality in the mind is masculine and what
quality is feminine. The Victorian critics could see that Miss
Austen's work was completely feminine; they said in her praise
that she was content to be feminine. The chances really are
that Miss Austen was far less feminine in her emotional life
than George Eliot. It was satire on a restricted scale she produced. We read it now and think how dull it all was, but for
her time Miss Austen was doing as daring a thing as Dorothy
Parker now does. She was making her contemporaries look
silly. So is Mrs. Parker. Neither of them has what George
Eliot had above everything else, compassion. Compassion we
elect to call a feminine quality because of its association with
the mothers of the race, with image expression of it in the
Virgin Mary, and in the Chinese goddess of mercy.

George Eliot could be deified as a most merciful spirit. That
is the thing that remains.

Her scholarship astounded the critics of her time. It was
unusual for a woman to have the grasp of foreign languages
she had. She learned quickly; she never forgot. She thought
nothing of learning a new language. She did it more easily
than we learn to drive a car. She thought nothing of reading the classics in these foreign tongues. Hebrew, which
is admittedly very difficult to get, she learned enough of in
two years to read the Kaballah. Mr. Cross noted in his biography the number of books she read each year while she was
writing. The number is astonishing. She knew philosophy.
She was a constant student of the mind. She disciplined her
own. She disciplined those of her characters. All of this the
critics chose to call masculine. Prodigious scholarship had been
unknown in women. But it was not going to continue to be
unknown. The Universities were beginning to open to them,

and it was noticed before many years that women students had an almost natural capacity for absorbing knowledge.

They called her masculine because she attempted work on a scale which was new to women. The Brontë work, though more ambitious than Miss Austen's, was still small in its outline. The critics were willing to admit that women could do a few small things well even in the nineteenth century. When a woman wrote about men as George Eliot ostensibly did, though not actually, and when she took the problems of men and dealt with them in fiction, they had to say the work was masculine. It defied all previous exploits of femininity. *Romola* alone was enough to set the critics hunting for some way out. But *Romola* is not a greater exploit than Clemence Dane's *Broome Stages*. All the work that women have done since bears out the femininity of George Eliot.

But more than anything else, it is in her portraiture of women that she is feminine, and when you take her work, book by book, and read it from the platform of to-day's knowledge, it is the feminine portraiture that stands out. Over and over again, even as Miss Austen did, she drew the portrait of a woman. It was herself. Over and over again she took this woman through experience, and the experience was always one that set up conflict within the woman. George Eliot was almost bowed down with her acceptance of fate. Fatalism grew upon her characters. She saw everything in relation to inner growth. Religion was necessary to the inner life, so religion held her imagination. The woman she drew was a passionate woman whom life hurt badly, and who sought to steady herself in her pain by philosophy and mysticism and the rigorous performance of duty.

Neither her central self-portrait nor the auxiliary women she uses are just women. In this George Eliot was different from the other women writers. That was due to her experience. She had no feeling of having missed things because she was a woman. She had grown up in a home where there was no sexual resentment; she had been an associate editor of a national mag-

azine for all that she was a woman; she had had a long-sustained
and peaceful relation with a man whom she adored. So she
was not full of pent-up sexuality, and therefore not indignant
about sex, and the women she drew were consequently concerned with more than their womanhood. They were human
beings searching for something that was not far away from
being religion. She was aware of no very marked difference in
either the need for inner sustenance or the way of searching for
it between men and women. So the main person of her books
alternated. Sometimes it was a man; sometimes it was a
woman; but always it was a suffering spirit. In actuality George
Eliot was carrying on in her novels the premise that Mary Wollstonecraft had set down—that there was no spiritual difference
between the sexes, and very little mental difference. She did not
say so anywhere. You may read every line she wrote carefully
and not find any flaming declaration of equality. But she assumed equality. There is just a slight shading of feminism in
The Mill on the Floss in the section dealing with Tom Tulliver's
education and the neglect of Maggie's. But it is very slight.
She touches again on the inequality before the law in *Romola,*
when she wrote down Romola's helplessness when her husband
undertook to sell her father's library. But neither the neglect
of Maggie's education nor the financial insecurity of Romola's
wifehood was the issue of her story. In both cases it was the
groping after the power within themselves to look quietly with
compassionate understanding upon life. It was the issue of
her own life.

For in twenty-five years of living with Lewes she was striving
to find peace of mind. She was an erotically satisfied woman.
She had the love of a man and she had it with martyrdom. In
her martyrdom she was an utterly Victorian woman. Victorian
women were trained for martyrdom. They must do their duty.
All George Eliot's heroines were martyred to duty. She was a
martyr to her need of Lewes; to the stupidity of the law. She
was just as much a Victorian in this as she was in her assumption
of spiritual similarity between men and women. Both were of

their time. Yet for all her philosophy and her satisfaction George Eliot was not a happy woman.

Her contemporaries describe her as being habitually saddened. She had an aura of grief about her that in a beautiful woman would have been very attractive. She was not beautiful, so her sadness seemed unnecessarily melancholy. John Cross said that her husky, amorous voice played upon his feelings, and that the strange saintliness of her gray-blue eyes affected him like a religious painting. But John Cross was a susceptible young man when he first met George Eliot, and he was quite a bit under the influence of George Henry Lewes. George Eliot tried not to be sad. She smiled when Lewes frisked. She laughed at his jokes; she loved the little man. They never quarreled. Lewes was much too clever a man to quarrel, and a kiss always soothed George Eliot. But the sadness always came back. It hung around her, persisting from the first hard years. Her health was never good, and the strenuous composition had not helped to keep it even. Lewes had bad health also; but his temperament was too volatile for more than a momentary depression, and in the years of his life with George Eliot he had become a professional bright lad. George Eliot had to be taken over her dark days on the exuberance of his spirit. That was his gift to her. It was not enough to be a lover to her. A man had also to be a harpist of sorts, and play David to her Saul. It was to her little harpist that English literature owes George Eliot. He knew how to draw the music. She was a person set going and kept going by a light-hearted clever man who rejoiced throughout at having a cause to tie down his own mercurial being. Her power to concentrate was tremendous. Once started on a subject her mind went on like a steam-roller. But it had to be started and driven. Her fame went on also like a steam-roller. At the head of it sat the gay little man, waving his cap, and shouting hurrah, and making everyone get out of the way for the oncoming greatness. He could not make it a royal progress, because he could not make it legal. Another man made it legal, and very nearly made it funny. It would

be entirely funny if we did not know it was merely an instinctive effort to cover a wound.

So her story goes. A woman with a voice of an *amoureuse*
and the hands of an intellectual. A woman with a heavy determined chin and very sad eyes; who wanted to be a success
in the world, but also to be a success in the inner world of the
spirit. A woman who was maternal and pitying, and at the
same time ruthlessly true to fate with its one law of retribution.
A woman who had lived a full woman's life, and a man's active
life, and found her romance in religion.

This, she would have said to Mary Wollstonecraft, is what
it comes to, whether we stay in our homes, or whether we are
pushed out of them. It is also what art comes to, she would
have reminded Miss Austen. For without the consciousness of
some mystic deep purpose, the fertility of women is a vain, sad
sacrifice. And equally sacrificial is the devotion that brings to
art finish and deftness and consummate grace. To the wild
Brontës she would have explained that neither in love nor in
the hunting for the one other who will blend imaginatively with
us is the meaning of life. It is in the descent of compassion
upon the soul. Whether alone, or together with one another,
or in the bright company of the people of the times, whether
as a man or as a woman, it must come at some time or another.
And mostly it was brought about through sin and the suffering that came from sin. What could any of them say to her?
They were all of the nineteenth century. What she was saying belonged to the age. She had had success. She had had
love. She had experienced an equality with men which would
have made Mary Wollstonecraft satisfied that she had lived for
a cause. George Eliot in herself was the proof of what Mary
Wollstonecraft had written. At least she seemed to be the
proof. Mary would have waved George Henry Lewes aside as
an accidental compensatory effort of nature; or maybe as a
shrewd speculator with a woman's talent, much like any other
showman. George Eliot had written books which disproved
Miss Austen's theory. A woman's mind had gone exploring

into a man's field and brought back fiction which the reading world of her time bought with extravagant enthusiasm. There had been no falling off in her sales for twenty-five years. And Miss Austen would have to have admitted that the first four of these books were technically perfect. George Eliot had known love of a man which poor small Charlotte Brontë would have gone straight to hell to have possessed for a little while. George Eliot had studied and written about philosophies, and talked to all the eminent philosophical thinkers of her time. Lonely Emily Brontë, struggling to get emotion out of the way of thought, would have been willing to have died several years earlier could she have had one fraction of the philosophical training. George Eliot had everything of which they dreamed. A woman of love, a woman of intellect, a woman with all the sorrowing feeling of women towards life, and above everything else, a woman of religion.

But as a doctrinal feminist story it is all spoiled by George Henry Lewes.

As a psychological story it has never been told. There is a mystery between men and women we are only just beginning to be aware of. There is a mystery between minds we are only just beginning to be aware of. There can be no doubt that George Eliot was subjective in her reactions to George Henry Lewes. It was very much as if he had given her mental children. She produced the children in order, and they turned out to be successful children. It was he who saw to it that they were. Lewes was versatile; he was volatile. But he was not these alone. His books were popular. They were also scholarly. The biography of Goethe has remained a standard biography to this day. We may turn the picture one way, and see a brilliant, sagacious man used by an ambitious, plodding woman. We may turn it another way, and see a really creative woman held back by her sense of inferiority, and released from that sense by the attentive love of a sympathetic man. If we turn it still another way, we may see a woman determined to justify herself, and determined to keep

pace with the man with whom she was living in sin. That was
all she needed to set her going. If we turn it once more, we see
a woman whose nature was bent early towards the way of the
religieuse, who, if she loved at all, would have to love as if she
were taking a vow for an order. Only a man whom it was difficult to love could rouse that emotion in her. She had gone to
Lewes with that mood upon her. It was martyrdom. But it
was for her beloved. Some of her emotion transferred itself to
Lewes. She became a cause to him. She remained a cause because it was profitable. Lewes was no fool. He was not made
for forlorn causes. But she was. She wrote her first four books
with a sense of failure within her. There was something forlorn about it. That was all it needed to get the emotional best
out of her. These first four books were her best. The next four
books were books she wrote to enhance her reputation; they
were done meticulously and quite grandly, but they have not
got the beauty of the first four, or the simplicity. Neither have
they the emotion. Through the progress of these eight stories
we may see the mind of the *religieuse,* feeling its way through
human woes and loves, stirred out of its brooding by the ardor
of a gay little man who thought love was a thoroughly human
art, and coming back at the end to its first preoccupation with
religion. In the progress the mind showed itself to be a gracious
feminine mind, with all the bitterness washed out of it by meditation, and brightness let occasionally into it by human love, but
preeminently a mind drawn to the consideration of inner things.
It was an aloof mind. But the aloofness was kindly and compassionate. It was the mind of the recording angel.

CHAPTER VI

OLIVE SCHREINER

Who Lay Listening to the Biological Drum Beating

IN 1882 A YOUNG WOMAN LEFT her home in South Africa to go by herself to London. She carried with her a manuscript of a novel.

The young woman was Olive Schreiner, and the manuscript was *The Story of an African Farm*. But the story of this young woman herself as she ventured alone to London, and as she stayed thinking and writing in England, as she returned still thinking to South Africa to write another book, is a far more interesting story than the one she set down in her youth. For her story itself was to catch in its tendrils the root story of womanhood everywhere.

Olive Schreiner was born in 1855 on a missionary station in South Africa. Her father was a German with a taste for metaphysics. Her mother was an Englishwoman of Puritan ancestry in which there was a Jewish strain. All these blended in Olive Schreiner to produce a reforming zealot. She lived a life of agony. Her health broke down early from prolonged and violent attacks of asthma. It was impossible for her to find a climate anywhere in which she could breathe comfortably. Yet she lived to be old and died in 1920, having witnessed two wars, and broken her heart over the ways of human beings in war.

She was one of a large family. It is not clear what drove her in her young girlhood to feel acutely the injustices to women. The only source of material about her is a biography written by her husband, Cronkwright-Schreiner, and a volume of her letters published by him. These, while valuable, are not quite valuable enough, as is always the case with family documents, and the secondary commentator therefore hesitates in any con-

clusions for fear there may be later published material to change
these conclusions.

She began to write when she was still in her teens. She
had left her home and set out to make her own way as a governess to children in various South African farms. Like her
great feminist predecessor, Mary Wollstonecraft, she was not
happy in her teaching experience. This, probably, is what drove
her inward, and made her a rebel against what society gave to
women in vocational opportunity, though she said herself that
it was her conversations with women from among the South
African native races which started her thinking. Her education was informal. She was a woman made out of the books
she had read by herself, out of her observations, and out of whatever she could learn from strangers who came her way. This
was just as well for the peculiarity of her power. Her intellect
developed naturally without the discipline of formal training,
and she took in daring instinctive leaps spaces of thought over
which academic discipline would have forced her to go warily.
She never, therefore, got tangled, as a woman of her endowment
might easily have got tangled, in the superimposed adventure
of sheerly decorative knowledge. It saved her from blue-
stockingism.

The manuscript she carried with her to England was the second writing of the story. She had written it once and sent it
to England. It came back with a criticism from a publisher
which drove her to rewriting. In its first form it had been
too wordy. She had poured into it all her young-girl feeling
about love and about the country of her birth. In its second
writing it came to the attention of George Meredith, and on his
recommendation it was accepted for publication.

The Story of an African Farm is a narrative impression of a
young girl set against the background of life on a farm in South
Africa. It is an exotic literary prelude, with the melody of
naïve feminine yearning playing through the unchanging background feeling of savagery. The heroine, Lyndall, was a sensitive young girl who grew up longing for culture in almost

primitive surroundings. She got herself books. She absorbed the knowledge of everyone who came casually to the farm. Then she went away to study. She could not rest content on the farm with its somber, almost animal immobility, while there was a civilized world beyond.

The story of Lyndall is not told in detail. It is left blurred. For a long time she disappears from the narrative, and life goes on within the environs of the farm without her. Strangers come and strangers go. The old woman of the place stays on. The life is almost sleepy, yet it goes on with great activity so far below the surface that its movement is hardly perceptible. Lyndall comes back into the story broken. She has sought in civilization a man to worship. She could not find him. She found a man who loved her. She wore his ring. She bore his child. But she left him. He was not what she wanted. The man is only a shadow in the story, a shadow that could not satisfy beautiful, naïve little Lyndall with her dreams of a man to worship with all her being. She thinks that she can set out again on her travels to find a man to worship. But life has been too much for her, and she dies. In her illness she is tended by a man who had loved her on the farm. He does not understand her. He grieves over her. In her need he takes the rôle of a nurse and sees that she has care. He has worshiped her, and so, the story implies, has the shadow man who had given her the ring and the child, but it was the feeling of worshiping Lyndall needed, and not the feeling of being worshiped.

This is the first instance in feminine writing of a declaration of the need in women to worship. Olive Schreiner caught the whole implication of the feminist tragedy in her ardent young imagination, for the higher the development of women the more difficult was it going to be to find for them men of worshipful quality. Which is to say that the greater the mental stature achieved by the new woman the greater would be the mental stature she would subconsciously demand for her fulfilment from a man. This was something that Mary Wollstonecraft had not realized when she launched her rebellion. This was

something Jane Austen stepped around cheerfully by creating
Mr. Darcy. This was something that the Brontë sisters eased
themselves out of by building for themselves in fiction amazingly dominant men. It was something that George Eliot refused to allow her women to contemplate. It was not the way
of wisdom. Olive Schreiner in her profound young imagination knew that in women the biological law was far more imperative than the sophistication of the worldliness they might
acquire, or than the fatalism of such submission to a moral law
which they might attain. And this biological law would cause
them to be unsatisfied with men who were less than themselves,
and less, therefore, than their dreams. It would mean tragedy
in the transitional stages for the new woman. For the wider the
learning of a woman, and the deeper her capacity for love, the
less chance would she have of finding a man greater than herself, and able, therefore, to dominate her. Mary Wollstonecraft
had rebelled against the subjection of the minds of women to
their biological purpose. Olive Schreiner rebelled against the
subjection of the minds of women to a purpose which was not
considered except very casually. The feminist cause in the
mind of Mary Wollstonecraft was a simple cause. It had to do
with women forcing their way into education which would prepare them for the professions. The feminist cause in the mind
of Olive Schreiner was much more complex. It was a twofold
matter of training the minds of women and training the minds
of men to realize the importance of the biological contribution
of women to the state. The feminist cause to Mary Wollstonecraft was a rebellion against a prevailing intellectual and political
injustice to women. The feminist cause to Olive Schreiner
was a rebellion against the much greater racial injustice. The
woman with the baby at her breast was the center of the race,
and the race went on with its wars and its inequalities as if
babies grew on trees. She was conscious from the beginning of
the depth of the problem which feminism would uncover. The
need of the woman for the man and the baby. The need of
the woman for her own protection of work that would give

her dignity in the world. The need to put these two needs together, and the difficulty of doing so under a system of competitive enterprise. She foresaw much tragedy for the new woman. Mary Wollstonecraft, when she wrote *The Vindication of the Rights of Woman,* was young enough to be buoyant. She tossed off the tragedy if she saw it at all. Olive Schreiner was young when she wrote *The Story of an African Farm,* but the blood of a very old race was mixed with her blood, and she was consequently not so buoyant. She was older when she wrote her *Dreams and Allegories.* She was still older when she wrote *Woman and Labor.* She was fully aware then of the biological depths and implications of feminism. They saddened her but did not destroy her courage. She was of all the brave women feminism has produced the bravest.

Little Lyndall, in *The Story of an African Farm,* is a figure of incredible feminine courage.

She was small, beautiful and appealing. She was young. She was essentially innocent. She was a spiritual Amazon. She went with her youth and her beauty and her courage out into the world. She wanted knowledge. She wanted distinction. She wanted to be loved, but more than this she wanted to love. There is quite a difference in the woman of high development between these two. Men wanted to love her according to their way of loving. They did love her. One of them wanted to give her luxury. Another of them wanted to worship her. But she was full of a dream about herself and about the love she might have for a man. The dream was still with her even when she held her very little baby in her arms. The dream stayed with her even until death came to her. She was too young to know death was coming. She thought she could grow strong again, and begin again her search for the man and take her place in the world. The scene in the story where Lyndall on her death-bed holds communion with her dream for women is a moving piece of restrained emotional writing. Olive Schreiner, when emotion was upon her, wrote prose that laid the heart open. And emotion was upon her throughout the whole writ-

ing of Lyndall's story.   The somnolent atmosphere setting of
the African farm is used with technical mastery as a still psychic
background for the struggle of the little growing dreams of
the girl and her courage in fulfilling them as best she could.

Critics have praised the book.   Contemporary critics hailed
her as one of the coming novelists.   They said that her atmospheric control in the background of the story was the mark of
the immortal litterateur.   There were those who placed her un-
reservedly in the class of George Eliot.   They encouraged her
to write again about South Africa.   There would be a sure
market.   England was interested in her colonies, and the very
distance and strangeness of South Africa gave in itself an exotic
substance to any writing about it.   The critics called attention
to the authenticity of her picture of South Africa.   With a few
powerful, sure fiction strokes she had presented the feeling of
the place.   They acclaimed the rugged masculinity of her characterizations.   With a few powerful, sure fiction strokes, the
people of the country took life in her book.   They drew attention to her tragic creative courage.   It was not the expected soft
romanticism of feminine writing.   It was no wonder, they said,
that she had hidden her femininity behind a pseudonym, Ralph
Iron.   They touched upon her emotional finesse.   She had
drama, exquisite sorcery with emotional effects, restraint in her
narration of the story itself, and an uncanny insight into
motivation.   She had every professional reason to go on writing
stories about South Africa.   She had probably every creative
reason.   She was a subjective woman, and her mind must have
been stored with impressions of both native and colonial life
in South Africa which she could have molded into fiction.

But she did not.   There has been quite an amount of sincere
critical lamentation that she did not.   From the point of view
of the esthete she was a fine artist ruined by the feminist movement.   For from that time on her writing was given entirely
to the question of the new womanhood, with the exception of
some definitely political writing after her return to South
Africa, and one unfinished novel published in its fragmentary

form after her death. What the esthetic opinion missed was that even in *The Story of an African Farm* the emotion of the writer was concerned with a problem peculiarly new to women. Everything else was of secondary importance, even the beautiful prose and the fine sway of atmospheric subtlety she showed in all her work. Probably she felt that all the beautiful prose and all the fine production of literary atmosphere was not going to be of much avail in the trouble of women. Women before her had written beautiful prose and produced fine atmosphere, and what had it done for them? Nothing more than earning them a little money and a little praise for being good girls to have written books that could stand up against the books of men. There was something else far more important. Being convinced of it she went into the feminist rebellion with all her ardent spirit. She was the bravest of many brave women. For she deliberately abandoned something that was all set for success, for something that was all set for trouble and derision.

For all the deliberation of the abandonment, it was emotionally inevitable. The signs of the inevitability are very clear within the text itself of *The Story of an African Farm*. It is not the story of a colonial farm. It is the story of a girl.

The girl was a symbol of Olive Schreiner herself, and of thousands upon thousands of young women who were starting out on the adventure of learning, poring over books long into the night, subjecting themselves to the discipline of liberal and professional education, preparing themselves for service to their state and their time. Some of them were to impair themselves nervously. But those who were to come out of their training unimpaired were women with an extraordinary equipment to offer men in companionship. They were to be somewhat impersonalized by study. They were to be free of the little irritating personalities of women. They were fulfilling the promise Mary Wollstonecraft gave—that educated women would be far more interesting mates for men than uneducated women. But they also were to fulfil for themselves the tragedy promised them by Olive Schreiner—that the more education they had, the less easy would it be for them to find mates interesting to them. It would mean loneliness and disappointment. But loneliness and disappointment in a great cause were an honor. It was the sacrifice of the pioneer.

This was the idea that obsessed Olive Schreiner from the beginning, and not literary form.

The Story of an African Farm was pure literature only through the accident of the author's talent with emotion set against strange backgrounds, and the further accident of her emotional feeling for style. It was a story that might have been written, except for these two accidents of composition, by any one of a great number of feminists of the time. But there is an inference to be drawn from it, which takes it out of the possibility of having been written by many contemporary women. It contains an idea that was distinctly ahead of its period in the feminist program, an idea which is only now beginning to be acknowledged. Lyndall admitted her desire to search for a mate. She had improved her status. Subconsciously the whole process of self-improvement was a gesture of search. She was not going to take what was at hand. She was going to get out of her circumstances. Somewhere there must be a big man, and she was going to be worthy of him. This was drawing a biological inference from the feminist movement. This was remarkable, coming as it did from a young woman with no experience of the world. She touched the fundamentality of the movement—which was that women were no longer content to take such men as happened to come into their environs. They were at last admitting their own business of mate-selection; and to get into larger arenas of larger mate-selection, they were demanding many new professional rights. No other of the great feminist leaders admitted this, and Olive Schreiner admitted it only as an inference which could easily be missed by the casual reader.

The professional push out of women had begun to be felt at the time Olive Schreiner brought her book to England. Miss Florence Nightingale had organized her training-school for nurses. Her idea was to provide an outlet for celibate women in service to the sick. She had been driven to her great nursing program by her observation of the unused energies of unmarried women. They must be given something to do. Nursing would provide them with an outlet for their frustrated maternal instincts. It also in time would provide them with an outlet for their talents in organization and management. Miss Nightingale's plan was the first admission in history, so far as we know, of the practical organizing talents of women. It was quite an intellectual step, as well as a practical move in the history of feminism. But what she did not know, and therefore could not admit, was that her plan was insured of success because of another great need in women. She had the older, definitely spinster woman in mind. She did not realize that young women on the great push-out to wider arenas would take to it in large numbers. Miss Nightingale was a Victorian lady, for all her deep human sympathy and her keen intellect. Biology was carefully disguised by Victorian ladies. So she could not know that women, no matter what they did, were subconsciously seeking mates. But a young woman from South Africa knew it. She had grown up close to savagery. The disguises of civilization were not spread over her imagination. It made a difference.

It was this difference that caused Olive Schreiner's work, for all its almost fragmentary character, and for all its emotional uneasiness, to be endowed with a significance far more permanently related to the course of the feminist movement than the writing of any other of the women of its first phase.

Mary Wollstonecraft set down the resentment of women against the persistent and unvarying labeling of them as sexual units. Jane Austen set down their pique at being summed up in mass and treated as romantic dreams or biological nightmares by men. She drew her women exactly as they were. The Brontë sisters set down the anger of women because their passions went unrecognized. George Eliot gave women struggling souls in conflict with many facets within themselves.

Olive Schreiner took the dreams of women and draped them around the infallible racial law. She knew that the dreams of women sank into impotency without the biological facts, and that the biological fact was cruelly stark without the dreams of women. She supported the protest of Mary Wollstonecraft. She accepted the romantic-reality of Jane Austen. She understood the tragedy of the Brontës. She responded to the spirituality of George Eliot. But there was another step in the feminist progress, and she took it. All that a woman had to give to a man and to the race, she said in *The Story of an African Farm*, could only be given when the whole nature of the woman was keyed to the emotional surrender to a power greater than her own. It was an unchanging law. In the transitional period many women would have to decide either for dreams or for biology. It would not be of any considerable help to complain in the meantime that men were blind, or vain, or in total ignorance of their own best personal and racial interests. Nor would it help to any creative degree to rest the soul meantime in the narcotic of hard professional activity, or in the sanitariums of religious retreat. As she thought it out in her youth, she saw no immediate way for the woman of unusual awareness of herself, so acknowledging her discouragement, she allows her heroine, Lyndall, to die.

It was the work of a woman who was young in years and actual personal experience. She could not tolerate emotional compromise. But neither age nor experience brought to Olive Schreiner the inclination to lend her emotions to compromise with civilization. She never tempered her dreams with sophisticated acceptance of things as they happened to be for women. The lot of women was awful. Biology heaped itself upon women and life went on for them as if biology did not exist. It was all wrong. And dreams haunted women. Yet life went on for women as if their dreams had nothing to do with them. It was increasingly wrong. Gradually as the years passed she felt she must do something about it.

London was engrossing to her. She lived in various attics

in the slums. She went wherever she would be likely to meet social thinkers. Frank Harris describes her in her early years in London as an eager, intense young woman, much too eager and much too intense for his taste in women, but a personality for all that. She was short and thick-set and dark. The asthma was already ruining her beauty, yet the flame remained in her brilliant dark eyes. She could not be overlooked.

The *Dreams and Allegories,* written by Olive Schreiner to aid the crusade of women, are among the finest pieces of emotional prose in the English language. They are published in two small volumes called *Dreams* and *Stories, Dreams and Allegories.* Nearly all of them brood over the condition of women. They weep over the sadness of human life. They touch upon the relation between men and women, and show how beautiful it might be, and how ugly it usually is. They shudder over the high price that has to be paid for the desire to love. One of the pieces called *Three Dreams in a Desert* has come to be the rallying music of feminists. It is an allegorical study of the attempt of women to lift themselves up from their biological burden. What she could not say in straight prose essay form she said in allegory. It was the Jewish blood rising in her, for the Jew when he is afraid takes instinctively to allegory, and Olive Schreiner, during the period in which she wrote her dreams, was afraid for women.

She saw in England at the height of its civilization that it was no easier for women than it was for the savage woman in Africa. The women of the slums were bowed down with incessant child-bearing, and each new child added to the family added to the economic burden. She saw the women of the middle classes also tied down, though a little more pleasantly, to their biological function. She saw wherever she went very little love and very little happiness. Children were born unlovingly, unwillingly, by women whose bodies were never their own. She saw nowhere any economic value whatsoever set upon the racial contribution of women. She saw women of society somewhat freer than other women, but restless in their freedom because it was not real freedom. For they, too, had to please men, and not many of them were happy. And there was no work anywhere that a woman could say was her own work, except the bearing and rearing of children, in whose bearing and in the matter of whose lives she had little or nothing to say. There was motherhood; there was the pleasing of men in sex; there were little odd jobs to be forced out of society like nursing and teaching. There was the slave toil of the poor woman. There were the excited social doings of the high-class woman. There was nothing else.

So she saw women in her dreams offering themselves to the race. She saw the lives of the pioneer feminists laid down one on top of the other to make a bridge that women in the future might cross over to a new life. She saw fine women unnoticed by men, bound to go unloved and barren through life because they would not stoop to the wiles and the guiles that men were used to in women. This she put into a strange story called *The Buddhist Priest's Wife*. A man and a woman meet for an hour in the attic of the woman. The man tells the woman she is wasting herself going to the far places of the earth when she might be the most distinguished woman in London. All the while they talk the reader knows that the woman loves the man but cannot tell him so, and as she describes to him the woman he must marry, her own heart is bleeding. He has not seen her as she is. He sees her as a new career woman without good judgment in her career. It is a pathetic story and probably it tells a good deal about Olive Schreiner and what made her write no more novels, but write instead pieces which she thought would have their part in the awakening consciousness of the race concerning women.

In *The Dream of the Wild Bees* she told about the wish of a mother for her next child. The bees hum as she sleeps and a voice asks her to choose for her child what quality it shall have, and she chooses, not genius or the power to attract wealth or popularity, but the fey sense—that to it what is imaginary shall be real. In this again she was telling a good deal about

herself. For by that time the Utopian dream of women had
so completely taken possession of Olive Schreiner that already
it was existing.

She talked to her friends about women. She studied every
subject that seemed to have some relation to the development
of women. South Africa and its problems faded from her mind.
No problem of any state was important beside the immediate
problem of womanhood. No state could achieve its even ap-
proximate Utopia while one half of the population was penal-
ized economically for the biological brunt it bore. She talked
to men about women. She found that men were also oppressed
by the condition of women. There was no freedom for men
while women had no freedom. The whole root of the trouble
was the economic dependence of women upon men and its
corollary—the dependence of women upon the happiness of
their relation with men. It bound women; it bound men. It
was sexual parasitism. A woman collected either lifelong care
within the marriage code, or temporary funds within the courtesan's code in return for real or simulated emotional response.
Having once responded she was held. There was nothing else
she could do. Having once assumed the responsibility of a
woman there was very little a decent man could do. The
vampires and the cads were the only ones who benefited by the
custom. Not even the children. For Olive Schreiner refused
to believe that children born of mothers held in economic
slavery and fathers held in economic unwilling responsibility
were children worth producing. The answer was the economic
freedom of women. She inferred that money was at the bottom of much of the sexual antagonism she observed. Men subconsciously disliked women they had to keep; and women subconsciously disliked men on account of their own economic
helplessness. Money involved in it caused the whole aspect
of the sexual relationship to squint.

There would have to be a grand crusade. Somehow or other
things would have to be rearranged, allowing women to pay
their own way by their own labor. But how this was to be

worked out in a competitive system she did not outline. She was interested, so far as her writing shows, only in the fundamental falsity of the prevailing family arrangement.

In this she was giving vent to her Hebraic tradition. The Anglo-Saxon practicality and the Teutonic talent for tying organization to metaphysical reasons for it did not seem to function at all in her. Her temperament belonged entirely to the people who wept for the sins of Babylon and the insult to their god. Her Babylon was the condition of women. Her god was the beauty and the sanity of sex. Her letters show that for years she carried in her mind a desire to write a book upon the sexual functioning of women throughout history. She seems to have taken the idea from Havelock Ellis, whom she met in England, and whom she loved.

There is no way of telling at the present how much she loved Havelock Ellis. She was, as we judge from her biography, her collected writings and her letters, a difficult woman to gage in any emotion. And, furthermore, a large part of her correspondence with Ellis was destroyed at her own request. In addition to this, it must be remembered that from her early twenties she was a sick woman, given to the wavering decisions of the sick and their always defensive protests. She accomplished only a fragment of what she felt was in her to accomplish. A lot of her energy was dissipated in the inevitable frequent moves from place to place in search of a climate which would permit her to breathe easily. More of it was wasted in the depression which accompanied the prostrating attacks of her disease. But no matter where she was, or how she felt, she always wrote to Havelock Ellis. And yet for all of this, which her husband states to be a fact, the drama of her lifelong attachment to Havelock Ellis is tantalizingly unfilled in with detail. So also is the other unadmitted drama which drove her to write *The Buddhist Priest's Wife*, and which must have been at the bottom of her preoccupation with the injustices of women. It needs hardly to be said, so obviously true is it, that no woman who is happy in her own emotional affairs becomes engrossed to such an extent and to the detriment of her art and her profession in the cause of women. There was tragedy possibly at the beginning of South Africa. There was unquestionably tragedy somewhere in England. For Olive Schreiner came to England a novelist. She met success. She had mastered a difficult technique. Critics told her repeatedly she was a great novelist. She was treated as an equal by the literary lions of her day. She left South Africa, as we judge from all contemporary comments, a sparkling, engaging, ambitious young woman. In England contemporary comments describe her as a bad-tempered woman. She never closed a door. She banged it. She paced the floor of her rooms hour upon hour on end. When she pulled out drawers she slammed them shut again. She knocked chairs over when they got in the way of her pacing. No landlady could tolerate her for long. It was not only her general noisiness. She had to have the society of men. Not of one man, but of many men. They came to her rooms and stayed far too long for the taste of Victorian lodging-house-keepers. When one landlady protested she moved, and the men came to the next room until the next landlady also protested. So it went on. She could not do without men. They stimulated her mental processes. They stirred her temperament. She had to talk and she had to learn. She liked men because they liked to teach. Whether through this ardor for learning from them, or through her own personal magnetism, Olive Schreiner was always attractive to men, even when racked by her disease, and after her youth had gone.

All these things—the poignancy of the drama, the preoccupation with the feminist cause, the nervousness of gesture, the intensity of interest in ideas, the need for men in numbers—point to a restlessness which was not just the restlessness of physical suffering. There was some experience of shock, and of frustration, which changed the life of Olive Schreiner in England. Her women friends said emphatically that the feminist cause diverted her from the novel. It may be so. It may be that out of conviction she laid down the form of writing belonging instinctively to women, and took up the traditional form of prophecy. But it is more likely that something happened in her personal life to create distaste for the novel. There are shocks which cause such a distaste, even to the extent of reading the novel. The spirit in its state of shock cannot tolerate the human story. It cuts into the bruise. It does not go in this way with every woman. But Olive Schreiner, it must never be forgotten, had Jewish blood in her, and the Jew in despair always turns back to the law which may be underneath the reason for things. She translated her own personal tragedy into terms of the general tragedy of women. She could only bring herself to look at love momentarily. She could write no more about love except in fragments, and even these fragments were wrapped around in allegory.

If the man whom she loved were Havelock Ellis, it would be surprising. No woman conducts a lifelong friendship with a man who has hurt her in love. No woman, however literary, writes to a lover of her past except to tell him about another lover. The relation to Ellis was unmistakably not this, but the pupil-teacher relation, and the letters she wished to be destroyed in all probability contained confidences having to do with an experience she wished kept concealed. Ellis was the sympathetic counselor, understanding the need of the woman, and suggesting with years upon years of patience that she turn herself to the writing of a great book upon the sexual functioning of women. And Olive Schreiner was the hesitating student, never sure that she knew enough, always delaying her writing until she had gathered in more knowledge. She outlined her text to him. He encouraged her. It was a very necessary book, and she was the one to write it. So it went on for years.

When she was thirty-two she returned to South Africa and married Mr. S. G. Cronkwright. She refused to surrender her name. It had been made, she said, and he, in gallant gesture, adopted hers, hyphenating it with his to commemorate their union, and was henceforth known as S. G. Cronkwright-Schreiner.

Olive Schreiner was blissfully happy when she found she was to be a mother. All the passion that she had poured into her writing about motherhood welled up in her personal experience of it. But again tragedy followed her. The baby died on the second day of its life, and Olive Schreiner was prostrated with grief. Her ailments increased, and her restlessness increased. They moved from place to place in South Africa, just as she had moved from place to place in England. There seemed to be no place in which she could breathe. She began to think again about her great book on women, and she began to feel acutely the political situation of South Africa. Her family was active in state affairs in the colony, and she turned her literary power into a propagandistic effort to avert the coming upheaval. She felt that, having lived many years in England, she could interpret the feeling of the colony to Great Britain. *Trooper Peter Halket of Mashonaland,* written in 1897, was a fiction indictment of British colonization methods in South Africa. A little later she wrote a pamphlet, *The South African Question,* which was an appeal to the British sense of justice. She was driven in these efforts not only by her South African feeling, but by a woman's terror of war.

But the war came, and among the things it destroyed was the manuscript of Olive Schreiner's great book. She had left it finished in a farmhouse on the edge of a South African village in the devastated area. Soldiers looted the house and burned all the papers they found. It was natural. She was a South African patriot. She had published South African propaganda. It was dangerous stuff. A friend who got through to the district brought her word that her desk and its contents had been destroyed.

She herself was under military observation, and in the darkened upper story of a barricaded house she sat down to rewrite as much as she could of what we now know as *Woman and Labor.* She could only remember a part of it. She was suffering. She thought she was dying at last. She thought, too, that civilization was dying. She wrote furiously. Some remnant of the great book must be saved for women. So she wrote in the middle of a war, and the writing came hot out of a torment of emotion. She saw woman—herself—creating over again what men—soldiers—had destroyed, and would always destroy.

This is a tragic, striking story.

But her husband says it is not true.

He says that she had never shown him the great book in its first manuscript, and reasons from this that it had never been written.

This, however, need not necessarily upset an admirer of Olive Schreiner. It might have been possible for her to have written the manuscript and have kept it secret. It is rather more than possible. For a woman who has lost a baby lives afterwards in fear of miscarriage, and is quite likely to become secretive about a creative effort. But if, technically, he is correct, neither should that upset her admirers. The story of the burned first manuscript—whether accurate or not in point of fact—was a dramatic piece of publicity for the second manuscript, and likely as not had quite some effect upon its reception by its readers. And aside totally from either of these reservations, the book as it was published shows unmistakable internal evidence of composition at the height of some tragic emotion. It was torn from its author.

Woman and Labor, as published, is a book of six closely connected essays related to feminism, and is dedicated to Lady Constance Lytton, who took an active part in the English feminist propaganda. It includes an introduction, apart from the six chapters, which tells the story of the first manuscript, *Musings upon Women and Labor,* and is in a sense an apologia for the relatively slight content of the published book. The introduction contains two very important comments for the student of Olive Schreiner. She narrates a conversation she had in her youth with a native Kaffir woman, which shows the awareness of the savage woman of the injustice of her condition, and also her submission to it because of the peculiar con-

ditions of the society of savagery. Olive Schreiner concludes
from this that women only revolt from unbearable situations
when revolt is indicated as being due because of changing conditions of society. This is the text of her book. For she infers
that the affairs of the world have so changed that a change in
the position of women in economic society is absolutely necessary if the race is to continue in strength. The introduction
closes with an appeal for understanding to future readers. She
wants passionately to be sure that women of the future will
comprehend the emotion which caused the upheaval among
the feminists. She wants passionately also to insure their sympathy for the actual small amount of change that was accomplished through so much feeling and endeavor.

Of the six essays three are upon sexual parisitism, one upon
the relation of women towards war, one upon sexual differences,
and one general chapter upon feminism, which is called *Certain
Objections*.

The three chapters on parisitism deal with the changing conditions which, according to Olive Schreiner's thesis, as inferred
from her conversation with the Kaffir woman, have produced
the feminist movement.

Women, under primitive conditions and in the civilization of
Europe broadly called the middle ages by the author, were in
the throes of constant child-bearing and child-rearing. It was
necessary, if the state was to continue. Many warriors were
needed. Many slaves were needed for manual labor. And out
of many children born, only a relative few would attain maturity because of the ignorance of health laws and the exigencies
which made it difficult to rear children. So the life of a woman
from adolescence until middle age was generally taken up by
the bearing and rearing of children. Attached to this there
was considerable manual labor. The household affairs were
run by women. Clothes were made by their own hands. Food
was prepared by them and stored. All of which meant that a
woman definitely earned her keep, and far more than earned it.

With the industrial revolution, fewer manual laborers were

needed. A machine tended and directed by one man super-
seded the labor of hundreds of men. And while the occupation of the manual laborer receded, a corresponding increase
took place in the occupation of brain workers. She gives one
example. The former one-man town crier of news was super-
seded by many men whose work was necessary for the production of a newspaper. She stressed the advisability of women
demanding at the onset of the change their equal chance and
equal preparation for chance in the new occupations. Otherwise there would be an era of sexual parasitism. That is, with
the household labor taken out of the hands of women by the
products of the factory, both in clothes and food, and with
the reduction of the period of child-bearing and child-rearing
to a comparatively few years out of a woman's life, women
would be thrown unconsciously into parasitism. There would
be, she said, undue strain upon intellectual workers among men,
one man earning by his brain effort the upkeep of female de-
pendents who had little or nothing to do vocationally with
themselves. She saw the period of child-tending lessening and
lessening in a woman's life with the need for children to be
prepared early for their professional part in the world, so that
the care of their mothers would eventually be brought down
to the time of babyhood alone. There was no sense, she maintained, in women pleading for the return of their old labors.
Clothes and food made in the home could not compete with
industrialized clothes and food. A child trained in the home
would not be properly trained for his social and professional
experience. If a child were in the future to be dressed and fed
and trained by an amateur in the home, he or she would only
be inadequately equipped to go out among his contemporaries.
Women, she reiterated, must demand their share in the industrialized and intellectualized life. But how this was to be organized to allow a short period of child-bearing, she did not
suggest. In this, as in all her writing, she was the prophetic
utterer of sound generalizations rather than the executive ar-
ranger of reform.

She hammered away at the evil of parasitism in women. She went back to history and showed how degeneration always set in upon a race as soon as it took labor away from its women. Even during the periods when women still bore large families. She believed in the spiritual dignity of labor. She taught that the kept woman—the woman who accepted up-keep from a man in return for sexual complaisance, either in legal marriage or outside it—degenerated, though often quite unconsciously. The sound of money drowned the sound of attraction. It altered the motive. And what children she might have were born from tissue made feeble by the parasitism of the mothers. Olive Schreiner, of course, was writing in broad generalizations. History could have shown her just as many cases of children of extraordinary power born of women who had sold themselves for money or position. Elizabeth Tudor was just one example. However, the point was very well taken on its large scale, and has its justification in contemporary history. For children born of relatively parasitical women lend themselves easily to the regimentation of military dictators, which is one reason why the military dictator always tends to push women back into relative parasitism. But there is another side to the modern issue which she did not foresee, and that is the need of men in the complicated modern scene of women whose nerves are not disturbed as their own are by the competitive struggle. It is this need which is at the root of the man's desire to shelter women, and at the root of the normal woman's instinctive resort to the life which Olive Schreiner called parasitic. There are services tendered by women which are not entirely sexual, but rather more in the nature of a solacing retreat. And it is partly because of such services that men keep women in marriage and also in love-nests. But Olive Schreiner was right enough in her assumption that that leisure was degenerating to the average woman. It demands a special temperament and highly specialized cultivation. The average women put into leisure gets into compensatory excitements, which further complicate her life and the lives of those in association with her.

She declared definitely that the male labor problem and the feminist problem were not identical. This in her time was a new idea. It was generally accepted that the women's movement, having originally come from a young woman, Mary Wollstonecraft, who was ardently involved in the middle-class revolt of the French, was part of the broadening labor unrest. She said that the readjustment of labor conditions among men, if it led to a more equitable distribution of wealth among males, might indeed diminish slightly the accompanying tendency to parasitism in the very wealthiest female class, but that it would open up exactly those conditions which would make parasitism possible to millions of women below the wealthiest classes. It was entirely a separate movement, and was based, not upon economics, but upon sex. Women were demanding labor in its new form, not for the sake of having money for themselves, but for the sake of preventing racial degeneration.

Chapter Four she devoted to a theme which was forced upon her through the experience she had of writing her book in the middle of war. Into this chapter her emotions poured themselves.

War, she wrote, was an insult to women, for women were the creators of life, and war was destruction. She believed that no woman could of herself support any war. She used her famous illustration of the sculptor. She said that if a city were besieged and its walls were full of holes, there would be one citizen who would refuse to let the holes be filled with the statues of the city. The sculptor. Women, she said, were the sculptors of the race, and if they had any say at all they would never allow the human bodies they had created and borne to be used in the defense of an abstract idea of state. This again was a generalization. It was a Utopian picture of women drawn from her own womanliness. She overlooked the capacity of women for jealousy of men, which in times of war leads them to urge men to go to war. She overlooked also the inertia of women and its resultant capacity for passive sacrifice of themselves and what they have done. The last war showed how easy it was to convince women to sacrifice their sons, and how many of them took pleasure in cheering men into battle. Olive Schreiner wrote her book before the Great War, though she lived to see it. But it lines itself with the thinking done by women since the war, and has had its place in the post-war era of feminist thinking rather than with the propagandistic era immediately preceding the war, when women cried for their political and economic rights. For women know now very decidedly that they are the chief sufferers from war and its resulting disorganization of the census. If she had been able to foresee a whole generation of men killed in four years, and a whole generation of women left without normal racial experience, it would have strengthened her chapter. But nobody could foresee war on such a scale prior to 1914. She saw it intimately on a small scale, and that sharpened her teaching. She saw it, too, as an organized political venture in which women had practically no share. She could not have foreseen it in all its psychological war-mania sweep involving women as well as men. So she concluded quite erroneously that all women would stand sternly aside from war, because it affronted their potential creativeness. She assumed that the possession of a womb indicated the passion of motherhood. It was a great pity that Olive Schreiner, like Mary Wollstonecraft, did not understand something of the intricacies of the mind in women. Women to Mary Wollstonecraft were suppressed human beings whom education and opportunity would liberate. Women to Olive Schreiner were burdened human beings whom the very fact of their burden had softened into an essentially fine apprehension of life. Women, in Mary Wollstonecraft's creed, stood in absolute need of life. Life, in Olive Schreiner's creed, stood in absolute need of women. Mary Wollstonecraft glorified equality and experience. Olive Schreiner glorified the racial passion of women. She understood biology in women. But she did not understand the psychiatric implications of biology.

This shows very clearly in her chapter on *Sex Differences*. Sex in her treatment was entirely physiological. Men and women were alike mentally. The male and the female were alike throughout nature except in one particular. The male animal and the female animal played alike, hunted alike, lived alike, were alike even in their seeking of their sexual opposite. Male and female alike would run all manner of danger to get to each other. The urge was equally strong in both of them. The difference lay in the attitude of the female to the helpless young. She nourished them and treasured them and hovered over them. The male went his way in unconcern. Men and women, she claimed, thought alike and felt alike. They differed only in their organs of reproduction and in their attitude towards the young. The apparent differences which made women peculiarly personal in their thinking were only incidental differences, and were caused by differences in education. Sex, she believed simply, had nothing to do with the brain.

This chapter is now completely outmoded due to the researches of the Viennese school of psychiatry.

But more than that, it is out of date with her own writing. *The Story of an African Farm* was far ahead of it in its comprehension of the force which led little Lyndall to seek for her superior in a mate. So also was the comprehension set down in many of the dreams. In *The Story of an African Farm*, and in many of the dreams, Olive Schreiner was writing subconsciously about women. In this chapter of *Woman and Labor* she was arguing a point in a debate. The opponents of women's suffrage were saying loudly that women did not have the brains necessary to make impersonal electorate judgments. They could not sit in Parliament or in the Law Courts. They could not practise medicine nor be good executives in business. They were secondary creatures mentally. History showed no evidence of exceptional mentality in women. Olive Schreiner and most of the women active in the feminist campaign fought back upon the obvious point. The implication of inferiority got under their skins. They refuted it. It was a great pity they did. For the implication really did not matter, and the very foundation of the cause lay in those very differences which they denied so strenuously. It was because there were differences between men and women that recognition of women in economics and politics was necessary. Women were half the population at least. They were a different half, and men could not adequately legislate for them. If women were exactly like men, there was no point in the demand. Men could just as easily legislate for them. It was unfair, of course, that being a woman prevented a woman from getting into public life if she had a taste for it, but the real root of the whole demand lay in the impossibility of one sex legislating for the other.

This chapter, however, was natural enough, as was the whole indignation of women at the taunt of inferiority. It was an indignation springing from uncertainty.

Difference did not necessarily indicate inferiority. But they did not realize that. The stressing of difference to them meant the assumption of inferiority, and from this point the feminist program took its impetus. Girls were urged to prove that they could distinguish themselves equally with men. They were urged to be a little more distinguished than men. It would take infinitely greater mental capacity on the part of a woman to take her place in the world with men, and at the same time fulfil herself biologically in the race. The contest was fixed with this in the minds of women. They must be very great. To be mothers and at the same time equals of men. But how it could be done neither Olive Schreiner nor any other of the leaders explained. They were thinking ahead and of a Utopian state of affairs which would make some necessary readjustment in the matter of taking care of women during child-bearing without penalizing them intellectually and economically for it.

The sixth chapter was a summing up of the platform of the feminists.

The opponents of the movement were bewailing the possible fact that equal opportunity for women with men would destroy the sexual quality of women. Olive Schreiner took that issue and said that sex attraction was the strongest thing in life.

She declared that it was far too strong to be reduced by the fact that women would labor in companionship with men for the state, or even in competition with them. It could be relied upon, so strong was it, to stand an incidental change in relationship.

More than that, she went on to say, the value of the female varied as her freedom. The male instinctively likes the female he has to make a big effort to get. He will pay any price to get what appears to be unpurchasable or of an exorbitant price. He instinctively begins to dislike the woman he has bought in finality. She foresaw a great heightening of the value of women to men through their economic freedom. She foresaw the liberation of sex from money. The woman who is kept, she believed, is not in any position to judge her essential emotions. The economic issue clouds them. She is prevented from making her intrinsic choice in men because she has to consider her economic future. Olive Schreiner rejoiced in the simple emotions of women. She resented the tangling of them with upkeep. She put her finger upon one point which has become increasingly important since her time—the difficulty in economics which bars the conscientious male from entering marriage on limited means. The economic freedom of women would, she believed, enfranchise love, and secure for the race the parenthood of the best men and the best women. She saw professional preparation taking more and more time, and marriage being put off and off, with serious loss to the race and serious sexual consequences. She maintained that love purchased by means, either legally or illegally, would vanish, just as love taken by capture and through superior muscles on the part of the male had vanished from civilized society. Love would come to be the response of affection and attraction. The women's movement, she said, in her conclusion, is at its heart a movement of the woman towards the man. The woman was bound in two ways to men—as lover and as mother. Feminism was not a rebellion but a decision on the part of women to make themselves more fit as lovers and as mothers, to free love from any element of purchase, from any bond of up-keep, and to endow motherhood with the joy of willingness, and with the greater power which would come from tissues strengthened through actual labor in the world. She ends with a bit of prose poetry which touched the very soul of her ideal for love and women. "Always in our dreams we hear the turn of the key that shall close the door of the last brothel; the clink of the last coin that pays for the body and the soul of a woman; the falling of the last wall that encloses artificially the activity of a woman and divides her from man; always we picture the love of the sexes, as once a dull, slow, creeping worm, then a torpid earthy chrysalis; at last the full-winged insect, glorious in the sunshine of the future."

Woman and Labor is connected in its idealism with the Labor movement, but its concentration upon the feminist aspect of the movement, as well as the sheerly emotional presentation of the doctrine of parasitism, removes it in relation to time from the Labor doctrines of the present. It is therefore not a text which has lived in its usefulness. It is already historical, and interesting, so far as its content goes, only to the historian of the feminist movement. Though it has perennial interest to the collector of prose.

Though in style it is not the equal of *The Story of an African Farm,* nor of the *Dreams.*

Olive Schreiner was an emotional thinker and an emotional writer. She could not so successfully bind her emotions into the context of an abstract idea. The idea of *Woman and Labor* was an abstract idea, immense in its sweep. Her power could not carry her through its sweep and down into its abstraction. It might be better to say that the doctrine she was seeking to put forward was one that demanded treatment of a concrete and practical order based upon sound abstract thinking. This was out of her field. Though she did not realize it, she was a writer who had to use images. When she put her feelings about women, which were part of the historic Hebraic feeling concerning the downtrodden, into small poignant pictures set in allegory, she was completely artistic and authentic. When she tried to mass her thinking into a cool substance composed of intellectual argument, she could not manage it. All she could do was to get the feeling over in rich, almost ornate prose. The effort piled itself into her composition, and *Woman and Labor* stands beside the heart-breaking simplicity of the *Dreams* as a heavily embroidered theme, carried by the emotion of its writer quite some distance beyond its scope.

She dealt in generalities with a subject which of its very nature needed a tentative approach, carefully guarded on all sides by admissions of exception.

One realizes at the end of it how little the generalizing mind ever knows of human realities. One questions whether for all of her associations with men Olive Schreiner really knew men. She seemed to have regarded them simply as part of the oppressing caste. And what did she know about the emotion of possession in men, and its relation to women, and the relation of that to the achievements of the race? Did she ever wonder what its absence might do to the efforts of men? It almost seems as if she were actually unaware of men. Certainly she took what inspiration she could get from association with them, but its effect she translated into the world of women. Women to her were the very center of life. It was a sincere conviction drawn from her biological awareness. So conscious was she of the mother with the babe in her womb or at her breast that it dominated her biological attitude. It was almost an Amazonian point of view, with a civilization in which men were only tolerated by women for their incidental infinitesimal part in actual conception. Women were the source of life. And life could rise no higher than women. The very ancient idea of women as vessels brought to the race—men—for its continuance seemed not to have entered into her comprehension. Nor the very modern idea of men as being the really potent carriers of the attributes of the race. She seemed hardly to consider the seed in her absorption of the field. She was the most feminist of all the feminists. For she far "out-feministed" Mary Wollstonecraft. Mary Wollstonecraft held a comparatively simple notion, fundamentally, that the biological interpretation of women was a foolish generalization concerning them. Olive Schreiner thoroughly accepted the biological interpretation of women, and considered that the whole of society should be reorganized to give it complete freedom of scope and operation. Her doctrine of parasitism was no revolt against biology. It was, on the contrary, the outcome of a desire to disentangle biology in women from economic attachments. She wanted it to function by itself; to be free to assert itself apart entirely from economic considerations. She saw woman as the mother with the baby in her arms. She stressed labor for women because she strove to find something to take the place in women of the ecstasy that follows the pain of child-bearing. This she knew to be the great moment of women when the child is first put in her arms, and this she saw to be the great need of women that the advance of mechanized life was very much to curtail. She saw children diminishing, and the plight of the childless woman and the hardly less serious plight of the almost childless woman. For what was one baby or two babies to a woman whom thousands upon thousands of years had made for the bearing of many babies? So must women find themselves labor, and Olive Schreiner wrote her great book to press home upon women their immediate need, and to suggest the work they might do for the race. There was war to stop. There was education to get and to foster, and there was a whole world needing to know something of the culture of love. There was plenty for women to do.

Her own life was over after she wrote *Woman and Labor,* though she lived a few years longer. She went back to England. She was there when the war came, and she fell under the suspicion of landladies again, but this time because of the German name she bore. She wandered from place to place, a woman of forlorn mind. The war distressed her. She did her duty as she saw it by attending what pacifist meetings managed to get held. And this did her no further good with landladies. Between the advance of age and the distress of her mind over the war, her disease became worse. She could breathe easily nowhere. But she stayed several years in England. Then she decided to return once again to her home in South Africa. She died one night by herself just after she had landed, and they found when they examined her body that her heart was stretched far beyond its size.

So she remains in our School of Femininity a woman with a big heart burdened with tragedy and feeling in herself all the sorrows of women, burdened with the burden of biology.

It was a fine sincere mind that belonged to that heart. It was an eager, ardent mind. It was above everything else a brave mind. And very tender. She understood women. She saw a little of what was before them. She was aware of what was behind them, and the pull it would have upon them as they struggled to be something more than their wombs wanted them to be. It was as if she had made herself a voice to encourage them, especially the young girl bending over books, and looking around for some place to put her mind in life. She wanted to explain to men that the new woman would be better than the old woman. She wanted men to understand that it was towards them that women were moving in feminism. She longed to avert, if she could, a war of sex in economics and the professions, as she had wanted to avert it if she could in South Africa. She wanted both men and women to believe that sex in itself was a beautiful thing, and that the mistakes associated with it were not of itself but only of people who barely understood it and were afraid of it or put too much emphasis upon it. She was a woman who was profoundly wise in her simplicity. She had seen savagery. She had seen war at her doorstep. She had loved and not been loved in return. She had loved and been loved in return. She had borne her baby and lost her baby. She had suffered agonies with a body which would not function as it should have functioned. She had longed for literary distinction and had accomplished it at the beginning, and sacrificed it. She had seen all her efforts fail to avert a war. She had lived through a much worse war. She had talked intimately with men. She had loved some one man with unbearable emotion, and because of her frustrated woman's heart she had turned to women and laid at their future a message which she hoped would be comforting in the hour that would be worst for them—that hour she vaguely felt when dictators and circumstances would take from them their new work in the world. Or in that hour which comes to every individual woman when she wonders if the work she has set out to do is after all too much for her, and if in working her way for herself she has made it too easy for some man.

It was an ideal Olive Schreiner set before women and before men. It was the principle of a great movement she enunciated as no other woman enunciated it. It was a principle that was very simple to her, but she set it down lest at some crisis it be forgotten. It was a principle that has much pulling against it both in men and in women and in the practical state of things. It is a principle that is only variously adaptable, but it remains, whether adaptable in general or not adaptable, the great initial and initiating principle of feminism.

Part II

THE TWENTIETH-CENTURY SCHOOL OF FEMININITY

CHAPTER VII

LITTLE GIRL PALS

Anita Loos—Dorothy Parker—Katharine Brush—Daphne du Maurier

THE BRIGHT YOUNG FEMININE things began to write after the war.

But before the war was over the army of little girl pals began to assert itself. The girls went to work at the jobs the men had given up to enter the fight. Work changed these girls. Men came home to them on leave from the front, and that also changed them.

Prior to the war women did not work. Prior to the war women did not do much thinking about themselves as separately functioning human entities. They were protected parts of a family. There were, of course, odd women of scholarly proclivities who forced their way into the centers of education. But after they had wrenched an education for themselves all they could do with it was comparatively little. They could teach girls. That was something, and they accepted teaching as a mission, and it was mainly through the women teachers and their bluestocking code that the undercurrent of the feminist rebellion was kept vital. There were, also, odd women with energy which no family interest could consume. These were the women who rushed after the standard of Florence Nightingale. But they were always careful to explain themselves. They yearned, they said, for human service. So they passed. Service was womanly. A few women began to go into offices and shops but this was considered a disaster. For girls to work before marriage was an admission of economic inadequacy on the part of the male members of their families. All this that has been written applies to women of the middle class. The women from the lower classes worked as they had always worked. Nothing was thought about that. God had ordained it. Because of them middle-class girls could sit waiting serenely for men to marry them. If they waited in vain they managed to hang on to the fringe of family society. There had always been aunts and sisters and cousins who never married. Nobody worried about them except themselves. Nobody thought anything could be done about it except to see that they had places to sleep in and a few clothes to wear and certain meals. Every middle-class family had its female retainers who were useful with mending and child-tending, and could always be counted upon to represent the family in church functions.

If a woman went out to work before the war she had to possess energy enough to fight her way to what she wanted to do. Her conviction about getting what she wanted had to be so strong as almost to amount to a paranoia. Very often even that conviction was not strong enough to batter down the opposition. It was women's resentment which brought about the suffragette campaign in England. Women got the idea that only through political representation, or rather through political recognition of them as persons in the realm would their wrongs be corrected. Behind the dramatic revolt of the suffragettes with its guerrilla tactics lay the anger of generations of frustrated women. It was a magnificent publicity campaign. It affected and involved a far greater number of women than is generally supposed. The funds collected by the party were enormous and came from women in all walks of life. It was a long-sustained and entirely deliberate campaign for all its apparent hysteria. It came in the end to be something approaching a sex war. Women were determined to make men ridiculous until they gave them what they wanted. The women who believed in their professional rights saw themselves as heroines. Women who had no professions thought about the freedom to be attained through professionalism and got into the fight. Men began to wonder about a social system which excluded women from almost everything except home management, especially when the surplus numbers of women were emphasized. There is an absolute relation between the suffragette campaign with its persistent feminine nagging and the rapidity with which women took over the work of men during the war. It had released the pent-up resentment of some women; it had educated other women; it had disturbed both men and women who previously had considered things comfortably arranged for them. It had been an efficient campaign, managed shrewdly and with a fine sense of publicity. The women speakers had made an excellent showing for themselves. Unquestionably there were brains among women. A few critics might point to a man here and there in the campaign, but the emphasis had been thrown upon the women leaders, and though cabinet ministers might call them hysterical women, the public remembered the peculiarly ridiculous aspect of men in power trying to escape these women. So when the war came the consciousness of women generally had been prepared. They were keyed for an effort. They were not to any extent bothered by a consciousness of inferiority, even if they still had a subconscious sense of it.

The war took all the men it could get. That left many jobs vacant. Somebody had to take the place of every man released to the fighting lines. So patriotism supplanted paranoia. Women worked because their work set men free. And they no longer had to push their way into positions. The positions waited for them. Girls who would never have thought of working felt they had to work too. It became unpatriotic to sit at home waiting for a man. Being unpatriotic it was no longer smart to be idle.

The girls went to the jobs with gusto. They began to dress to them. No girl could hop busses and street cars in a soft trailing gown. She could not carry what she had to carry if her coat were elaborate. She could not make her way through crowds wearing a big hat. So skirts were shortened; trench coats became modish and small hats were worn. Towards the end of the war women's long hair came off. It was a gesture of utility. Long hair was not likely to remain attractively tidy through a day of work.

There emerged a boyish young woman.

But it happened that there was more than work behind the boyish appearance of the young working women. Men fastened to the lines of fighting month upon month thought in the nature of things about their own sex. The war lasted long enough to effect in one generation at least a subconscious, if not actually conscious, homosexuality in men. The women, subconsciously, if not actually consciously, responded to an intuitive understanding of how it was with their men by appealing to them boyishly. The emancipated war girl had adjusted herself with amazingly rapid dexterity to the temporary inclinations of men. It worked. Men on leave found an army of little girl pals ready to entertain them. They found them amusing. Work by the day had no apparent effect upon the sexual pattern of the night. It cheered a man to see that his women could make their own way. The self-sustaining, casual young girl was the popular girl. She understood her men. Men took her as she was, and nobody did any amount of thinking about the future. Men towards the close of the war had become fatalists, and accepted things as they happened to be at the moment. These new girls were comfortable girls with whom to get along. They were real. Men did not have to play the humbug with them. They were jaunty little pals.

The jaunty little girl pals began to use cigarettes and make-up.

Prior to the war the odd woman smoked. The aristocrat and the Bohemian and the very old women among the poor. The aristocrat was a law unto herself, tempered only by a sense of obligation to her class. The Bohemian did what she liked, provided what she liked would shock society. The poor old woman smoked because it was comfortingly sedative to smoke. But no good woman among the middle classes smoked—certainly not admittedly. There was a time when no man could smoke in front of a woman he considered good. He associated such freedom with ladies from the brothel.

Prior to the war no good woman made her face up. There were whispers about what professional beauties among the aristocrats did to preserve the illusion of color on their cheeks and lips. Stage women frankly painted themselves. So did the women of the streets. But a middle-class woman who used such artifices did it in great secret, and used it sparingly. To use it admittedly was a sign of moral decadence.

Behind the sudden addiction of the little girl pals to tobacco and make-up lay a mixture of motives.

The jobs they had taken on set them free of parental control. If parents raised strenuous objections to what they did they could quite easily set themselves up by themselves. Many of them did. Tobacco and make-up became symbols of self-reliance. So they smoked and made up extravagantly.

But there was more to it than this. There were many men at the front who, when they thought of women, thought of them in terms of the demi-mondaine. The little girl pals knew with the inherited intuition of women that they were competing, not only with homosexual inclinations in men, but also with the traditional attractions of the whore. Being instinctively practical, they set out to rival both the young lad and the whore. They were playing safely for their men by appealing to both possibilities. They accomplished their appeal with gestures which would leave both the young lad and the whore gasping for breath.

Everything that savored of pre-war femininity and parental control went out.

No nice girl in pre-war days crossed her legs in public. No nice girl lifted her hands to rearrange her hair in public, for the pull of the arm upwards brought the pectoral muscles into play and featured the breasts. That indicated a mind offering a body.

So the little girl pal slouched in her chair, went in for the cult of the leg, and lifted her arms frequently. How else could she light her cigarettes?

No nice girl prior to the war was actually informed about

her anatomy. Girls were kept virgin through ignorance, it was thought. The little girl pals considered this interesting if true. They began to compare notes. They also began to be hungrily curious about the secrets of the demi-mondaine. They must have secrets. They were very simple secrets after all. And by a miracle of timing a lot of gathered biological information began to seep through to interested inquirers. The thing was not such a mystery as had been supposed. The little girl pals began to laugh among themselves. They laughed hilariously. Somebody had played a joke on them. The joke could be turned backwards.

So the little girl pals emerged painted young things dressed in boyish clothes, smoking and laughing girls who occasionally did a bit of thinking. They fascinated the men returning from the fight. No wonder. Were they girls, or were they young lads? The boyish clothes necessitated slender figures, and the cult of slimming came into vogue. The boyish figure and the boyish styles set against the rampant femininity of painted cheeks and lips produced an exotic appeal probably never before achieved in history. Masculinity of dress and attitude set against utter femininity. It was bizarre. It was tantalizing. There was no escape from it.

It was an entirely new development in femininity.

After the war the bright young things began to write.

The excitement was over; the world had changed and a lot of young men were dead. Whose fault was it? The fault of the old men who governed the world, and the old women who applauded old men and their governments. The attitude of the young towards the old and the world they had made became pointedly and bitterly critical. How had the old got that way? Through believing in things. Through believing in the romance of things that had no reality. The way out, then, was obviously not to believe in the romance of things. And what was there to believe in anyway? More than that, who could believe in belief of any kind? Religion was a pretty enough story except that it cramped the style of living. It was focused upon death. The world had had too much death. The family was an outmoded institution and contributed mainly to the talents of the middle-aged for petty tyranny, and had more than a little to do with the neuroses of existence. The state was no great government plan, but rather a muddle of vague stupidities. The race—well, the race went on, anyway, due to the sexual desires of men and women. Why make such a to-do about it? There would be reason enough to make a to-do when the effects of contraceptive knowledge began to be felt. That was going to be the great biological joke. Maybe a joke on God. What was left? Oneself and cigarettes! And neither to be taken too seriously. A little bubble in the universal stream. A little puff of smoke. Soon out. Meanwhile why attempt to make it stay put and lasting inside silly beliefs and foolish customs? Everything was pretty damn awful. So the young things smoked on and on. The women smoked more violently and persistently than the men. They seemed to need it more. Perhaps something had to take the place of beliefs with them. Cigarettes were handy, and at least there was something one always wanted.

With their imaginations emptied of the major beliefs, the little girl pals took to story writing. One story taken out of life had to be replaced by another story put into it. The bright young men were writing jeeringly about things as they had been and do continue to be. The little girl pals had to keep up with them. They found the new game amusing. It passed the time, and something had to pass the time. Jobs were not so plentiful as they had been. And, anyway, it was fatuous to work steadily at building some kind of occupational security. Old men sitting in easy chairs could sweep away that security. And as for old women—they knew nothing about anything. What could they know about a shattered generation? For by this time the little girl pals had learned that their world was broken. They said among themselves—well—to hell with it—what does it matter?—the only point to remember is not to let one's heart get broken. Be nonchalant—that's it. Yet they longed for a world that would be safe for the nonchalant.

The bright young things were a generation brought to maturity in violent shock. The war was one shock. The peace was another shock. A whole generation felt it had been sold. It went to war to protect some notion of race and boundaries. It took jobs at home and made itself over to suit a revolution in ideas. Nothing came of anything it did. Medical folk said that sexual expression was necessary for the maintenance of nervous poise. That was another sell. Sex went bitter on one. It seemed to need something else. Nobody knew what the something else was. Maybe it was a sense of security. Well, there was no security to be had, and nobody but a fool looked for it. So maybe one had better enjoy the bitter.

This was the mood in which the little girl pals began to write.

It would seem as if they and their young men had absorbed all the tragedy of the world of 1914-1918, and the worse tragedy of the years following. They reacted by refusing intellectually to admit feeling of any kind. They laid over themselves a hard crust. They developed a sales resistance against emotion. This was the cause of the brittle shell which covered all the writing of the survivors of the war. They saw themselves inheriting a ruined world with no prospect of rebuilding. All building was doomed to destruction. They held nothing to be sacred or lasting. They looked purposely for the worm of doom in the apple, and when they found it they laughed at the wiggling it did, and laughed, too, at the horror on the faces of their elders. That, in fact, was the biggest part of the pleasure of finding the worm.

Most of all they laughed at biology and the pomposity with which the old people dodged it, or went round corners to get it, or camouflaged it with all kinds of pretty stories.

ANITA LOOS

The biggest laugh at biology came from Anita Loos when she wrote *Gentlemen Prefer Blondes*.

It was a laugh that was both a snicker and a guffaw.

The subject was a lady who made monkeys of men.

The book was a natural gesture from a generation of disillusioned young women. It was a book from women for women. It acknowledged the perverse enjoyment women take from the antics of men in pursuit of biology and their pleasure in seeing them taken for a ride.

It was the diary of a professional gold-digger written in vivacious wise-cracking short sentences. It was a little book and could be carried conveniently in a pocket or slipped neatly behind other books. Everybody read it. Only the hypocrites took exception to it. The girl was a hilarious mixture of classical hedonism and modern rapture over business deals. "A kiss on the hand is very nice, but a bracelet lasts forever," was her motto of operation, and how she went about persuading gentlemen concerning bracelets and their equivalents proved, as delineated by Anita Loos, to be a full-time career of absorbing interest.

The theme itself was a punch in the battle of feminism. It was a deft and devastating punch. For the eternal attraction of men for light ladies who could make them feel lordly and compelling powers in creation turned out to be, as revealed by the diary of the blonde, only the attraction of the fly for the spider's web. Seriously considered, it did more for the moral issue of such goings-on than all Mary Wollstonecraft's indignation about the appeal of the courtesan, and all the righteous anger of respectable women down through the nineteenth century. It made them funny.

The blonde was an expert huntress. The lure she used was her blonde hair and adept beguiling, thoroughly studied ways with the "big boys." Not one of them mattered personally to her, but only what they possessed, and what they possessed solely in relation to the possibility of transferring an adequate section of such possessions to her.

It took away the last citadel of masculinity—that when he was on the loose a man was playing hell with the girls. The truth was they were playing hell with his pocketbook. It was

the eternal joke upon men. It was the eternal joke of biology—
women using men for what they could get out of them.

Anita Loos may, or may not, have intended this.

Probably she did not intend it at all. She saw, for all that
we know to the contrary, merely an extremely funny situation,
and out of it created a rollicking story. The United States at
the time was full of gentlemen familiarly known as "butter-
and-egg men" with their pockets full of variously collected
gold. The United States was also full of ladies with blonde
temperaments in possession of adroit talents for picking male
pockets. On both sides it was easy money.

Anita Loos wrote in the vernacular of easy money. She managed her snappy phrases with astute skill. She penetrated the
smugness of society with cheeky sorties upon a so-called sordid
enterprise. The blonde was no "wronged" girl. She was a high-
pressure sales-girl and what she sold for magnificent returns was
only something of no intrinsic value to her—her virginity. Any
female could do it. And it paid. It always paid. The only
thing was to watch out for love. Love, as the blonde said, never
did any girl any good. It made her forget the gate receipts.
The blonde giggled up her sleeve at women running here and
there being the equals of men. She hooted at the excitement
over virginity. It was not as if a girl could only sell it once. It
was a constantly turned-over article of merchandise, and the
world was full of prospects. She brought to her game the zest
of youth for adventure, and an appetite insatiably greedy for
the expensive things to be had. There were so many expensive
things. A girl need never get bored. She felt no terror of the
disdain of respectable women. She knew what it came from.
Respectable women were women who were not well-equipped
with what men wanted. They stayed out of the game because
they knew they would lose. They cheered themselves along
by being holier than others. The point every woman was to remember was to be better with men than other women were.
Men still had the money, and that was the only way to get

some of it. The really clever woman studied herself and her own interests with the modulated sharpness of the thoroughly trained confidence person. The blonde was herself so thoroughly trained and so whole-heartedly devoted to her own technique that she would take on any competition, even the competition sustained by coronets in international circles. A few wise remarks did for most of the competitors, and a few pretty ways did for most of the prospects, in addition to the merchandise display of blonde hair and promissory biology.

Underneath the sinister social aspect of the story, and underlying its humor, was quite a lot of information for women. It was the diary of an expert with men, the record of biological and commercial success, a text-book of sexual competition, pleasantly disguised by genial comments upon things in general, and garnished by a genuinely native wit. It was the first popular appearance of wit in women, boisterously presented, but containing an undercurrent of subtlety.

Gentlemen Prefer Blondes was a best seller in its time. That means that it hit a receptive spot. It came at a time when nobody wanted to be sad, or to see anything tragic in life. There had been too great a tragedy. It came at a time when many women were without men and this during their prime. In defense they were glad to see the insistent affair of biology as something that was funny. It came at a time when the men who were left were inclined to be put out by the natural pursuit of them by numbers of women. They hardly knew what to do about it. Good women waylaid them; bad women allowed them no peace. It was all preposterous. It was a relief, therefore, to see it set down plainly as a joke that was commercial rather than a tragedy that was biological. It was a time of terrible awareness of money as the only reality in life. Sex-starved women took all the romance away from the relationship of the sexes. Sex-bored men saw no romance in women. It came at a time when women saw the first flush of their keen interest in new jobs fading, and they were ready to look back consideringly at the old biological stand. It came when men were beginning to resent the problematical presence of women in their particular stamping-grounds. They were ready to look back appreciatively to the one reality concerning women. There was even more than this behind its popularity. Every woman thought to herself, "I could do this—if I buried my virtue." Every man thought, "Well—she gave them a good time—which is more than a virtuous woman does." Having her mind fixed upon money, the blonde went light on emotions, and it is the emotions of women in their relationships that men find trying. So it happened that every woman who resented the to-do she had made over some man, and every man who resented the spot some woman had put him into over a little matter of sex read the book and found it engaging.

In the historic feminist movement and in the school of literary femininity it is very important.

It was the first of the portraits of courtesans done by women.

The courtesan as portrayed by women is a different being entirely from the courtesan portrayed by men.

Painted by men the courtesan is a suffering, yielding, loving creature, dying for the most part of tuberculosis, beautiful beyond dreams, for the possession of whom men will start wars and wreck careers, not to mention the homes and children they will desert if need be for her. The traditional courtesan of masculine literature is a wish fulfilment. Men like to muse upon a woman who lives for love alone. Most of them get tied down to women who bind love about with all kinds of social taboos. Men set the courtesan with tragedy because tragedy promotes poignancy of feeling, and burns it into the imagination. There is no man anywhere who has not yearned in his spirit, and with his body, for a woman he could never altogether possess, and who sustains his emotion by surrounding herself with art and sorrow and the immutability of a great passion.

Painted by women the courtesan is a calculating hussy.

If a woman of the nineteenth century had tackled a courtesan in writing she would in all likelihood have described a monstrous female, prowling around the dregs of humanity for what she could pick up.

She would have treated her as the enemy of all good women, and the emissary of His Satanic Majesty with reference to men. This was the conviction which made the women of all countries and all classes dominated by any form of puritanism refuse to adopt personally any of the decorative or comfortable habits of the courtesan. In the estimation of the good woman it was very necessary to preserve the lines of difference. Bad women painted. Therefore no good woman painted. Bad women smoked. Hence when the little girl pals began to smoke a shudder went through their elder female relatives. The attitude of women towards the sister they designated as fallen was made up of a mixture of motivations. Part of it came from a quite sensible fear of the sexual pirate. She was a menace to the home. Part of it came from a not quite so sensible apprehension of sexual parasitism. Good women have always shrunk instinctively from living entirely for their sexual functioning. Part of the attitude came from a quite insensible jealousy. Men had set the courtesans with romanticism. It was an insult to all good women. It implied that the courtesan was the sexual expert, and this implication bruised the self-esteem of virtuous women.

This attitude descended upon the little girl pals, though they did not mean it to. A whole generation of new women had tried to loosen up on sex. They found, most of them, that it took a highly specialized temperament. Most women could never attain that temperament, hard as they worked at it.

Unquestionably there were bruises and cuts underneath the nonchalance of the little girl pals. They were amateurs at an age-old profession. Men, they found, were not in the main properly thankful for the talents of the amateur. The little girl pal in trying to be an equal, and in all ways a decent fellow with the boys, hit hard upon the stupidity of men with emotion.

It hurt her. She expected men to know just what she was doing and what it meant to her. The courtesan had never expected such a miracle. She was contained in herself and men were by way of being audiences, and nothing more. If the audience got the point, that was cheering. If the audience failed to get the point, that was as it happened to be. The toll was paid anyway.

So the little girl pals dealing with courtesans are not much in advance of their predecessors—the good women of all countries and all classes suffering from puritanism. The courtesan gets the impact of the ancient female resentment, fear and jealousy. The work, therefore, is touched with malice.

The bright young masculine things dealing with the courtesan are not either much in advance of their predecessors—the male romantics. It is true that the writing boys no longer call these ladies courtesans. They are prostitutes. They no longer die of tuberculosis to music, and surrounded by flowers on soft divans. They live in tawdry rooms; they do not always get enough to eat; they are on the whole a somewhat depressing species, but none the less good fiction material. The boys do not mean to be sentimental. But they are. Their prostitutes are subjects for delineation because they are part of the downtrodden masses, helpless bits of wreckage, woebegone elements of humanity, usually possessing hearts of gold roughly concealed behind a hail-fellow attitude. They take them in the gesture of crude defiance. For all its crudity it remains just as much a gesture as the dying gesture of the romantic ladies who lived for love and art.

The bright young men paint them in failure.

The little girl pals paint them in success.

There is a whole universe of sexuality in those two simple literary facts.

Though conceivably the little girl pals might jeer at the sexual interpretation of an incidental presentation of material providing tasty and good selling copy.

DOROTHY PARKER

Certainly Dorothy Parker would jeer, as she might well jeer at any idea pulled slightly out of its context.

Dorothy Parker is the little girl pal gone professionally critical and professionally witty. She is a Nell Gwyn columnist with a dash of Vashti added. She is a wag who will not do what she is expected to do. She is probably the most quoted woman in the world. She is an amazing dynamic kinetic force. She is queen of the little girl pals.

She is half Jewish and half Scottish. Which means she has the cast-iron effrontery of the Jew when put up against the world, and the cast-iron sense of superiority which is the temperamental inheritance of the Scot. It also means that she has the knife-blade bitterness of the Jewish tongue put together with the emotional economy of the Scot. This leads her to set her remarks within the smallest containing phrase and to aim them at the bull's eye.

On a very slim actual amount of publication she has made herself a person to be reckoned with. A few short poems, a handful of short stories, a few columns, many remarks of her contemporaries, and she has become one of the best known of the critics. The darling of all the weary young things; the pal of the intelligentsia of New York; a very famous woman indeed.

In her written work she uses a short, devastating, driving sentence. She pushes it out with the cynical precision of the Jew for the weakest spot, and the well-concentrated muscle-power of the Scot. The result is a knock-out blow, with the awful reverberations of the hellishly clever wise-crack.

For all of that, it is utterly sentimental work.

Pause for the jeers.

Repeat—it is utterly sentimental work.

She is striving with her time. She hates a lot of what she sees. Only the sentimentalist ever strives with any time. Only the sentimentalist ever hates anything. The sentimentalist wants things to be different. Therefore the striving. The sentimentalist wants things to be perfect. Hence the hating when they are not. The sentimentalist believes that things can be brought nearer to perfection, and accordingly spends an amount of energy trying to bring it to pass. The. first step in improvement is to be aware of deficiencies. The writer who yaps at the heels of humanity is fretting over humanity's deficiencies. Dorothy Parker is a persistent "yapper." Ergo she is continually fretting.

The Jew is a congenital fretter and the Scot is a habitual "yapper."

The Jewish prophets fretted over their own people, and the Jews as a race fret about the world. Jews get annoyed when their own folk fail in spiritual and temporal grace. They feel badly about the judgment of the world concerning them.

The Scots are native exhorters. John Knox thundering about idolatry was only one of them. They believe that people should be made to be better.

Little Mrs. Parker, behind her Nell Gwyn-Vashti make-up, is a combination of Jeremiah and John Knox, with the addition of a quality peculiar to the twentieth century and to women. Jeremiah comes out in the undertone of spiritual despair; John Knox comes out in the zeal for calling attention to flaws; the twentieth century shows in the placing of what she has to say in smart perversities; the femininity is exhibited in the emotional scratch and hiss. What a show! She keeps the show going because it has turned out to be a good show, and because of a feeling she has never been able to conquer—that it is her duty to "yap" and jeer and snicker the people out of their complacency.

She writes and she talks in the nervous staccato of her time. Her thoughts go out with a machine-gun tempo; shot after shot in rapid rhythm. It contains no melody but a lot of noise. It is exciting and powerful and neat. Where it is directed it finishes. It is a triumph of consistent follow-up shooting completely mechanized because a woman has said to herself, "I will be modern."

Anita Loos and Dorothy Parker both represent the little girl pal in a phase of getting something off her chest. They personify the hooting and the jeering, the sniffing and the grunting. They are girls with a gesture—thumbing their noses.

Both of them are sketch portraitists using caricature. The caricature of Anita Loos is vulgarly human and the caricature of Dorothy Parker is sadistically inhuman. Anita Loos has no intention to hurt. She only intends to get a laugh. She is a show girl. Dorothy Parker has every intention to hurt. She also plays for the laughs, but it is for the self-conscious laughter of the punctured hypocrite. Anita Loos hits upon a human peccadillo, such as the taste of gentlemen for pirates, and takes it as it is—excellent show material. She is essentially creative and entertaining. Dorothy Parker is essentially critical and informative. Neither is in the strict sense artistic. That is, they do not draw their pictures for the sake of the picture itself, nor do they say what they have to say for the sake of the saying itself. Anita Loos has her ear cocked for the laughter of the gods; Dorothy Parker has her eye fixed upon the squirm of discomfort in the front rows. But both of them require an audience.

Neither of them has lived entirely for her printed work. So there is an amount of work from both of them which cannot be tabulated in the School of Femininity. Anita Loos belongs to the screen and screen creativeness. Dorothy Parker belongs to the press. Both of them have had an influence far out of proportion to their actual publication in book form, which is the result of the positions they have achieved in two of the three most volatile media of modern thinking and feeling, including the radio. Both of them belong to a period which is, so far as may be tentatively judged by contemporary appraisal, somewhat on the ebb. But both of them will live, certainly in any collection of feminine contribution to history in literature. It is possible that they may also live in history itself because of their personification of an emotional attitude of a whole generation.

The bright young men and the little girl pals discovered early in their careers that spiritual nonchalance was acquired through forcing the imagination to see human doings as fiction. They could stand beside a dying friend and observe for future reference all the details. It was separation of oneself from life, but it worked. They could take the ups and downs of emotional experience with resiliency if they could manage the trick of seeing everything objectively as fiction material. It is one way of escaping. But it is difficult to accomplish it neatly. Whether or not it was accomplished neatly and fully on a wide scale, the attempt to do so created in a generation a taste for objective portraiture in fiction, and it produced a regiment of new young writers who tend to believe, and in some cases do not mind declaring, that the writing done before they made this great discovery was all so much "blah."

Among the young women there are not so many writers of this class. Objectivity is in the nature of things harder for a woman to capture. Because of her womb life lives inwardly with her. If she holds feeling on its external edges she is likely to produce frigidity in herself, or a debilitating inversion. Yet objectivity in writing has been successfully handled by women.

Katharine Brush is an example.

KATHARINE BRUSH

Katharine Brush is a young writer just getting into her stride.

But even at this stage she ranks high, not only among the younger women writers, but also among all the women writers. The high ranking is justified by the technical control and the depth of her fidelity to her subjects.

She maintains a touch of the suave *élégante* with the sharply impersonal matter-of-factness of the little girl pal. She is a commercially adapted young writer. There is no lonely attic atmosphere to her compositions. She intends them to sell. They do sell. But for all that, there is not the least descent in creative fidelity to the sodden emotional tastes of the general public.

Her portrait of the courtesan, *Red-Headed Woman,* is to date her most outstanding contribution.

Red-Headed Woman is done with more pigment than Anita Loos' portrait of the blonde. It is a full-length, lifelike, ruthless picture of a ruthless young person, who improved her circumstances man by man. She had never heard of love. So she never bothered even to say it did a girl no good. She was a pleasant-tempered hussy, greedy for the luxuries of living, and quite ready to exchange for them the gifts of nature. There was nothing more to it than that. When she got what she wanted she frankly reveled in it. So it was only decent according to her code to revel in what she had to barter for it. Men stroked her, and she purred, thinking of what was in their pockets. She comes to no bad end. She wrecks homes incidentally. She never has any remorse. It is all a competitive game, and somebody has to lose. So why should the winner feel sorry for the loser? It was better to put in the time filing one's nails and painting them. Once again the courtesan emerges from her portrait by another woman as a sound business woman, an expert merchandise display person, a slick collector of gate receipts; with a capacious appetite for business and an enormous talent for elbowing her way; with a thoroughly elaborated finesse for flattering the trade, and a very astute understanding of advertising psychology. And all combined with the essential laziness of the crook. As well as combined again with the natural gusto for conflict of the pirate. It all simmers down to the excitement of self-interest in a world of competition.

Put this against the gorgeous-creature effect of the courtesans done by old-fashioned men, or beside the drab-creature effect of the prostitutes done by the bright young men. There is quite a difference.

Romanticism comes into the picture because it is a success portrait. The red-headed woman was a menace and a prowler.

Realism comes into the portrait because it is done with virility, coming itself from the suppressed hatred of the author's sex. For all its objectivity there is an unescapable element of feminine disdain. It is too accurately aimed to have been an innocent character promotion. The story is pulled from its beginning to its end through a mold of definite purpose. It is stark and humorless. It is without tears and without laughter. The red-headed woman is an automaton managed by her greediness. The total effect is a warning and a campaign, though it should be said that the warning never pinches unpleasantly, nor does the campaign ever intrude itself jarringly throughout the progress of the story. It is an excellent story. As all the stories from Katharine Brush are excellent.

She has concentrated upon contemporary portraiture of women. It is concentration worthy of her talents. For women have never been in history more interesting than they are to-day. Women may try anything, and the backgrounds of new attempts set off traditional femininity in many kinds of new angles. There is the young woman of business, the young woman of society, the young woman of high professional standing. How they hold their new interests timed with the old, old interest of men and marriage to men is absorbing to such a writer as Katharine Brush, and to the great army of her contemporary readers. This field of fiction dominates the commercial avenues of publication, but no woman writer has taken hold of it with such consistent success as Katharine Brush. She is sharp as a well-trained reporter, and faithful as such to her story. She is objective as a well-trained reporter, and abides by that objectivity. The critic has to search minutely to find traces of subjectivity. She shows her training in the media of commercial publication. In such characterization of women as they fulfil themselves, or do not quite fulfil themselves against the background of their time and their circumstance, she is extraordinarily able. Her women live unto their own personality and against their own time with startling likeness to life. But when she folds or melts them into relationship with men, she herself falters. That is because she is primarily a writer of her time, and of a generation of women peculiar to a period. Women themselves, through the stretch of feminism, and through the need to make their own way competitively with men, have strained to develop personalities which will tell in their endeavors. To roll that personality into some agreeable blend with the personality of a man in marriage or its equivalent is an uneasy proceeding. It eludes its consummation in life, as it does in most of the fiction of the young women. An author such as Katharine Brush, who is by temperament and by creative purpose faithful to her own generation and its time, finds herself temperamentally and historically handicapped. She has to leave her subjects in the middle of their struggles if she attempts at all to blend them into a full story relationship with other mortals. This blurs their image. The blurring is particularly unfortunate in her case, because her power lies in her precisely indicated characterization. Her women, standing alone against their world and period background, are striking personalities, produced by striking artistry. When they move on into life lived in the small group of the family, they are helpless beings, unable to adapt themselves in the historic old way of women. This effect is increased by the inability of the woman author to present men convincingly in fiction. The result is that the problem is given to the reader without enough to warrant it. The men never make themselves felt in the general fiction of women, so the real force of the situation cannot be sensed.

DAPHNE DU MAURIER

When the women writers set out to portray men they also have to isolate them. Daphne du Maurier, who has drawn the most convincing portrait of a man as yet attempted by a woman, had to isolate her subject.

The Progress of Julius is her third book to be published.

She is an example of the little girl pal who has put aside the defiance of her generation. That is, her technical form shows a mind which is content to find freedom within conformity. Her prose is even and conventional. The subject of her first book, *The Loving Spirit,* was the traditional subject of feminine literary endeavor, the abiding love of women for their men. Her second book, *I'll Never Be Young Again,* was the study of the development of the temperament of the out-and-out *amoureuse* in a young girl. The author sketches rapidly and poignantly the hesitating rebellion of the virgin girl of the period, awakened by pure and utterly feminine devotion to a boy, and gliding almost imperceptibly into the current of heady sexuality until her need and her demand had no relation whatever to the personality of any particular boy or man. This was a book of its defiant period among young women; yet it contained a tragic warning to all young things. It showed the dark and powerful forces within human nature into which the young things were stepping in gay ignorance. It suggested the old wisdom behind the cautious moral rules. The older writers taking such a subject inevitably related the tragedy to the price demanded by conventional society from its outlaws. The woman paid when she encountered the disapproval of her fellows. The little girl pals had jeered at such a price. Moreover it hardly affected them. Their whole generation was involved in the rebellion, and for the opinion of their elders they gave no thought. The elders had bungled too generally to merit any serious thought from a clever young thing. But the payment within oneself was quite another matter. This book was the outcome of certain among the generation who were appalled at the significance of their rebellion when they saw it rolled out in front of them. Sexual anarchy was terrifying. But so was sexual humbug. Maybe maturity following upon sad knowledge gained in youth would lead to some amount of wisdom. Certainly maturity following upon blind ignorance sustained through youth would lead to no wisdom whatever. It would remain to be seen. That was the meaning of her title. She left the subject and passed on to something no woman had ever altogether accomplished, the portrait of a man. *The*

Progress of Julius placed her in the ranks of the virile few.

She told the story simply. She threw off all the clouded experimentation of her contemporaries. She did no dallying with the stream of consciousness. She took Julius from the sternly objective view. He was a man who made himself a force in the commercial world with strict conservation of his emotions and by a strict concentration upon one idea. She began with his childhood and his background. He was a blend of peasant French and Algerian Jew. He was a small child during the siege of Paris by the Germans. His French peasant grandparents taught him to bargain. He witnessed his mother's infidelity and his father's anguish. It gave him a low opinion of women. He saw his father murder his mother. He saw it unmoved, believing that she deserved it, as did every unfaithful woman. He was an Oriental. But he decided that no woman would ever rouse him to such a pitch of emotion. All his ardor went into building himself a fortune. He got to England. He built the fortune. He played with women; he bullied them; his treatment of them paid off the consistent subconscious desire for revenge upon the mother image in himself. He loved no woman until he came to love his own daughter. His love of her paid off all the stored-up accounts of his own emotional starvation. When she told him she was going to marry a man, unreasoningly he considered it infidelity to him, and murdered her. Thus was the line of his fate fulfilled.

It is the work of a mind which courageously has brought itself to realize the impossibility of dealing with emotion. It is a sincere and serious admission. It defies all the nonchalance of the rebellious generation which naïvely believed that the only damage came from repression, and proceeded to toss over all the repressions. It defies also the doctrine of the diversion of emotion into the profitable economy of personal career. It carefully avoids the inconsequential though tantalizing foibles of emotion differentiating between the male and female expression of it. The mind of this young Du Maurier accepts emotion as a great implacable mystery taking possession of men and

women in one way or another, at some time or another, as
something that comes down upon them and throws them from
experience to experience. A power like wind and rain and
the heat of the sun. Not to be placated. But maybe to be
worshiped. Certainly to be endured with fatalistic submission.
What she says with clear young courage the psychiatrists are
also saying. And wondering if worship in religion or in romance is the key to the answer. If emotion comes down upon
the life with religion, the spirit is steadied by contact with the
vast body of faith before it and around it. This is the blessing
of religion. If emotion comes down upon the life with romance,
the spirit is steadied by its own heroism. It sees itself as part
of the great story. It pursues its story bravely and beautifully,
literally drinking the cup to its dregs. Religion and romance
give their own peace, and the votaries of both know ease with
themselves. They have not said to emotion, "Do this," or, "Do
that"; they have said, "I follow."

The Progress of Julius is technically magnificent.

It rises from its beginning to its culmination with simplicity
that is Greek in its austerity and modern in its power.

There is no waste of its form or its virility in unnecessary
decoration. It is gaunt and strong. It is pure. Out of it
comes a man given by a woman. Daphne du Maurier fulfilled
the desire of her womanhood, which is the desire of all womanhood—to produce a man-child. She fulfilled the desire of her
generation—to see man as he is. She fulfilled the desire of
humanity—to reach some place of creative invulnerability
from which they could survey with composure the history of
men and women, contemplating sin and disappointment and
failure without tears, tracing the steps in their inevitability.
And maintaining themselves somehow intact for all of a
willingness to be broken if need be in the ascent to and the
descent from that place. For unquestionably it is a place of
momentary stopping. Humanity is in constant movement,
and the permanency of emotion lies in its acquiescence to the
impermanency of its aspects.

CHAPTER VIII

GO-GETTERS

Edna Ferber—Fannie Hurst—G. B. Stern—Rose Macaulay

BEHIND THE WAR GENERATION and the post-war youth lay long centuries of feminine silence and economic helplessness. The ghost of it still haunted the race. Emancipation was so recent, it was confusing. The ghost appeared in the confusion. When the emotionalism of the war faded, and the excitement of the new emancipation gave way before the necessity of making some program for women, a very real problem came up. There was a generation of women left over from the war. When the war casualties were counted, and the war-wrecked men were admittedly of terrifying numbers, it was seen that a whole generation of women would have to go through the remainder of their lives without any kind of what had been previously considered normal relations to men and to family. Two possibilities faced these women. They could take the place of the men who had died, or who were shattered. If they did not, the old men would carry on far beyond their time, and the world would be worse off than ever. Or they could look upon themselves as already dead along with their male contemporaries, and get whatever relief the dead presumably get in surveying the sufferings of the living. Sexually they could have no normal future. It was celibacy, or inversion; it was a "catch as catch can" sexual relationship with the strong men left, and this of necessity likely to be shared with other women, or it was relationship with the broken men who survived, or with the unfit who had not served, or with the very young if they could be had, or the very old. Whichever way the individual woman decided, there was no use at all in setting up once again the old romantic standard. It would be too painful. Also it would be futile.

It was fortunate, or unfortunate, whichever way we may choose to see it, that at the very time when a generation of women realized their sexual predicament, the sexual foundation of nervous disorders was broadcasted to the public. The subject of sex and all its ramifications in society became the dominating subject of contemporary thinking and writing. People had turned bitterly away from both national and international politics. There was no solution in sight. The deeper one delved into state relationships and humanity in the mass, the worse the general human situation appeared. People on the ebb from the illusionary emotion of the war accepted the hopelessness of things on a big scale. The interest in sex was in one sense a mark of a retreat from the large to the small. More than that, it was something that appeared to be new. War and social conflict were old subjects, and completely baffling to the human spirit, but men and women saw some possibility in a new attention to sex of arriving at some understanding of themselves in particular. They tackled sex with pioneering intensity. All the historic figures came up for reexamination. They were discovered to be historic neurotics. Women saw feminine history in a new light. They saw their contemporary situation in a new light. It was not a soft, flattering light. It was a light which threw into utter clarity all the difficulties before them. It convinced them of the need to revalue. It gave the revaluation the emotional purposefulness of opening up new territory. It intensified the original feminist rebellion. The little girl pals had taken one step in assuming sexual nonchalance. The go-getting women into which some of them evolved took another step in assuming a sexual determination and a corresponding determination to pull the world round into acquiescence concerning an entirely new type of femininity.

It happened at the same time that the commercial world became conscious of women. This fact made a world of difference for the go-getting female. The world was her dish. The great cosmetic firms and the great dressmaking firms sprang into commercial power almost overnight. The little girl pal had painted herself for her boy-friend. The go-getting woman painted herself for the sake of her own morale. The advertisers told her that a woman was only as old as she looked. Cosmetics, they went on to say, defeated time. The little girl pal dressed herself to remind her boy-friend that she was a good fellow. The go-getting woman dressed herself to remind herself that the world was her dish. The right clothes made a lot of difference to the woman approaching her prime. The little girl cut her hair in defiance against her elders. The go-getting woman kept her hair short because it was convenient, and also "youthifying" —a new word used by the advertisers. The little girl pal smoked because it was a shocking thing to do. The go-getter smoked because smoking was a kindly sedative, and also, so it was said, a help in the matter of fighting fat. For women had come to look upon fat as their worst enemy. Commerce helped them in that viewpoint. All kinds of contraptions appeared for women in their struggle against pelvic padding. The little girl had kept slim because it was boyish. The go-getter kept her weight down because the less she had to carry, the keener was she in the game. The little girl went pagan sexually as a gesture of contempt to her elders and their sense of propriety. The go-getting woman went after what sexual outlet she decided she needed because it was part of her equipment. No woman could afford to insult her glands.

The little girl pals looked at one another incidentally when there were no boy-friends around. The go-getters look at one another appraisingly.

The reason is obvious—the inherited sense of rivalry among women. This has been sharply intensified by the new rivalry in business and professional experience. The instinctive fear of a woman that any new woman might attract the attention of the man has added to it a new fear that every new woman may be getting along in the world better than herself. The old biological fear led women to imitate other women. If a particularly attractive woman wore her hair in a certain attractive way, the women who were subconsciously afraid of her followed the style. The old biological fear always made women examine one another interestedly. It was sound business. It was study of the competitor. The new fear has not pushed the old fear out, but has intensified and amplified it. One of the incidental, if not altogether main, reasons why women attend their own clubs and go to meetings and to social affairs is to take in the appearance of other women. It is to be seen in any public place, even upon trains and street-cars—women looking one another over. It is not seen among men. Men look at women in public places where both sexes meet. When they go to men's affairs they go in boyish good fellowship to foregather merely with their own kind. Women, except for the out-and-out declared nymphomaniac, do not in public places examine the men. Which shows that their minds are concerned with their competitors.

Men have sometimes said impatiently that women are like sheep; they do what any style leader or success leader does. This has been off the point. The point has always been respect for the dangerous competitor and her methods, and every woman who is honest with herself knows what the point has been. It is this constant watchfulness concerning competition which has made women difficult in general in their business relationships with one another. It is sound on a small scale. But it is unsound in larger issues. It tangles and complicates. It makes it hard for a woman to concentrate upon an impersonal issue, or in other words, to attend to the game for its own sake. It makes it hard for her to applaud when another woman makes a successful run. She relates that success to her own failure.

The feminists explain this tendency in their sisters as part of the inherited technique of the harem. They hope that after a few generations of feminism it will disappear. They make a rapid rationalizing twist, and point to the increased interest of women in the doings of women as a growth in their feminist appreciation. It is a very doubtful rationalization. It twists in a circle back to the old study of the competitor camouflaged.

The magazines are full of the work of enterprising women interested in this new phase of femininity. They are writing murder stories and stories of business, with possibly interrelations with the domesticity of women. They are writing history, or rather rewriting it. They are handling any kind of fiction and assignment they think an editor will tolerate. Most of them stand securely on two feet. One foot is modern and daring; the other foot is safely conventional, for the good reason that the magazines and their readers prefer conventionality. Most of them do not use characters; they use handy types. Most of them do not produce atmosphere; it is much easier to concoct a set-up. They invariably have their eyes on the screen, and when they write a story about a woman the mark of the screen star is upon her. They write with a background of a mahogany desk, a cable address, two telephones and stacks of memo sheets. They are business women making shrewd use of fiction because it is an excellent paying business once it is established.

Ahead of this go-getting fleet there are several women of definitely magnificent fiction proportions.

The first of them is Edna Ferber.

Edna Ferber

Edna Ferber appeared when women first appeared on a big scale in business and careers through the English-speaking world.

There were great candy-makers, great cosmeticians; there were great corsetières, great women dressmakers, great dieticians. There was an army of women selling insurance and real estate and all the things that women want to buy. There were lawyers and doctors and the odd female preacher. Every one of them felt joyously at the beginning of a great new era in history. They regarded themselves as pioneers.

This was the feeling of the years. It was the breath-taking decade after the war. Women drove cars and airplanes. They directed enterprises. They made money. The world was theirs.

The magazines said so. If one judged by the advertising, there were no men in the world at all, or, at the most, men who were decorative appendages to such women as might still feel the need of them either in perpetuity or temporarily. It was the decade of hilarious divorcing. No woman had to stick a relationship that bored her. She could make her own way. She could also make the man pay up for having had her a while. The law was on her side. It was a decade of strong women and adventurous women. It was as if all the stored-up female energy of the ages suddenly blew off.

Edna Ferber's first stories had to do with women who pushed their way into competition in business with men. She glorified the woman commercial traveler and the woman producer. They were case histories of actual go-getting women, and she related them by her astute journalistic sense to the subconscious opinion which all women were holding of themselves. The combination was excellent for her own bank account, and excellent stimulus for the progress of feminist enterprise, and excellent also for the increase of the primary documentary sources of the feminist movement. Unquestionably, future historians will turn to Edna Ferber for the gathering of vivid first-hand reporting of the time in fiction. She is, therefore, to an almost final extent, the supreme feminist.

Whether it was out of utter feminist conviction, or out of the accidental attraction of the keen journalist for good material, only Miss Ferber herself will know. But whatever the conscious, or subconscious, motivation might have been at the beginning, she stands now as the supreme fictional annalist of careerist women in the heyday of their careers.

She has used a characteristic technique which by a lucky strike related itself to the intellectual methods of the go-getting women of the first post-war decade. It is a shunting technique.

"Shunting" is a technique which allows the story to pull forward and backward leisurely.

It was what a lot of women were doing until they got up full steam to go ahead. It is what women in the past had done with their lives. More than that, it is the way women had thought. No woman had ever taken off immediately and cleanly and clearly into a career. She shunted around for years with biological possibilities. She gathered experience and the experience had inevitably to do with the career of some man before she was convinced that she should be at her own career.

This is what makes the shunting technique popular with women and native to them.

More than that, it is a technique which belongs to the new world and to commerce. The new world was opened up by railways, and the courier of the new world was the commercial traveler. Without any exaggeration it can be said that the rhythm of the new world was the rhythm of the train shunting up and down in railway-stations. The movement of the train got into the thinking and the talking of the commercial gentlemen who sat by the hour in smoking cars and exchanged stories with their fellow travelers. When they got back home to their wives and families the rhythm was still upon them, and all that they said was said in the shunting manner of their traveling.

Women started to go upon the road. They took the primary materials of millinery and dressmaking out from the big cities to the little towns and the villages. Laces and buttons and artificial flowers. Corsets and lingerie and ribbons. A new order of women. A change in the trade. They fraternized with the traveling men on the trains. They exchanged stories with them in the small commercial hotels all over the country. They spoke the same language. It was a language of sales approach and order lists and the conditions of trade. It was these women who as fiction material first attracted Edna Ferber, and before any other author had realized the story wealth of them, she tumbled into their portraiture, telling her stories in the manner of the good fellow sitting in the smoking room with the boys, and influenced definitely in her narrative rhythm by the shunting movement of the train. She was influenced also by another train effect. The commercial traveler telling a story was under the necessity to get his story told quickly. Some of the boys

would have to get off at the next station. The superimposition
of brevity eliminated all the decorative literary or philosophical
additions to a story, and produced an interesting technical combination of bare story detail with a shunting movement from
point to point instead of a general progression of plot.

This, so far as the new world is concerned, is a fundamental
story form. The story in the new world is in its origin a traveler's narrative. Travelers who met casually on the road had
no community of interest for conversation, and in place of the
gossip usual to people contained in a familiar small community
or group, they put the story. It was invariably struck in its
beginning from some accidental comment, and shunted backwards and forwards from that comment into a sequence of
events which had some relation to the thing which provoked
the original comment.

This peculiar technique comes out of and belongs exclusively
to a country which has only recently emerged from pioneer
experience, and which is unequally developed. That is, there
was always some vacant land in the great stretches of the
North American continent which called out the people of
pioneering temperament from the already settled districts and
lured them away into the primitive delight of trekking and
pioneering. So it follows, because of the law of the association
of ideas and emotions, that the story form most intimately connected with these people would be the traveler's narrative told
in the familiar traveling rhythm. Throughout the United
States and Canada there were still places to which the traveling
salesman came as a messenger from the big world. He was received as minstrels formerly were received in the great castles
of the old medieval world. He represented movement and
news as well as commerce. When Edna Ferber's stories began
to be published, the motor-car was just beginning to be popu-
larly available. The American people were on the edge of
possessing machines to gratify their inherited taste for the trek,
and also on the edge of receiving new entertainment through
the ether and the silver screen, but neither of these was quite

ready for the popular wide market when she swung into fiction. She caught the tide of familiarity. In her technique and in her material she was altogether American. She combined the new energy of women, which was a pioneering energy, and the trekking sense of the continent, and she did it with more con- centrated fidelity, with deeper sincerity and more primitive simplicity, than any other American writer.

There is nothing in her stories borrowed from Europe. There is no shadow of sophisticated weariness. Sometimes there are touches of naïveté, but these touches come from the author's sense of the zest for living, which is the breath of any new civilization.

She writes as if none of the authors of Europe existed. From the classical standpoint she has no style whatever. But from the vital standpoint of how style is associated with the emotion of time and place, she has perfect style.

Apart entirely from her fidelity to the rhythm of primitive pioneer story-telling, and apart entirely from her absorption in the current of the American scene, Edna Ferber is of towering importance to the School of Femininity. She belongs to the great procession—Austen, the Brontës and Eliot—who presented the feminist picture.

Serena de Jong, the heroine of her greatest book, *So Big*, belongs with Elizabeth Bennett and Jane Eyre and Maggie Tulliver. Her other women are like the other women of Miss Austen, the Brontës and George Eliot. They are the Elizabeths and the Janes and the Maggies out in a new world on the make, selling lingerie, performing on show boats, running newspapers and raising prize asparagus, struggling with emotion and finding themselves relief in action. But there is one great difference, and it is the difference between the nineteenth-century lady and the twentieth-century woman—her women are not de- pendent upon men for the adequate conduct of their lives. Elizabeth Bennett, had she been disappointed in Mr. Darcy after marriage, would have been in an emotional whirlwind, and Miss Austen, had she tackled such a situation, would have been

hard put to it to find a neat conclusion. Little Jane Eyre, if
fate had not taken the wild and fascinating Mr. Rochester by
the scruff of his unrighteous neck and handed him over to her,
would have been a flattened out little mortal. Poor Maggie
Tulliver had to be drowned after a purgatory of isolation because she had magnetism which she could not use to her own
advantage. But Serena and all the women of Edna Ferber take
erotic disappointment in their twentieth-century stride and do
not expect anything from men. They say to themselves—
men are like that—and find plenty to do besides looking around
for another hero or getting drowned. And this in spite of the
fact that they are women of deep emotions and strong passionate attachments. They observe their husbands; they mother
their sons and their daughters, and expect no undue amount
either of love or of great stature from any of them in return.
Life to them is worth what it brings in experience. They live
in the feminist era in the new world.

Serena de Jong, facing disappointment both in her husband
and her son and raising the best asparagus in the State, is a
symbol of the new woman. She is not a romantic figure in the
old sense, yet she is a woman of new romance, courageous, real
and vital.

In all Edna Ferber's work there is an undercurrent of dissatisfaction with men which is characteristic of all the general
writing of the modern School of Femininity in its present phase.
It may be a half-way phase. The woman of the next phase
may come to the conclusion that her real work for the race is
to maintain at all cost and with great creative effort the illusion
of romance and greatness in men. But for the present she
seems to be of the general opinion that men are weak, or that
at least the men of this period are not strong enough for the
women whose strength has been bred of the feminist pioneering
era. Serena de Jong met no man who was as strong as herself,
and this is true of all Edna Ferber's women. It is the plaint
of all strong women, and women for the time are through with
the nursing of an illusion. There is too much to do in the big

impersonal world. It is the tragedy which Olive Schreiner
foresaw when she wrote *The Story of an African Farm*. Men
would inevitably be a step behind the new woman. But it is
an even greater tragedy than Olive Schreiner foresaw. She believed in the race. She taught that strong women would breed
strong sons. Edna Ferber shows her women disappointed in
their sons; for the sons are never quite so rugged in fiber as
their pioneering mothers; and the conclusion is that strength
needs more than one parent. So has the feminist story reached
one of its plateaux of experience, and what is to be done about
it? For nature created women normally incapable of happiness
in companionship with men weaker than themselves. Meanwhile there remains much of the world yet to be conquered for
women, and this is the real love of the women she portrays in
the height of their powers.

Fannie Hurst

Fannie Hurst is a graduated sob-sister concerning women.
Her knuckles show through her technique. She knocks at her
story and slams it down and rolls it through with the intensity
of a prize-fighter. If she likes one particular adjective, or verb,
or adverb, she trots it out with exacting frequency. She has in
the classical sense no style whatever; yet the complete absence
of any regard for classical correctness gives a style of its own
to her writing, and along with her determined emotionalism,
produces a characteristic power that would be recognized
through any number of pseudonyms did she care to use them.

She likes to write about the under-dog. It is her Jewish sympathy with the oppressed. When she ventures away from the
under-dog and away from women, as she did in one story,
Five and Ten, she is not nearly so successful. Her success has
been with studies drawn from the racial melting-kettle of
America and in poverty. She understands its color and its
rhythm.

The sob-sister is a go-getting woman who has shrewdly estimated the intermixture of sadism in the human response to a sad story.

She realizes two things—that when we shed tears, or prepare to stir up the feelings that send them coursing, it is partly because we have miseries of our own and like nothing better than to see other people having a good dose of them; and that also we like people when they have more miseries than we have, which comes from a decided taste for seeing other people suffer, and in part from the indulgence of our sense of superiority. The sob-sister, for all that she "douses," to use one of Fannie Hurst's favorite words, upon us her sympathetic presentation of human woes, is subconsciously cynical about the reactions we who read her stuff get. She is under no illusion as to why we enjoy sob stuff.

The ordinary sob-sister becomes automatic, and while we read her dish of woe we are, if we read analytically, aware that she herself has never got immersed spiritually in the suffering she relates. She has seen it all as a spectator, astutely calculating its story value, and wisely sensing its provocative emotional appeal, and going to it, pressing down the spots that will hurt, and letting out a wail of sound.

The great sob-sister like Fannie Hurst is never automatic. Her dishes of woe affect her as much as they affect her readers. She lives through the suffering with her people, and because of this they emerge from her treatment of them real and inescapable.

Fannie Hurst is creatively a friendly, energetic, talkative Jewish girl. Her technique is drawn from the family group. It takes life from a kitchen center, with children bustling to tell their stories while the mother portions out the soup. Her gestures and her exclamations are racial, and so is the emotional rhythm of her narration. There is no shunting in her way of getting into her story. She is into it with one jump, and it proceeds with amazing speed. She includes only the dramatic high and low spots, and between them she leaps and gestures. She uses no levels. She pitches into the feeling of the story and carries her details along only as properties to prolong emotional effect. She tosses everything aside except the fundamental emotions, and she is at her best with stories of simple people because their emotional enterprise is less complex. More than that, she is in sympathy with simple people. They are the people who get the worst of it in life. She thinks subconsciously always in terms of the Jewish mother portioning out the soup and the family gathered together in the security of racial solidarity. No alien is present. So tongues rush into phrases and bodies sway into gestures and stories get told, including an amazing amount of drama in an amazing short space. She tells stories that would be understood in that kitchen, of human grandeur under great stress; of the stoicism of the poor and the misunderstood; of the discomfort of the rich in their comfort; of the lonely wages of sin among the sinful; always again and again does she return to some form of the story of racial misunderstanding. *Lummox*, the story which is her best work, brings into its space of telling all these issues so dear to the Jew. A poor simple girl, working among the rich and tending them spiritually, though they never realize it, while she tends them physically, is the heroine. She is the legendary "dove woman" functioning in an awkward body and with an almost inarticulate mind, but responding in dumb ecstasy to the memories of beauty she has known somewhere in her blood-stream. Fannie Hurst follows her through her experience, going down with her to her horrible dirty cleaning jobs, up through her situations as cook, or general servant, keeping pace with her as she bears her child from the one fine cherishing rapture of love in her life and as she surrenders her child for adoption; on and on through her service to people, going here and going there, as if in response to the string of fate, never expecting either appreciation or reward, and not even any slight amount of understanding. It is a Messianic story—the beloved story of the Jews.

It is the apotheosizing of the sob story. It contains a trace of the prophet call, and more than a trace of the minor Hebraic song of sorrows. The Lummox is the feminine order fulfilling the Messianic dream—one born conscious of connection with God, and under some strange compulsion to be like God in relation to other mortals, never taking, always giving, and in the end enduring the cross of misinterpretation. The story is left there in traditional Hebraic strength in all its misinterpretation and tragedy. The traditional Christian anti-climax of recognition and its consequent worship is not added. For nobody among all the people she tended ever saw the Lummox as more than a rather peculiar servant.

Fannie Hurst writes with familiar conversational simplicity. She uses the vernacular. She recognizes the general taste for repetition. She has undoubtedly listened time upon time to the conversations of people on buses and trolleys. She knows how popular phrases become. She takes the hint. She repeats her phrases. When she is in a hurry she never bothers to finish her sentences. She lays down a phrase like a poker player slamming down a hand. She takes it up again. She gets it again in another sequence. She writes in emotional jerks. It is the nervous staccato of the twentieth century with an undersound of emotion coming from people to whom the English language is new, and among whom English has been learned in trading, and has therefore a trading color with the odd inclusion of a sonorous book-taken phrase. Her form is a curious blend of middle-class newspaper sentimentality and proletarian inarticulate realism. The blend is presented with a power which is again a blend of the newcomer's vivacious zest for the new life, and the melancholy shadow of sufferings remembered from the old world. It is the attitude of a subconscious mind which, though it tackles life again in a new situation, knows because it is only a generation removed from the old life that life itself never is altogether new. Particularly not for women. Despite the apparent newness of feminism in the new world.

Fannie Hurst, like all the go-getting women writers, will try almost anything once. She has drawn the old-fashioned mistress, the traditional kept woman living in the back streets of a successful man's life, and tasting all the sorrows of her

social sin; she has drawn a multimillionaire's wife; she has drawn
a woman who has stumbled into a great business career; she
has drawn innumerable ordinary men and women in her short
stories. She has the knack and the will and the audience. She
can put anything over. Her style, with its punch and its
oriental flamboyance, makes any theme and any situation real.
But her natural inclination is towards the women who slave
with shawls over their heads and large flat boots and wide bearing hips. These are her women—the women of the slums in
great cities. The other women are drawn as if in contrast.
Behind the millionaire's wife and the financier's pathetic mistress and the daughter of a genius and the mother of a soldier-
musician and the career woman in love with a younger man,
the reader feels the woman who remains in Fannie Hurst's mind
—the root woman of the race—fertile, kind, superbly emotional.
She appears even if only in side drawings in most of her stories,
always busy at her soup-kettle, or at her cleaning, or with her
nursing of children. Her heart is always wrung in its maternal
vague and patient longing to understand. Her children grow
up; her sons marry strange women; her daughters have strange
desires; but sometimes there is a genius child, not a more comfortable child than the rest of them, yet who somehow makes
it all worth while—the child who takes up the thread of the
spiritual remnant.

This is what lies underneath all Fannie Hurst's portraits. It
is a song of womanhood sung in the lazy but vivid way of the
modern woman, staccato yet romantic, and aimed at the melodramatic senses of the masses.

Edna Ferber writes for the women who are adventurers.
She is concerned with go-getters. Fannie Hurst writes for all
women. She is concerned with the reading public. Ferber's
women are new women. Hurst's women are women who are
neither new nor old. Ferber's women are women who have
fallen back upon themselves through a defense of themselves
against the hurts of men. Hurst's women are women who have
accepted the traditional lot of women—suffering and giving—

and who never take thought for any defense against feeling. It is interesting to note that both of them are Jewish women. Ferber's work interprets the pioneering passion of women packed down in a particularized era upon themselves. Hurst's work interprets the racial passion of women as it functions in the sifting and blending of races in the new world. Both of them caught on with their racial astuteness to the consummate drama of women in the new world. Neither of them has paid much attention to her own people. That is the influence upon them of life in the new world where the races met.

G. B. STERN

G. B. Stern is also a Jewish woman, but she writes in the old world where the racial lines of separation are more intact.

She has outdone all the writers who have applied themselves to writing family books. Her saga concerning the Czelovar and Rakonitz families of Vienna and Paris and London embraced bigger crowds of people than all the other family sagas, and she kept the manifold lines of her story clearer than most of the other authors who tried the experiment managed to do. She is a versatile writer. She outdid all the little girl pals in her nonchalant story called *Debonair*. Her heroine was a naughty girl and the very spirit of the rebellious generation. She has written about crime and about the feminine temperament. Everything she does is put over with a gusto that is peculiarly her own. She has a hard glittering surface. She never sobs her story. She presents the picture of the effective go-getter in her Continental connotation. There is quite a difference between her manner and the manner of the two outstanding Jewish women writers of America. The sob-note would not go over with her Continental audience. Therefore it would not be good business to produce it, though certainly she could if it were useful to her. For emotionalism is never buried very deep in any daughter of Israel. Neither would the high pioneer heroism of Ferber's women go over in Europe. Continental women who have made much of themselves in this era

have not done so out of a will to pioneer but out of the necessity to take the places of lost men. In a sense this is true of
Edna Ferber's women. All of them lost their men, but the
loss was individual and brought with it disillusionment; while the
loss in the case of Continental women may be said to have been
catastrophic and not individual. It makes a great difference.

The books of G. B. Stern are important to the go-getting aspect of the School of Femininity because of the theme—the
growing strength of women. The Czelovar and Rakonitz saga
shows the increasing dominance of women. It is a matriarchal
study. The patriarchal tradition—even of the Jews—crumbles.
In these families the tradition disintegrates as the family assimi-
lates into Gentile life, and out of the assimilation the matriarchs came. Her saga therefore belongs rather to the feminist
tradition than to the purely Hebraic tradition. It is a powerful
study. It begins with the violation of the family law by the
first Matriarch through her marriage to her own first cousin,
thereby weakening the family by the production of delicate
children and grandchildren. The Matriarch in her youth put
passion before family, and in her age put family before everything. It was the law of balance and retribution. The second
matriarch, her granddaughter, took up the retribution, and saw
personal passion as a very small matter beside the great command
of sustaining the family. Between these two women lies a
magnificent family annal, which is chiefly concerned with the
women of the family.

The Czelovar and Rakonitz women of the first and second
generations of the saga were women completely spoiled by their
men. They reached for jewels; they reached for big houses
and gorgeous furniture, rich hangings and sumptuous gowns.

The men of the first and second generations went on making
more and more money, and when reverses came they did not
tell their women. One after another the men died ruined.
When the men died the women became men-women, which is
go-getting women. They went into business like their fathers
and grandfathers before them, and their businesses prospered

because of their inherited financial skill and an innate zest for it. After they had conquered business the family got them. They looked round for means of holding it together and building it up again. They were still Jewish women, though they worked in a Gentile world.

The theme of the saga is the theme of both Ferber and Hurst—that women rise to their power in adversity. But Stern has an additional theme which is a hang-over from the little girl pals. It is the playing of women upon men, and failing them, with the world. She likes to watch it. She enjoys looking back at its late nineteenth- and early twentieth-century aspects. She delights in examining it as it is now. If there is in the feminine composition any capacity for selfless devotion to a man—either father, husband or son, G. B. Stern is not aware of it. If there are Jewish women living who fulfil the pattern of womanhood as laid down by the author of Proverbs, they were not born into the Czelovar and Rakonitz family, and G. B. Stern did not become acquainted with them. So far as she is concerned they do not exist, and her very modern mind would say, "Well, why should they exist?" So you find a galaxy of aggressive women, accompanied by men who dally with finance and taper off into forlorn relics of masculinity, all of them dying early from lack of initiative to live.

Stern puts her mosaic together in rich colors and with exaggerated, rather swaggering line. Some of her women are robust comedy characters. A few languish into semi-romantic quarreling with their relatives. All of them keep count of the marriages and the babies in their wide-spread family. Each one of them lives violently within herself, and with as much impingement of her personality upon the rest of them as she can individually manage. They undergo dramatic ups and downs of fortune. Sometimes their men pour emeralds upon the dining-table for them to grasp. Sometimes they have to hurry around for jobs. But somehow they survive, and their zest for experience survives even down into the generation which has taken the brunt of the first Matriarch's rash intermarriage. None of these women ever sits quietly meditating upon life. Not one of them ever says anything about the long sad history of her people. No woman ever lights the candles at the descent of the Sabbath, or thinks of the spiritual force which has kept the race alive through centuries of persecution. They are all practical women who look neither to a man nor to an unseen God for guidance. They are women who estimate values with solid economic sense, and estimate pleasures in solid good times. Her women represent the temperamental volatility and the mental shrewdness of the Jew minus the melancholy, the art and the mysticism.

The technique of Stern is itself volatile and shrewd. She is innately histrionic. The women she puts into print are unquestionably impressions of femininity as she sees it objectively. She leaves the soul alone as an unproved quantity, and certainly as an unseen quality. The femininity she presents is extremely modish with the bizarre touches of the frankly vital Jewess. Like Ferber and Hurst she hurries her tempo. It is the prevailing mode of the time. But there is a difference. Ferber proceeds like a shunting train and stays on the observable surface. Hurst goes underground to the emotions. Stern whirls along with the motion of a bus. It is an intimate motion. It snuggles in and out of the rest of the traffic. It catches up on people when they are unaware. It is in the movement of life, yet sufficiently and safely apart to see the rest of the traffic in perspective. What she sees is something that is not romantic yet is not sordid in its reality. Her writing belongs to the middle class, and her people are juggled together, some strong, some weak, some dull, some brilliant, but all of them put together into a lively stream of traffic. Nobody could be bored watching with her. She has a vivacity which makes most of her work thoroughly entertaining. She is not spiritually tired. She is not sorrowful. She has seen perhaps as much of the struggle as Fannie Hurst, but it does not touch her emotion. She is no sob-sister. She is more like a crack reporter, pulling all the lines of her story into a well-substantiated whole, and presenting it not to strike at the feelings of her readers but to hold their interest issue by issue. She has seen perhaps as much of the romance of women as Ferber has, but it does not elate her. She has felt perhaps a little of the same engrossing will to power in modern women, but it does not take possession of her. It comes down to the difference which has been touched upon before—the difference between women of the new world and the old, even when interpreted by daughters of Jewry. The new world and its feminists still believe in and produce sincerity. It comes from the inescapable atmosphere of the new world and its essential acceptance of the *second chance of humanity,* as the French explorers put it. The atmosphere of the old world remains faintly skeptical, and its writers are under some compulsion not to be silly with sincerity. Its people have suffered too much and too long to see suffering as a heroic gesture. It is something that is, and therefore is taken without much intensity. Nothing to them ever begins again. It merely goes round and round in the same human circle, and though the circle is interesting and worthy of use in art, it is nothing about which to be emotional. And this is the great difference between Ferber and Hurst, and their racial sister, G. B. Stern. If Ferber had written about the Czelovar and Rakonitz women, they would have been great striding women lashed to some creative idea, patient with the deficiencies of their men, and lonely in the midst of success. If Hurst had written about them, they would have been brooding sad women weighted down by their need to minister to the race, not expecting very much from anyone, and strangely comforted in the midst of trouble. As Stern has written about them they are just women. She has skipped any temptation to glorify her race, and also skipped any temptation to be prophetically indignant about what failings they have. They talk a lot; they weep a lot; they do quite a bit. And it all makes an absorbing picture, which is not intended to be taken as one of the immortal presentations. Stern is a woman of careful common sense who indulges herself in a flair for exotic, somewhat exaggerated superimposed personality. And all because it is good business. It is the good business she takes seriously and not the careful common sense or the exotic exaggeration.

The go-getting woman, after she has gone and got what she wanted, is inclined to be bored. She has bagged her game, and in our time the game has been the substantial proofs of success in a man's world. That is all that women really wanted out of feminism. It was the need of the suppressed to show their equality. After it has been shown there is nothing else to do. For the business of taking an interest in things after conquest is a very old business which in all likelihood takes centuries to implant in people. Women have not been trained for it. Not even in their very own business of procuring husbands were they trained for more than the catch. What came after, and the long fine art of taking interest in the game after it was in the bag, was left untaught chiefly on account of the determination of civilization to keep women blindfolded about biology.

All this affects the psychology of women as they go out to challenge a world which men have designed to suit themselves.

The world of men looked at the beginning like a great adventure for women, calling out of them all their powers. At closer acquaintance it did not look like such a great adventure. It looked more like an illusion sustained by a lot of tricks. And it was boring.

Rose Macaulay

Rose Macaulay is bored. Her writing is emancipatedly spinsterish. The whole human enterprise reads to her like a tale *told by an idiot*. She does not even give it the dignity of insanity. It is all sheer idiocy. It is neither touching nor amusing. It is just silly. She looks the scene over, and is aware of no brooding presence in fate. Only a crazy unpatterned hit-or-miss conglomeration of events into which human beings are drawn because there is nothing else for them to do. She sees a stream of traffic going nowhere. In places the traffic shunts about for a while; in other places it goes down underneath and gets up a great speed below the earth; in still other places it rolls along on top of the earth making a roar. But it is all the same traffic, silly mortals being carried here and there to nowhere at all. There is nothing to do about it.

It is not even a good show. It is dully silly. The watcher is bored. Look, she says, this is how it is. And she takes us back in *Told by an Idiot* to the late nineteenth century in England, when all the thinkers were drawing long breaths of delight in a new age. It was a modern new world. The old Queen had reigned a long time. Art was flourishing. Education was flourishing. It was a grand world. Women had grasped at last after a century of feminist propaganda the fact that they were individuals. Religion was flourishing. Religion, in fact, was rampant. Everybody believed in something.

She turned a few pages. She presented a comfortable high middle-class family. The father was enamored of religion. He tried them all one after another, from the Church of Rome to the esoteric cults from the East and back to the simple sects of Protestantism in England. He had a fine adventure with God. His wife followed after him, not out of any conviction, or any ability to share the adventure, but with marital docility. The children were all enthusiasts after their kind. One daughter loved art and fashion. One loved learning and the new opportunities of women. Another loved dogs and horses and the solid earth of England. The remaining daughter, Rome, was enthusiastic about nothing. She did not possess sufficient energy. She, Rome, is the spokeswoman for the author, Rose Macaulay. To Rome it was a tale *told by an idiot*. One son becomes a practising journalist full of ideas about the improvement of things. The other son makes money and so is enthusiastic about keeping things as they are. The daughter who was artistic and fashionable marries correctly, produces a large family and takes life generously. The daughter who was feminist marries into the "illuminati" and finds marriage an uneasy arrangement. She finds freedom again in divorce, and dedicates her new freedom to the promulgation of the general freedom of women in the world of men. It was a cause sufficient to absorb the talents of any enthusiastic woman in the early twentieth century. The daughter who loves horses and dogs marries a farmer and devotes herself to increasing the sustenance to be found in the earth. Rome does nothing. She does nothing gracefully. She sits back and contemplates the scene. She observes her feminist sister and her fashionable sister. They chase rainbows. The farm sister at least has attached herself to something tangible. So far so good. Except that life never remains tangible very long. What with winds and storms and crop failures.

The portrait of Rome is the one definite example in the School of Femininity to date of portraiture of the purely cerebral woman. It is indubitably self-portraiture. Rome in the story did not bother to write. Rose Macaulay presumably would have preferred not to have bothered herself. Intrinsically she finds nothing about which to write. Only living in a go-getting age when women before everything else have to do something to keep a position in intellectual society, she writes. She writes well. Rome would have written well. She was a woman of intellectual style, who commented upon people with highly civilized disdain. She was a woman of complete disillusionment who had not arrived at her disillusionment by the usual route of too completely tasted illusions. She was born disillusioned. She preserved herself intact by watching the show instead of playing in it. To her there was nothing new under the sun. She was the veritable feminine Ecclesiastes.

The story rolls on. They are left well on in the twentieth century, with the second generation muddling their lives with twentieth-century blending of gusto and weariness. Rome herself is to die of cancer, and all that she wants is to die without any heroics. There was nothing new about death, so why fuss about it?

Told by an Idiot is the key book in the case of Rose Macaulay. That is, it gives the key-note to her performance.

There is a key book in the case of every author, past and

present, male and female. For there is one initial drive into writing in the personal history of every writer. It lies, as cannot be said too often, in self-portraiture. The urge to paint the portrait of the self, which is, in most histories, self-justification, and in some cases a wish concerning the self, is the motive which sets writers writing. The motive pushes forcefully into the key book of each writer, and in most cases it is only one book we need out of even the most persistently creative writer's many books for understanding that writer. The key book may be the first book. If this be so, the other books are parts of a commercial follow-up program, or creative amplifications of the original theme. If the key book happens to come later in the career, the earlier books were undertaken subconsciously as means of getting up creative tone and speed. Looking back at the early women writers in the English School of Femininity, the key books may be seen clearly. Jane Austen said what she had to say in *Pride and Prejudice*. Charlotte Brontë put herself into *Jane Eyre*. Emily wrote everything about herself in *Wuthering Heights*. George Eliot's great book was unquestionably *The Mill on the Floss*, which came third on her list.

In dealing with the modern writers it is not quite so easy to see the key book, because the work is contemporary and the evidence is not all in. But even with such a reservation in most cases the key book is already before us. Some of these contemporary women writers abide precisely with the key pattern. Others vary it. It is all a matter of creative versatility. Some of them under discussion are at the zenith of their creative output. Others have passed it, and still others are still in approach to their full powers. All critical comment, therefore, has to be held in tentative restraint because of the difficulty of estimating the exact individual position of the writers in relation to their zenith.

Rose Macaulay is one who has remained precisely with the pattern set in *Told by an Idiot*. She wrote books before this; she has written books since. But all of them have struck the same creative sound.

It is a sound of definite sharpness. It is the definite sharpness of an observing, skeptical, practical woman, than which there is no more devastating sharpness. It belongs to a mind which has laid aside its beliefs and its illusions even as society has laid aside swords and chariots. Beliefs to such a mind are pretty but archaic. Like swords. Illusions are attractive for emotional pageantry but useless in a business world. Like chariots drawn by decorated horses.

She has one of the very few feminine mentalities which has arrived at the impersonality of the surgeon. She writes with the neatness and the rapid sure stroke of the surgeon. Her characters are laid bare with a scalpel, and they bleed amazingly little from the laying bare because of the dexterity of the technique. A small incision; a few drops of blood, and the ailing sore spot of stupidity is uncovered. The woman who is the surgeon sheds no tears and exhibits no astonishment. She expected to find the sore. Neither does she laugh. Stupidity is no matter for laughing.

Her technique is the consummation of the go-getters' technique in writing. Without waste of either energy or emotion she opens her story and presents the histories of her people. It is the narration of a sequence of events in all cases under her delineation proceeding from an initial stupidity. Upon this sequence she has trained her powers of observation. Enough detail is given to indicate the characterization without causing the least hesitation in the narrative outline. Like all the go-getters she covers an amazing space in a short time. She uses a technique relatively like the other go-getters in that it is narration seen in passage. She differs in the slant of her sight. Ferber lingers a little to stress the heroics; Hurst lingers a little to feel the emotions. Stern lingers a little to amplify the dramatics; Macaulay does no lingering. Not even to emphasize the follies. She knows they will speak for themselves.

It is go-getting writing in that it is writing done by a writer who does not have to write. Conceivably Rose Macaulay, like every other writer, toys with the idea of putting herself down in portraiture. Conceivably all the go-getters toy with this idea. But no pressing need to feature themselves forces them into literature, and consequently though they use their own portraiture in writing, they use it as a lens through which to see the world objectively. That is, none of the go-getting women is obsessed with herself to the extent of digging deep into her own psychological resources. This is a differentiation between the go-getter and the other women writers which the reader has to sense. To sense it at all demands the possession of an extra and purely literary sense with which to separate the writing of writers who write because they are so moved by the mystery and entanglement of the soul in life that they have to set it down for relief, from the writing of such writers who write because they see a good story. The go-getting writer belongs to this latter group. She writes because God has presented her with a story-searching eye. And because she has focused this eye in a certain line. The go-getter therefore selects what she intends to see. In such a light she is subjective; but in no other. Having surrendered to subjectivity in her subconscious selection of what she intends to see, she leaves it and becomes in all other matters exactingly objective.

Edna Ferber chose to see the heroics of femininity. She saw it and set it down for all the world as if it were a passing story picked up on the way. Fannie Hurst chose to see the primitive emotionalism of women as unchanged and always unchanging, and precipitating women into an unconditional surrender of themselves to emotion. She set it down as if it were an incidental notion picked out of a welter of excellent human-interest stories—the sob notion of women. G. B. Stern chose to see the civilized practicality of women. She set it down perfunctorily as something everyone would be likely to accept concerning women as she spun out a few good yarns about their doings in families and outside of families. Rose Macaulay chose to see the copy-cat tendencies of history as particularized in modern women with a consequent inevitable boredom to the observing watcher. She set it down judiciously as a casual fact while she turned out a story or so of the illusions people call events in their lives.

None of the go-getters concedes any profound significance to the force of biology in women. Ambition is the driving element in Ferber's women; sympathy in Hurst's; the economic grasp in Stern's, and a rather fatuous pseudo-intellectuality in Macaulay's. The men in the stories of the go-getters are type men, drawn in relation to the women. The scene is always Amazonian. It is the stage-setting of a feminist paradise, though the play may proceed either in utter heroics, or in the poetics of emotion, in sheer dramatics, or in the irony of boredom. Reading the go-getting work the future critic might very well assume that in the feminist era women did pretty much as they cared to do without undue concern about whether or not it happened to please the men; that it was an era of strong women and weak men, and that no woman ever thought to lament unduly the lack of strong men; there was too much else to occupy her attention.

The go-getting picture is a picture of society taken by strong-grained women of a particular kind of strong grain. It is the grain of sexual self-sufficiency; the grain of the dominating female. They differ only in their surface temperament. Ferber has heroism in her strength; Hurst has primitive human feeling; Stern has more Continental tolerance than either of these two, and Macaulay has a more complete disillusionment. But all of them are alike in their refusal to admit the emotional dependence of women upon men. So far as they are concerned God might just as well have omitted men from His scheme. Men flop so far as the emotional nuances are concerned. They die easily; they break easily under strain; they degenerate easily under racial crossings. Business and sports and war mean more to them than the actual living. And even these they bungle. Women for centuries assumed that men were great and strong and heroic because they went out and dealt with a world that was closed to women. "Blah," say the go-getters. The truth is quite otherwise.

Chapter IX

MATRIARCHS

Dorothy Canfield—Margaret Ayer Barnes—Storm Jameson—Phyllis Bentley—Phyllis Bottome—Sheila Kaye-Smith—Ruth Suckow—Evelyn Scott—Kate O'Brien

The matriarch is a woman whose emotional center is in her regard for arranging and re-arranging the affairs of the people around her.

The historic matriarch was a woman of stanch self-assurance who manipulated the destinies of her family. She superintended the education of her children and her children's children. She arranged their marriages. She studied their households. She considered herself their head. The family was an order and she was its mother-superior. The family was a community which had to be directed, and the children within it remained children under her tutelage. Matriarchy in its historical significance was a transference from the original tribal authority of the patriarch to his wife. It occurred when men went out and got themselves killed in wars. It occurred whenever men let themselves get interested in affairs outside the family. It occurred always in periods when nature slumped in her production of virile males.

We are at this time unquestionably entering a period of matriarchy. It is inevitable. A generation of men was killed. A generation of women was left. And the war generation of women is now at the age when the matriarchal emotion begins to manifest itself. It is gradually appearing everywhere except in such countries which have yielded themselves to the control of the dictator, and in the countries which were least affected by the war. The dictators, one and all, admit its likelihood by

taking deliberate steps to control women and keep them in domestic subjection.

It is not the family matriarch they fear. They have infinite
faith in the subduing powers of child-bearing, child-raising and
nourishing upon the energies of women. They emphasize the
need of the state for children. Women must bear children.
That is the purpose for which they were created. But this is
secondary. The first point is that on no account must women
be allowed liberty and leisure enough to get into state affairs
or into business affairs. There are too many of them, and in
every woman lies the possibility of the dominating female whose
matriarchal tendencies might drive outward into gathering gradual control of the state. But what the male dictator forgets
everywhere is that the more does he absorb into the state the
males of the large community, the more inevitable is the development of matriarchy in the small community of the family,
and that there is such a thing as indirect control. They also
overlook the intrinsic vitality of women which can survive
child-bearing and child-raising and have something very powerful left over.

The English-writing School of Femininity, however, has had
so far nothing with which to cope from dictators, and even a
casual study of its output will convince anyone that it is for
the most part a school at the present of matriarchal writers.
The matriarchal woman dominates the writing field. By far
the greatest percentage of the women at present publishing
books and getting stories into the magazines and on the screen
and over the radio, and even on what is left of the legitimate
stage and into the activities of the little amateur community
theater, are women of matriarchal tendencies. It is quite easy
to detect them. Their work is always serious and the seriousness is always noticeably organized.

In the groupings of the women writers prior to this group
into little girl pals and go-getters, and in the subsequent grouping into helpmeets, sophisticates, priestesses and artistes, the division and listing is in no case arbitrary. The greater a woman is

in her contribution to the School of Femininity, the more likely is she to be a blend, yet a tentative listing and grouping may be laid down thus far—that in most of the writers one thought-sound dominates.   Among the little girl pals it was the sound of derision.   Among the go-getters it was a touch of determined commercial swagger.   Among the matriarchs it is a very definite appearance of seriousness in relation to the lives of the people who are laid down in print.

The world which the matriarchs survey is a world at which they long to get.   It needs straightening out.   The matriarch who does not write does as much as she can do with her immediate family.   But the family is badly disintegrated at the moment, and there is very little respect for central authority either patriarchal or matriarchal.   To begin with, families are smaller.   And space is much smaller.   Children do not need to stay at home.   They do not stay at home.   No mother can know what her children are doing.   They go much earlier to school.   In up-to-date families they go to nursery schools almost as soon as they are out of babyhood.   In their schools their health is watched by experts who never assume that maternity provides knowledge along with pain.   When the children get into their teens they also get into motor-cars and moving-picture houses.   The all-seeing maternal eye cannot follow the motor-car, and the actress on the screen is quite likely to be a far more interesting model to the young thing than the mother at home.   Yet the mother at home remains in possession, after her few children are born and sent to school, of an amount of energy which will send her to a psychiatric physician unless she can find some outlet for it.

She goes to clubs, she gets on committees, she sits on executive boards, she drafts new rules for the community which interests her.   She attends current-event classes.   She reads all the new books.   She subscribes to magazines.   She reads the papers. She watches editorial policies.   She keeps her eye on government.   When she can she gets into party politics, and sometimes she receives nominations and runs for election.   The result is a society dominated by the mature woman who can no longer dominate her family. The result is a community taking the place of the family to literally thousands of women. The result is the passage of laws and ordinances which will appeal to the mature woman voter, and another result is the censorship of this and that after the familiar old manner of the elderly female alarmed at the temptations of youth. It develops into more or less of a struggle between the matriarch woman, who wants power as much as she wants a properly organized society, and the go-getter and the little girl pal, who want freedom for their own affairs, and, if necessary, danger with it. It comes down to the age-old battle between the conservative mind consistently aware of the group and the need to protect it from the rebel, and the individualist who believes in the divine right of the ego to stretch and initiate and experiment.

The matriarch who takes to writing always chooses a group study, and usually it is a family group. There are hundreds of books coming out at the present written by matriarchal women, and they all have to do with family or community groups, and they are always handled with deep seriousness and brought to profound conclusions. They are invariably moral. The sinner is always punished, if not by society, certainly by inner torture. The wise always are sustained by the comfort of their conduct, and the foolish learn through their folly.

The matriarch, like the go-getter, finds the world of the present exactly her dish. It invites her activity. It needs improvement. The matriarch has, like the go-getter, swallowed the idea of a feminist age, and not until there are as many great businesses run by women as by men, not until there are as many women doctors, lawyers, judges, teachers, professors and parliamentarians as there are men, will the matriarch be satisfied. And not until all the laws are redrafted to admit that women, like men, are responsible citizens. And not until marriage is recognized as a duty women may take on, if they care to, in addition to their other duties to society and the state. And not until the last vestige of the idea of women as property of men disappears from the face of the earth will the matriarch rest in her doings. So she has quite a history before her. And she is in constant danger from the wiles of the dictator, whose ideas, once they get into force anywhere on the globe, tend to spread like a toxic infection. So she has quite a campaign in front of her.

When she tackles fiction she has all this in mind.

But her greatest enemy she hardly ever considers.

It is her own biological nature.

The full force of the matriarchal urge rarely hits women until they have passed middle age, and with that passing there comes to most women an imaginative rigidity which interferes with their humanity. They forget their own youth. They forget their own early maturity. They do not remember that human beings enjoy bungling along through experience. They do not see human activity as kinetic. They tend to regard life as a house to be regulated by a good housekeeper.

They see themselves as excellent housekeepers. And so they are.

But life is not a house to be regulated by a housekeeper. This is hard for the matriarch to realize. She always thinks that things and people can be tidied and cleaned and disciplined into their proper spheres. It is an age-old instinct with her. Now, with no wool to card, or linen to bleach, or household goods to polish, or much food to store against winters, or many children to train, she has to do something else. In society we see her doings in the great increase of social welfare activities. She hates slums. She hates to see children growing up under the influence of dirt or poverty or vice. We see her influence in the passage of laws relating to child welfare and child labor. She would take away, or literally put on a very unreachable shelf, all the habits of the race, like drinking and smoking and betting, and even spitting on the streets, which tend to injure the heritage of children. What she does is not always wise. What she causes to be done is not always wise. The prohibition law of the United States was one example. But the motive is always pure.

The matriarch when she gets to writing is aware of a social mission. She sets her story down as a map. She drews it meticulously in reference to its inspirational use. She believes with all her stored-up matriarchal passion that life, if it is left to itself, will go wrong. If things were as they formerly were she would not bother to write. She would bustle around her estate and see that everyone stuck with duty. With all the power of the tradition behind her she longs for her former estate. She hungers for its intimacy. The community which has taken its place for the modern matriarch has no such intimacy. So far as it goes it is an adequate outlet, but in it she is under the social necessity of working with other people. Which hampers the speed and the efficiency of the matriarchal type of mind. It is a "boss" mind, and does not take easily to cooperative maneuvering of affairs. In her fiction that "boss" mind gets out in full swing. She lays down her story squarely. Usually she goes back to the original family plan, but often she pulls the family out into community histories, and a story comes forth which is serious and sedate and human, with an undertone of practicality, and often containing quite shrewd comment upon the business of living together in groups.

The depression in the United States has brought to the surface a small battalion of matriarchal writers, looking wise and saying, "Mother knows best." One and all they go back, generally to the foundations of a particular family, and trace the growth of the family up through the building and the losing of a fortune. They all of them insist upon some manner of return to the original simple thinking and simple living of the early settlers. They assure their readers that America during its years of wild prosperity just after the war was not America, and not really happy. It had imported a lot of foreign ideas about thought and about life in exchange for the manufactured goods it exported. These writers promise us gravely that the suffering will renew the national tissues and restore the communal health. It has been excellent news for a confused people who in their confusion turned back to the racial fountain of maternal wisdom. The editors, knowing this, literally grabbed the matriarch stories.

For editors needed what she had to say, and needed the form she used. Magazines had to have serials—many of them per year—and the matriarch took to serial-writing naturally.

It was no wonder. For the serial story is the direct descendant of the story form used from the beginning of time by women telling stories to their children. And the matriarch is before everything else a mother.

The mother telling stories to her children in a simple society is always busy. She has no time to sit down just for story-telling. She must be knitting or sewing. She may even be ironing, or washing the dishes, or setting the table, or paring the vegetables. There comes, therefore, an automatic break in her story as she pauses to make some slight alteration in the movements of her hands. She may have come to the end of a seam. She may have to fit an armhole. She may be folding a tablecloth, or emptying the dish-pan, or getting out the plates, or covering the pots on the stove. The story pauses. It is the end of an instalment. If the children are interested, which means if mother is a good serialist, they will say, "And what happened next, Mother?" So exactly, if the readers are interested, which means if the matriarch is a good serialist, they will remember to buy the next issue of the magazine. This is the commercial reason behind the fashion in magazines for the serial story. Centuries of adapting story narration to a rhythmic break accompanying the rhythmic break in the occupation of the hands is behind the talent of the matriarchal writers for serialization. And the popularity of the serial form with most readers goes back to racial memories. "What happened next, Mother?"

The serial as women write it is a story form which comes down from the middle classes. For the women who told stories to children using the rhythmic work break were women who

tended their own children and did their own work. We see,
therefore, that in countries such as the United States, particularly in the northern states, the serialists can break into instalment form story-material which by ordinary first glimpse would
not break naturally. They are following an inherited subconscious narrative tendency. In other countries where stories were
told to children by nurses we see the serial form used with much
simpler narrative material, though a change is noticeable which
makes this no longer a safe contemporary generalization and is
due to the commercial opportunities. That is, all writers now,
aware of the returns from serialization, strive to put their stories
into form which will break serially.

The matriarch writers as a group are not so interesting as the
other groups. Neither is the matriarch as a woman so interesting as other women. She is too serious, too solid temperamentally, and too much focused upon the idea of pinning down
into a decent form a substance which is inherently kinetic and
volatile. It cannot be done, and the attempt to do it brings
stiffness to the human being who tries to mold the race into
fixed lines. The matriarch in plain language is a female boss,
and authority sits unattractively upon women. It is as if God
did not mean it to be. History has shown that the great women
placed by dynastic lines in power have always chosen to disguise their power. That was the case of Elizabeth Tudor. So
far as can be assumed from the maze of contradictions that
baffling woman set going about herself, she was a woman in
whom there was an undue masculine content, and this she
worked hard to hide by wearing the mask of a most frivolous
femininity. The women who let their content of masculinity
go wild into careerist go-getting and matriarchy produce in
themselves a matter-of-fact temperament which is too plain
and sensible and powerful to be interesting. The work which
they turn out is plain, sensible, powerful work. They tackle
their fiction as the historic matriarch tackled her household and
its supplies. They produce fiction as their great-grandmothers
produced linen and preserved food for the family. They col-

lect facts about the race as their predecessors collected produce of all kinds against the long winters. They order their fiction families as the matriarch ordered the affairs of the family. The precision and the concentration destroy the glamour of the story.

DOROTHY CANFIELD

Dorothy Canfield's stories have all had to do with family life set in middle-class professional circumstances in the United States. They are the families of professors, physicians, nurses, school-teachers, set for the most part in small communities. The family histories and community narratives show meticulous care of detail and meticulous seriousness of purpose. They are the product of a sincere hard-working woman ordering the ways of her fiction people into quiet effectiveness.

Her first important work, *The Bent Twig*, has to do with the premise of the home—that as children are shaped in their formative years, so will they be in after years, no matter how changed the circumstances may be. She portrays the family of a professor in very middle circumstances. The children are taught by their parents to respect knowledge and character, to take part in the labor of the household, to follow honor, and to care more for the intangible substance of human relations than for material comforts. When the children go out into the world they meet their temptations and handle them in accordance with the training of their home. They abide with what has been gently instilled into them. *The Bent Twig* is not an exciting, moving, fascinating story, and neither are any of the stories which have followed it. Another story, *The Bonfire*, even more than *The Bent Twig*, shows the matriarchal mind at work in fiction. Again it concerns professional folk, but the scene has altogether to do with their adult life. The center of the narrative is a district nurse in a small New England community, her brother, a young doctor, and the various people associated with their destinies. It is a conscientious picture of New England life in a community which may be taken as typical. The nurse and her brother belong to the place. Their family had belonged to it for generations. So, in a sense, the communal life is family life to them. The nurse is a typical example of the matriarchal tendency in women gone into its modern expression of social service. She takes her work among the people with intensive seriousness. She sets out to cure the sore spots, and in her cures and the working out of them destinies get twisted, but they all untangle in the end, as is almost invariably the case in a matriarchal novel. The matriarch is usually not content to paint the picture and leave it, or even to paint the picture and make comments upon it. There are exceptions to this rule, but in general the matriarchal story is brought to a successful finish, and the people who were disturbing the currents of their lives are all brought to their senses, and the right people get married to the right people. The tentative mistakes are all corrected by destiny itself. That is the picture of life which the matriarch likes to see, and which she brings to pass in fiction when she cannot manage it in life itself. If she does not see it around her, she sits down to consider how it might be brought about. A push here, and a move there, a pull in one direction and another pull in another direction, a word spoken in time, or a word withheld in time, and everything set going in its right way of going.

Dorothy Canfield is the pre-war matriarch. That is, her mind matured and took its style before the upset of the war, the post-war excitement, and the post-excitement depression. It is a mind stamped with matriarchal dignity. Her stories unfold slowly and gather their force slowly. There is nothing hectic, or impatient, or really ugly in them. So far as she is concerned in her writing, the world runs by a law which in the end smooths out everything hectic and impatient and ugly. It is the social-service point of view. Things can be cured, and it is the business of serious superior minds to take upon themselves the mission of "keeping" the silly lesser minds. Sex she features as mostly a trap.

The pre-war matriarchal mind is indicated by the constant return in the picture to the idea of sex as a trap set for the young men in the story. So far as the women and the girls are concerned it hardly exists, and the sons and the brothers are always getting into situations with unworthy women on account of the sexual urge, and often as not they have to be lifted out of these situations by Machiavellian finesse by mothers and sisters. This is the genuine matriarchal note—that men cannot safely be trusted to manage their own experience, but always there must be the watchful, careful, competent matriarch ready nearby to dispense with the sex-harpies who lie in wait for the unwary man, and he walks into a trap which will ruin his social career and his character. Always a matriarchal hand must be put out determinedly to save him.

This, of course, was the feminine pre-war view of sex, except insofar as it related necessarily to neat and contained family lines. The post-war matriarchs have altered their conception slightly to include its power over women, but the mark of the matriarchal attitude comes even into this, for the new matriarchs merely treat the "erring" girls and women exactly as they treat the "erring" boys and men. However that is something. It is a feminine gain.

Dorothy Canfield writes with sedate and unemotional vigor. No wild passion really tears her people up from their roots. It merely shakes them momentarily. No wild passion ever touches one of her sentences. Or colors one of her scenes.

She builds her story adequately with meticulous attention to the details of character and movement. Yet for all that, there is a feeling throughout of compelling order and quiet. You see them all as if you were a visitor in a remarkably well-run establishment, in which, though there are little individual trials, the current is never disturbed noticeably. You become aware gradually that the precision and the competency have come from the operation of a kind and motherly, yet obviously "boss" mind taking infinite care for the welfare of everyone, and determined upon the maintenance of comfort and security. In this respect Dorothy Canfield is the very personification of the matriarchal writer at the height of her maturity. She is old enough to know that the small troubles of life settle themselves, with a little wise handling, if they are not treated to undue drama. She is old enough to be able to say with conviction that it is in the sustaining of order and peace that the ultimate human satisfaction lies. To the restless adults she holds up a warning finger—"Remember the children." To the children she explains that discipline, though it is hard, is good in the end, and assures a reasonable happiness throughout the whole of life. It is in all ways the wisdom of a woman who has lived long enough to be certain that a good meal helps almost anything, and that a good sleep on a quiet, well-made, well-built bed will alter the aspect of almost everything. She refuses to look too closely into the apparent tragedies of frustration. If she does glance at them it is cogitatively, taking into her thought the practical possibilities of resolution by means of lifting a weight there, or rearranging a pressure here, and then standing back to see what difference a few touches will make.

Work of this type is interesting only to the matriarchal mind. Women of her own period and her own type take naturally to them. It is a picture they can understand and appreciate. For women of her type and her period are astonished, and more than a little disgusted, when they are confronted sharply, as they frequently are now, with fiction which presents in reality the jagged edges of all human relationships at any time, but definitely emphasized as at this particular time. They look upon the generation below them as awkwardly unfinished, prating wildly about frustrations, under the impression that sex and all its amplifications are a startling post-war discovery and the only fit subject for intelligent adult conversation. Sex to the pre-war matriarch certainly, and to the post-war matriarch tentatively, is only the cement of the family, very important naturally, but not so important as the thing it holds together.

Work of this kind, and a mind of the matriarchal order, are never truly literary. For the purely literary mind never has any conception of the great benefits to society accruing from order and good government. The literary mind is a kinetic mind, and as such is far more likely to be attracted to the dramatic possibilities of the elements which tend to pull society apart rather than to those which tend to pull it together. It watches always for drama. It sees infinitely more drama in the individual who shocks the pack than in the individual who settles snugly into the ordered laws of the pack. But in spite of this the matriarchal work has its place definitely in the School of Femininity, inasmuch as there will always be a large proportion of matriarchs among the female population. The matriarch is essentially racial, and essentially feminine, despite her masculine tendency to govern. If the men in their government impressed her favorably she would show no tendency to govern. It is when she believes men to have failed that she comes forward.

There are plenty of them coming forward at the present. The conclusion, therefore, is unavoidable. Women think that men have failed.

MARGARET AYER BARNES

Margaret Ayer Barnes is an example of the younger American matriarch.

She is aware of the confusion of the period because she is in her chronology involved in it. The people she writes about are people who have gone through the war, through the enthusiastic era of much money following the war, and through the terrifying depression. She watches her people lose their bearings, and she gathers as many of them as are left after the deluge back into the fold of a purely matriarchal sanity. She is a young matriarch in that she permits her people to rage in emotionalism, or what passes for emotionalism, and in that she has a complete modern knowledge, the modern courage of admission of the sexual force, both in men and women. She even suggests that it is possibly a little stronger in women than it is in men. She does not step circumspectly around the issue. But she does treat it with therapeutic impersonality. She looks upon

the women of her time in the relatively new and unfamiliar
throes of a force which may disrupt the family. Therein is she
matriarchal. Furthermore she is matriarchal in her implication, clearly to be seen in all her stories, that men will do exactly what women want them to do. If women determine that
the preservation of the family and an ordered community is of
far greater consequence than the short happiness of individuals
in fulfilment of sexual chemistry, then men will fall in line,
as they have always fallen in line, in the main, and in the end,
even though they have always, and probably always will, stage
small sexual revolts. And likewise, if women in the tumult of
suddenly discovering themselves to be sexually as rebellious as
men, and equally as impatient individually of the restraining
family ties, do shake the ordering of society in a trifling attempt
to get something that looks like happiness for themselves for
a while, men will again fall in line and agree with them only
too quickly. This is primarily the matriarchal point of view—
that the woman leads and the man follows, even though it might
appear down through the centuries that the reverse has been
true. The matriarch has always believed in feminism. The
modern post-war and post-depression matriarch like Margaret
Ayer Barnes portrays her people in the midst of their racial in-
decision, and gives due place to all the forces that encourage
disturbance, and at the same time, brings into play the other
forces that tend to settle the upheaval, but in the end they
all come out on the side of the family and security and order.

One book, *Westward Passage,* shows a woman in the middle
of an emotional debate. She had divorced her first husband because he was not a good husband or a good father. She had
married a second husband because he was racially to her matriarchal taste. The first man appears again in her life and tries
to take her away from the second man. Individually he sat-
isfies her—which is to say—sexually—more fully than the second man; but racially he does not. He is utterly irresponsible.
She decides in the end for racial security. The women's magazines are full of stories of this type at the present. Margaret

Ayer Barnes just happened to write what is probably the best of them. Stories pour in to the editors of women's magazines written around all the aspects and ramifications of this one theme. It would almost seem as if every married woman in the country had been called upon to decide, or would like to be called upon to decide, whether or not to stick with her husband or run off with a lover. This is quite new; at least it is quite new on such a scale. The struggle of the man, whether to stay quietly with the woman of his household after the romance has been worn off, or to run to the strange woman of new glamour, appears also in great quantity, written by women. It is merely another aspect of the same story. It is more than that; it is the outlet of women who have always known that men yearned to stand on two emotional feet, and it is, further, an outlet for the decision most women have made some time in their lives concerning which manner of women they would be—the woman of the household, or the woman of strange, strange glamour outside the household. There is nothing new in this variation of the story. But it is new in that women admit that the decision concerning themselves is never quite over. For just as surely as a woman decides concerning one man that she is a woman of the household, will she decide concerning another man that she has decided courtesan leanings. She, like the man, finds that she can interpret passion in two ways—for the race— and for herself, and never it seems in both ways with one man. The problem is—what is she to do? When the man steps out it does not shatter the race, because his woman stays to maintain order. But if the woman steps out she pulls the race out with her. So, where is equality? It is the matriarchal women who are concerned with this theme. It is the terror which separates her generically from the little girl pals, the go-getters, the helpmeets, the sophisticates, and even more definitely from the priestesses and the artistes. None of the others cares as much, if she cares at all, about what may happen to the race. They do not see the family as it builds into the community as the center of civilization. The matriarch does. They do not see them-

selves as having anything more to do with the race than anyone else. The matriarch does. She always does. The young
matriarch, like the old matriarch, waits for the sexual fire to
burn lower. In her family stories, *Years of Grace* and *Within
This Present,* Mrs. Barnes takes her associated groups in both
cases through the war, through the post-war excitement and
through the post-excitement depression. She falls back upon
the familiar idea that so long as American society remained in its
true American perspective of pioneer simplicity it was not
psychically difficult. Women married men and tended their
homes and families as matters of destiny. But when society
plunged into new wealth, and women found themselves in possession of leisure, the family hold began to loosen, and they
began to look around for something to which to give themselves. They discovered the sexual hunt. In each case she
shows the family returning after three generations to its original
simplicity, and this emphatically is the matriarchal note again.
It is not exactly accurate, but it is what the matriarch would
like to be accurate, and to which, when she recovers herself,
she bends all her energies in order to bring it into some
semblance of accuracy. Certainly she brings it into print in
all the magazines.

Margaret Ayer Barnes is one of the most perfect mistresses
of the serial technique in activity. She has absolute rhythm.
She has absolute instalment timing. Her people hold together,
and rise and fall together in response to the author's sense of
story timing. She has movement and suspense. But she always
subjects her characters to technique. Her people are human
but are not markedly individualized, even when in the stress of
highly individualized problems. They are era people and group
people. They are parts of a whole matriarchal aspect.

They are, when you come down to a final study of them,
magazine people. That is, they are the people one meets in
magazine fiction and perhaps nowhere else.

They consist of a grandmother who remains watchful in her

own native wisdom and simplicity; a mother who struggles in her loyalties between a hard-working, thoroughly dependable husband and the attractions of a hovering lover; an aunt, maybe, who tries to find peace of mind in spite of a husband who philanders and keeps mistresses; the cousin who is rather mannish and makes good in a career; the young daughter who is exactly like her grandmother and is never quite in approval of her mother. Around these women the gallery people circulate who live beyond their means and wonder how they can pay their bridge debts and have as many clothes as other women; women who concentrate upon helping to build the careers of their husbands, and worry over dinner parties and having their children's tonsils out; men who commute day after day; men who fail to turn up to dinner, and telephone about business engagements holding them in town; wives who worry about blondes; men who talk things over with their wives; men who carry their loads in secret; lovers who telephone ten minutes after the husbands have telephoned about business engagements; lovers who write plays or music or books and send flowers. None of them needs a name. They are magazine people. They vary only slightly in their dialogue and their settings. The matriarch writes about them because she is interested in getting some appearance of order out of the prevailing confusion, and when things get down into writing they look simpler. She writes as she would cut out a pattern. With her material laid flat on a flat surface, and her pattern pinned securely over it, with her lips pursed in determination and her hand firm in the grasp of her adequately sharpened scissors. She never, or rarely, varies the pattern. It is safer, she knows, to follow it implicitly. And usually before she has laid it out upon its flat surface she has looked at a picture of the finished product in a book. This, she remembers, as she cuts, is what the finished work will look like if all the rules are followed. It is true, for the finished work is just such a garment as women have cut for themselves for centuries—the garment of the race molded for the family.

STORM JAMESON

The most comprehensive study of the matriarch as an individual woman has come from Storm Jameson, and is contained in her trilogy, *The Lovely Ship*, *The Voyage Home* and *A Richer Dust*.

It is a great feminine portrait, and a tragic consummation in femininity of the feminist urge. The matriarch, Mary Hervey, has the emotional craving of Mary Wollstonecraft for self-expression, the emotional thirst of Maggie Tulliver for love, and the emotional hunger of Olive Schreiner for her children. She has them all and in the end has none of them.

She set out in her youth to build ships. Her family had built ships. There was no man in her generation. So she took on the man's duties. She married at fifteen, was a widow at eighteen with a little son. This meant that she also took on a woman's duties. She must bridge a generation and hold the business for her son. Work and her son were not enough. There was passion. So she married again, and Hugh, her attractive second husband, was unfaithful out of his need for a lesser woman. Mary was too strong.

It was the Wollstonecraft story with Imlay over again—the everlasting experience which haunts all great women. Hugh was jealous of her ships and jealous of her creative energy and unsatisfied because he could never, he thought, dominate her. He loved her, but he had to be a hero to some women. Mary was temperamentally incapable of playing the *élégante* with emotions and sharing her man. So she turned all her passion to her ships while her children grew up. Another man came into her life. He was already a broken man; broken up by another woman. He loved Mary and he loved her ships and he helped her and then left her to return to the other woman. Again the saga of the weaker woman. As she grew older the ships became to Mary a symbol of family and, in a still deeper sense, of her family's contribution to the state. Hugh, her husband, came back home and taught himself to find her and her corporation worth living for. He tried to make the children feel it too. But he could not. The children went away from her. One by one they recoiled from her determined government of them, and from the business in which they found no glamour. The story carries on through the war, and into the generation of the grandson in whom she tries to instil her emotion for ships. She could not do it. Mary at the end of her life knew she had been a failure. She had built a great business; she had ruled her family. She had lived through the middle and the end of the nineteenth century and on into the second decade of the twentieth. She saw all the changes, and she survived them. But when her grandson failed her she was through, and she sold her magnificent line of ships and he went into the antique furniture business. She saw all her children and her grandchildren repeating in their lives the mistakes of the various family strains that had entered into their blood-stream. She saw that there was no such thing as preserving a family destiny. Individuals lived and died, and all their living, and even all their dying, came in the end to be only the repetition of vague blood memories. What she forgot was that she herself and all her energy had entered into the blood-stream and would appear again later, recalled into the blood and focused into one individual, bound to repeat itself because once it had been there.

Storm Jameson, as can be seen clearly from this brief outline of her trilogy, has portrayed the final overwhelming sorrow of the matriarch—the eternal mother doomed to see her glorious dream hanging upon a cross. She does her portrait with the restraint of the English writer, as well as with the English writer's brooding awareness of history. It is writing such as follows after emotional torture and belongs to the stillness that comes after pain, when the human spirit has learned to accept its burden of disappointment. It is writing which is characteristic of thoughtful women living through colossal tragedy. Tragedy pressed down upon the women who were emotionally mature during the war in England. They saw everything

taken from them. The incidental new freedom it brought to
women meant nothing to them. They were too old and too
mature to be taken in by the enthusiasm of something that
appeared to be new. They had learned that there was no such
thing as freedom for women; that women were bound to the
race, and that women suffered acutely when the race entered
upon a period of calamity; and that no amount of work and no
amount of success in that work could ever make for a woman
compensation for the descent of the race into hell. A whole
generation of men had been swept out of the stream of living.
And a whole generation of women were left who could do
nothing but stand and watch the stream go on past them. The
matriarchs had nothing to do but to look at the emptiness of
everything. Life had no need of them any more. Yet they
themselves went on living with the terrible attachment to life
which is in women. It is so hard for them to die. For women
have been endowed by their biology with some awful power to
remain alive when every reason for living has gone, and all that
there is for them to do is to watch by the empty tomb. Storm
Jameson is the very voice of these bereft matriarchs. Though
the individual woman she drew had everything for awhile that
a woman could desire, she came in the end to have nothing,
and the story took its emotional urge not from the beginning
but the end of Mary Hervey's life. It is—the whole trilogy—
an attempt to provide a negative kind of compensation to
women. It says to the childless woman that it is all useless,
anyway—that life itself is not worthy of motherhood—that the
lines of life will never follow the pattern of the matriarch.
Mary Hervey was wrong, she is saying, and wrong upon three
counts. She looked for happiness; she worked like a man; she
believed in the destiny of the family. There is no happiness
except in short moments of illusion, and these must be paid for
by the suffering that haunts all happiness. No woman could
work like a man. Her whole nature asked only for racial blos-
soming and the peace that it needs. Children born to a career
woman have their teeth on edge because they were not born in

peace. No woman should seek to order the destinies of a group of associated individuals. She was no appointed vice-regal to God. She was only a vessel of the race. Her mission was fulfilled when her last baby was weaned; life might go on from then, but it could only go on in watchful contemplation. For from her nothing more was to be expected.

It is a portrait taken at a long view. It is far-seeing. It is spiritually remote. It is intellectually composed. It is work that could only have come from a generation of women who had to become remote and composed. And this is true whether or not Storm Jameson herself is remote and composed out of personal necessity. The real writer draws from the population of his or her time the subconscious fiber of thought. We see again and again instances of books held back in their publication until the immediately appointed time, and marked cases of authors who seem to be caught in their creativeness by an inertia of waiting. This is because the real writer is essentially subjective to the race and seems to receive in some strange way from the undercurrents of life unspoken messages of desire. It is in response to these messages that their books are written, laboriously put together from peculiar, hardly touched substance within themselves, or torn out of them in agony which is of the spirit and tears the spirit as human birth tears the body of a woman. Storm Jameson is unquestionably one of those psychically obedient writers, weaving in and out of herself texts that belong to the race.

She writes simply and yet on a grand scale. She has made no attempt to be smart and modish. She does not experiment with style. She is preeminently the sensible middle-class woman of England, devoted to wearable tweeds and sturdy shoes and the traditions of her class and her race and her time. No light remarks fall from her. No passing mode snaps her into its restless cynical pattern. George Eliot could have read her books with understanding. And so also will some unknown woman years from now. It is work of painstaking balance and genuine humanity. As such it belongs to women of all centuries.

PHYLLIS BENTLEY

There is a large collection of matriarchal writers from England. They are serious women who put their passion for racial construction and reconstruction into rather more literary form than do the American matriarchs. They also put it down in plainer language—that is, it is easier to see the matriarchal tendency in them than it is to see it in the Americans. Their motivation is simpler. But at the same time they have less vitality. The Americans as a race still think that a wise woman may do quite a bit of good in the world. The English women are not so sure about it, and it is this tentativeness which destroys some of the vitality of their composition. And at the same time gives it greater literary power. Because literature is always a tentative approach to life. And good writers usually write because there is something they are not altogether sure about, and are driven by a desire to see it down on pages for better and clearer reconsideration.

Among them is Phyllis Bentley. She is the young matriarch gone economic.

She is interested in the pattern of the family, but has transferred her pattern to the community. Problems of labor readjustment engross her at the expense of compact family or personal emotion. Storm Jameson touched gently upon the dilemma of capital tied to the world's need for more and more goods, and the new necessity of bringing the laboring classes up out of a position of slavery. But she subordinated the dilemma to her initial purpose, which concerned the matriarchal woman at the head of an industry and a family. Phyllis Bentley, on the other hand, subordinates her characters and their stories to the industrial problem. The world problem she appears to believe will bring frustration to everyone until it is solved.

Her first book, *Inheritance,* was taken from the history of a family involved with the business of weaving cloth, but it was not so much a family history as it was a history of the economic issue with particular relation to that particular business. The second book, *A Modern Tragedy*, pulled abruptly away from the family setting, and went over entirely to the baffling question of the time—labor and capital and the balance, if any, between the two.

Miss Bentley is neither an aloof observer of the situation nor yet an ardent advocate of any set method leading to possible resolution. She comes in between the two, which is rather a matriarchal attitude because it is practical. She takes, probably without being aware of it, the attitude of the mother dealing with factions among her children, and while one child may be her emotional favorite, she holds her judgment in reserve, and stands by her first duty, which is to maintain the peace of the family. In writing this is manifested and carried out by an effort to interpret one side to the other. This, in brief, is her text in both books—that there is a simple way out of a complex situation—only human nature in its exaggerated extremes of emotion fails to see it. She pointed out in *Inheritance* that down through the generations there always appeared a mind capable of leading the people out of their dilemma, and that it was always a mind which was endowed by some miracle with a capacity for seeing both sides of a question. Because of this very quality it always drew persecution from the people who could only see one side. She shows each generation in its blind emotion pushing away the leader who was wise in his impersonality, in favor of the demagogue who always fanned the emotions, and through fanning increased the confusion and further entangled the problem.

It is the everlasting tragedy of the human race; and her story is another of the everlasting cries of women waiting at the foot of the cross, weeping because of the spiritual immaturity of the race they have borne.

She leaves it as such, but while she sets it down she paints the portrait of a time and a problem which is in itself quite aside from the underlying text a valuable historical document. *Inheritance* was sound social history of a very high order, and an

example of the mind of a woman entirely graduated from the
usual personal preoccupations of women. It follows the tradition of the English bluestocking women, sincere, scholarly,
utterly devoted to the issue under discussion. It is undec-
orated. She never lingers to play with her phrases; she never
pushes her characters into the duty of entertaining the readers.
She is intent upon their fulfilling a definite destiny, which is to
remind the readers of something they need to consider. It is
the work of a matriarch concerned with the welfare of the
human family and preoccupied with it to the point of being
much too serious for pure literature. She responded subconsciously to the layer of oppressed life, mowed down impersonally by the industrial machine, with hardly enough life left
in it to assert itself, and yet containing the element of resentment which once roused may ruin the pattern of humanity.
She writes out of this sympathetic response as with a warning
and a prayer. She is a woman deeply conscious of her duty.
She represents a mass of English women aware of the currents
which sweep the human race helplessly into danger. She represents their sorrow and their indignation.

PHYLLIS BOTTOME

Phyllis Bottome is a matriarch who has reached hopefully for
the help there is for the race in the new discoveries of the
psychoanalysts. She has many books, but the key book is
Private Worlds, which takes the reader into a psychiatric hospital.

Private Worlds is not an absorbing piece of fiction, but neither
is the work of any of the matriarchs. They all write with too
definite a racial purpose to turn out engaging fiction.

But it is a very important book in the development of the
School of Femininity for one simple reason. For the first time
the career of a woman is accepted by an author without apology,
without any sense of treating a cause, and entirely as an accepted fact. She starts from that premise, and discloses with
sharp precise lines a new variation in the eternal theme of

woman functioning as a mother. The heroine is a medical woman upon the staff of the psychiatric hospital. Without being at all aware of it herself, and quite free in her own judgment of any sexual implications, she gradually attains a matriarchal power over her associates and in particular over a brilliant young co-worker who is married to an ordinary, nice, harmless girl. This girl, through what she feels to be unfair competition intellectually with a more powerful woman than herself, slides step by step into a mental breakdown, and is rescued by the superintendent of the hospital, who has no taste for women in professions. He recognizes the matriarch in the woman doctor, and determines to free his hospital from her influence. This is the central point of the story. The author introduces other issues more or less relative to the conduct of a readable piece of fiction, but it is upon this one point that the story turns, and is the contribution of Phyllis Bottome to the school of feminine portraits and self-expression.

It is in no way great fiction, but it shows conclusively the mind of the modern woman grasping at every phase of discovery which will aid in the development of a finely balanced feminine mind. More than this, it is a decided step in purely feminist, as distinguished from feminine, history.

The history of women has been a history of superimposed ignorance. The subjection of women was maintained and sustained by their ignorance of themselves. What makes the twentieth-century scene of absorbing interest to the observer is the effort of women to throw off the fascinations of ignorance. They have arrived at a definite amount of information concerning the workings of their bodies. They definitely depreciate the attempt of any organized institution to keep information from them. They are also arriving at a definite amount of tentative information concerning the effect of biology upon the mind, and, conversely, of the effect of the mind upon biology. They want to know themselves, and from that to get more for themselves out of life, and again from that to have more to give to life.

Phyllis Bottome's sincere and guarded story of a matriarch practising her profession and her matriarchal tendencies in a job ranks as one step more in the progress of women towards full, or relatively full, understanding of themselves. It has opened a whole new field to women and the thoughts they think about themselves as they function more or less completely through life. In a sense it carries on the story of Lyndall where Olive Schreiner left it off. Jane, the heroine of *Private Worlds*, is a Lyndall who has completed her particular self-appointed job of making herself through study the equal of men. Like Lyndall she believed that friendship on equal terms was possible with men. Like Lyndall she wanted for her own emotional experience a man who was just a little better than she was. She found him, and when she did find him, she submitted to his dominance after the old manner of women, though at first she was bothered by a resentment coming out of her immediate struggle for equality. The inference of the story is that after her emotional submission to him they would go hand in hand to work together at their chosen work. Whether or not it is possible, some future feminist recorder will have to say in such time as the evidence of such an experiment is all gathered in with sufficient time having passed for its consideration.

At the moment it seems a very questionable point. For a woman when her emotions are roused reverts to one of five very sharply marked divisions among women. The man she loves will make of her a helpmeet, a sophisticate or a matriarch. If she cannot love a man with peace, and is emotionally baffled by this lack in her experience, she becomes a go-getter or a priestess. Unless a very rapid result occurs from the use of psychoanalysis among very young women, it does seem that so far as the immediate future is concerned there is little hope of a woman attaining normal love of a man and normal outlet for her own work in the world with any considerable equality.

The original purpose of the feminist movement was the demand for equality of opportunity. It was initiated by women who believed that equality of opportunity would change the

whole sexual aspect, that economic and intellectual readjustment would alter the sexual current. It is almost needless to
say that these women were in almost total ignorance of the
sexual force and its effect upon women when it got into its
full force. The generalization concerning equality of an un-
awakened woman, of a congenitally cold woman, of a woman in
whom traumatic shock had produced inversion, of a woman
with a lust for government, of a woman with a passion for the
images of religion, has almost no value when applied to a woman
whom nature has endowed with a capacity for completely natural sexuality. During the first phase of feminism it was the
abnormal women who did the writing and the talking. They
were justified. They had every right to claim freedom for
themselves to appease their abnormality in some chosen field of
work. The mistake was in the sexual leap—that is, they pulled
into their demand for equal professional and economic opportunity another demand which had, strictly speaking, nothing
whatever to do with the first demand. The plea for sexual
equality was a plea formed out of the dreams of starved or
frigid or inverted or priestess women. It was the plea of the
indignant abnormal, releasing itself in a reach for the biological
impossible. It set the movement back, or rather it held it back
inasmuch as the emphasis being placed upon the wrong aspect,
it stirred biological resentment in men, and it also stirred biological complacency among satisfied women and further made
the few who were wise hesitate. It made a sexual crusade out of
something that was a simple request. As such it caught in its
crusading hysteria any number of young women who did not
realize for what they were really searching, and caused them to
assume, often with infinite emotional havoc to themselves, that
it was the right to distinguish themselves.

SHEILA KAYE-SMITH

This was shown admirably and clearly by Sheila Kaye-Smith
in *Susan Spray*. The novel is set back in time and the setting
was taken from the laboring classes. But it is built upon a

theme which belongs to all time and all classes of women.
Susan Spray was a girl who was reared in an atmosphere of
poverty and religious excitement. She manifested early in her
childhood a tendency to play for attention. The only audience
she could have was the audience of the little religious sect to
which her parents belonged. She made the most of it. She
saw remarkable visions. She spoke in the meeting. She married a man who admired her. The play for attention went on
apace. Though the author does not say so in plain language,
it is inferred that Susan's marriage was no great upheaval of
passion to her. The man died. Her baby died. Had the baby
lived, all her dissatisfaction would have veered into a Messianic
fixation upon the child. She was injured at childbirth and
could have no more children. The visions and the preaching
continued. Then she met a he-man who took her to London
with him, amused her, and gave her emotional heaven and emotional hell, and generally treated her to a period of intense
femininity. She did no preaching during that time. The man
was unfaithful and she left him, and all her visions returned.
Step by step she rose to them and became a power in the religious form to which she was accustomed. The man was presumably drowned at sea and Susan found another man who had
money enough to endow her with a temple for her adherents
and the position of religious authority and utter superiority
which she craved. Just before her marriage to this man she
learned that the other man had not been drowned, but so intense
was her need for the attention she would get from her temple
and her leadership that she went through a bigamous marriage
and trusted to her luck to see her through. For by this time she
was in the full power of her fantasy and saw herself anointed
by God, and in no need, therefore, to trouble about the small
laws of mankind regarding marriage.

This is a powerfully drawn portrait of abnormal functioning
in woman as related to sexual and play satisfaction. Susan was
the plain girl child. It was her only chance for attention and
she took it. It was suspended while she was living with her

second husband. It was resumed in a revenge-defense mechanism when he failed her. Her whole life after him was to be a revenge-defense mechanistic gesture. She insulted him by her bigamous marriage. She became, according to her own lights and in the only way open to her, a famous woman. Sheila Kaye-Smith by this portrait proclaimed herself a deep student of women and of their psychology. It is probably the history of many women who have achieved fame or what approaches fame in their own immediate circle. It portrays unquestionably the preliminary stages of the development of religious matriarchy in a woman. For indubitably Susan Spray would come to rule her believers with the matriarchal rod. It opens up a whole field of speculation upon the data behind any woman who in our time has reached a pinnacle of power in religious sects and their platforms. It is, for all its literary power, a grave study of matriarchal danger. Step by step Susan was led to see herself as the center of a group. From a simple need for attention she moved out into a complex need for dominance until the whole universe so far as she was concerned had to revolve around her satisfaction.

Though the story is set back in an earlier century in its time element, it belongs to the present because of one unescapable fact—the lost generation of men—and the corresponding generation of women who are under the necessity of finding abnormal satisfaction. Whether in religion, in business, in the professions, or in the community life generally, there is full cause for the development of matriarchy in women. Power is relatively easy to get. And the matriarchal temperament slips up on women almost imperceptibly. Professions such as all the amplifications of social service lie temptingly open to women in which they can so easily forget the fine art of minding one's own business. Social service is only a step or so away from community control, and community control is only a step behind a matriarchal society and government. It might be admirable. Certainly it would be a change. But every woman who heads that way should be under the compulsion of study-

ing her own private affairs and determining the position of the
thin line between her own need of dominance and the good of
the public. And the greatest help in this lies in the tentative
doctrines of the Viennese school of psychotherapy. So much is
this true that unquestionably the whole development of the
present phase of the feminist movement will lie in the acceptance, whether partial or whole, or the negation, whether partial
or whole, of these tenets by women.

If we are to judge by the writing of women in a School of
Femininity, it does appear that the present phase of feminism
will branch quietly away from its first phase. Though possibly
not for a time. That is, not for a time insofar as the reality is
concerned. For society generally lags behind its writers slightly
in point of historic fact. It is perhaps unwise to attempt to
draw conclusions as yet, but it does look as if the women who are
writing are inclined to lament the emotional poverty which
drives the women they portray into fields which can eventually
only be barren for them. They handle the fiction they use as
they would handle an experiment. They are careful what they
set down. They leave an escape. It is as if they were aware that
another generation and its outcome may change the whole
scene and all their conclusions. They write for their own time,
yet they have their eye also upon a new generation who may
laugh, or pity, or ignore. But if, in all their tentativeness, their
gravity, and their sincerity, they manage to get over just one
facet of the feminine story, they have accomplished well. And
if that facet turns out to be, as it seems as if it might, that
equality is a cry for satisfaction from women who as things are
cannot be satisfied; and if they point out that sex with its emotionalism and its inverted emotionalism is a subject belonging
absolutely to the feminist program of teaching, then they will
have done what certainly needed to be done for women in this
Western world.

Meanwhile a certain type of matriarch, of which Ruth
Suckow may be taken in illustration, waives all the tentative

social psychiatric experiments aside, and contents herself with
setting down family life as she sees it.

RUTH SUCKOW

Ruth Suckow is a family thinker. She is absolutely concentrated upon family. Not so much out of conviction that it
is the backbone of society as that it is still a good quarter section
of humanity as it lives together, and in which individuals develop character or are frustrated. The family as a social unit
is undergoing a period of change, but as means for study for
human close-up it is still the best medium.

Ruth Suckow approaches it as such. She is a modern matriarch who is interested in the avenue to the adult through the
child. Her latest book, *The Folks,* is about a family in the
middle-western United States. It begins with the children
and traces meticulously all the conversations and actions which
affect the psychology of the children. It is almost a treatise
in child training. One of the children, the elder daughter, ties
the hair ribbon of her little sister one morning in a way of
which the mother cannot approve. The mother unties the ribbon
and does it over again properly—just one incident in a family
life—but it leaves a bruise upon the older girl. She concludes
that nothing she does will ever suit her mother. Out of that
she develops a neurosis and is forever under a strange compulsion
to do things her family will lament. Another of the children,
the elder boy, is sent to fetch this girl home from the backyard
of a playmate with whom the mother does not wish her to play.
Another incident, familiar enough in family life, but out of it
the boy develops a brooding sense of constant self-apology.
The story is heavily built up; the details are massed; the human
understanding of the author is hardly able to illuminate the
heaviness. It stands as the work of a matriarchal mind which
has taken enthusiastically to the study of interrelated human
psychology, and knowing that the future of the family as a
social unit is under some process of change, is content to portray
it as she has seen it.

Like most of the matriarchs during this era, she is in the depths of disappointment. Life eludes the fixing hands of the matriarch. The mother in *The Folks* lives to see the children she bore and reared suffer inner frustration. She has to realize that nothing can be done about it. This is the new note in matriarchy. The older matriarch would have brought, at least in fiction, some appearance of inner order to her story. She would have rounded them all in the end into decent happy citizens. The younger matriarch knows that it is impossible. So she does not attempt it. To see clearly the change which the last years have produced in women of this matriarchal type, one needs only to read any one of the novels of Dorothy Canfield and after it *The Folks*. With Dorothy Canfield the work of the matriarch is never over. With Ruth Suckow the matriarch is realizing that all she had to do was to bear and nourish her children; that psychological scars are inevitable in any kind of group life; and that some form of frustration is the general human lot. It is the difference between the nineteenth-century and twentieth-century mind as functioning in the matriarch. Or rather it is the difference between the era of hope and the era of despair. But they have one thing in common, and this makes them matriarchal—they both take it seriously and a little sadly.

EVELYN SCOTT

Evelyn Scott is more than a little sad, as well as serious. She is a matriarch who surveys the world instead of her family. The world as she surveys it is a plague-ridden spot. The war urge hits it like a giant wave, and goes through the people leaving desolation in its wake. This subject she dealt with in her historical tome about the American Civil War called *The Wave*. Vice comes to the population and spreads through the interlocked lives of people. Vice that is really human ignorance. This she treated in another tome called *The Calendar of Sin*.

Evelyn Scott is a steam-roller type of writer. She "steam-rollers" her subjects over an immense territory, and when she is finished there is nothing left to say. Her great machine is equipped with all the modern psychological gadgets. She understands how men get caught in the fight and how women get held in the mazes of their own twisted imaginations. These little gadgets serve to make her progress the more certain. They tell her when she is coming to a curve in the road, and how to take the curve. She treats the human race in big fiction masses. She piles up her masses and rides them down. She is not an entertaining writer. She is under no impression that the duty of the writer is to entertain. She is a determined woman who sets her readers down to a table groaning with material for eating. She sits at the head of it and sees that you take each course as it comes to you without any flagging of appetite. If you do not like it, then the inference is that you do not know what is good for you.

What is good for you is to comprehend that life is a many-ringed spectacle, and that minds circle and circle about the rings; that you may watch one ring for a while and turn to the next, and back to the first, and again to the next. The riders may have done a few more turns and added a flourish or two, but they are still doing the same thing, going round and round; birth and death and suffering in between, with maybe a love or so, all of which come in the end to be like every other love. If you have any idea that the spectacle is grand it is an idea that does not last as you read Evelyn Scott. She tells you didactically by means of her massed material that it is in the end a shoddy show; and she makes you wonder if even the magnificent path taken by the planets in the heavens would turn out on a close look to be shoddy too. Certainly if all the planets were to be like this planet.

She is a matriarch in the great-grandmother rôle. She looks at human antics from quite a long way off. Her romance about it all has gone; her endeavor to assist it to improve is gone; her sympathy for what might be interpreted as an effort to grow is gone. She is past all these, and has come to the time when she sees it endlessly repeating itself. She has no time left to value the infinitesimal movements in character. They count for too little in the planless plan. She merely looks on and registers within her the fact that the silly story still goes on. She writes as if she were the hard-worked secretary of the recording angel, with the trained impassivity of the secretary, and without the recorded compassion of the angel. She may have the compassion, and in all probability she has. But she would never get her job done if she allowed it to gain possession of her. She writes on and on and on. It is all that is left for a matriarch to do after she has gone through many stages of matriarchy, and has seen families disappear and empires fall and change come over everything.

Out of the change one thing remains unchanged—the need of the human heart to worship at some shrine, and to find that worship supported by some infallibility.

KATE O'BRIEN

Kate O'Brien, the Irish matriarch, offers the shrine and the infallibility of the historic Roman Catholic Church.

Her first book, *Without My Cloak,* was a matriarchal drawing of family life in the upper middle class of Ireland during the later part of the nineteenth century. The second book, *The Anteroom,* is a dramatic episode in the history of one branch of the same family, the Consadines.

The work of Kate OBrien is interesting on several counts.

First, it is so far the only outstanding feminine writing during the present Renaissance of Irish drama and letters. As such it is in itself worthy of close examination. The men writers of the Renaissance in Ireland are one and all revolutionary. Kate O'Brien is not. Her stories go back to the time before the Revolution and the emotion of her people is centered upon their family life and upon the Church to which they cling. The young men of Ireland have gone realistic. The sound of guns is in their writing, and the nervousness of suspicion affects them. It is writing done by human beings still mentally "on the run." Kate O'Brien, so far as her work has gone, writes as if nothing had happened in Ireland, and out of a matriarchal consciousness concerning the relative unimportance of revolution. Wars come and wars go. Old wars are finished and new wars begin. It is always so. Maybe it will always be so. But one thing remains unchanging—that human beings must be born of two parents—a man and a woman, which constitutes family, and that they must worship God with dignity, which constitutes the place of the Church in life. This is primarily the belief of the woman. Nothing else matters very much.

The work of the young Irishmen shows families split upon varying social and political ideas, and bitter young patriots ready to sacrifice family and love and all emotion for the sake of an idea in statecraft. Ireland as a political idea is the center of all feeling and all devotion. Nothing else matters. If their womenfolk stand with them side by side it is fine; if they do not, they dispense with them. "Wounds for Ireland; imprisonment for Ireland; death for Ireland," as the young men say in O'Casey's *The Plough and the Stars*.

We do not know yet how Kate O'Brien would write about the actual time of the Revolution, but it is significant that during a period when every Irishman with the hunger for words writes about war, this woman writes about family and the power of the infallible Church. It is a matriarchal answer to the little games of men; the little towers they build out of blocks; the little states they build in the sand; the little ideas they have about this country or that country and what it may mean in the general plan.

In the second count her work is interesting because it is profoundly Catholic. There has been no writer in our time who has put into writing the sheer romance of religion as she has given it in *The Anteroom*. Life, she is telling us, is the anteroom of death. The soul must go on alone to its great adventure, and to take this experience well it must not cling during life to the things that seem to make life good. And all through life it must prepare for death, and let the doors stand open. This is the meaning of all the symbology of the

Church. The sons and daughters of the Church go humbly to their services and their confessions, and each service and each confession opens the door gently and the soul wanders while still in life into those regions to which it will go when death comes. Candles are lit, a bell rings, incense is wafted through the air, the people respond to the prayers of the priest, and songs go up from the choir and a fragment of wisdom is uttered from the mouth of the representative of the great office. It is nothing more than that. Yet the people go out from it washed of their sins and aware of the littleness of their desires and their rebellions.

The story of *The Anteroom* is slight. An Irishwoman, the mother of a family, is dying. Her children gather around her. One daughter is in deep sorrow. She is in love with the husband of her sister. She cannot pray for the ease of her mother with this sin upon her. So she takes her problem to confession. The priest tells her that religion is romance; that no human being is in utter need of a certain other human being, but only in need of God. The burden of it lifts from her. Not the tragedy, for it remains with her. But the importance of it has gone. The priest had given her a greater romance, and the lesser sank down into something that was a passing fancy.

The story works out to a dramatic culmination. The young brother-in-law does what to him is the supreme act of heroism, but is in reality the supreme act of defensive cowardice. He ends his own life. That is all there is to the story of this branch of the Consadines.

The other book, while fuller and more detailed, is also a study of the little renunciations of living. The Consadines put aside their individual tastes in romance for the great cause of the family and the Church and its laws.

It is to be seen from this brief consideration that Kate O'Brien is a woman saying to the race—*remember*. The highly individualistic doctrines of the day—the usurpation of authority by self-appointed dictators—the mechanistic facts which stand in actual war against the individualistic urges of the time—all these are things to be adjusted. Two things remain unchanging. The need of the race to continue—and the need in the human heart to get away from its little self to the great mystery of it all. The family and the Church. It is the work of a woman who sees the human race remaining for the most part as children; children who have to bring their sorrows to be healed, and who, if left to their own inclinations, make an untidy arrangement of things. A lot of children following their own tastes produce the bully. The only answer, therefore, is a historic hierarchy set over and above all the little nationalistic states. It is to this she turns in her writing and portrays a picture of the benign influence upon immediate human problems. All else is of little passing significance.

The spiritual idea of the Roman Catholic Communion is matriarchal, and its practical effect upon the lives of its communicants is matriarchal.

So in presenting a story deeply imbued with the passion of Catholicism, Kate O'Brien presented the supreme manifestation of matriarchy.

The Church gathers her children to her beneath the Image of the Eternal Mother. The Church remains through the ages unaware in her actual being, or rather unaffected by the temporary rebellions of Protestantism or agnosticism or atheism. She remains unchanged, yet peculiarly adaptable. She provides a wealth of emotional relief for her children. Her doors are always open for the sanctuary of prayer. Her discipline is stern and at the same time easy. She expects spirituality from her children yet at the same time leaves ample room for the inevitable human inconsistencies. With the celebration of the Mass she calls them to her; with confession and absolution she keeps them with her. Her breast is warm and comforting. Those that are weary with sin; those that are weary with much thinking; those that are weary with the confusion of human relationships—all may come to her. From the simplest mortal taking toddling steps through life to the complex mentality of a mind like Newman's, they come to the refuge of the ages, drawn back to the mothering arms. Always in front of them, she keeps the vision of the gentle Mother whose head is slightly bent, listening to the troubles of her children and ready to lay in their arms for a moment the Christ child who is her faith in the race.

This is the secret of the long history of the Roman Catholic Communion. For the human being never forgets the comfort of the mother's breast and is homesick through life. In pain, in worry, in joy and achievement, and in the fear of death, he remembers the mother's sheltering arms. He is no longer a baby, and the mother is gone, but the Church is there, waiting for that moment of nostalgia, ready to draw him to her. The figure at her shrines stands waiting too, with her gentle understanding eyes and her gentle bowed head. And the tired mortal comes to her as to his mother.

This is the supreme matriarchy.

Chapter X

HELPMEETS

Edith Wharton—Helen Grace Carlisle—Mary Borden
—May Sinclair—Margaret Goldsmith—I. A. R. Wylie
—Kay Boyle

THE HAUNTING ROMANTIC MYTH of femininity is the desire innate in the gentlewoman to lean against the protection of a man who loves her.

It is not a myth which haunts every woman. It never was. It is a myth not now in good standing with women. For this is not an age of gentlewomen. It is a period belonging to little girl pals and go-getters and matriarchs. The gentlewoman when she does appear among us is an archaic creature. The great lady whom the gentlewoman becomes with sufficient worldly experience is still more archaic. For the circumstance which produced the gentlewoman, and the worldly experience which developed her into a great lady, was a peculiar circumstance which is almost unknown now.

The gentlewoman is a woman who shrinks instinctively from elbowing her way either with men in emotional relationships, or with the world in careerist ventures, or with society in an effort to get the limelight. She is a creature who has evolved from generations of protected women. Her femininity has come from sexual, economic and social guardianship. She is usually the result of a long line of family and social caste, including economic ease. She comes to maturity believing in the chivalry of the man who will take her for himself. She trusts her own romantic feelings about him. Against the economic struggles she is helpless—a lamb among wolves. In society as it is now she is lost. For breeding has produced in her a tendency to understate herself, and faced with the vogue for overstatement she will be puzzled.

This is a woman doomed to suffer.

The helpmeet women are not all gentlewomen in actuality. But they are intrinsically, for they all have the qualities of the gentlewoman. They are self-effacing, faithful and, in the old sense of the word, womanly, which is to be interpreted now, unambitious for themselves.

The simple helpmeet type of woman can attach herself in her youth to almost any man who takes notice of her. She will so lose herself in her relationship with him that she is completely fulfilled emotionally. These are the simple good wives that we saw around us a generation or so ago, with an extraordinary talent for making their men comfortable, and an extraordinary contentment with a little house, a little affection and a little piece of a dream. These are the slipper-fetching kind of women, who always have the dinner on the table for their men, whose menus always consist of the things their men like, who dress to suit the circumstance and the taste of their men, who read what their men read, and attend their men's churches. They usually married comparatively simple men who themselves were content with a little comfort, a little affection and a little piece of a dream. They were men who found all their adventures in going daily to their businesses and returning nightly to their homes. They were men who never thought of looking speculatively at other women, and who rarely had the energy or the money or the temperamental adroitness to contemplate a double life.

Such women as these, married to men of their own kind, were fortunate.

Unfortunately there are not many of them now.

For the education of girls and the pressure of the economic system which puts off early marriage even among intrinsically simple folk tend to emphasize complexities in women, and produce in men a distaste for simplicity in women. To most men of the age the simple woman would not be a satisfying companion. Or so it seems. And women, accordingly, try very hard to be the reverse of simple.

The girl who, by some peculiar set of circumstance, grows up in this age to be a gentlewoman, is an image-worshiper.

She has been reared on a romance rather than upon a reality.

She has matured under an assumption about life which is no longer, if it were ever, actually a reliable assumption. That is, she has been taught to believe in the attractiveness of gentle femininity. She is in the grip of a legend concerning strong men. She is under some compulsion of an illusion about gracious human living.

This is the woman that life gets after.

She is never aware that her illusions are illusions; that her beliefs are beliefs; or that legends are only legendary.

Her biological nature uses her illusions and her beliefs and her legends to send her into experience. She never quite sees a circumstance as a circumstance, or a man as a man. She sees everything in imagery and in symbol.

This is the woman who goes eventually to the psychiatric physician.

For the first impact of reality upon her imagery is usually shattering to her nervous system. She finds her images will not absorb shock.

Yet this woman, if she can learn to ride her illusions and to use her image, can be the happiest of women.

If she has courage enough, and artistry enough in her femininity, she can use her imaginative bewitchment to create romance. It is a matter of learning to project her own romanticism upon the object of her emotion. And she can learn to sustain the romanticism in spite of any shakings and totterings from reality. Which is to say that such a woman, having had an illusion about a man, may continue to have it, for her own benefit and his, regardless of spots where it does not quite fit. She may so tend the romance that its magnetism will transfer itself to him, and gradually he will become, out of a strange spiritual gratitude to her for the romance, the prototype of her image. This is not romantic nonsense. It is sound racial and sexual truth. The man, in love, seeks the woman who rouses in him this sense of his own fitness for love. This is what makes the young girl seek her hero, and makes the young lad seek the girl who makes him feel like a hero. It is natural to natural youth. But it is the hardest thing in the world to sustain through mature experience.

The danger to the gentlewoman is that she is unprepared for reality. The first shock brings intense disillusionment. She has believed that romance lives of itself. Often as not with the first shock she lets it die. If she is married she rushes if she can to the divorce court. She cannot live without romance. She must be free to seek it again. Some of these women will go through several marriages and several divorces. Others of them go off men for the rest of their lives, and find romance in causes that are religious or social or artistic. Or they may make a cause of themselves. Women all around us run to dress-makers and cosmeticians and milliners and perfumers and shoe merchants and jewelers. They are making causes out of themselves. Sometimes it may look as if they were making frantic efforts to hold some man by their appearance. But that is usually a false trail. What they are really doing is transferring ardor from a man, or men, to themselves. The motivation is always mixed and baffling. The woman may think she is making herself fine for a man. But even if she is actually doing this, the emphasis is placed upon the wrong point. Desirability in women only affects men in relation to its reaction upon themselves. That is, a man looking at a woman and thinking he would like to possess her is motivated by a subtle reversion of interest in himself. She looks like a prize; therefore the man who has her must be quite a man. That is the story. And the sequel to the story is that it is in the power of a discerning woman to make a man feel himself to be quite a man in the possession of her without in herself being much of a prize. It is all a matter of projecting to him an image of himself as seen through her eyes. This was the eternal trick of the old-fash-

ioned woman, whether expressed in so simple a matter as bringing the lord his slippers, or in the still simple, though often
heroically self-controlled, business of looking at him as if he
were a big hero boy. It is not a technique to be laughed at.
In its varying ways it was an art, and the idea behind it was to
elevate the consciousness of the man concerning his own man-
hood by putting across to him an appreciation of grandeur in
him.

The new woman scoffs at the technique of the old-fashioned
woman. She lets the man fetch her slippers, or she calmly gets
her own, and expects him to get his own. It is not just determined independence. It is part of the new cult of fairness in
sexual relationships. She leaves the slipper fetching and the
baby blinks from the eyes to the clinging vines and the baby
vamps. She thinks that no man of any intelligence would be
taken in by it. At least not for long. She sets out to be a
decent companion who has put away forever all the shoddy
appeals of the slave-market and the harem. If the man shows
that he does not want to "stick around" she lets him go. She
will not descend to tricks to hold him.

This is where the modern scene is somewhat tragic for women.

Fairness is a lovely bright doctrine. But it presupposes
equality in love. And there is no such thing. Nature itself
says so. The biological load is upon women. To carry the load
at all it has to be of infinite importance to her. And further to
be at ease in her mind about the infinite biological importance,
she, if she is sensitive, has to surround it with romance and the
imagery of romance. Men get off lightly by the ordinance of
nature. Men, excepting only the Don Juan and the priest,
fundamentally care very little about women. Most of them
are gauche in their relationships with women. No image ever
becomes them. At least not naturally. Men, except in their
momentary mating urges, are interested in their particular game.
They like business; they like war; sometimes they like politics;
and sometimes they like golf. They do not really like love
affairs. They never quite see why women cannot take sex as sex

and let it be; yet somehow they never quite trust the woman who does. It reminds them of the courtesan. It is all emotionally confusing. Women want men to feel all the fine nuances of love. Yet they never quite trust the man who does. It reminds them of the Don Juan, and it implies many women. Women want to turn with absolute confidence to the man who is strong and who understands them. That is a hunger for the father—or the priest—yet such men are never playfellows for one woman. They belong to the world, are aware of responsibilities, and women find them in the end tantalizingly hard to get hold of for themselves in perpetuity. It is all emotionally confusing.

What comes out of the confusion is the general rule that the average man takes a romantic relationship awkwardly and with all the unfinished gaps in the technique of the amateur. If he gets himself related to a little girl pal everything is easy enough. The little girl pal takes him as he is and tries to be like him herself. If he gets himself somehow tied up to a go-getter things are still easier, for the go-getting woman is much too busy to bother about trying to change him, or worrying about why he is not different. If he gets into the designs of a matriarch things are even better. He is just what the matriarch expected him to be, and she can use him for her own plans. But if he by any chance is involved with a gentlewoman and a helpmeet it is too bad for both of them. She wants so much more from him than he can give, and if she can adjust at all after her first disillusionment, the process is likely to take some length of time, during which anything may happen. She may see another man; or he may see another woman.

This is the theme of many of the books coming from women of the helpmeet group.

The stories written by the helpmeet women are more thoroughly autobiographical than the stories from any other group of women writers. This is ordained by the intensely personal attitude of such women. They are invariably preoccupied by a completely feminine problem—which is the finding and holding of romance with one man, and pursuing it through the experience of marriage or its equivalent.

It is because they have been puzzled by their experience and confused by the fluctuations of emotion within marriage, or any sexual relationship, that in general the helpmeet women take to writing. They do not take to writing for itself. That is, they are not careerist women. They are women who, if all goes well with them in their sexual relationships, concentrate upon the career of the man to whom they are attached. Given a reasonably happy situation and a reasonably understanding man, the helpmeet woman is a valuable asset. She is the talented second-fiddle person, with a genius for background. She is a fine home-maker; she is never restive about not getting her due, and never restless concerning an outlet for herself. She is as a rule socially adept, a marvel of tact and good nature. In the simpler ranks of society she is a sweet woman, very easy to live with, and always ready to cooperate with her man in his plans and his enterprises. In the more complex ranks she is usually a woman of extraordinary social charm, and a very feminine person. But reasonably happy situations and reasonably happy sexual relationships are not just as prevalent as might be thought, particularly not for the gentlewoman, because of her tendency to undervalue herself and understate her qualities.

And so they take to writing.

Women of this type during the nineteenth century wrote sheer romance. Over and over again they wrote about the great theme of women—the approach to marriage. They treated it with glamour and romanticism. Writing in the twentieth century, even in its simplest form, has to be sustained by some semblance, at least, to reality, and the prevailing writing habit among the helpmeets is to begin where the early romanticists left off. Which is, for the most part, after the ceremony of marriage. The business of joint living engrosses them, and what they put down about it is not romance, but documentary evidence. It is as if they were easing something in themselves by taking a look at it outside of themselves and upon paper.

This preoccupation with the marriage theme is natural and is the outcome either of experience or the total lack of it with a corresponding complete desire for it.

The woman in the home, whether of average, of more than average, or of less than average circumstances, has the walls of her home closed in upon her, and she can never get away from the fact of marital success or failure, or the compromise between the two, which is the general experience of matrimony. She can never get away from the fact of it, unless she has an outside career which takes at least half of her nervous energy, in which case she is not exactly in the helpmeet group. Or unless she has an absorbing family passion, in which case she is matriarchal and not a helpmeet essentially. In the case of the go-getting woman and the matriarchal woman, the immediate success or failure of her own marriage is not of imperative painful importance. And this is the reason that the feminists have stressed through the nineteenth and twentieth centuries the need of some kind of labor for women as a safety-valve and to take the place of the industrialized household task. For women, the feminists say, who do not work technically become kept women, and it is bad for their nerves and consequently bad for the race. Romance the feminists assumed to be an intangible substance, and inevitably evanescent, and romanticism in itself no career for an intelligent woman. A woman, according to the feminists, must have a second line of defense. To live by emotion is not enough; to live for sexual giving and taking is dangerous. This may be as it may be. It is a subject upon which a lot might be said on both sides.

But a few women remain, the gentlewomen, who have not swallowed the feminist dogma wholly, and who insist, subconsciously if not consciously, upon the right of women to seek romance, and when they have found it, to make the nourishing and protecting of it a career in itself. It may be admitted that it is a career full of danger to the nerves. But so is any career that is absorbingly creative upon an intangible plane of being. The romanticists among women build over and over again, and spend their lives watching over their structure, caring for the weakening spots, filling them in, and covering them up, and if their structure should tumble, then building again upon the ruins. These are the women who abide by the old tradition of femininity. And some of them who cannot actually rebuild upon the ruins build again in fiction.

They have in this period every encouragement to build imaginatively in fiction, for the women's magazines are increasingly interested in stories about marriage, and the interest of the general woman reader remains still very much focused upon the marriage theme. In the language of the publication vernacular, there is a wide market for their wares.

EDITH WHARTON

Edith Wharton is the outstanding early example among the American women writers of this group.

It is the relation of the woman to the man in the helpmeet association which is her prevailing theme, though it would be easy to miss her creative point because of the meticulous care she has given to her settings. They are so thoroughly drawn in their detail that she might conceivably pass as a portraitist of eras and social classes rather than of people. There is something else to be noted at the beginning. She places her sympathy, though very delicately, with the men. This does not set her outside the helpmeet class of writer. On the contrary it encloses her completely within it. For the helpmeet is essentially a man's woman, and was so, particularly, during the period when Edith Wharton was reaching her creative maturity.

The key book in her case is *The Age of Innocence*.

It is a post-war book with a copyright date of 1920, but it might have been written in 1890, except that the man who is the hero is a twentieth-century man, in spite of the historical date setting of the story, which is the late nineteenth century. One woman, May, whom he marries, is the conventionalized presentation of femininity popular in the late nineteenth century in fashionable New York. The other woman, Ellen, whom he

really loves, and who renounces him in fine dramatic self-
sacrifice, is a portrait of the beginning of what we have always
called with no real discrimination the new woman. She was a
woman who violated the customs of her social group—an individualist.

The story winds in and out of fashionable life in New York
at the time, and the man wavers between the failure of his wife
to provide sustenance for all sides of his nature, and his attraction to Ellen, whom he thinks would give him all that he wanted
from a woman. He was a modern man in that he wanted more
than a woman's body, and more than her social technique, and
more than her good housekeeping. His wife, May, was an innocent girl who was allowed, or rather forced, to grow up in a state
resembling sleep-walking. Marriage was something that was
ordained. Once accomplished it remained fixed. She had no
idea at all that it demanded a subtle art, and that it was her job
to make it a success or a failure, or a dull compromise between
the two. Ellen was distinctly a man's woman, experienced, deft,
and interesting, knowing instinctively and also from acute observation of men when to come forward in invitation, and
when to retreat in order to allow men the pleasure of the chase.
In her own daily life she did exactly what she pleased. And this
gave her the sparkle of personality. May, in her daily life, did
what fashion and her group dictated. And this made her personality dull. It ruined her marriage because her husband was
a man who was drawn to art and thought, and even to independence of judgment. The maintaining of her superior status
in her group was more to May than the sustaining of the delicate relation between her husband and herself, and for this the
author sets out to punish her by allowing her gradually to
realize that the love of her husband has gone to Ellen. But
nevertheless May wins, and she does it by appealing to Ellen
when the crisis arrives and the husband is ready to elope.

It was not, however, her own wits that saved her situation,
but the chivalry of the "new woman."

The struggle of a man in attraction towards two different

women, the woman who follows the pack and the woman who refuses to, is the general theme of all the Wharton novels. Following her program, men seem invariably to marry the first type, because in their youth they are attracted to the conventionalized picture of the female, and fail to realize that such a woman loves the society in which she is placed rather than the man with whom she lives. Such a woman will bend all her powers towards keeping him within her circle. Later, and it is always too late, he feels the attraction of the other woman, and it is through this woman, who is the real helpmeet because of her adaptability to him, that he could reach his fulfilment.

In her early books Edith Wharton held with the note of sacrifice and renunciation. The "other woman" knew sorrow. The man always stuck to his bargain, and missed what he always would believe was his destiny. In her later books, of which *Hudson River Bracketed* is the key book, she has taken cognizance of the American attitude towards divorce, and allows her people to adjust their lives. But again she stands by her type, and shows the man coming into his own, and the woman living her life for him, altering its current to suit his needs, and spending all her energies making his life what it should be. For all its modern setting this second period of her writing is no more feminist than the first period was. The women she draws are women who would find no happiness for themselves in a career. Their well-being consists in surrendering themselves to men. They are women whose maternal passion is utterly bound up with their sexual passion in a composite emotion which goes out in its whole force to one man. This is the design for femininity against which the feminist movement was a revolt. It was precarious. But it was heroic and rather glorious. It was an attitude of an emotional gambler. The eggs were all in one basket; but what a basket it was! To take them out and put them safely away in places was to the romantic the action of the coward and an acknowledgment of lack of art in carrying the basket.

Edith Wharton is a romantic and a gentlewoman. Her

writing is the writing of a gentlewoman with generations of ease and cultivation behind her. She is in no way under the influence of the press. She writes leisurely as if the world were still a place where people had time to read beautifully balanced sentences and to contemplate exquisitely involved ideas. She writes as if readers still lingered over phrases and could savor pleasantly the backgrounds of the characters under discussion and watch patiently for signs of pulling away or pulling back into the hold of the background. She has style. In her short stories she moves over into the artiste group, and on the whole she has a distinct tendency in that direction, but in her novels she is pulled back into the helpmeet group because of their prevailing absorption in the old design of femininity. It is the gentlewoman's answer to the feminist program. In her eyes the careless dull woman of fashion is not very different from the careful, deliberately brilliant woman of career activity. Both of them are focused upon themselves. Both of them ignore the great need of men for the ministering woman, and sniff at the need if they admit it.

The sophisticate is also deeply interested in the relationship between men and women, but the distinguishing difference between her and the helpmeet gentlewoman lies in seriousness. The sophisticated writer is interested in her art for its own sake, and incidentally for its returns. The helpmeet writer believes that somehow this thing between men and women should get settled with dignity and happiness. The problems it meets sadden her. The same problems amuse the sophisticate. In some cases the line is thin-drawn and wavering. But is observable.

HELEN GRACE CARLISLE

Helen Grace Carlisle uses the experimental technique of the little girl pal and the go-getter. But she is not one of them. She is too completely concerned with her subject. Her stories plunge into movement, and the movement shunts around a little. The story itself flits with the unsubstantial ease of thoughts, and at times it is as incoherent as thought. She is uneasily emotional. Like all the young moderns, emotion sits on her heavily, and she gives the impression of trying to repulse it, and not being quite able to manage the repulsion. She writes in jerks which sometimes surprise the reader by suddenly sweeping out into an even narrative flow. She does not mean to be even in her narration. She prefers to be unevenly staccato, but what she is saying gets beyond her and the story takes its own course.

There is quite a bit of the sob-sister in Helen Grace Carlisle, and accordingly the work is not exactly that of the gentle-woman. That is, it is not the work of a gentlewoman of the old tradition, and yet it is not the work of the go-getter. It lies between the two. She has a peculiar subjectivity which is never found in the go-getter, and she has a peculiar starkness of emotion which is never found in the writing of the gentle-woman. It is as if the writer herself were quivering with pain, and was more intent upon finding relief for the pain in writing than upon rousing a sense of it in others. She would be thankful if she could feel no more pain, and never again see anguish, and she seems to be far more engrossed with the progress of that pain through lives than in telling an interesting story. Because of this interplay between a gentle shrinking from suffering and an almost masochistic attraction for it, her stories are definitely certain of a place in the School of Femininity. She is the self-pitying woman in person. And she is terribly sorry for all women. All the generations of women who have lamented in secret, or to the torture of their associates, because of the fate which made them women, seem to have risen from their shadows and forced themselves into the writing of this woman. They make quite an emotional army behind her.

Love as Helen Grace Carlisle presents it between men and women is a doomed thing.

Her heroines rush after it, and clutch it and are themselves doomed. Or rather, they rush after something that looks like love, and having clutched it to them, find that it is not love. Or if by some miracle it does turn out to be love, there is still tragedy. The woman who is the central figure in her story,

The Wife, is a woman who after sad experience with something
that she thought was love, finally comes upon the real thing.
It is enduring and beautiful. She should be happy. But she
develops tuberculosis. Before the germ gets her completely
under, she has had time to think about the engrossing passion
that love is to a woman, and to do some further thinking about
the balance between love and a career in a normal woman's experience. It is these thoughts of the heroine that make the
book valuable in the School of Femininity.

She had loved three men. Two of them disappointed her. She
had built a career for herself out of her disillusionment and in
compensation. She had met success. But she had never learned
to add and subtract her emotional losses and gains. She hated
erotic failure. The sense of having failed in love twice cor-
roded within her. No wonder she got a germ. She hated the
hold of eroticism upon women. She struggled with it in herself,
and went down again and again in spite of her struggles, and in
spite of the compensatory success. Then she met the perfect
love and lived with a man in legal marriage and thought it
would bring peace to her. But she found there was a great
price to be paid for that peace. She no longer cared about success. She became a woman whose time was given to ordering
her home. It had to be. To be a good wife she had to be a
helpmeet. She had to live the man's life. He could not live
hers. And no joint life was possible. Seeing to his comfort,
entertaining his guests, furthering his career interests through
adequate social activity, interfered with the progress of her own
work. And she was finding to her amazement that it was not
disturbing her that this should be so. She thought about all
the dogmas of feminism. Her husband was no demanding
egotist. He was proud of her work, which was in the sphere
of art. He wanted her to continue. It was all within herself.
She was learning that the erotically satisfied and emotionally
happy woman did no work of her own. She lived for the man.
She neglected the second line of defense. She felt no need of it.
She set down no dogmatic conclusion, but she led her own

thoughts quietly to face the assumption that success to a woman is never more than the answer to a need for compensation, and that all career efforts are compensatory in their motivation. In other words, she suggests that women have to be driven to achievement by tragedy, that the happy woman does nothing, that her whole purpose is fulfilled when she lives happily with a man.

Helen Grace Carlisle is not saying anything new.

But that she does say it now indicates a turn in the feminist thinking. Maybe the ardent feminists would be right to resist such suggestions and to label them as counter-feminism and counter-evolution and highly dangerous doctrine for women to be reading at this period of their development.

The point they—the feminists—might make is this: That it is only in books that the perfect romance is met, and therefore only in books is it safe for women to lay down their second line of defense. The heroine in *The Wife*, the feminists might very well say, was tired not because of the terrific effort she had made to create and sustain her second line of defense, but because of the germs latent in her system. She failed to carry through a joint working life with her husband, not because it could not be done, but because she was herself sickening with infection. She was appalled, not by the ravages of emotion within a woman, but really by her own growing weakness. And further, the feminists might say the perfect romance with the husband had not lasted long enough even at the end of the story to be submitted as evidence. There remained a possibility that the heroine might very well need her second line of defense.

The feminists would say emphatically that it is during the inertia which happiness does admittedly bring for a time to women—even waiving aside possible latent germs—that women should prepare themselves for what may come after. Work is their great emotional insurance. Not compensation. That the man's life absorbs the woman's life is a transitory social thing which is likely to pass as time passes, and women get used to the idea of work for itself.

This is the fundamental argument of the feminist from Mary Wollstonecraft down—that through not having work to do in the world women have placed undue importance upon romance and their personal happiness, and that this left them defenseless. The whole program of the feminist movement has been to build for women slowly and carefully a place of their own in the social structure which does not depend upon their permanent or momentary attachment to men. This is what has made the feminist cult a warrior's creed, and the movement itself a crusade.

It sounds as if it were intensely practical. It is in fact essentially idealistic.

The anti-feminist view, such as that presented by Helen Grace Carlisle, is a pacifist's creed. It sounds as if it were idealistic. It is essentially practical.

Its doctrine is this—that the feminist argument is great and splendid. It looks as if it were the emotional salvation of women. But it does not happen to be so. For the very simple reason that women are too naturally practical to be inwardly content with a substitute, or an insurance, and that in concentrating upon the building of a second line of defense too much energy is taken from the protection of the first line of defense. Women, the anti-feminist suggests, might just as well admit that once the enemy—fate—and the psychology of fate—gets through their first line the struggle is over and defeat is accomplished. Concentration upon the second defense of work emphasizes the second line too much, and develops in women a psychological expectation of failure and defeat in the first line. The anti-feminist believes that the trouble has not come from the lack of sufficient work defense, but from lack of sufficient attention to the feminine nature. Girls should be taught from the beginning all about their own femininity, and as much about masculinity as can be assimilated by the female. Traditional sexual judgment should be handed down. Traditional sexual knowledge should be preserved and some of the principles that there must be somewhere concerning mating should be considered and disseminated. There would not then be nearly so inevitable a likelihood of the enemy—erotic disappointment—getting in to a woman's experience. As we concentrate upon the second line we pay dangerously little attention to the important first line, and its weakness is what makes the retreat to the second line almost general.

All this revolves around the anti-feminist idea that no woman is really happy when driven back to her second line. She still thinks about the first line.

Helen Grace Carlisle does not say all this. But it is implied in all that she has written. The women in all her books are women who have suffered through love, or what appeared to be love. They are most of them emotional experimentalists, forcing themselves to have courage to experiment, but not experimenting with any instinctive taste for experiment. Back of all her writing is pity for women. She believes that fate is set against them. Through all her work there is a sound tone of the sexual awareness of women—the undertone of the need in every woman for her mate. Nothing else matters very much to women. Yet nothing very much can be done about it. Women are by their eroticism made helpless. What she never seems to realize, for certainly she never suggests it, is that men also may be left defenseless. Or would be had they not adequately equipped themselves with many back lines of defense in business and sports. How little do women know about the erotic disappointments of men. They do not talk so much. It is just possible that many a man ravages his nervous system through too persistent dealing with business, or plays too hard at some sport, or philanders, out of disappointment. It may be that the very insistence of the man upon a casual attitude towards all *amour* is a defense. For the man is quite unable to create an illusion in romance. It is the art of the woman, and if the woman he takes into his life knows nothing of the art, there is nothing he can do.

MARY BORDEN

Mary Borden is one of the very few women writers who see romance in relation to both a man and a woman.

Love as she wrote about it in *Flamingo* is the rarest thing.

She almost seems to believe that two souls come forth from the essential creative substance together, but get lost, and have to find each other. Her lovers in *Flamingo* only meet for a short while at the end of the book. They have met in their childhood. And a few times the man saw the woman in various places in Europe, but was never able to speak to her. In the story he was the active seeking soul. By some mysterious process his spirit followed hers and he saw many things as she would see them. He was an American architect, and she was an Englishwoman married to a cabinet minister. He built a house in the United States which was the replica of her house, which he had never seen actually with his eyes. Without her he was a pitiful being, entirely lost and not knowing what was the matter with him. His nerves were the nerves of a genius, unsteady and painful. Life was a desperate business to him, except when he could lose himself in the planning of great new buildings or in wild orgies of terrible dissipation. He married a rich young woman who was as cold as she was wealthy. The Englishwoman also found life a desperate business, but she had steadier nerves. She went about her duty of being the wife of an eminent man, and was bored. She also did not know what was the matter with her. Life that should have been interesting was flat and tasteless. The man she married was too strong really to need her. God had made her a strong woman, and she needed to be with a man who was not so strong. In her married life there was no complement. It was a case of two positive natures being put together and making a negative. Her husband was sent by his government to negotiate with the government of the United States. At the end of their stay they met the architect, and were guests in the house he had created so mysteriously to be like her house in England.

It is a story of tragedy. Dark forces play against the love that could have been between these two. Everything happens to prevent their meeting. All the lines get crossed. But when recognition does come it is no use. The woman was too bound to her duty to put it aside. The architect threw himself off his own great skyscraper as her ship was leaving the shores of the United States. It was no use. All his upward reach in art had been an attempt to assuage the loneliness and the hunger of his spirit. He goes to death, and the woman goes back to her routine life. She was dead too.

Flamingo is a book which will live entirely outside of its part in the School of Femininity. It is a magnificent interpretation of New York and its life as felt through the sensitivity of the Englishwoman. A great dashing, daring, heroic city built up out of the courageous new vision of people who have come to a new world to live again. A city of Continental sophistication balanced by a remainder of Puritanism, and balanced again by the sheer primitiveness of the negro population, and balanced yet again by an Oriental blend of astuteness and mysticism in the Jew, and balanced yet again by the elemental responsiveness of the Irish. A city the like of which the world has never seen before. Strains as old as the world in its blood blended together in one new consciousness of life. Against this background the old, old tragedy of love plays itself out in people who die because they cannot say, "This is what means most."

Mary Borden's interpretation of attraction is a purely spiritual one. It is a matter of secret chemistry. It is as if she were putting her finger gently upon a substance as yet entirely unguessed at by all the romanticists. Love as she treats it is something that has little to do with the body, except as the body by its differentiation between male and female admits that each by itself is unfinished. In each of the two marriages of the story she shows people fumbling to find the cause of their unhappiness, and it remaining a simple thing—the wrong halves have got together and do not make harmony. She handles it almost breathlessly, as if she were before a deep faith of her own.

Such a faith about the meaning of the sexes to each other sets aside entirely all the art of femininity in love, and all the preaching of the feminists upon equality. There can be no point to all the art a woman may lay at the feet of her own experience with sex, and there can be no point whatever in all a woman's cry for freedom, if the whole of life is a search for the one other half of one's being. No art can conceal the mistaken placing together of two halves; no freedom to express oneself in a career of one's own can atone to the lonely spirit for its loneliness. This belief, which is the ultimate romanticism, is so simple as to reduce most thinkers upon the manifestations of eroticism to quiet amusement. It is the instinctive belief, they teach us, of first love. The need of a man for a woman and the need of a woman for a man are so deep they create of themselves an illusion of permanency. The lover cannot face any idea of existence without the loved one. Nor can the lover face any compromise or any substitution. The body with its constant sad change tells about impermanency, and out of longing that there should be some permanency the spirit makes its own myth. It is a gesture of defiance and a gesture of faith. So love legends arise concerning the attraction of spirit for spirit, of which the sad changing body is only a symbol. First love and last love. Spring love and autumn love. Both of these partake of the legendary quality. Other loves are more reasonable. The love written down by Mary Borden in *Flamingo* is autumn love; the man and the woman are neither of them young. They have achieved all they can achieve. They have tasted the young half-flavored fruits of spring, and they have seen the fruits go bad under the hot sun of summer. They have come to the last fruits of the autumn, and these, with their peculiar autumnal richness, do feed more than the body, because of the knowledge that goes with each taste of the long, long winter that is ahead.

Flamingo is, so far as the School of Femininity goes, the peak of the helpmeet philosophy of love. These were two who stood in absolute need of each other. The career of the man impinged even upon the ether surrounding the woman, and caught its vibratory nature. It is a drama of the subconscious minds of the two as they met entirely unknown to their ordinary consciousness. The woman gave subconsciously to his life work, though all she was aware of was an innate attraction to the engineering of new things, to steel and to creation with steel. When she came to the great city of steel she felt its strange pulling upon all her nerve centers. She saw his great buildings and she asked, "Who did them?" This was a woman whose conscious life was spent in political doings and who took it as if she were walking in her sleep.

The story thus in its way is the fulfilment of the dream that is in the heart of every helpmeet woman—that somewhere there is a man who has need of her, not just for love, but for the making of him, and that he would know that need, and ask of her all that she has in her to give him. This for the helpmeet woman is supreme happiness. And without it she goes unfulfilled. Of herself she can do nothing. No career of her own has any power over her. It never seems of any importance. She is the helping, mating woman, but with that helping and that mating she must have the understanding of the man concerning what it all is.

Flamingo is a bruised story. It is tragedy. As well it might be, inasmuch as the story of any helpmeet woman is often as not a bruised story. For the history of sex is somehow a general history of failure, with the wrong woman getting in with the wrong man. It is particularly marked in the cases of helpmeet women of the more sensitive type. We see them all around us. And we see men all around us needing the helpmeet women, and with perversity walking into marriage that chemically is not suitable.

MAY SINCLAIR

This is the theme that haunts May Sinclair. If we were to judge society by her stories we would conclude that it is made up of ugly marital mistakes. Her fiction world is a world of suffering men and women, and invariably her sympathy lies with love that is illegal love. She goes into all its heroic details.

There is nobody so frank as a woman who has decided to be frank, and nobody so sexual as a woman who has decided to be sexual. May Sinclair is baldly frank and heavily sexual.

She seems to be under the impression that the whole subject of the sexual relations of men and women needs to be treated in fiction. And treated quite apart from romance. Certain men are attracted to certain women. Certain women feel they must have certain men. It is all a matter of glandular tastes. The men are invariably held in holy wedlock with women they no longer crave. There is no tragedy about it. They are all phlegmatic people who admit things to be as they are, and they are always ready to talk it over frankly with the one for whom they no longer have a craving. It is a world of the sexually "big and free." Probably it is on the whole a healthy world, and much saner than the sophisticated hide-and-seek of most of the extra-sexual arrangements. But it seems quite naïve as it reads in fiction. Or maybe it is just the Utopian picture painted by a woman who believes that hard and fast matrimony as related to sexual attraction is in itself an absurd arrangement. And a good deal of a standing lie. Much better then to talk it out. Which is possibly quite true among people who are sexual rather than emotional. The subject is infinitely more involved than one would gather from reading Miss Sinclair, though it has to be admitted that she is aware of the involved situation in *Arnold Waterlow*.

Arnold Waterlow is a man who marries a woman who wants a career of her own. The career is musical and includes leaving the husband and going off with another musician. The husband meets a quiet helpmeet woman and lives openly with her, always making it clear to her that if ever his wife should need him and return he will take her back. The wife does return, broken and disappointed, and the helpmeet woman, feeling that life for her is quite over, lets herself die with the first germ she encounters. This is unquestionably a fiction slap from the helpmeet "other" woman, who while she submits to the dictum of the man, resents the "tyranny of the weak over the strong," and expresses the resentment in death.

In *Anne Severn and the Fieldings,* she again takes up the saga of the "other woman." She fills in a definite course of attraction. The heroine of the story had always been in love with the man. But she was not able successfully to put her love across to him until he had married and been unhappy. She, in the meantime, had had no men at all in her life, but had looked after his brother in such a way as to make it appear that she was the mistress of the brother. She cared nothing about the world. She had missed the only thing that mattered to her, and she finds a perverted kind of pleasure in being a martyr in the doing of duty to his family. Recognition follows, and she becomes the secret mistress of the man she loves. Though she accepts the half-loaf, she is emotionally in a state of tension. For she is not the courtesan type, and cannot adjust easily to the relationship. Nature had made her a helpmeet woman.

May Sinclair writes primarily as a sexual rebel. There is something Whitmanesque about her presentation of sexuality in women. Underneath her studies of women held in emotional bondage to an image stimulated by one man lies a suggestion of restrained pity. They can so rarely find that image in a man who can be married to them. And they must have it. She looks upon the surface to be making quite a fiction objection to the bonds of matrimony, because her heroines find love outside of it. That might be true to an extent, but it is a subordinate point. What really bothers her is the image-making of the truly helpmeet woman. This, and not marriage conditions, is what drives the women into tragedies. All of them would have been comfortable socially as well as psychologically had they been able to banish their image fixations.

May Sinclair is an English writer who matured before the war. Her sexual rebellion therefore came from something that had nothing to do with the problem which has since arisen for a whole generation of women—the terrific numerical majority of women over men. This problem has in itself altered the whole sexual point of view of thousands upon thousands of women. They, if they are normal, must have what is called on the screen and in polite conversation love. They take it wherever they can find it, and manage to keep it. The great to-do of the triangle has therefore smoldered down.

The altered situation brought about through the war has produced in the women who were left unmarried a fatalistic attitude more or less resembling in its intrinsic emotional essentials the attitude of the Oriental woman about sharing a man. It is not exactly the harem mind, for the reason that women have work and their place in a plan of things which includes them. It is also not altogether the harem philosophy in that while a woman may get herself a man without the benefit of the law, she cannot produce children casually without the benefit of the law, though there was immediately after the war a body of thought among women which was inclined to accept the right to go into motherhood as the last of the women's rights to be demanded. This, however, did not grow in strength. It was nipped by the still newer current of thought concerning the right of children to normal experience including both parents, and by the discoveries of the Freudian school of psychotherapy in relation to the damaging effects of too concentrated mother-interest and mother-emotion upon children.

This situation created by the war has not produced a generation of courtesan women. The courtesan is a woman of highly specialized temperament. It has rather produced a generation of respectable secondary wives—women who in their peculiar way augment in a man's life the ways of his wife. These are women who in themselves as a rule are helpmeet one-man women, who out of the necessity of the period accept the half-loaf, and make it into something reasonably satisfying to them. It looks upon the surface to be a gala period for such men as were left from the war. Which is not always true, inasmuch as men having for the most part had wives, look for the courtesan in other women, and find themselves involved with the secondary wife with much emotional inconvenience. What they do not know is that the courtesan is as rare as an orchid, the product of an exotic temperament, and many women willing to enter a liaison are totally unequipped temperamentally for the rôle.

This is the plaint behind such writing as May Sinclair's. On the outside she seems to be lamenting the tight bands of matrimony. She treats the baffling human situation of two people tied together, with character developing in unexpected ways, and the evanescent thing which drew them together vanishing, but the social bond remaining. It strikes her as socially an anachronism, as well as being devitalizing to the nervous organism of the people involved. But in the main the problem she treats comes down to the emotionalism of the outsider who approaches and forms a triangle, and who invariably cannot adjust to the social situation. She leaves it as it stands.

MARGARET GOLDSMITH

A younger woman, Margaret Goldsmith, in a story, *Belated Adventure,* pulls it very much away from where it stands.

Belated Adventure is the study of a woman who married a man and found it impossible to be a helpmeet to him except by allowing him to get his amount of sexual adventure apart from her.

She was a modern young woman who had had her own affairs. She earned her living. She was a successful lawyer. When she married she was in the mood to settle down. The man, she thought, was one with whom she could join her life on all its planes. She found that he had been unnaturally repressed, and the story goes into a frank discussion of their relationship. This book is another case of the frankness of women when they do become frank. A case history from the records of a psychoanalyst is treated to fiction-handling with all its nervous details. It is as much as anything a study of repression. The man wrecked the marriage through his prolonged virginity. That is made very plain, and this in itself is a long step from the early books; or even from the tenets of the early feminist program, which insisted theoretically upon as high a standard of absolute purity—or inexperience—from men as from women. The repression is followed out to its psychological conclusion. The man, having been impotent with his wife, had, when at last he got himself into condition, to prove his power with women by other affairs. The wife, being an experienced woman, and knowing her Freud, understood him, and permitted it, or at least made no fuss about it. But he was driven by his utter need of bolstering his male vanity to taking a woman who was closer to her than a sister. This was a shock to the wife. All her knowledge could not support her through the surrender of her best woman friend. The two involved considered they had entered into an immortal love affair, but the reader, along with the wife, sees that it is part of the course of a repression, and accepts it fatalistically, though with sorrow, as the wife did.

This is probably the most stark presentation of the man and woman presented in the whole of the modern School of Femininity. It is a long pull away from former presentations of the theme. It is treated entirely apart from the superimposed moral point of view concerning sex and its amplifications. There is no aggrieved wife, wrapping herself round with resentment. There are no heroics on her part, and none that are obvious on his because she came to him not a virgin. The situations are built up with sound psychiatric appreciation of their underlying causes. There is no sentimentalizing about restraint and renunciation. There is no solution offered, except the implied idea that the more men and women know of sex and its manifestations and its expression, the less likely are there to be situations such as this one turned out to be. When in the early part of the story the woman consulted an eminent physician, he chided her for walking into a marriage blindfolded. He said that in this period there was no excuse for such biological stupidity. It was taking too big a chance.

If you put this book against a nineteenth-century book by any woman, a great writer or one of the lesser writers, you see instantly the distance that has been traveled by women. You do not even need to go back to the nineteenth century. It is enough almost to take any pre-war novel. Even such rebels as May Sinclair would never have considered such a problem. The early rebels thought that they had accomplished a shocking revolution in thought when they got as far as writing it down that men and women had been known to be unhappy in marriage, and to find attraction in others. They treated it as if it were something quite beyond control, and they progressed far enough when they threw overboard the hypocrisy and the "yapping" about love outside of legality. What brought men and women together was a mysterious bond of attraction impossible to analyze.

Belated Adventure presents the bond as being entirely sexual. This, according to the story, is the neglected center of romantic interest. According to its assumptions the business of finding a suitable helpmeet is involved and baffling in its sexual connotations. There must be absolute union and a blending of forces in the biological nature. All else—intellectual companionship, temperamental understanding, cultural tastes in common—fade back into relative unimportance beside the great primal point of sexual exchange of magnetism. This new attitude towards the subject admits the triangle, but admits it casually. Life is not a neatly arranged business. It is a series of mistakes through which the individual may grow, or be frustrated, exactly as he or she allows himself or herself to function. It follows that in the matter of sex one's judgment is wavering, especially in youth. The older code forced human beings to abide by the judgment upon which one gambled most heavily and to the extent of making public vows. The newer code is still in the making. It is because it is in the making that all these books from women which are documentary books are so interesting. They are contributions towards some relative final solution. They state plainly their experience, and this experience marks certain sign-posts upon the road.

The helpmeet woman, however, in general holds back from the modern sexual program. She is afraid, as well she might be.

The normal woman brings to her marriage the shadowy suggestion of her mother and her grandmother and her great-grandmother that the moral code imposed upon sex was necessary to
keep men in reasonable social control—that without it they
would be lawless sexually and socially irresponsible. The
woman and her children must be protected, and any loosening
of the code, even if she should come to the place of wanting it
for herself, would boomerang upon her and upon all women—
that the only gainers from it would ultimately be men. This is
an economic picture, of course, and psychological to the extent
of estimating the emotions of women as being social rather than
sexual.

It is based upon the idea that a woman prefers, when she has
to choose, her place in the matrimonial sun safe and secure, for
the sake of her standing among her associates, and for the sake
of her children, to sexual fulfilment. It is founded upon the
belief that a woman is happier when she is thought well of in
comfortable society than she is with purely sexual joy in relationship with the man who might suit her better than all other
men. Sex, according to this doctrine, was not meant to mean
very much to women. A woman when she marries accepts it
more or less graciously, and never allows herself to wonder if
she has got from her man all there is to it. The man, on the
other hand, continually wonders if he has done the best he
could for himself. He is curious, if nothing else, and this leads
him to experiment.

The new psychiatric thinking laid bare the information gathered through the investigation of the minds of thousands upon
thousands of unhappy women, that sex does mean a lot to
woman, and that when it does not it is the result of frigidity
which has a cause. This was heady information. It made
women wonder. But in the main women are restrained by their
inherited fear that any change that might be made in the code
would give the plums to men. All around us now we see women
who are married wanting to step out. They play with the idea

flirtatiously, but they rarely go very far because they hesitate about the reaction upon the men who provide for them.

It is a thoroughly involved subject. It is so involved it is labyrinthian. Once you get into it you cannot find your way out of it.

So we find many of the helpmeet writers sedulously leaving it alone.

I. A. R. WYLIE

So much so that a writer like I. A. R. Wylie thinks that the sex element can be left out of the man-woman relation. Her book, *The Silver Virgin*, was the story of a soldier who was totally incapacitated through injury in the war for sexual experience. The girl who married him remained with him, thinking she could accept his tragedy as her tragedy too, but as time went on she found herself attracted to another man. She went to live with him. Then she found that despite sexual satisfaction her imagination was living with her husband. It was he whom she loved. He had meanwhile retreated to a lonely place to think the problem through, and to get himself a philosophy which would help him. The story from then on becomes a mystical, half-poetic story of two torn human spirits arriving in the secret world of spiritual peace. The woman returns to her husband carrying the child of the other man, and the husband tells her that inasmuch as it is her child it is also his, and that he will rear it as his own.

In all the work of I. A. R. Wylie there is a spiritual fabric. Life to her is not biological but implicitly of the spirit. Her lovers in *The Silver Virgin* draw themselves beyond the hold of the body. It is life precipitated a few years ahead of the inevitable tearing out of the spirit from the body. Their earthly experience therefore resolves itself into a preparation for the life of the spirit which comes after death. Her lovers yearn for each other in spirit, as the dead yearn for the living, and the soon to die.

They learn to accept their peculiar fate in love. They learn more than acceptance. They assume an attitude of spiritual

election which is far deeper than resignation. They realize in
their flesh that the flesh is a veil over spiritual reality. And
having realized this the flesh has no more part in love.

This is the ultimate teaching of religion, and is what lies behind the injunction of celibacy which the Church of Rome lays
upon its priests and nuns. It is what is behind all the occult
laws which stress continence for the purpose of heightening the
psychic powers.

The Silver Virgin is the most spiritual work of an English
woman whose work maintains throughout a spiritual content,
and a technical purity, and at the same time is of extraordinary
intellectuality. Yet for all that it is definitely popular. I. A. R.
Wylie appears in many magazines with short stories, serials and
articles. She is an excellent reporter of current national situations. She has courage; she has insight and the power to portray what she has seen. Her writing substance is always full of
thought, and she has writing style. There is never any degree
of light-heartedness in her productions. She is profoundly serious. She wants unmistakably to give the best she has in her for
the information of and the restitution of spirituality among her
readers. There is relatively little emotion in her work. What
emotion there is remains intellectualized and spiritualized. She
is a blend of the helpmeet and the priestess, but more of the
helpmeet than the priestess by reason of her application of spirituality to definitely individualized problems and also by reason
of her consistent refusal to mold her writing into any kind of
teaching.

The Silver Virgin seems to be the ultimate word of the helpmeet woman upon the love relationship of a man and a woman.
It simply lifts the great problem of sex up to a sublimated plane
of soul fulfilment.

A man and a woman, it implies, do not find themselves drawn
together because they are variously equipped with organs which
in themselves need complementing. There is something else.
There is an attraction of soul for soul, and the need of a soul
for a particular other soul which may take the body incidentally

in its stride of fulfilment, but at the same time may dispense with the body. The soul comes to its earthly experience alone and seeking that other soul. It goes out of its earthly experience blessed by life if it has found that other, to another experience which is likely to include the soul of the loved one in still another substance of living. The story stresses the inward need. It does not ignore the sexual hunger. The woman feels it acutely, and has to deal with it in herself. She has to go through the humiliation of surrender to it, and to come back up out of her humiliation. She finds her loved one waiting, understanding, ready to forgive, ready to comprehend, ready to accept the burden of her mistake. This experience, the story suggests, can only be possible to such mortals as are in the spiritual mood to put themselves under the discipline of religion. For only the faith of the mystic can see them through their crisis while still habilitated by the flesh. This is in the mystical sense the ultimate meaning of marriage, and its outward semblance is only the crude symbol of the reality.

Yet it is not the ultimate meaning of marriage, nor is it the ultimate word of the helpmeet woman concerning the relation of love between a man and a woman.

It is a story that has come out of the deep fear of helpmeet women that love may not last. Because the romance of love is so fragile and wavering, she lifts it up into the realm of the spirit. There presumably it stays put.

KAY BOYLE

The ultimate meaning was put into a little story by an Irish-American girl who allowed no fear of impermanency to distract her. The girl is Kay Boyle, and the story is called *The Year Before Last*.

Kay Boyle emerged from distinctly arty small stories which were highly stylized fiction protests and belonged with the writing of the little girl pals. But *The Year Before Last* is one of the sweetest romances ever written. It is written as if it were created out of the amazement of the little girl pal at finding that love really is, and changing her with the blessed wand of a good spirit into a loving helpmeet woman.

The love is told as music is told. The Celtic ancestry of Kay Boyle pulled at her until the story came through like a tale out of Irish romance. The prose sings. It is a delicate melancholy story of a love that was not long for this world, as the Irish say, and for which the world was well given up. Before the lovers lies parting. Death is coming for the boy. Around it lies poverty. Neither the boy nor the girl has money. Behind lies trouble. The girl has sacrificed her own marriage for this love. It rests a moment in our hands, a lovely intangible bit of feeling set down in the passion of a man and a woman for each other. The world outside does not exist. Neither does the death that is coming, nor the failure behind, nor the difficulties that are present. Everything is taken up in the love. The sick man is a poet and the woman is his audience and his muse and his mother. There is very little actual body to the story. It lives through its feeling. There is no plot at all, and nothing in it that could be retold upon the screen, and hardly a bit of it to be put into a synopsis. It is a story that successfully eludes the reviewer's comment. It belongs to love, and the world of love is a silent world that lives for itself and does not lend itself to other worlds. By subtle use of suggestion and atmosphere set down in little half-phrases Kay Boyle presents two who were made into one for a while by the gentleness of great feeling. It is a story of the hours that are more to lovers than the years that roll up and are gone.

It is a story told with the immortal half-gestures of a woman in love. A woman busy and at peace with her task of human cherishing. She keeps her dear man in her heart with the passionate tenderness of Irish women towards their men and their children. In its little-girlish nonchalance about a situation called sin, in its modern use of conversational technique, the story gets itself told as a new kind of story. Yet it is very old. As old as poetry. Underneath it has the singing tone which the Irish can never keep out of their prose when love sends them to writing. And underneath too lies the gallantry of the Irish in love. What if the love be short, and what if it be hard? Maybe it might have happened the year before last, and this is now another year, and before it went still other years, but to the girl it would always remain the one love when she knew what love could do to a woman. For nothing else mattered to her then but the sweetness of giving. A story told in the dark, a hand put out in the dark, an hour of realization, a moment of reconciliation with life, and all this known only to those who for a little while had been together.

This is love told with courage as well as sweetness. With no attempt to build a defense. And with no attempt to make it comfortable. Love taken just as it is. Without past or future. Without any laws set up to protect it, and with no need whatever to do anything to honor it. And a woman completely fulfilled. To help and to meet, and to cover it at the end with romance.

CHAPTER XI

SOPHISTICATED LADIES

Ellen Glasgow—Mazo de la Roche—Margaret Kennedy—E. H. Young—E. M. Delafield—"Elizabeth"—Victoria Sackville-West

THE SOPHISTICATED LADY IS feminine but with reservations. The reservations have to do with her emotions. These she contains cleverly within her technique. She is engaged always with the picture she presents of herself.

She goes back in her history, whether she chooses to make the admission or not, to the ancient courtesans. She uses, whether she knows it or not, the technique of the trained courtesan, which was a technique of the concealment of the emotions and of the presentation of an art of the senses.

The Greeks at the height of their culture divided women arbitrarily into three groups: the woman of the home, the hetæræ, and the priestesses. Below these, of course, there were women of the slave class, but they, like the men of the same class, had little or nothing to do with the program of life in Greece. From the women of the home the Greek civilization expected nothing but child-bearing. No Greek was simple enough to demand scintillating mental companionship from a woman engrossed in the business of carrying and rearing children. So the hetæræ were ordained. They were courtesans of a particularly cultivated type. The men turned to them, not only for the pleasure of their senses, but also for the exchange of intellectual ideas. The place of a great woman among the hetæræ was a gathering place for great men. She was skilled in the art of drawing men out. She let them talk; she listened; she made herself a person; occasionally she herself talked; she made intimacy a gracious thing. From her the Greeks expected beauty and culture and charm.

The priestess was still another kind of woman, and was ordained out of the acknowledgment of the presence in women of a mysterious intuitive sense. This was developed through a special kind of living, and to the priestesses men turned when they were in doubt about grave issues.

We do not know how it was decided to which group a woman belonged, or if the decision lay with herself, with her family, with society, or by an accident of fate. It is likely that among them, in spite of all their wisdom, there were many women in the home who had the tastes of the hetæræ, and many hetæræ who would have been more fully contented had they been given to the race. We know almost nothing about the priestesses except that they did exist, and what led a girl into the order we cannot say with any accuracy. It may also have been that there were women who, despite the arbitrary division among them, were in themselves blends of all three temperaments, and were therefore only partly happy in the lot of their lives. This division of women forced them to play certain parts all through their experience, so far as outward manifestation was concerned. What they thought about it secretly is not known. But taken on the whole, it was possibly a simpler arrangement, and much easier to fulfil than the modern version of womanhood, which demands of the normal woman often much more than she can give. The woman of to-day, if she has a thoroughly full life, finds herself obliged to be wife, mother, hetæra, priestess, and in some cases a slave also. It is no easy rôle. It calls for magnificent vitality of body and mind, as well as imagination and skill in technique.

The hetæra, we may assume, was usually beautiful, certainly in the shape of her body, if not in her face. There was no point in a plain woman or a badly-formed woman entering the ranks. The legendary hetæra was always remarkably beautiful, or managed through her ability with backgrounds and the foreground of her own personality, to present the impression of ex-

traordinary charm. To carry on with her profession successfully she had to make the most of her original endowment. She
had to make her audience feel some enchantment in her presence.
And to do this she had to have a glamorous conception of herself, which is to say she had to tend an image of herself.

The idea behind the hetæræ found another expression in
France at the height of the Renaissance and post-Renaissance
monarchs.

Society gathered itself about a few brilliant women who maintained salons. These women were not courtesans professionally.
They were great ladies, but they took up the essential idea of
the hetæræ. They provided places to which the illustrious men
of the time might come and talk. The salonnière was the ultimate hostess. She had to have personal magnetism; she had to
have a definite amount of wealth; she had to be cultivated; she
had to be a diplomat. She studied her settings; she worked
upon her own personality; she knew her way through the ideas
of her time, and also through social standings. She taught herself to give men the impetus to talk. She knew when to put a
word in herself, and when it was wiser to listen. She became
an adept at getting the right people together. She developed
finesse in handling her social crowd. And what relations of intimacy she might enter into with men were distinctly her own
business.

With the famous mistresses of the French Kings we have
women who used all their talents to further themselves into
power. Some of them rose, after the traditional manner of the
courtesans, man by man until they reached the first man of the
realm, and then they focused all their talents into the exacting
necessity of holding what they had achieved. They became
profound entertainers of men. Some of them combined the
talents of the hetæræ and the priestesses. They amused their
Kings; they also offered them counsel. A few of them were the
virtual rulers of their period of ascendency. What the Kings
did every man in the realm felt he might do. It was the heyday of the mistress. What the great mistresses of the Kings

did most women, unless held back by personal purity, did also. It was a particular form of courtesanship that was not exactly courtesanship. It was not professional. It was rather the adventure of the great lady and of all women who desired to be great ladies. It set the style for intense personal cultivation. For no woman could go far in the adventure unless she polished herself to the last most infinite point of her capability. She had to have what men wanted to begin with, and she had to hold what she eventually got through the sheer use of her wits.

When the scene changed, and royalty and the aristocracy came into disrepute through the rise of the industrial middle class, the scene also changed for the great lady. The mistresses of the French Kings had been wildly extravagant, and therefore were considered to have been wicked women. Most of them were wicked socially. The classes below them did not exist so far as they were concerned. They were hated. As well they might have been. But the hatred was not pure hatred. The men in classes below the aristocracy resented the possession by the upper-class men of these beautiful charming extra women. The middle-class women subconsciously realizing the subconscious envy of their own men, took the only stand they could take—moral superiority. They said such women were nothing more than prostitutes for all their graciousness and their personal loveliness. Such women as were left having the temperament for erotic adventure degenerated into the kept women. It became a shady profession. There was no art to it. The men of the middle classes rarely knew how to treat these extra women. It took generations of leisure and of cultivation to adapt to the extra relationship. When middle-class men wanted another woman it was usually only a momentary rebellion from domesticity, or a momentary desire to be superior to the ordinary men of their class. All the art the extra woman might have was lost upon them. So it followed that the women who continued to enter the dubious ranks entered it with the new idea of giving as little as possible for as much as they could get. They became commercial, and except for the excitement of the possible returns of the business, it was a dull way to live, and could not possibly interest a woman of culture or charm or of histrionic temperament.

The whole picture had changed. Men got deeper and deeper into the game of earning money. They found that they could lift themselves out of the class and circumstance into which they had been born. They worked feverishly for it. They were altogether taken up with it. They no longer had the time or the energy to pursue women, and women, accordingly, had to hunt them. The woman who wanted a man either for biological or economic reasons had to manage to be in the places where men were. The prostitute waylaid men in the streets. The other women approached them socially or through getting into the businesses of men.

The radical doctrine of the recognition of the still lower classes of society sweeps away the great lady, the courtesan, with her variations of mistress and kept woman relationship with one gesture that includes the feeble imitators of the aristocracy, the middle class. The radicals say that any woman whose expenses are paid by men is a kept woman, regardless of the legality of her status. Any woman who takes money or its equivalents in up-keep from a man has sold her sexuality and her social self-respect. The radicals say it is no matter what her motive may be. A woman may marry and accept the financial support of one man because through him she wishes to be a custodian of the race. That is the purest of racial motives, according to the old standard of womanhood. It is entering a vocation. But in the eyes of the radical it does not justify the fact that she does not do her share in the labor of the world. The radical does not see this woman as having surrendered her own life and blended it with the life of the man she has married and whose children she bears. A woman may enter into an arrangement of up-keep with a man because she believes that femininity is a sheer and lovely quality which she cannot do justice to in the wear and tear of economic competition out in the world with men. That is a relatively pure motive, but to the radical it is an alibi for taking the easiest way for women. It is a sale of the sexual function. Women in the radical program must do their share in the world's work, and what they contribute to the race is their own affair, or, still better, the affair of the state generally, and not an affair of the man who has joined her in her racial purpose. And as for any undue cultivation of feminine charm, that in the radical view is a pernicious hang-over from the old order, and women cling to it because they are slower than men to change.

So for the moment the case of the woman who down through history has cultivated her personality for its own sake, or the sake of what it may bring to her in social prestige, rests.

But her tradition remains, and in an intellectualized form something of it remains among the sophisticated ladies of our time.

There are two types of sophisticate among women.

There are the simple personal sophisticate and the intellectual sophisticate.

The simple personal sophisticate is a lady who shrewdly estimates the world as still a place, for all the radicals may wish it to be different, wherein all the plums go to the best showman, and wherein women only get such bites out of the plums as they can inveigle men to give them. The best way to get a plum from a man is to flatter him. That is sound thinking, things being as they are. It is practical. Such a woman is distinctly a man's woman. She has no use for women because women do not usually have the plums, or if they do have them, are cagy about sharing them. So she gets herself ready for the men. And the plums. The plums may not be necessarily in checks or bank-notes. They often are merely jobs and chances of jobs. Such a woman puts paint on her face, a wave in her hair, lipstick on her lips and lacquer on her nails. She buys the clothes that she thinks will hit men in the eyes. She uses her figure so it will be noticed. She adds perfume. She trains her eyes to look admiringly upon the lords of creation. She thinks of appropriate remarks. She watches for the best moments to bring them out. She cultivates personality plus. It is no wonder. All the magazines tell her to. The advertisers insist that she have a success appearance philosophy. She cannot possibly interest any man unless she uses a mouth wash and a fine-grained peach-bloom powder. She must have long lashes; she is well advised to have thin arched eyebrows. It is to be hoped that she will have pearly teeth. This is a deliberate appeal to the remnant of the courtesan that is in every woman, as the advertisers suppose. The films take up the insistent story and feature women of exotic personalities. They set the styles, and every woman tries to look and act like some star of the screen. They dress for business carefully, and the women in the homes are reminded how much the women in offices do care for their persons, and are cautioned to follow their example. So we find an era of women playing the part in appearance at least of the very sophisticated ladies of the past. Even though there are those among them who have no idea whatever of what they are doing. But those who do know play themselves off assiduously.

Their tricks are quite obvious. They brighten when a man enters the room. They overlook the women. They enjoy conquest. Usually they feature their conquests. The world as it still is to-day is comparatively an easy place for these women so long as they have their youth. Some of them get along very well indeed. Men can still be taken for rides and the sophisticated lady of simple designs upon men has lots of opportunities for getting away with her designs.

The intellectual sophisticate is quite another woman. Her designs upon men are not tangible. It is a matter of admiration. She is like the second type of helpmeet, an image-builder, but the image is built around herself and not around a man. Therefore she is, all things being equal, likely to be happier than the helpmeet. The image is comfortably attached to herself. She is under no necessity, therefore, to go hunting for some being to whom to fasten it.

She is self-contained, and it is in this self-containment that the reservations of her femininity lie. Much as she likes, and to an extent needs, admiration, she is never entirely intent upon getting it. She always has herself upon which to fall back. She realizes her own self-sufficiency. Admiration is a pleasant tribute and is always graciously accepted, but she will never go unduly out of her way to get it, and because she does not go out for it, she usually gets it.

These women are never capable of love as the helpmeet is capable of it, and certainly not as the priestess. They cannot become engrossed with a man. The image of no man ever completely fills their imaginations. They treat such men as they take to themselves as audiences. As soon as any man in relation to a sophisticated lady begins to take her for granted, she begins automatically to look around for his successor. Though very often the little look around is all that is necessary to put an end to the casual acceptance of her. She holds her man by the very fact that he is not absolutely necessary to her. Her attitude is psychologically one of self-assurance. Because she is ready to lose him, the sophisticated lady rarely loses her man. Except when she wants to.

She is a woman who through incapability of love for a man is able technically to promote an atmosphere of *amour* which is far more satisfying to the normal male than intense love. He feels more at home with it. The man never knows her mind though he may know her body. For the woman who is really intellectually sophisticated, and adept at *amour,* is mysterious. Da Vinci painted her once and for eternity in the Mona Lisa, with her still sensuousness and her secretive withdrawal into her own personality.

The withdrawal of the sophisticate is an outcome of judiciously cultivated skepticism, and the skepticism is the outcome of a desire for self-preservation.

The helpmeet in love is helpless. Everything she has is open to the inspection of the man she loves. Her hands are held out to him. The sophisticate controls her hands. She keeps them quietly folded within her sleeves.

The attitude of the sophisticate is not natural to a woman, for neither the desire for self-preservation and its corollary, skepticism, is innate in the normal woman. The very existence of the womb within a woman denotes instinctive belief. For to take life within the body is to believe in life, and to nourish it there is to imply a permanent acceptance of that belief, and a corresponding indifference to self-preservation.

It is possible that there are women who started out as natural loving women, and as helpmeets, with an image in their minds, and finding no man to fit the image, gradually became skeptical about men and the habit of expecting image fulfilment from them. In other words, the helpmeet sometimes becomes a sophisticate because she has suffered through some man, or through men. If this is so, she puts herself under some manner of discipline planned to eradicate from her system the inclination to lay herself open to the wounding of men. Such a woman from then on plays at love with men. All the ardor she may want to feel she will deliberately divert into some other form of expression. All the glamour of which she may be aware in the presence of a man she will gather into herself to make her the more glamorous. She will never permit her lover to touch her soul. She will preserve inviolate some center of her being. Because of this inviolability she is free to play with love as no other woman is free to play with it. It preserves her sight. She comes under no more illusions. If she does meet an illusion she raises her eyebrow skeptically and reminds herself cryptically that she herself is all that counts. So she remains in control of her emotions, and therefore can use them. She knows when to be moved, and when to be unmoved. She becomes a complete technician. She knows when to be tentatively conversational and when to be tantalizingly silent. She knows when to come to the edge of tears and when to be casually amused. She keeps an eye on the responses of the man, and always remembers that in every love affair she must be the gainer, if not in actual cash, certainly in her own opinion of herself. So she sets out according to the particular status of the affair to be the sophisticated lady, whether as wife, or mistress, or little girl pal, by the way. She is under no illusion that the man is hers by destiny. She takes him as a matter of biological course, but knows that he is hers only so long as the mood will last, and she makes it her vocation to sustain the mood by whatever means she has, and all the time she herself remains mysteriously aloof.

The sophisticated lady in writing surveys the scene skeptically. She does not believe altogether in what she sees. She looks for the thing which if understood would change the whole aspect. Therefore she never is emotional about what seems to be seen, and is never surprised when something else comes to the surface. If what comes to the surface is something that is quite upsetting, she is never upset. She is faintly amused. And out of her amusement she writes. She makes delicate entertainment out of it for her readers. Her own deft aloof mind controls the story. She tells it with a side glance.

Whether she deals with a sophisticated situation or a simple one, does not matter at all. It is how she presents the situation that counts. The presentation is always ironical, but never obviously ironical. The irony lies not in the story itself but in the slant she gives it in her writing. The story she tells never quite gets her. She does not allow it to get her. She is never riotously funny as some of the little girl pals are. She is never completely objective as others of them are. She is never enterprising in her search for new material, as some of the go-getters are. She is never bored as others of them are. She is never tragic as many of the helpmeets are. Nor is she ecstatic in her emotionalism. Neither is she serious about the plan of life as the matriarchs seem on the whole to be. She is merely interested in seeing what there is to be seen easily, and in what is not so easily seen. In some cases she is close to being an artiste, but in most cases she willingly sacrifices art for the ironical effect. She is in all things an emotional dilettante.

ELLEN GLASGOW

Ellen Glasgow leads her people into conventional situations in their place of residence, Richmond, Virginia, and proceeds to the truth concerning their unconventional emotions. She treats marriage as if it were a trap out of which all manner of neuroses grow.

In *They Stooped to Folly* a man and a woman live an outwardly perfect marriage. The home management runs with charm and efficiency. The man never stays out. He never has business engagements which keep him away for dinner. He sits at the head of his table with poise and apparently complete satisfaction. Underneath he realizes that he has missed everything that he wanted from life. The woman presides over her duties with precision. She has attained control over everything except the thoughts and feelings of her husband. She has reached what all women are supposed to reach—the satisfaction of a husband and a home. She has attended to the future and served the race. By all counts for women she should have been content, yet she is vaguely discontented. A woman comes back to the community who has been a romantic memory to the husband. He contemplates the romance which has always been a regretful image in his mind. It is there no longer. The woman tries to waken it again to life. But it cannot be done. She is even willing to take what crumbs might be gathered, but he has reached utter disillusionment and refuses to hand her the crumbs. When his wife dies he turns to her best friend, a spinster who has always cherished a romantic picture of him, and he decides to warm himself by that fire. It is more sustaining. After all, he has lived many years without feeling anything himself, and he finds that more vitality comes to him through the admiration of another, than through any feeling he might try to stir in himself. There is no story in the book other than this.

In *The Sheltered Life* another conventional marital situation is taken. A beautiful woman has married a handsome man, and has set herself two tasks—to preserve the illusion of her beauty and to preserve for the community the illusion of a perfect marriage. The first task collapses gradually through the inevitableness of time; the other collapses violently through a sudden emotion. The husband in this case has always been a philanderer. When he turns his speculative attention upon a lovely young girl, the wife shoots him. Even then she preserves the appearances, and it goes down as an accident with a gun. There is no story in the book other than this. In both cases it is story enough. Step by step the writer takes off the semblance of things and uncovers dreadful neuroses. It is unhappy work without the compensating emotion of great tragedy. They are a set of human beings, in both stories, who are unable to promote themselves through their suffering into spiritual greatness, and are also unable to rest gracefully in littleness. They want the unattainable without having the spiritual energy to pay the cost of attaining it. They all subconsciously resent their own failures without being inclined to feature the failure in itself, which, if they could manage to do, would bring them inner peace. They are therefore a group of torn people. The author treats them with circumspect aloofness and gentle humor. This, she is saying, is our human race, and is about as far as it will ever get. We strive so diligently for order and shelter behind conformity, and underneath it lie unresolved emotions which eat out the heart or dull the intellect, and in the end tear us to shreds.

Ellen Glasgow writes with conformity herself. These two books which are chosen from her later work are books that have come from a mature woman protecting herself and her feelings carefully from the excitement of causes, and all undue seriousness. She observes the scene in front of her with a slight smile. She presents it with a slight shrug of her shoulders. Both the smile and the shrug are in excellent literary taste.

So also are the contours of her story in excellent taste. There is no touch of melodrama, or exaggeration in any form whatever. It is the work of a gentlewoman who by reason of sheer thinking has come to expect consistently little from human beings. The tempo of the work is leisurely. It is Southern. It is suave. And it is gracious for all its irony. She is cynical without being addicted to wise-cracking cynicism. She is disillusioned without being disappointed. She is aware of the parts of the apple that are in the process of decomposition without being upset about the parasite that set the process going. The apple would have been eaten anyway, if it had not been bad. The characterization in her books is among the best of the characterization done by women. Her men and her women are equally real, and with relatively little concern about plot she leads them into fiction which insinuates itself into the imagination. Her atmosphere is genuine. There is no artificiality.

The mind behind such writing is distinctly a mind that has turned aside from the old preoccupation of women with romance and the race. And also from the new preoccupation with finding places for the activity of women. It is a mind that is free from any sense of sexual injustice. Men and women suffer alike from the conformity fixed upon the sexual relationship. The spirit coming into life to learn and to experience finds itself tied down to the pattern of civilization, and while outwardly establishing itself with that pattern, inwardly knows no peace. It came to experience and to experiment, and because it cannot fulfil that purpose it is tortured.

If Ellen Glasgow were matriarchal she would have smoothed out the torture in fiction. She would have pulled in all the ends and clipped off all the uneven edges. If she had been a helpmeet she would have given her people a glimpse of something enduringly constructive in their relationships. If she had been a priestess she would have shown them that beneath all the pain there was a truth pushing to the surface. But she is none of these, and neither is she quite the artiste. For underneath her stories there is a hint of a smile at the expense of the people whose stories they are. They are, we know from reading her version of them, precious fools. It is just this that makes her the sophisticate in this phase of her writing.

Mazo de la Roche

It is this also that makes Mazo de la Roche a sophisticate. She has greater virility than Glasgow, which may be the result of having grown to maturity in the simpler community, culturally speaking, of Canada. Yet for all its virility, it is also aloof work. It has come out of the watching rather than the participating mind. Her fame has been built upon her family sequence written around the Whiteoaks of Jalna. But for all that this sequence has to do with a family saga, and features one of the most exciting matriarchs in all literary attempts to portray the matriarch, it has nothing at all to do with the matriarchal writing.

The sophisticated quality of De la Roche is exhibited not only in the ironical twist of the story sequence, but also in an obvious impatience with women. In her stories they are all prize fools. She portrays them bungling their affairs with the men, and cannot restrain a smile. And it is the historic smile of the great sophisticate. It is a gesture of superiority from the expert concerning the amateurishness of other women with men. In addition to this, Mazo de la Roche flatters her men. The whole Whiteoak sequence hangs upon the virility of a he-man called Renny, who is like a fox. He is a strong man— a veritable colonial. He likes his women submissive. He rules the family with an iron will, and remains the master of the house of Jalna. He marries his brother's wife after the brother has deserted her, and he is unfaithful to her as a matter of course when she fails to understand him. It is the privilege of the male, as every sophisticate knows and expects, and subconsciously admires. For innate in the consciousness of every sophisticated lady is a taste for the lordly male, and a consequent distaste for any man who gets under the thumb of a women even to the extent of being faithful to her. It is upon this point that the woman sophisticate differs sharply from the woman of the helpmeet temperament, with her dreams of a man who would be faithful as she is. The sophisticate enjoys a hard game. She wants to compete with all her powers for the attention of the man who is difficult to hold. Any other kind of a man makes the game too easy for her, and her interest flags. Love never enters into her point of view on this matter. The game is not of the emotions with their swing and push, but rather of technical skill in *amour*.

The wife of Renny in *Jalna* and its sequels is a stolid young woman. She is baffled by the exuberant masculinity of her husband, and takes refuge in an almost querulous devotion to her child. The child repays her by being frankly in a state of preference for her father. It is a girl child. Around Renny there is a family gallery consisting of as hilariously funny a group of characters as has appeared in fiction since Dickens. It is the gallery that has made De la Roche famous. They are melodramatically unforgettable. The old grandmother with her perversities and her defiance of time pursues the imagination and holds it in this period of many books and many fiction characters. She cannot be overlooked. She stands out with garish coloring and raucous sound. De la Roche is a mistress of the old melodramatic trick of persistent repetition. The grandmother has set phrases which are used in the story just as in the first films certain phrases of music were used to accompany and to accent the appearance of certain characters on the screen. Whenever Renny appears we are reminded that he is like a fox. He even takes to a mistress who raises foxes. His uncles and his brothers all stamp themselves into the reader's memory with similar fiction tricks. You know exactly what they will do at given moments in given situations. They swagger and brag and stagger through the chapters. All of them lead their women a merry dance. The children are puckish little devils, and tighten the tension of the story through their complete devotion to themselves and their immediate wants.

The ironical glance of the sophisticate in Mazo de la Roche's case ends in being very nearly a leer, and is accompanied by a hoarse chuckle of derision. The work is that of a mind which considers the human situation as neither tragic nor glorious, but on the whole rather tawdry and inconsequential. The people portrayed are in no way rounded out in bland or fine humanism. They are caricatured almost into cartoons by a woman who has twisted her artistry into a desire to entertain herself and her readers. The result is a collection of human beings within the environs of a family who are as full of antics as a cage of monkeys.

The technique of the writing is extraordinarily good. The chapters are obviously carefully planned and fulfilled. Nothing extraneous to the story and the development of the characters is allowed to enter. The author has put herself under hard literary restraint, and she relieves the writing tension in herself by her amusement at the expense of her people. It is as if she had taken possession of them in order to make fun of them, and the fun is carried through with a gusto that is infectious, except where in spots it offends circumspect taste. De la Roche has a grain of Rabelaisian zest in her composition, and there is an undertone of suspended sexual excitement through all the *Jalna* sequence. The reader feels in the hot atmosphere of people who are just on the point of committing hectic indiscretions without the least measure of reluctance. They actually do commit a few of them during the space of the sequence, but they all sail through even up to their deaths with a ribald verve concerning their own doings.

MARGARET KENNEDY

Margaret Kennedy set out to write the answer to every romantic lady who ever thinks to herself, "How wonderful it would be to be living with big people—people who really do things and are not dull and ordinary and provincial!"

The Sangers in the Sanger sequence beginning with *The Constant Nymph* lived for music and incidentally for love. The head of the clan, old Sanger, was a man who had some kin to De la Roche's Renny. He is a swaggering male, and dominates the tribe. He is a law unto himself and his music, just as Renny was a law unto himself and his farm and his family. The children have variously inherited his characteristics. Beyond their devotion to music they are ordinary mortals, but differ from the rest by their conviction that nothing matters at all except getting down into form the music of themselves. Women have a hard time with them. It is the men of the family who write music. The women have all they can do looking after them when the big moment takes them in composition, and in the worse times in between big moments when they prowl in bad tempers looking for more music to write. The Constant Nymph is the most sensitive of all the girls. She is very young in the story, but has been forced into a premature spiritual maturity through the hothouse of art in which she has been reared. Much too early she falls in love with a man who is also devoted to music. Margaret Kennedy allows herself a little elbow room for tragedy. She causes this man to be married by a woman who takes great pleasure in his artistic eminence and the social prestige marriage to him will give her, but she has no real understanding of the way to live with a musical genius. She likes her house to be run properly. She likes people to be on time. She likes them to go to bed at the proper hour and get up at the proper hour. And naturally she does not enjoy a lot of other women in her own house. Not very young women. However, she cannot control the whirl-wind of emotion that produces music, and she cannot manage the genius of musical composition. She, like the rest of the world, has to stand still while it is getting put down. The man inevitably turns to the very young Sanger girl. She under-stands. She was brought up to understand men who write music. It is all she does understand. They are her world. There is no other world. School is funny; games are funny; conven-tions are funny. Her mind is quite ready for love and the emo-tion of it, but her body is too undeveloped and the nerves that hold body and mind together suffer in the torment of the triangle. She dies in the midst of a grand elopement.

It is for all its tragedy not tragedy. It is an ironical story of the human clumsiness of genius. A man may write gorgeous music in an incomprehensible mood of artistic awareness and remain a queer human being with no more sense of a man's responsibility than to rouse feeling in a little young sapling of femininity. A man may write gorgeous music under constantly coming moods of greater and greater awareness and remain a child himself in relation to the human beings dependent upon him. It is a picture of an artistic circus—the Sanger Circus, she intimates it is called. No romantic lady could live in it. Any lady to stand it at all would have to be born in a similar circus, be as indifferent to ordinary things as the Sangers themselves were, or be strong enough to take the attitude of the matriarch in all concerning them except in the moods of creation. Then she would have to maintain the aloofness of the sophisticate, waiting with her hands in her sleeves for the mood to pass. And she could not maintain the aloofness of the sophisticate without being one, and no lady of sophistication would willingly be ignored as the geniuses ignored their women most of the time. So what manner of women it would take to fill the rôle, it is hard to say. Not the helpmeet, because such men have no real need of the helpmeet. They create out of a volition which has nothing to do with their surroundings. They function under a law of their own.

Margaret Kennedy had a fine time writing the story; her enjoyment of the predicament of the women is genuine, giving where no need of giving is; loving where no need of loving is; suffering where it is futile to suffer. This is romance among the artists. Women have no place in it. And always think they have, for the artist attracts women as children do.

It is a good story. It has tempo. It has style. The author is vivacious. She has creative power. The world of the Sangers is a high-cylindered world where everything is dramatized slightly beyond itself. It is breath-taking and trying and immensely interesting. It has feeling too. Music lives in it, dominating the bewildered mortals who are instruments of music, and giving them moments of sheer wonder that atone for the human stumbling they do.

E. H. Young

E. H. Young has a knack with simple satire which is the first of its particular kind since Jane Austen. It is not as immaculate writing as Miss Austen's. It lacks her spontaneity. It lacks her melodic dance in its prose rhythm. But it has her way with the ordinary affairs of everyday living. E. H. Young would have been a helpmeet writer except that she has the sophisticate's inclination towards more or less polite satire.

Miss Mole is her key book to date. It is the study of a spinster with a sharp tongue and the memory of one sinful interlude. The interlude had strengthened her perceptions and elaborated her distaste for illusions. It has done almost nothing else to her, and she came out of it wondering why so much to-do was made about the chastity of women. She was as much a spinster as ever. She left the man living in her house. She had taken him in after the war, and had no heart for turning him out. So she went out herself. That is a modern note struck in the story, and it is the one note which separates her from Miss Austen. After she left him she went from position to position, keeping house and being attentive to old ladies and children. She decided after ten years of recovery from her interlude that she would marry the first man who looked as if he might be caught. As she remembered, the relationship had its moments, but her chief point in favor of getting married was its social and financial advantages. Lone women had a thin time of it. Especially if they could not compare legitimate notes with other women about the men with whom they had lived. Before she married she took one last fling at a job. She was recommended by a cousin who was in convenient ignorance of the interlude as an eminently suitable housekeeper for a non-conformist clergyman left a widower with children. The clergyman was a pompous individual. Much as she enjoyed looking after his children, Miss Mole ruled him out as a possible husband. Even though she was in excellent propinquity for her designs. He was, however, an enticing target for her wit. So she had quite a round with him, and this is the main body of the story. In his congregation there was a man who fell into line with her plans. And he came to her rescue in fine time when the clergyman found out that his housekeeper had had an interlude with sin.

The matrimonial design of Miss Mole, however, is only the icing on the cake. The cake itself is of delightful nutty and fruity consistency. It contains bits of spiced surprise and a richness of starch base which makes it thoroughly palatable. The insight into human motivation is its most interesting quality. There is no wash of pale sentiment, and yet no depressing bitterness. It is very matter-of-fact. She has the same faculty as Jane Austen had for producing the effect of reality both in small groups and large. Her parties are lifelike, and so are the conversations around the dining-room table of the ministerial home. There is also a sensitive appreciation of feeling, and all the scenes used are acutely sensitized for the over and undertones. The irony of *Miss Mole* is a superimposed patina rather than an ingrained attitude of mind. It is the patina of a mind that has set itself to the smoothness of an amused *laissez-faire* through life. It is not in any way the unconscious defense of mental laziness, which is so often the truth about irony. It is an attitude assumed out of courtesy to her own intellectuality and in deference to life itself. Her own intellect is astutely aware of the foibles of human nature; therefore she nourishes it with continued attention to those foibles. Life provides much variety, and it is the duty of the mind to acknowledge the variety gratefully, and to take pleasure in what is set before it. In addition to this she has the sense of her audience. She realizes its collective weariness, and she stimulates it gently so that it may rouse itself to an enjoyment similarly enlivening to her own concerning the engaging foolishness of mortals. This is her adaptation of the sophisticate's talent for presenting an entertaining stage.

All the while we watch we are gradually becoming con-

scious of the deftly attractive mind which is conducting the
entertainment.

E. H. Young has photographed herself. A woman, not too
young, certainly old enough to be subtle, and old enough in
that subtlety to know that there is no flattery like the flattery
of slight irony shared. The ironist consistently flatters the
reader or the companion in conversation. Irony presupposes
superiority of mind. You do not spread it before fools. It is,
therefore, as it manifests in a woman, essentially part of the
equipment of the sophisticate. It is a supersensual appeal which
acts downward upon the senses. More than that, it catches the
participants off guard. The personality of the ironist then has
a chance to seep through to the listener. And further still, it
never cloys. So no reaction ever sets in, as it sets in from direct
flattery. It is a kind of perversion of flattery, creating a delicate
new interest, and holding the attention by means of a concentration upon a possible next ironical remark. The sophisticated
lady among men is a lady so intent upon holding her own that
she can afford to appear not to be intent upon holding it. The
sophisticated writer is a writer so watchful of the attention of
her readers that she can afford to appear not to be so very
watchful. She tosses off her bids for attention as if they were
merely something that amused her by the way. She succeeds
in holding attention by this very talent for engaging disinter-
estedness. For both men and readers are skittish creatures, and
run when too deliberately pursued, and elude when too determinedly held. To do this the sophisticated lady and the sophisticated writer have to be persons of preeminent self-control. This,
inversely, is highly attractive to men and readers. Nowhere do
you find it so thoroughly elaborated technically as in *Miss
Mole*. And Miss Mole herself is a person, one of the saucy
immortals of ironic literature.

E. M. Delafield

E. M. Delafield has the same self-sufficiency in her writing.
In *The Diary of a Provincial Lady* she set the reading English

world smiling about the funny slant of an ordinary woman's existence. She has written other stories which in their way are good pieces of experimental portraiture of women, but none of them has the ingenuous sparkle of the provincial lady's record of her affairs. She has no affairs. She has a husband who hides behind his newspapers when she wants to talk to him, and reaches for his hat when the question of more money for household expenses comes up. He is a nice husband, and does take an interest in the things that go on in his home. He is nice, too, about allowing his wife to write in her spare time, but he is only a man, and a woman has to have some outlet for her thoughts other than a man. The book is significant for all its slightness because it is possibly the first time a woman ever set down the doings of her day-to-day life in all their simplicity, and attached to them her own tentatively philosophical conclusions.

The writing might appear at first glance to be the writing of a helpmeet. Certainly it is the writing of a woman painting the situation of a helpmeet woman. Living in honorable matrimony with a man, rearing his children, attending to his house. But the sophisticated element raises its signs in the fact that she thinks her own thoughts as she goes through her days, and also in the fact that these thoughts happen to be amusing thoughts. She is under no psychological strain about the unfair emotional relationship between men and women. She is under no need to worship her man. But she wants to be entertaining. She must be entertaining. So she in her limited circumstance makes a fine story out of the irritating visits of the rector's wife, and the daily struggle with inadequate help in her own house. It is all a great game to her. The husband is varyingly attentive to the entertainment she provides. He reads his papers. He gives a snort or a grunt as the case may be, and he sees fit to be amused or disgusted, but the show goes on whether he applauds or not. He sticks and that is the main thing. He pays the bills, which is another thing, and it is up, therefore, to any lady to make it all seem extraordinarily interesting. Which is exactly what she does, and while she does it, she draws a picture of the life of an average couple together after the tense emotion of romance has died down and the long business of pulling together in harness has engrossed them to the exclusion of almost every other consideration. It is more to the point that there is enough cream in the house for the tea than that a woman have power to rouse all manner of fine feeling around her. It is more important for a man to be able to pay the coal bills than to have power to drive a woman to distraction over the stray thoughts he may be thinking. The helpmeet woman would be concerned about the subsiding of the feeling. She would be digging and prodding into the reactions of the man—"Are you happy?" "Do I satisfy you?"—the sophisticate is practical. She takes it for granted that the man is happy, and she sees to it that she does her part to satisfy him. This is the example without par of the sophisticated lady handling the prevailing matrimonial situation in complete normality. It is a lady of the ingénue type, playing her simple part with all its funny nuances, easy on the emotions, easy on the mind, gentle yet lively, full of fun, yet full of technical appreciation of every least little movement there is to be taken with it.

"ELIZABETH"

"Elizabeth" is a woman of the same generic type in her writing, but carrying her point of view into the ramifications of a different stratum of society.

Elizabeth and her German Garden is the study of an English woman living in Germany, the wife of a German aristocrat prior to the war. It is a story-book atmosphere, but there is no story. The man is a shadowy background. The woman herself is a ghostlike personality, wandering among her gardens, watching for the first lilacs, catching their rain-drenched fragrance, watching the glint of the sun on the grass, taking books of poems down to read by particular spots. The world of the garden, with a man in the background and three babies.

This again is the self-sufficient feminine mind. The man

might as well not be there, except that with precision he comes forward occasionally with this law or that law concerning the estate. He was Lord of the Manor, and unquestionably it was what his wife wanted him to be. The woman assumes his happiness and his comfort and withdraws into her own pleasure with the garden and her thoughts. The picture of the woman is entrancing. She is a woman with peculiar balm in her spirit, a quiet woman aware of beauty, and drawing the man and the reader to her by presenting a banquet of sweetness. Along with the sweetness there is a touch of gentle irony. It is a mind which, though encased for the time within the walls of a garden, is a mind that belongs to the world. It has the aloofness which only comes to the completely sophisticated. It has the impersonality which only comes from much cogitation upon life in all its aspects.

"Elizabeth" carried her German garden through a sequence, and through the studies the same woman glides mysteriously, showing a thought here, and a feeling there, appreciating the fine taste of things, the perfumes and the delicate underplay of psychic atmosphere.

When later she turned to straight fiction, she was not quite so happy. The irony which was well controlled in her early studies got rather too much force in the later books. She moved into a less aristocratic setting. The woman she drew in *Love* was a baffled woman to whom love came too late. She was a widow, who in her maturity attracted the devotion of a young man. She married him, and found it increasingly difficult to keep pace with him in passion. She had longed all through her first matter-of-fact marriage to know the great emotion, and when it came she could not stand it. She spent her days in beauty parlors struggling with the lines left upon her face. It was useless. Until her second marriage she had remained youthful in her appearance. She had not really lived. Life had put nothing, therefore, upon her face to tell her story. With the second marriage life got at her, and told the story on her face.

She has followed in this the pattern of the sophisticate's

familiar thesis, which was summed up in the wise-crack of Anita Loos' famous Blonde, "Love never did any girl any good." She has followed it in other books of this period, and for all that she is following a pattern that is tragic to the women involved, she carries it through with the ironical shrug. Love is, as far as the woman herself is concerned, something from which to steer meticulously clear. The technician cannot afford it. It gets into the mind and muddles one's technical mastery of a situation. So long as the woman does not love she has control of herself and the relationship. If she loves she is helpless and she loses sight of the salient little points upon which every sustained relationship is built and maintained. So she paints a woman losing her beauty and consequently her dignity and her essentially feminine prestige over an incalculable emotion for a man, who after all is only one man out of many men. It is all so futile. It is the sophisticate laughing up her long mysterious sleeves behind her hidden hands at women who let themselves go. Far better is it to read poetry in particular spots in a lovely garden, and to watch the flowers as they come out in their seasons. Only with the emotion cleared of devastating fixations can a woman be free to enjoy what goes on round about her, and be in a position of feminine invulnerability in the relations of the sexes. What if she does long for the grand sweep of what might be? The point conceivably may be that enjoyment may be utterly in the longing and not in the realization. And it is just possible that the woman who longs to love and will not let herself love does exude from her own personality the perfume of that longing, and with far greater aphrodisiacal effect upon her associates than any perfume there is among all the flowers in the garden.

VICTORIA SACKVILLE-WEST

That women have their own gardens to tend and that marriage often as not keeps them from it, is the theme of Victoria Sackville-West's *All Passion Spent*. But before she published this book she published *The Edwardians*.

The Edwardians was obviously written in order to balance the great mass of middle- and lower-class work of this period by an adequate picture of the aristocrat during a particularly hedonistic period of aristocracy. The book subconsciously undertook to explain the aristocratic principle, because at the time of its writing aristocracy was already unmodish. The hero was a young man born centuries too late. He contained in himself all the passion of feudalism, with its devotion to those dependent upon that devotion, and with its instinctive consciousness of being a law unto itself in matters of personal conduct. The author carries him through stages of erotic adventure, first with an equal, a titled woman of almost professional beauty and poise, next with a middle-class woman who repulsed him with virtue absolutely astonishing to him. Then he discovered an artist woman, and after her he investigated the servant class. By that time he was ready to consider his family and his duty to the next generation, and was on the point of putting his marriage through when he was reminded by a thinker that in this age the feudal concept was out of date, and he had only duty to himself as an individual.

The book is a noble attempt, but missed its fire for the sound reason of a woman's usual fallibility in the portrayal of a man. The young Duke reads as if he were a young Duchess. The author therefore did not come into her writing maturity until she published *All Passion Spent*.

It is a vital contribution to the School of Femininity.

It is a poignant story of the heart hunger of a woman who had given her whole adult life to the support of the career of her husband—a great man in his own state and his own time. She had what appeared to be an unusually full life for a woman. But it had been a life lived for the position in society of her husband. She had never done one thing that she wanted to do. When he died she was an old woman, and all passion was spent. But she decided to grasp the time that remained to her. She found that her children expected her to live for them. She astonished them by taking a small flat of her own, and luxuriating in solitude and such friends as she chose to take to herself for their own sake and her own.

That is all there is to the story.

And it hardly suggests its importance as a document of femininity.

Underneath the bare story is a whole field of thinking by women concerning the separated personality of married women, which under the existing social system has to be completely suppressed, or to be so featured as to be emphatically accented out of harmonious proportion to the lives of the men associated with them. Which is to say—that to preserve an equitable relation with a strong and aggressive man a woman must be a sweet yes-girl, or if her nature is itself strong and aggressive she must attach herself to a nice yes-man. There is, or appears to be, not one middle way. A woman is to be a helpmeet or a sophisticate or, failing this, a go-getter.

The writing of this book would have classed Victoria Sackville-West among the helpmeet writers except that it presents a hedonistic philosophy with regard to women fulfilling themselves at any cost. The old lady at the end of her life encourages her granddaughter not to surrender her own career when she surrenders herself to love. For all the gentleness of the writing, and the graciousness of the picture of the old gentlewoman, the study is ironical. It is a woman's laugh at what life does to women. The old lady taking her soul out for its last airing on earth shows how lonely the soul of a woman can be as she lives her full woman's life with a man, bearing his children, tending his place in society. It comes out at the end as a challenge to the helpmeet woman, and all the women who long to be helpmeets. It questions the honesty of the woman who thinks there is no greater life for a woman than to live with a man and obey her racial instincts. It treats marriage as a burden laid upon women. It uncovers the awful nostalgia of a woman in search of herself, and unable to search very far on account of the restrictions of her marital situation. The woman is very old. All the illusions of love are gone, and all the illusions concerning the happiness of racial projection have sunk into fancies that are unreal. The man has gone; the children have left her breast. She has had no life apart from them, and her soul must face its impending crisis alone. It is conscious of not having tended its own fibers. It is aware of having evaded itself in devotion to others.

The story is the eternal tragedy of women handled with quizzical aloofness. It is a deft renunciation of an idea cherished through the ages by women, and deliberately publicized for them by men—that happiness for women consists in the laying down of the self in the race. What utter nonsense, the old lady says. She confesses bravely that the surrender is impossible—that the real truth about women is that biology possesses them before they have awakened spiritually to themselves, and that when they do wake it is too late because they are imprisoned by an iron code of society, and also by their own instincts. The old lady surrounded by her children and the children of her children thinks of her lost self, and all the passion spent without returns to herself.

The placing of *All Passion Spent* among writing done by sophisticates is admittedly drawing the analogy slightly beyond its depth. Though where else could it have gone? It is not helpmeet writing. Certainly it is not matriarchal. It is not the work of a go-getting business woman. Neither has it anything to do with the sprightly nonchalance of the young things. Maybe it has a blend of many qualities, even as some women have in themselves the blend of the sophisticate, the helpmeet, the go-getter, the matriarch and the little pal. It is not the work of the priestess temperament. It contains disappointment. It contains irony. It contains a modern point of view about women which relates itself back to the point of view of century-old women who rebelled against the holding of themselves to one man and his affairs. The old lady had drawn romance from other men. She had never been able to take it for herself. She had loved art. She had never been able to study. She could think. She never had had time to think anything out to a conclusion. She had been a perfect wife. She had been a fitting mother. She had had no actual part in the creative part of her husband's career. He went his own way with men and government. She had furnished a beautiful domestic and social background—the Governor's Lady. As she added up the columns of her life she found nothing she could set down on her own side of the ledger. A blank life, and far, far too late to add anything to it now.

This was perhaps the point of view of the women who chose the sophisticated way in the historic times. They lived to themselves. They, if they were high in their caste, could choose their men. They cultivated themselves. They took their part in the creative thinking and doing of the men with whom they were associated. They had no racial obligations. They had no social obligations. Their shoulders were free. Their personalities were free. They could cultivate themselves in whatever way they pleased. When they became weary of a man, they could stop the relationship, and even if that only involved, because of their profession, changing to another man, it was a semblance of liberty which could pass for liberty.

It is definitely the point of view of many women to-day who, though not in themselves go-getters, choose the career way for women. These are women who go to the professions and the arts, and even to business, with an urge to be biologically free. And no economic pressure, and no strain of competition with nerves not adapted well for competition, will ever bring them to the surrender of themselves to something out of which they cannot move quickly. This is intellectually the way of the sophisticate, and if these women do enter into relations with men they enter them with circumspect emotionalism. They watch carefully to see that they do not get down deeply into the emotional current. They side-step biology in its ultimate law. They are out to tend their own gardens, and the men who come to them come as men came to the ancient sophisticates. But they are further on than these women were. For dealing with themselves in the world of men, they have developed still further the mysterious hidden sophisticated hands, and the fingers of these hands curl often in movements of delicious derision. Yes, they may have their men. Yes, they may have their careers. But above all they have themselves and the self-sufficiency of women when they have tended their own gardens.

CHAPTER XII

PRIESTESSES

Pearl Buck—Radclyffe Hall—Mary Webb

THE PRIESTESS IS THE "DOVE" woman. She is a legend all through time. The Hebraic tradition has her as Esther surrendering herself for the good of her people, and using her innate wisdom in diplomacy for the benefit of her race. The Christian tradition has her in Mary, the Mother, whose soul was pure, to whom Gabriel spoke, and to whom the Blessed One came a little child for mothering. The Chinese have her in the Goddess of Mercy, with her thousand arms held out to human beings. The Greeks had her among the priestesses of Delphi. Artists have painted her and put into the faces of their Madonnas and saints and angels a feeling of incarnate peace. Her symbol stands in every Roman Catholic church, the lovely legend of womanhood, holding the Babe with humility, a reminder to all women of God's wish for them, and, kneeling in faith at every cross, a reminder to men of what God has given to them in women. We see the face of her in passing women, in women who wear the robe of the nun, in women who wear no robe of peculiar office, and sometimes in women with the fashionable clothes of the world upon them. It is a face that never can be passed over casually. It is full of wistful beauty. It appears oftener in some races than in others. It seems to belong to people such as the Jews and the Irish and the Italians, because perhaps they care deeply for religion, or have cared in their past.

The Roman Catholic Communion made provision for the priestess woman in the orders of the sisterhood. The young girl with the fey look of religion upon her is taken to a convent, and there she may stay, in peace, if she feels it is her vocation.

But before she takes her final vows she is given a discipline which makes certain her sustained desire for the life of a nun.

Feminism has provided for her by forcing open the professions of service for women, and the teaching and nursing and social-service ranks have many women among them with a touch of the priestess in their faces.

The Greeks provided for her in a legendary order of priestesses. And more than this, they used her strange temperament for the enlightenment of the race.

The priestesses of Delphi, so far as we may gather from the fragmentary story of Greece, were women whose intuitive powers were developed to their highest possibility.

Students of occultism claim that there are secret records concerning these women, that they were mystics, that the great men of Greece consulted them, that wisdom was uttered through the lips of the priestesses, that in a subjective state their minds could be projected through time and space. If this be so, they were a school of feminine clairvoyants living in some manner unknown to us which induced psychic awareness.

It has been generally accepted that women as a whole are more intuitive than men, though why they should be so has had no explanation other than the worn-out theory that the intuitive senses develop when the conscious brain is not irritated too much by quantities of information. It was one of the arguments of the anti-feminists that scholastic study and prolonged vocational training for women in competition with men would ruin the intuitive faculty of women, and thereby incur grievous loss to the race. The answer of the feminists was that this was entirely suppositional, and that research showed no evidence of the intuition of women being allowed at any time or in any place to function for the benefit of the state. The counter-answer to this was that the signs of the influence of women coming from their intuitive senses could not be traced; that it was intangible; yet a very definite force in society. There is no saying what was true. There was no need to attempt to decide what was true. The industrial change settled it for women, that, intuitive or not, they had to contribute to the work of the world, and time would tell whether or not intuition would fade under the pressure of competitive occupation.

The Greeks evidently believed that life in the world did affect unfavorably the intuitive tendencies of women. For they protected their priestesses by enclosing them within a recognized order. In all probability the priestess, like the nun, went through a disciplinary test, and upon taking her vows was sworn into a life which stimulated the unknown senses.

What the rule was concerning the sexual life of the priestesses is nowhere set down. There is not even a legendary inference. They may have been sacred courtesans. But it seems unlikely in view of our knowledge that wanton living deadens the intuitive faculty. They may have been celibates. But that also seems unlikely. For the Greeks, we may assume through the very fact of the ordination of these women, knew something about psychic phenomena, and therefore would have recognized the mysticism produced by absolute continence as pseudo-mysticism, and in psychiatric reality not more than simple visionary compensation. There must have been some carefully chosen middle way of life and of love for the priestesses. It would have been necessary, for any heightening of the mystical nature increases the sexual magnetism in any human being, either male or female. But whatever the secret was, it was kept.

Putting the findings of occultism together with the findings of psychiatric investigation, we assume now that the priestess is a woman who has accomplished a complete flight from the world of reality. She walks upon the earth and uses a body, but lives imaginatively in another sphere, which seems to be a beautiful sphere, inasmuch as it radiates itself through the beauty of her face, her personality and her conduct.

Something showed her at some time, probably quite early in life, that living as mortals usually live would prove to be a bad experience. Maybe it was a too premature view of the human jungle. Someone was at hand who taught her about God and another world and the mystery underlying creation, and to that world and that mystery she fled for protection. Yet she remained in her body, and remaining there she proceeded to translate the experience of life in relation to a life that went on before the body and that would go on after the body, or maybe went on in spite of the body. She would look for a mystical meaning and find it. Life therefore became a symbol of something else. And keeping fast hold upon the symbology she would be able to go through life with inner peace. This accounts for the peace in the traditional face of the "dove" woman, but it does not account for the beauty, unless a face of utter peace, being rare, interprets itself as beauty. Nor does it account for the strange fey effect upon other people, unless peace in itself is magnetism. In some aspects that seems all the explanation needed, for human beings writhe and are torn in their discontents, and the soul that has found peace is focused and therefore has force and something so different from others that it is called beauty.

As a woman to whom this has happened goes through life she will do one of two things. She will turn to the race in pity. Or she will retreat from it to think.

The pitying priestess spends herself trying to mend the torn places in life. Human beings need her. She never craves the needing of her own man as the helpmeet does. She never craves the needing of her own family as the matriarch does. She never builds an image around one mortal as the helpmeet does. Nor does she strive to organize the ways of other human beings as the matriarch does. Her concern is altogether with the little balm she may pour upon the cuts and bruises.

Such women are always present when there is sickness or sorrow in small scale or big. It may only be flowers the priestess brings, or a portion of food. It may be a book, or only a visit. It may on the other hand be great service on national or international scale. It depends on her circumstance. Sometimes you see the priestesses working in offices in close association with men of high caliber. They do their work quietly. They never elbow their way. They never care unduly for their own success. They sense the need of their associates. Sometimes you see them in the rôle of the wife. And even occasionally in the rôle of the mistress. Men depend upon them for their intuitive judgment, though often they are hardly aware of the dependence, so self-effacingly is the service given. They are women who see life as the substance of an immutable universal plan, and not piece by piece in relation to themselves. They are always patient and always understanding. As a rule they are distinctly impersonal, though they may conceivably give themselves into a personal intimate relationship with some man. If they do this it is never for their own benefit, but in the fulfilment of some need to which they respond. They are always ready to surrender the relationship. They subconsciously guard themselves against fixations in personal attachments. They do not reach out to fasten other human beings to themselves. Neither do they ever care greatly about enhancing their own personalities. They rarely offer the wisdom they know, and only give it hesitatingly in response to much asking. They are always afraid of gaining control over the destiny of other beings. They remember the law of varying human experience. The world to the priestess is a place of suffering, and the human beings she meets are sufferers in need of something she has to give. When the giving is no longer sought she moves on kindly. There is always more and more need of her in more and more places and from more and more people.

The thinking priestess is a woman who retires to discipline herself. She looks upon the world as a sad planet in which people seek to control one another without first learning to control themselves. She is a hedonist in the spiritual sense of the word. She feels that she came herself to earthly experience for the sake of enriching her own spirit. She becomes an adept at minding her own business. What she knows she protects secretively. Often she will pose carefully as some other kind of woman. She does not want the world around her to know that she is different. She is afraid of the group hatred of the lone one who is unlike the rest of them. Invariably, through much thinking, she is able to see all the sides of the human problem.

She can never say that one point of view is altogether right. Therefore she is usually a woman of no fixed allegiance. She calls no person friend.

She guards her associations circumspectly, and even in such relationships as she does admit she holds most of herself in reserve. For she is aware constantly of not being exactly as other women. The fibers of her being become too acutely sensitized to tolerate intimacy with any but a select few of her relative peers, and even with these the door must be always open for escape. In such relationships as she does assume she takes a peculiar rôle. She interprets all that happens as having some relation to the law of her own being, that is, what is done to her in injustice she interprets as a test to her spiritual fiber. She watches her own thoughts, she watches her emotions, she watches her words and her actions. She looks upon the ordinary reaction of mortality as it expresses itself within her own self as unfinished unadult edges in her evolution. She is ashamed when she finds herself burning with resentment. She is appalled when she finds herself seething with jealousy. She expects more of herself than this. She deals with her resentments and her jealousies by teaching herself that all things have their time and their place and all mortals their own experience. Gradually she becomes totally unresentful and completely fatalistic.

Between the meditation and the drilling of herself, the thinking priestess develops her intuitive senses to a high degree of insight. She comprehends what goes on around her when she does come out among people. She is aware of their conscious thoughts. She is often aware of their subconscious processes. Sometimes she can trace the lines of their past experience. Sometimes she is vaguely aware of what is in store for them. She can feel the vibratory nature of a room when she enters. She can read the impressions people have left upon the etheric waves. In a negative state she is a receiving-station of mind. In a positive state she is herself so magnetized that she dominates the attention of people in any place she chooses to go. If she is wise she learns how to turn on and off the negative and positive states, and sedulously conceals from her fellows her "second sight."

The great historic priestesses have been blends of the pitying and the meditative priestess, with the pity slightly in the ascendent.

St. Joan was one of them. So was Florence Nightingale. So too was Mary Baker Eddy. And perhaps also Helena Blavatsky. And all women who have had an idea which would, if applied, relieve the inner or outer suffering of humanity.

The writing priestess is both pitying and meditative.

The pity makes her want to give. The meditation makes her want to give in a form which is a peculiar form of giving, and that will not react upon her personality except to set her still further apart from the rest of humanity.

The writing of the priestess is always close to being pure artistry. This is because the ear of the mystic is always highly sensitive, and the sensitivity of the ear shows in awareness of sound in language. This awareness dominates the writing style. In separating the work of the women held to be priestesses and the women acknowledged as artistes, a very fine line is drawn, which may be in some opinions totally imaginary.

In listening for the sounds of separation one listens for halftones and shadings and for alterations in phrasing which are so slight as to be almost indiscernible. There are those who maintain that the pure artist is always a mystic, and that the absolute mystic is always an artist. To such thinking the use of the words, mystic and artist, in separated connotation is an affectation, and creates an artificial boundary line with no excuse for doing so. It should also be remembered before we proceed further that there are also thinkers who believe that there have been no pure artistes among women and no absolute mystics, and that those women who appear to be artistes and mystics are only helpmeets or matriarchs or sophisticated ladies who give a slight additional touch of finesse to their completely feminine preoccupation with the race as it affects them personally.

However all this may be true, half true, or not true at all, it

may certainly be said that there are women who have entered
the fields of mysticism and art. Whether or not they are superb
in their fields in comparison with men is quite another question.

Concerning the division between the priestess and the artiste
among these women, there is one suggestion for submission. It
is that though the artiste may contain the mystic, and though
the mystic may be essentially an artiste, there is a motif of reconciliation in the written work of a mystic, and an altered
motif of interpretation in the writing of the artiste. The mystic
is focused upon life for its meaning. The artiste is focused upon
life for its simple being. They may meet and blend in individual
cases. It is this possibility of meeting and blending which is
baffling to any set division. Yet the separated qualities which
do meet and blend can be resolved to their origins in the
cause of any tentative catalogue of type. In enclosing a group
of the great women writers under the listing of priestesses I
have listened for a conciliatory undersound. In all cases they
are gently calling the attention of their readers to something
they wish to be understood. They are both healing and teaching. In the other writers this sound is so submerged as not to be
audible. The difference is almost negligible, yet distinct enough
to make it a difference.

PEARL BUCK

The sound of conciliation in Pearl Buck, artiste though she is
in her form, is unmistakably present.

She is a veritable Goddess of Mercy from China. She reaches
out a thousand arms of pity to the women of the world. Underneath the purity of her English lies the clangor of Chinese
sounds. Her phrasing, taken though it is from the phrasing of
the Hebrew scriptures, has the stylized intonation of Chinese
utterance.

Pearl Buck is passionately and devoutly feminine. It is as if
the women of all ages, all races and all countries took possession
of her and poured through her all stored-up anguish and racial
patience. It sets the tone of the sacred mission to all her writing.

She draws the women of the East and the West together in the
bond of common womanhood. The woman with the baby at
her breast, and in her heart the love of a man out of which she
made the baby, is one woman the world over.

The first of her books to touch the hearts of her readers was
The Good Earth.

It is about two peasant Chinese, a man and a woman. They
labored together in the fields. They endured poverty together.
They endured famine together. The woman brought forth
children. She grew old and bent and ugly. After a while the
man prospered and in prosperity his thoughts turned to women
who were not useful but just beautiful. He wanted one of them
for himself. He brought home a girl from a brothel. He
could not help himself. He had been starving for beauty as he
toiled. It was not that he showed disrespect to his wife. He
honored her as the mother of his children. The wife did not
take it as disrespect. The man had not cast her off. And
she knew her own lack of beauty. He had been good to her
within his powers and in accordance with his doctrines. Her
pride lay in the welfare of her children, who grew up and married and were a credit to the family in their own individual
ways. The story is told as evenly and as fatalistically as the
story of Job. It is the simple story of simple folk living close
to the earth and its reality. It wakens in the reader strange
feelings. There is a memory sound within it of the Biblical
narratives. Pearl Buck uses her narrative details as the Hebrew
narrators used theirs. The simple facts of human living, toil
in the fields, labor to bear children, the eating of food, the
hunger for food, sleeping, breathing, pain and the eternal
separation of human spirits one from the other are treated with
simple dignity. There is no side-stepping around human issues.
There is no exaggeration of one issue at the expense of the others.
Her people live in China, and the atmosphere of China is all
about them. They are Chinese. They endure what they have
to endure with placid endurance. They hardly know they are
enduring. It is life to endure. They never know that they

have accomplished great heroism. They have just lived. She uses color and line to produce a picture of a grade of living in the country she knows well. But more than this, she uses flesh tones and bone lines to produce a picture that is a symbol of all living.

Mrs. Buck took a similar theme and a similar manner of narration in *The Mother*. But more definitely than *The Good Earth* she makes it a woman's story. It is about a woman's long wait for the return of her husband, her patient long look down the road he had gone and on which he would return.

The feeling of the waiting of women comes into the work of Pearl Buck over and over again. It is a sad and beautiful little melody in a minor key occurring and recurring. The woman waiting for the man to come to her; the woman waiting for her child to be born, for it to learn to walk, for it to grow up; the woman waiting for the man to return to her; her long, long waiting through history for understanding.

The Mother is a simple story of womanhood in the peasant ranks of China. The man went away and the woman was left to till the fields and feed the children, one of whom is blind, and to provide for her mother-in-law. The neighbors wonder. She makes up a story. The man has gone away to earn money for her. She goes to great trouble to write herself letters that are to all inquirers letters from him. She even sends herself money. The story follows her descent into sin with the land agent, and the payment she makes for the sin, and it follows the spiritual graph of her gradual absorption in her motherhood. The children grow up; the old mother-in-law dies; the children marry. The blind girl child goes to an unhappy life and dies. Something dies, too, in the mother. And all the while the man never returns. He has vanished from the life that knew him, and almost from the mind of the woman who lived with him. For a long time she waits for her son to have children, and when at last her grandchild is placed in her arms, she knows that she has done her part. Life will go on.

The story pulls at the heart. It is a woman of China. But

it is a woman of all countries, from all races, from every age. It is every woman who has taken a man to her in trust and finds how strong is the hold of that trust upon her. It is every woman who has given her flesh to children and finds how strong is the hold of their flesh upon her. It is every woman who has worked long years that something may be brought to its end, and in that work has not known all that she was doing, and not even why she was doing it, but only that she must fulfil the command within her own spirit and body. It is the woman throughout history, eternally creating, and eternally, in the end, alone in that creating, while life tears up what she has created, forcing her to create again and again. It is the woman of faith in the tradition of womanhood and staying with it no matter what suffering is upon her in its fulfilment.

Besides the novels, Pearl Buck has written a number of short stories which are collected in a volume called *The First Wife*.

The title story is about a woman in a class many strata above the peasant class. But this woman also waits. She has been given in marriage to an ambitious young man who, after his racial duty in the matter of children has been accomplished, goes out to foreign countries to study. The wife waits at home for the return of her husband. But when he comes everything is different. He has gone modern. He does not want his wife. He wants a modern woman who can converse with him and understand his ideas and build with him into the fabric of new China. More than this, he wants his children to be reared in the new conception of things. He does not think their mother is fit to bring them up. Her ideas are archaic. For him the self-effacing graciousness of the traditional Chinese woman of caste is not beautiful. It is pathetic and useless. Her lovely quiet movements are lost upon him. Her simple worship of his masculine wisdom means nothing. She is not educated as he counts education. Therefore her admiration is not interesting flattery. It is merely the gesture that has been trained into her, the gesture of the Chinese wife of the old tradition. The wife realizes that her life is over. She kills herself. That was to her the way out and the solution of the tragedy—to remove herself that her husband might be free and that her children might take their places in the modern world. In the writing of this poignant story Pearl Buck tries gently to reconcile the reluctant past to the conquering present. The story shows the author a woman stricken with feeling over the resisting and pulling centripetal and centrifugal forces of history. She lays down her feeling simply and profoundly into her phrasing. It meets our feeling. The human heart, she is saying, is a universal heart, and the universal woman engrossed in her task of creating finds it hard to understand the restlessness of men, and in like manner the energetic adventurous universal man finds it hard to be patient with the fatalism of the creative woman. She feels for the poor among folk, and the poor in China reach out in her stories to the poor everywhere else. China rousing itself from its centuries of fatalism appeals through her stories for the sympathy of the enterprising West.

The material in itself was enough to leave its impression upon the sensitive reader; with the addition of her peculiar style, the effect was overwhelming. In a time of sharply sophisticated writing a woman began to write after the manner of the Hebrew narrators. The English she used was the English of the King James Version of the Scriptures. Her phrases had depth of tone; sound was placed in conjunction with other sound in a way that produced a strange vibratory inflection. The gestures throughout were dignified. The meaning was spiritual. The human race in a time when it was the style among writers to mock and sniff was treated with simple grandeur. Those who read felt again the wonder they had felt years before when first they heard the Scriptures read by their mothers. It brought them back to the mother and the mother's faith. It was a mother speaking about God brooding over China, though not making any direct use of the word *God*; China, a land of mystery as the Holy Land was a land of mystery to the narrating Hebrews and the listening children, yet where women suffered for their men, and men suffered for the want of something more

than they had, and children were born in the unchanging way.
The brooding and the suffering and the mystery of life that is
everywhere. It moved in a peculiar rhythm of its own, and
underneath was a faint singing tone. It took the mystic sense
of the reader like the intonation of a prayer from the lips of a
priestess.

RADCLYFFE HALL

Radclyffe Hall is an example of the inability of the public,
even of the reading public, to hold more than one idea about
one writer. She published *The Well of Loneliness*, and it
doomed her to be remembered in her own time only as a student
of sexual inversion. All the beauty and power of her prose
was, in general, lost in the popular reaction of horror to her
theme. The book was banned by opinion terrified by a frank
study of abnormality. It refused to consider the book as a valuable document set down in parable form. It does not happen
to be a valuable document when considered psychiatrically. It
opens with a curious psychiatric error. The writer submits an
artistic theory concerning the peculiarity of her heroine. She
assumes that a girl child could be born out of the normal sexual
plan because of the prenatal influence of her parent's desire for
a boy. If this were so, nearly every girl would be born out of
the normal sexual plan, for nearly all parents long for a son in
preference to a daughter, which is in no way unflattering to
a girl, but is only the natural hang-over from the old tribal
necessity for plenty of male warriors. For some reason Radclyffe Hall avoided the traumatic shock findings of the psychiatric investigators in relation to the sexual invert, or if she
did not avoid it in thought, she could see no way apparently of
dramatically presenting shock in the course of her story. The
heroine grows up longing to have been a boy, and when she
comes to sexual maturity she discovers in herself the normal
male's attraction to the female. The tragedy goes on from
there.

But she did manage to get over one documentary contribution—that the whole problem of Lesbianism needs to be con-

sidered coolly and justly in relation to the present doings of women in the world.

There is an astonishing amount of it, both actual and implied.

Lesbianism has infinitely more facets of expression than the actual sexual taste of certain definitely inverted women who wear suits and collars and ties and fedoras, for little, very feminine fairies. It may be found later, when the subject has been tackled by experts, that all aggressive women who are playing the man, whether in an apparently normal taste for dominating weak men, which implies a desire to put men in the position of women, or in a tendency, against which most of them struggle more or less successfully, to prefer the society of very feminine women to that of strong men. It might even be found that an extraordinary number of successful women are implicitly, if not actually, Lesbian. It just might happen that a careful organization of the subject conducted after the gathering in of honest data would uncover astonishing facts about the so-called new woman. It is just possible that it might be discovered that the whole feminist enterprise as it manifests itself in this age is to a large extent the result of a sudden subconscious determination on the part of the Lesbian population to assert itself.

The Lesbian, we know now, is a woman who, through some early shock, developed a distinct distaste for the feminine rôle towards men. She sets up in defense a psychological process which leads her in its culmination to avoid the engulfment of herself in the biological consummation of women. She subconsciously refuses to hand herself over as a vessel to the race, and nature takes it out on her by twisting its plan and producing a woman with an attraction to other women. If she likes women she will dislike men, and that dislike will save her from the biological consummation of women. Subconsciously she is aware of shame. So she makes a tremendous effort upon a mental or artistic or professional plane to show that she is not less than the normal woman but more. It drives her to achievement. In a sense it saves her for achievement. She never sees the golden apple of romance which sidetracks the normal woman in her run for the goal of success. She never sees the golden apple of the baby which so engrosses the normal woman that it takes her as a rule right off the track which leads to success in the world.

The novels of women at this period indicate an almost general impatience in women with men. The novels, taken as a whole for consideration, set down an almost unanimous conviction that men in an emotional relationship are unsatisfactory and unsatisfying to women.

This is the surprise of the feminist movement as it expresses itself in fiction. It is an indirect admission either of the inability of women to take the traditional rôle of women towards men, or of the failure of the new man to come up to the desires of the new woman. There are, of course, exceptions to this among the women novelists, but in the main it is a general fiction fact.

It must have a cause. The cause must lie somewhere in the period of feminism. The traditional woman always took men as they were, and expected from men some difference in the attitude towards the romantic relation and towards the race. She let it go at that. The new woman is not content to let it go.

The new woman who takes to fiction is in the main not romanticizing her relation to men. She treats it resentfully in realism. To this, it must be stressed at the risk of repetition, there are many and notable exceptions, but it is on the whole a safe generalization.

It is just possible that there is a chance of the fictional resentment having come from the exposure of all women of the day to the infection of latent and actual Lesbianism. The Lesbian always maintains that men are poor lovers. The women who are writing resentfully may have no idea that they have gathered in from the etheric waves the dominating thoughts of inverted women, and still may have gathered them in.

Lesbianism is admittedly flourishing in either its implication or its actuality in an astonishingly large number of women.

Whether the largeness of the number is to be accounted for by the world shock sustained by the war and post-war generation of women, and the sickening of the civilized mind against the animality of war, and consequently with all other phases of animality, is a subject for thought.

This is a period of high nervous intellectuality.

In periods of high nervous intellectuality Lesbianism and its masculine counterpart appear. Whether this is due to the effort of the intellect to lift itself above the animal body, or whether it is merely a sign of the devitalizing of the emotional nature following a great war, is a problem that has to be left. It might be that inversion has always been innate in certain numbers of the population, and is only acknowledged on a large scale in such periods as those following a great war, because large scale killing demands from nature some compensatory effort to balance sexual manifestation, or because war, by its very terror, awakens in the race its submerged courage, and thus leads people in the aftermath of the excitement of bravery to admit what under other circumstances they would not admit.

Whatever the suppositional cause, the second and third decades of the twentieth century have produced a body of fiction by women which seems to regard the historic position of men in the race as being decidedly overestimated. It is interesting because so far as we know to the contrary this opinion is being set down for the first time in history. The one point is—is it an innate opinion of women—or is it a period opinion? And this has to be left unsolved.

And the second point is—how likely is it to be an opinion insinuated into the thinking of normal women by abnormal women and their thinking? And this also has to be left unsolved.

Radclyffe Hall suggests without actually declaring it that the women of the Lesbian group with which she deals in one section of the book are women of out-and-out muscularity of brain. It leaves the reader with still another question in mind, and that is the possibility of mental muscularity presupposing a

definite amount of masculine content in a woman; and the
corollary that the woman who uses her brain in the struggle of
accomplishment becomes more and more masculine with time.
And that question also has to be left unanswered inasmuch as
the history of feminism is still too young to indicate any reliable answer.

Apart altogether from its psychiatric implications, *The Well
of Loneliness* produces an artistic impression which is somewhat similar to the artistic impression of the Greek tragedies.
The Greeks accepted inversion in all its variations as being of
excellent dramatic substance.   The Greeks were able to separate
their intellectual curiosity from their instinctive regard for the
preservation of the normal, which fact alone makes them stand
out in history a superior people.   Radclyffe Hall set herself the
mission of portraying to the normal the sufferings of the invert in society.   She pleads for pity and for understanding.
She says that mankind, having only just begun to find the laws
relating to sex, may in a relatively short time discover that
there are biological accidents producing inversion.   Her heroine
she presents as a victim for our sympathy.   The pity note in the
book is pity that goes out to all creatures who are not able,
through her theory of biological accident, or through the
psychiatric theory of trauma, to partake of normal experience.

There is pity also for the race which, through its terror of
the abnormal, punishes the victims, and may thereby lose valuable services in fields that are other than racial.   She believes that
these people, because of their peculiarity, have something else to
do for the race than to continue it.   She stresses their acutely
sensitized nerves—the nerves that always go with beings of high
capacity.   She dwells upon the invert's susceptibility to sound.
Radclyffe Hall herself writes with mystical sensitivity to tone.
Her phrasing shows it.   Her words are put down in relation
to their sounds set against other sounds.   She produces by this
means a disturbing emotional effect.

The importance of her fictional comment upon the situation
of the invert lies in this—that inasmuch as inversion, by reason

of its distortion of nerves, can at least be tentatively held to be
a nervous disorder, the invert should not be treated as a pariah,
but rather as a person who through no fault of his or her own is
suffering from nervous excitement coming from the kinetic response of the whole human fabric to change. It can be drawn
from her story that only the highly sensitized members of
society take shock acutely enough to be disorganized away from
the normal, and that in the long run it is only the highly
sensitized members of society who are in the spiritual sense
valuable. The race goes on. The normal people see to that.
But art and religion and thought and science have always been
maintained in the race by the variously abnormal, and meanwhile they suffer tortures through being unable to adjust themselves to normality.

The priestess tone in Radclyffe Hall developed through the
tone of the invert. She comments in her story upon the attraction of the invert to religion, and that very comment in itself
suggests a world of inquiry concerning the old historic orders
of the priestesses and concerning the priestess temperament itself. It may be that the attraction of any young girl to any
order of the priesthood, implied or actual, presupposes inversion certainly to the extent of a marked shrinking from normal
experience. Radclyffe Hall fulfilled the essentials of her priesthood when she wrote *The Well of Loneliness*. She showed
the invert striving to find reconciliation to her fate. She pleaded
with the world for understanding and patience and sympathy
concerning its inverts. And having fulfilled that mission she has
moved deeper into her destiny.

Her latest book, *The Master of the House*, portrays a man so
enamored with the Christ that he himself partakes of the
earthly experience of the Christ even to the extent of suffering
upon a cross during the war. It is a study which goes into the
phenomena of the stigmata and the indrawing of the personality
regardless of time or place within the very details of the lives
of the saints. It is a purely mystical presentation of the idea
that what we love, we are. The hero, loving the Christ, be-

comes step by step a Christ. This is the intangible law behind the symbol of the sacrament.

The Master of the House, like *The Well of Loneliness*, deals with inversion. While the heroine in the one book lives the life of a man within the body of a woman, the man in the other book lives the life of a Christ within the body of a mortal. Neither of them has any concern with normal experience. They should be kept together and read together. They are part of the same mysterious saga. Some process was started which had to be fulfilled in crucifixion. Radclyffe Hall in her studies has come to the edge of something that is not as yet comprehended. She puts her observations into parables because parables suggest rather than proclaim. These things happen, she believes. A woman gets tangled biologically with the being of a man, and maybe also spiritually. She loves women instead of men. A man gets attached spiritually to the being of a Master, and maybe also biologically. He loves mankind instead of an individual. The woman begins to look like a man. She wears the clothes of a man. She acts like a man. The man begins to look like the Master. He wears in his flesh the marks of the Master's suffering. He takes it upon himself to live in his mortal flesh the life of the Master. Both of them are under some impulse neither they nor anyone else can understand. Yet both are sane; and both in their way are great. The woman was great artistically; the man was great in spirit.

The work of Radclyffe Hall, including these two books and two others which also touch upon the spiritual mystery, *Saturday's Child* and *Adam's Breed*, is serious, profound and beautiful work, in no way doctrinaire, yet thoroughly indoctrinated. Her emotion is still yet deep. She is like a quiet pool of great depth. She is ageless. It is work that might have come out of Greece. It is work that might have come from India. It seems to have nothing to do with the modern Western world and the flair of that world for the nonchalant, the bizarre and the funny. It has nothing to do with Victorian sentiment. It has nothing to do with Elizabethan delight in living; neither has it anything to do with eighteenth-century sophistication; nor yet anything to do with the romance that belongs to all centuries. She is preoccupied with the mysteries, as the priestesses were, and she pities the human race as it passes them by for things that can be added up and multiplied and subtracted and divided.

The priestess with the first urge to set her thoughts down does not as a rule take the narrative form. The ecstasy of spiritual realization belongs to poetry. It is a strange emotion which in its first implication unites the feeler of it to the world of nature, to the world of nature's sounds and colors and beyond that even the world of silence. It is an incommunicable awareness of cosmic life, and it feels its way out to expression in verse form or music or dancing. It is a spiritual song in the soul. It comes at the beginning suddenly. It stays at the beginning only a short time. The communicant is never able to sustain it. The form of expression is therefore a burst of feeling into melody and into rhythm, and usually is short. When it is over the soul seeks for it again, and wonders how it may again come to pass. It moves in search of the spiritual law, and as it does this the thoughts behind the experience begin to come out in the form of the mystical essay.

The mystic in first communion with the feeling and the law of life is separated from other men and women. The atmosphere of unity includes only the immutable changeless substance of life—the swing of the planets in their orbits, the return of the seasons, the beat of rain, the soft falling of snow, the silence of the forests superimposed upon the little sounds of animals' feet, bird songs and flight, and the murmur of leaves, the glinting light of the sun, the shadow of the twilight, and the slow undulation of fields of grain in the wind. So rapt is the mystic in all these that mankind seems to be something that lives upon the earth an alien.

It is only after a period of time that the glory spreads to human beings and the mystic sees the light in the eyes of a child, the sweetness of human love, the beauty of the bodies of

men and women and the dignity of death. It is then that the
drama of human effort and failure takes possession of the soul,
and all the little inconsequential things of life begin to unfold
themselves in pleasure and in pain before the eyes of the watcher.
And the form of expression moves on to the narrative. Men
and women set down in their impermanency against the strange
permanency of the universe.

MARY WEBB

Mary Webb, who is the greatest of the women mystics writing in English, began as a poet. The story of her development
is told by Thomas Moult in his fine study of her life and
work.

She was a Shropshire lass, born in 1881, and dying prema-
turely in 1927 of pernicious anemia induced by a glandular disturbance.

Her name was Gladys Mary Meredith. On her father's side
she was of Welsh ancestry. Her mother belonged to the Scott
family of Edinburgh, distantly related to the family which had
produced Sir Walter Scott. Which means that there was a large
amount of the Celt in her racial composition. And further
means a tendency towards mysticism, it being almost native to
the Celtic imagination.

The tendency in her case was increased by constitutional delicacy. The glandular disorganization showed itself when she
was twenty years old. And she struggled the rest of her life
with sickness and fatigue. The first round with the trouble
laid her out for a long time. She learned then intimacy with
death, and felt the awful surprise of the spirit when the
body is helpless. She reached out eagerly for compensation.
She found it in meditation upon the life that went on within
her without much cooperation from the body, and upon the
still greater life that was life before she had been, and would
still be life when she had gone. She forced herself into com-
munication with that life, and put down what came to her in
verse, and then in prose essays and finally in fiction.

When she was in her early thirties she married Mr. H. B. L. Webb, a schoolmaster. It was a happy marriage, though there were no children, and in spite of very little money and the poor health of the wife. Marriage was the link she needed for the realization of her mysticism in human experience, and it was not until she was married that she wrote fiction.

There was something about Mary Webb that was like Emily Brontë. She was shy in ordinary social ways. The rich and the powerful failed to stir her. To the poor and the lowly she responded. When she was well she visited the aged and the needy. She read to those who could not read. She gave generously from her own slender resources of vitality and money. Like Emily Brontë she needed a lot of solitude and cared very little for her appearance. Like Emily Brontë she craved always for her own country. She was homesick away from Shropshire. It seemed as if she had to have the influence upon her of the place of her first mystical impressions. She could write as she wanted to write nowhere else. She differed from Emily Brontë in that she definitely cared about the publication of her work. She felt it acutely when reviewers and readers did not see what she was doing. She was ecstatically happy when she received praise from people of the caliber of Stanley Baldwin. She differed again from Emily Brontë in that she could enjoy the society of her peers. She liked going to gatherings of literary folk now and then. However, a little of it went a long way with her. She could never for any length of time do without solitude and the familiar places of Shropshire. But most of all she resembled the mystic of the moors in her recoil from cruelty in any form. She hated the hunt. She felt the agony of the poor puzzled fox, and more than this, she felt in her fibers what the hunt did to those who took part in it, reducing them in a moment to creatures of one horrible instinct—the instinct of the killer. She hated injustice. That was at the basis of her reaction to the hunt. There was no need to kill the fox. The fox was not overrunning an estate, and the hunters were not in need of food, or of fur to protect them-

selves against the cold. She hated persecution in any form and
the preying of the sophisticated upon the innocent and of the
ignorant upon the wise. She hated war. She began her first
novel the first year of the war. It was the creative gesture of
a woman determined to save something of the spiritual remnant
during a time when destruction was upon her world.

Thomas Moult in his study shows how she developed novel
by novel. *The Golden Arrow, Gone to Earth, The House in
Dormer Forest*, until she came to her great book, *Precious Bane*,
the meaning of which is *The Sweet in Much Bitter*. The first
novels were in his estimation means of tuning her instrument,
and she gathered all her force and all her message into one
glorious whole when she wrote *Precious Bane*.

Precious Bane is the story of a girl, Prue Sarn, who is marked
by a harelip. In scarring the face of her heroine Mary Webb
followed a psychic principle. The human being who becomes
a mystic is always handicapped in some measure. He is low
born, love born, or deprived of some one of his senses, so that
never upon the path of experience can he be led away from his
mystical destiny by the approval of the pack. He is one set
apart, the child of God with knowledge of God. This is the
fact which causes the psychoanalyst to trace all manifestations
of mysticism back to a human lack, and to a fear of the pack
induced by a difference and a failure. There is only God who
understands, and to God the marred one turns for safety.

The story is set historically in a period when a harelip is interpreted by the folk of the country as a sign of the witch, and
Prue Sarn knows fear from the beginning of her individual
consciousness. No man will ever want her in marriage; people
will always watch her suspiciously; her family will always consider her dubiously.

Out of the fire of her sorrow and out of the wash of her sensitive inner life she emerges a sparkling white spirit, and the
author sets her a symbol of spirituality against a black background of materialism and sin. The story is told almost alle-
gorically in the first person. Prue narrates her own experience

with simplicity and grace. And never once did Mary Webb slip technically in her use of the difficult technique of the first person singular narrative. The story is fulfilled with consistent plausibility.

Prue Sarn lives with her parents and her brother in an old house. Mary Webb over and over again set her people against the foreboding background of houses that contained evil in themselves. She produces the same impression of hateful implacability in a house that Emily Brontë produced in *Wuthering Heights*. The house presses itself down with all its stored-up bitterness upon the fate of its tenants. But it was foiled by the presence of the bright spirit, Prue, and her discovery within it of a sanctuary in which no evil was. There was an unused attic in which the apples mellowed, and where the weaver when he came did his weaving. It was a place unsullied by human spite, and to it Prue went for her meditation, and there she realized the awakening of her spiritual sense.

Old Sarn, the father, dies in a storm of anger at his son. Young Sarn bargains with his mother for the possession of the place. He will be the sin-eater for his father if she will give him the house and its land. Sin-eating was an old custom of speeding on the dead and loosening them from an earth-bound tendency by acceptance on the part of a mortal still living of the sins and their consequences left behind by the dead. Young Sarn, by the very fact of tying this ritual to a bargain gainful to himself, put himself in league with the devil. As the story progresses he becomes more and more tangled with the notion of material success, until he will do anything to accomplish his own will to power. He forces Prue to work in the fields with him. He forces his aging mother to overwork in the house. When she sickens he arranges for her an overdose of foxglove tea, but sees that somebody else is the medium of giving. He will have nobody around him who slows up the course of his purpose. He had a chance to reconsider. Love of a girl brought him to the spiritual crossroad. But blended with the love between him and Jancis was the hatred of her father for Sarn.

This hatred dominates. Jancis and Sarn were married in reality but not by the preacher. The father of Jancis burns the crop at Sarn in revenge. Sarn repudiates Jancis, but later she returns to Sarn with her baby. When he refuses to acknowledge her, she drowns herself and the baby. Sarn is haunted by her and drowns himself. The people of the place blame all these deaths upon the harelip girl, and are on the point of drowning her for witchcraft when she is saved by the Weaver.

Against the one story of darkness and sin and tragedy another story of light is set. Prue had met the Weaver at the love spinning for Jancis. She recognizes him instantly as her love. All her spirit goes out to him in worship. He is the Master of her being. She saves him when the people turn upon him because he has interfered with their sport of bull-baiting. She writes him love letters, though they are to all intents the letters she writes for her brother to Jancis. Jancis, she knows, will take them to the Weaver to be read to her. The Weaver lives in her heart, though she never believes that he could love a woman with a harelip. The body of Prue was light and beautifully formed— the shape of a fairy—and once she had done a fearsome thing and the Weaver had seen that body. The queer old father of Jancis posed in the district as a magician. He could, he said, summon the body of Venus out of a bottle. He commanded Jancis to be Venus and come up out of a trap-door for the entertainment of the young Squire. Jancis was afraid. Sarn, she told Prue, would disown her if another man saw her. So Prue was Venus that night, and in the darkened room the Weaver sat with the young Squire, and saw how like a pearl the skin of the girl was, and how exquisite the shape of her was. Being an observant man, he knew whose form it was he had seen. What with the memory of that night, with the lovely words of her letters, and with her rush to save him regardless of her own safety, and a few conversations, the Weaver came to realize the sweetness of the woman that was Prue Sarn. The love between them lived unseen but felt, and it threw a mantle of charity over the mind of Prue as she played her part in the destinies of those under compact with sin.

The story is woven in between darkness and light. The gentle mind of Prue takes pleasure in the rural life in which she is placed. She revels in the beauty of the natural world. She revels in the peace of a simple life. The fire by night, the purring of the pussy-cat, the coming of the sun, the sheen of the dew on the grass, the gold of the grain. Again and again she returns to the mystery of life itself. The struggle of the dragon-fly to get out of its chrysalis suggests to her the struggle of the spirit to reach God. The hum of the bees suggests to her the cosmic hum of the worlds as they obey their Maker; the fragrance of the ripening apples suggests the fragrance of the universal spiritual substance.

The girl seeks with her mystic senses for the Master. To a nun it would have been the Crucified. To Prue in her simplicity it was a man who came and was known in the community as the Weaver. He would have none of the sumptuous females around. He saw the white shine of Prue, and when he does the spiritual story is linked with human romance. The Weaver is molded in the design of a Master. He suffers persecution. This blended the mysticism and the femininity of Mary Webb. It was another version of the age-old Messianic dream of a woman—to hold the Christ in her arms, to weep at his agony, to be the first in the garden upon his reappearance. So strong is the Messianic passion expressed by Mary Webb in the faultless Weaver that the reader pauses to wonder, with admitted blasphemy, if perchance the whole Christ story could have come out of a woman's great Messianic hunger—or if in its symbolic drama it explained to women the search for something in a man to worship and to save it in its remnant of legend after the world had done its worst to him. Or maybe, putting aside the blasphemy, the great story has so dominated the emotionalism of women that they seek the Christ in their lovers, and maybe set up the Christ image within the lover's image, and by holding tenaciously to that image do bring something incredibly healing to the pain of loving.

The young Prue, conscious of the Weaver when he came into a room, and hiding her stricken face so that he might not see it, writing him letters, pouring out her adoration in the relief of phrasing, humbly grateful when he came her way, symbolizes once and for all the woman's consciousness of herself as marked by the very profundity of her sexual functioning by what seems to be a burdened fate. This is the priestess point of view—that the man is free biologically, that the woman, doomed to bear the burden of life, loves the man yearningly and wistfully because he is not doomed, and out of her love for him reconciles herself to her lot.

All this is pressed into the simple story of tragedy and love and spiritual communion set in the archaic life of a small community. The story is slightly unreal considered in a modern sense, and yet in spite of the unreality it is humanly warm. The warmth shows in the sustained bits of character-drawing throughout. The gallery of people around the principals is whimsically attractive. The humanity shows in the romantic ending. Had Mary Webb followed her spiritual drama through, she would have let Prue die a victim of group fear. That she did not was a priestess gesture—she wanted to give to the mortal Prue what she desired.

Precious Bane is a beautiful story. The style of the writer is immaculate. There is music in every phrase. There is drama in every situation. There is rich fulness of body in the characterization of everybody in the story except Prue and the Weaver. They are spiritualized creatures wandering for a time among mortals. They are creations of Mary Webb's imagination; Prue is her own imaginative self, and the Weaver is the fine drawing of the spiritual woman's dream of a man. The other people she took straight from the countryside. She had seen them. She had talked to them. She had lived among them. And apart from all this excellency of pure fiction in the story, it is a record set down in a form akin to allegory of stations in the spiritual progression of a soul. It presents through the story of Prue and her blemished face the story of the enlightened spirit lifting itself up after its bruising, and gradually becoming aware of its mission, seeing itself in symbolized relation to other human beings. The spirit takes its hurt and is reconciled. No longer does it shrink. It comes forward to give, and to live again and again, and in the giving the hurt is resolved into a blessing. This, when it is followed through, is what turns a woman into a priestess. And also what makes her put down in narrative form the feeling she has for humanity. When she writes verse it is the feeling of God that goes into metrical pattern. When she writes essays it is something of the disciplining she has given herself that puts itself into thought in prose. But when she turns to the race to give, she uses, as all the great mystics have used, the light veiling of the parable. It is truth as she has received it set down in symbols that are familiar, love and hate, birth and death, struggle and submission, and all the interplay of human beings individualized.

This she can do because, as Mary Webb herself said, it is the saint who understands sin; it is the mystic and not the sensualist who understands human love; it is the "dove woman" and not the sophisticate who understands sex; it is the priestess and not the matriarch who understands motherhood. The mystic in Mary Webb's mind was the final reconciler of life, for all others in their interpretation left it half-told for lack of awareness of "the sweet in much bitter" and "the glory from the other side of silence."

CHAPTER XIII

ARTISTES

Katherine Mansfield—Willa Cather—Clemence Dane
—Virginia Woolf

THE LITERARY TEMPERAMENT IS
part of the artistic temperament, and is not normally the temperament of women.

A normal woman, either in ancient times or modern, is a still, deep sexual being. She is a biological force under a compelling instinct to find a safe place to lay her babes, and before that she is in subconscious search for a man who will give her the babes and help her to find a place to lay them.

The literary temperament is a baffling, elusive kinetic force which finds no peace anywhere, and is content nowhere. It feels a strange momentary pleasure in the creation of mood in the sound and the color and the meaning of words and their form in phrasing. It goes its own peculiar way through life, leaving broken experience behind it, and the wrecks of relationships that will not suit its volatile need. The litterateur, like the artist, the musician and the thinker, is a creative explorer of living, and when one place is explored and a record made of it, another place has to be explored.

How can these two go together?

When a young woman takes to writing, it is because something has hurt her biologically, and she tries to escape the fate of womanhood.

This may also be true of the young man who takes to writing, but there is a great difference. He has nothing fundamentally from which to escape biologically. It is true that some aspect of the world around him may have hurt him, and he may feel the need to create for himself a world which will be

339

better than the world he has experienced, or he may feel a need to make fun of the world, or to protest against it by drawing it as he has seen it. It is true also that gradually as he learns to write he may become so completely overpowered by the creative forces he has set working within himself that he lives entirely for them. But in living for them he is not going very much against the biological currents of his nature in their fundamental expression. To go from experience to experience for the sake of savoring and recording experience is not alien to his original masculinity. For men, if we are to judge by their biological tendencies when undisciplined by the restraints of domesticity under Western civilization, were fashioned for the purpose of wandering from place to place and from experience to experience. It is only the holding need of a woman attached to him, or some acquired sense of economic duty, which keeps a man still in one place, or fastened to one evolving experience. It is just possible that it is because men have been held still against their original instincts that they take so quickly, so blindly and so zestfully to the wars which come up. For war means change and movement and exploration of a kind. And men take to them generation upon generation.

It has been seen in the lives of the historic women writers that all of them were damaged biologically in some form. They were, all of them, girls who looked into a mirror and said to themselves, "No man will ever like me." They were not all of them plain women. Mary Wollstonecraft was handsome. Jane Austen was actually pretty. Emily Brontë was distinguished-looking, and George Eliot and Olive Schreiner were both of them disturbingly full of personality. They were all, however, in some definite way decidedly out of the ordinary. And in their times, as in all time, it was the average sweet little girl who received the attention of the little boys, and upon whom parents and relatives and probably teachers impressed the notion of desirability. The little girl who was different, as George Eliot plainly showed in the story of Maggie Tulliver, was bothered continually by the implied, if not always actual, criticism

of her elders and her contemporaries, and this, in spite of the
fact that her very difference was a quality likely in her maturity
to make her a biological winner. But traumatic shocks, as we
know now, have slight relation to any actual reality, and a sense
of inferiority may be developed entirely unrelated to any actual
inferiority. More than this, the slightest degree of unusual
quality in a child induces a sensitivity highly susceptible to
wounding by the pack. The little girl who is thus wounded
subconsciously seeks relief in a world of her own creating, and
in some cases this leads to writing. And in some cases the relief
is so effective that nothing would make the girl give up her
writing.

It may be that the young man who takes to writing also has
at some time looked into a mirror and said to himself, "No girl
will ever like me," and thereupon subconsciously set about a
compensatory activity which will distinguish him. But there
is a great difference. What he does to make himself different
actually does distinguish him biologically as well as intellectually. It adds to his sexual appeal. He becomes attractive
to women because he is different. He is something worthy of
their game. For the illusion of success is there, or at least its
making. No woman sees him as having anything about him to
prevent him from becoming her mate if she decides upon him.
And most women considering him are inclined to consider as
an added asset their own possible part in helping him to attain
his place in the literary, which is to them the success, world.
Biologically they estimate him as being good with his distinguished elements for the making of babes if he can be steered
into success which will insure safe-keeping for the babes. He
may go on being possessed by his need for expression and distinction. A woman may still possess him, and the more elusive
he is of possession the greater will his erotic value be to her, and
the harder she will work to get him, and having got him, to
hold him. There is only this to add—that the stronger the
need in him for distinction the less likely is he to allow himself
to be got, or, having been got, to be held in perpetuity. For as

literature advances upon him he will find that people and things can only remain real to him until they are written down.

But in spite of this elusiveness, he can still come down, as no less a writer than Branch Cabell has pointed out, hungry and amorous, and find some woman waiting to feed him and love him, and regretfully allow him to return to his writing when the mood returns to him to write.

It is not so with a woman, though there are women writing who declare that it is so with them.

Writing is a vocation involving a long, hard novitiate, and the woman who enters it cannot come out hungry and amorous and find some man ready to serve her. If she does find a man, it is not likely by the rules of her nature that she will return, at least not in the fulness of her being, to her writing. Why should she? She has achieved the result for which subconsciously she was seeking when she first started to distinguish herself in a world of her own making. If, through vanity, through habit, or through economic necessity, she does return, it is likely to be only with a fraction of herself held over professionally or avocationally. In the general normal case she will not be likely to return at all, if her life with the man is a full woman's life, including child-bearing and child-rearing and the duties of home-making. She will return, it can be said more or less safely, only if the man by reason of his circumstance cannnot give her the full experience of love and of marriage and economic security. This does not mean that she will not write at all. It means that she will not be in the state of living for the sake of writing, which state is almost absolute to good writing.

The young woman who writes is in a condition of suspended waiting. Because of her womb, if she is normal sexually, she is biologically holding herself in waiting for her man and her children. What she does in an art or a profession is a way of putting in time, or a way of atoning to time for her searching, or a way of enhancing herself. This is dealing with the woman biologically and not intellectually. There may be a thousand more or less intellectual reasons which appear to be the absolute reason for her activity, not to mention the economic reason. But biologically it is certain that the more furiously a young woman works, the more likely is it to be true that she is subconsciously dealing with time or with ornament for herself. She thinks and she hopes, subconsciously, that the time will be short and the ornament effective, and the greater the necessity then to do what she has set out to do with speed and with result. Because of this under-implication of waiting, she hardly ever goes out in search of material. She takes what lies around her. Or, discarding what lies around her, she pulls at her imagination and produces a world such as she would like herself to be in. If, discarding both of these, she forces herself out into experience in the manner approaching the manner of a young man in search of material, she does it against the censure of some law in herself. Always she strains against a dictum, "I must not do this." She is psychologically in the subconscious condition of the pregnant woman. If she does this, it will affect the baby; if she gets into that, it will disturb the baby. She has an inevitable deep sense of having to save herself for the child, and it is always a restraining element interfering with her own individuality. It makes her a racial vessel. If, through an iron will to accomplish, or through an abnormal will to ignore the baby and the racial destiny of women, she can break through this restraint, its fragments when breaking are likely to pierce her own nervous system. She will wonder what it is that ails her. She will curse the caution that shadows her leaps into experience. She will be bothered by regrets. She may try very hard to shake off the racial attitude innate to her, but she will have a difficult time doing it.

If she persuades herself that she has the experimental way with experience, and, for the sake of experience, lives with a man either with marriage or without it, she finds herself contending, in spite of her carefully controlled attitude, with the terrifying emotions produced by the sex relationship. Before she knows it she is into it much deeper than she anticipated. All her sense of art is transferred imperceptibly and almost without volition on her part from writing to femininity. While she may persuade herself that she is living with a man as an experiment in the primary source of fiction, she will eventually and inevitably not feel her experience quite so scientifically. Nature did not organize her for emotional nonchalance. Emotional nonchalance is the particularly acquired psychic preventative of the courtesan. Its technique demands specialized training and application. It does not come easily to the normal woman despite the centuries of practise. A young girl playing with the idea of emotional nonchalance finds it quickly eluding her at the first onset of actual experience of sex. The normal woman, and even the woman with courtesan tendencies, finds sexual experience not conducive to the solitary and arduous labor of the mind necessary to writing. Living with a man she will, if she is even tentatively happy, find herself tending not to think, but to dream, to dance and to sing and to play, and none of these with the determined intensity of histrionic effort, but spontaneously because the deeps of fulfilment in her are stirred, or at least are beginning to be stirred. At the start of love she will think of clothes with which to enhance herself physically for her man, and what to do with her hair and her skin and her figure. She will not listen for a voice within her but for his voice on the telephone. She will not think of stories to write, but of letters to him, or of phrases to say to him in whispers. As love moves on from its start to its full current within her she will not continue to plan success for herself, but for him, and for the children she will find herself desiring, if they are not already with her. She will only turn back to her writing if for some reason no babies can be born to her, or if there happens to be a situation between them which prevents her active woman's participation in his career, or if on some account the man keeps her in a state of uncertain tension concerning himself.

None of this applies to the elderly woman, to the wholly or partially frigid woman, or to such women in whom hereditary or environmental influence has produced the temperamental proclivities of the courtesan. Nor does it apply to the rare case of the woman whose will to write is strong enough to dictate its will to the biological depths of her.

Eliminating such women, it may be said with security that it is always tragedy connected with her biological nature which sends a young woman to writing. It should also be said that there are cases in which the woman herself is not always consciously aware of the tragedy. For to be fully aware of sorrow one must have known joy. And to be fully aware of lack one has to have known fulness. Yet both sorrow and lack can be present and produce an effect upon the biological nature without registering themselves as such upon the conscious mind.

It may also be said with security that it is a hovering sense of tragedy which keeps a mature woman writing. She knows that she must save a remnant out of her experience for the comforting of herself.

She is a woman who in the midst of love remembers the sorrow that always in some form and at some time finds love, and who thinks in the arms of a man of the time when she will not be in his arms, and so works in those days at the perfecting of a technique in order that in other days she will have something to contain her in her sorrow.

The normal woman in her first love never does this, and never realizes the impermanency of emotion. If she thinks at all of tragedy coming to her love, she thinks that far rather would she be dead than safe with something to sustain her through it.

Even with tragedy the normal woman does not write easily, no matter how ready her technique may be. It is like writing in the presence of the dead, and it is a woman's nature to weep beside the dead, or to do the little things that help to hide death. When she writes it is because she is driven by a need to save from her experience the remnant of it.

Writing, then, is a kind of spiritual exercise to her. It is a schooling which enables her to enter willingly into experience for the sake of what she may be able to salvage from it. It is a discipline which trains her to look quietly back upon what has happened to her, and to look quietly around her for the sake of balancing against the experience of others her own experience. Setting down experience is laying out its pattern, and laying out its pattern is often the solution of suffering. It gives to the spirit the detachment which brings peace in the midst of attachment. Romance to such a woman becomes something which remains in her own giving and her own making. It is a quality emanating from her own spirit, and what she puts down upon paper is the residue of understanding proceeding from the human relationships of her life. This woman is the artiste.

The artistes are women who have let themselves down into the passionality of living, and have brought out from their own passionality the wisdom which is the remnant. The things that matter to other women never matter very much to them, and in another sense matter much more. They see romance as the giving of romance. This heightens and at the same time lowers its hold upon them. They see motherhood as the giving of experience, which heightens and at the same time lowers its pull upon them. They see writing as the giving both of romance and experience in a form which variously approaches a more lasting form than love and than motherhood, and therefore they are without tension as is no other woman. If these women have men of their own and children of their own, and still write, it is because there are things which even to their men and their children have not been told and must be told. If they have no men of their own and no children, they write because there are things they would like to tell those who are not with them. Poetry may catch the fragment of the feeling of such women; essays may catch the fragment of the wisdom they have sustained through experience. But fiction contains the residue of both feeling and wisdom, and it is to fiction that these women usually turn. Some of them turn also to the drama, but the drama is a form which for its ultimate success necessitates experience of the theater and a professional interest in it. Fiction is a form which may be studied and practised apart from any professional association.

The woman of the literary temperament is a woman who has emerged an artiste out of the contention within herself of two conflicting forces. Her womanhood wants to be at peace with itself. It needs for its peace to be lost in the race. The litterateur in her wants no peace. It wants change and movement and complete containment in itself. Self-containment as it grows in a woman tends to make her less attractive erotically and it resents any use made of her as a vessel of the race. The pull of the race in her resents the onset of self-containment. If the pull of the race is stronger in her, it makes the litterateur in her an amateur litterateur. If the litterateur wins the contest, it makes the racial element in her an amateur element. She is never then a professional wife and mother. If by some miracle of adjustment the two forces in her can be held in a perfect balance, then it does happen that the racial pull in her heightens her sense of the story of experience, and the pull of the litterateur deepens her sense of the meaning of the racial experience. She becomes thereupon a greater writer because she is close to biological reality; she becomes a better racial vehicle because of the wisdom she has gathered through the disciplining of herself in thought and art. If this miracle happens she is truly an artiste, and she has a contribution of her own to make to the residue of the ages set down in literature.

To such a woman a home is not a secure haven, but a laboratory of experience. A man is not to her a sexual possession, but the sharer of her experience. Children are not creations of her own, but aspects of a racial trust. A religion is never a compact group of fellow believers, but a substance taken from the insubstantial. A book is never a professional achievement, but the surviving element of her life as it relates to the lives of others and to the main body of the racial stream. If she thinks of herself at all it will be not either as a woman or as a litterateur, but as the custodian of the remnant, the spiritualized art

remainder of life kept for the race by its most cherishing hands
—the hands of a woman who is also an artiste.

KATHERINE MANSFIELD

Katherine Mansfield as a little girl felt femininely inadequate
beside her beautiful mother and aunt, and also beside her little
sisters. She was pale. She was too sturdy in build. She was
difficult temperamentally. She was forced because of a sense
of inferiority to call up from within her something which
would sustain her in her isolation.

She was born in New Zealand, the daughter of Sir Harold
Beauchamp. Her name was Kathleen, and the family called
her Kass. Prior to their immigration to New Zealand the Beau-
champs were goldsmiths. Pepys mentions purchasing a tankard
from Mr. Beauchamp of Cheapside. There is said to be a Jewish strain in the racial composition of Katherine Mansfield, as she
chose to call herself when she began to write, Mansfield being
the name of her maternal grandmother. Certainly there is a
Jewish quality in her dark eyes and in the intensity of her
capacity for suffering.

Intensity of feeling shows itself in her early diaries and letters. The published personal notes belonging to that period present an almost fierce desire for compensatory distinction. It
was an absolute case of a girl driven to make herself gloriously
different because she was already conscious of being different.
Writing was the way to the glory. Writing was also an outlet
to a troubled spirit, words gradually becoming friends who
never failed. Her intensity of feeling increased as her health
failed. The later journal and letters are the outpouring of a
spirit which had to atone for the body which was slowly giving
up its strength. Writing was the way to atonement. It made
her life mean something. It was also a friend never failing to
bring comfort.

Mansfield said of herself that she saw life in little glimpses
only. It is little glimpses that her stories are, and fragmentary
bits of mood.

She was in England during the height of the suffragette campaign. She was writing during the war, 1914-1918. She went on writing after the war, when the world turned this way and that way trying to bring order to itself. But not one touch of the turmoil of any of these times enters into her writing except as a slight background of agony. In the foreground she put a little creative island, built up out of a few short, intensely vivid memories. It was a sanctuary made out of short fiction, and to hold it as a residue of human experience became her particular task for the time that was left to her. All her stories have a feeling of short time. She finished her work quickly. She made each story get itself down and off, not knowing but that it might be the last story she could write. She incorporated her glimpses into forms which would hold them securely. She finished each story meticulously.

The stories reach out over most of her experience. There are incidents taken from the solitary journeys to the Continent in search of sunshine and warmth. There are stories taken from the happier trips when she was not alone. But most of the stories go back to the years before she became acquainted with pain and weakness. As she lay sick she had to think back to such times as went before she knew the persistence of ill health. She could only get away from the depression of her own personal situation by pulling up from her memory scenes that had no association with sickness. For many of her stories she went back to her childhood, finding in her memories of New Zealand a rich fiction content.

The work of Mansfield considered as a whole is intrinsically feminine and whimsically feminine. It is perhaps the most feminine of all the writing done by women in English, using the word feminine to denote femininity in the sense of the quality of women highly cultivated in order to be different from the masculinity of the male.

It is the way of women to build from very little a great deal. They do it in love. They do it in coming to decisions. They do it consistently through life. It is something they have had to do because of the very little they were allowed to see and know down through the centuries of subjection. Sometimes it makes them distinctly intuitive. Sometimes it makes them superficial in their judgments. Sometimes it makes them incline towards illusions. But whatever else it does, it provides them with the natural equipment of the short-story writer. For the first essential of the short story is to suggest from a short incident a world of character and feeling. From a glimpse of the present the past shows itself, and the future hints at the way it will go. Mansfield did this in her stories, touching the natural woman's glimpse of life with an artistry of expression which she molded as her own over years of patient work. The stories are spontaneous and simple, yet they show the rewrite of the craftsman. Not one word is left in them which is not a necessary word. Not one feeling that is alien to the situation ever creeps in. The story as it is printed is the perfect story of its kind. It is a woman's look at an event, reading from the event the way of the world.

The little glimpses Mansfield had of life opened to her the characters of the people she watched. She described what happened. She tells how the people were dressed, what the day was like as they walked abroad or stayed at home. She writes down what they said, and suggests what they were thinking. She was an artist in dealing with the moment. Because her time was short she was intensely aware of the moments in life that slip into other moments and yet stand out by themselves because they indicate something within something else. The outstanding example of this is in the story called *Bliss*. A woman woke suddenly to the feeling of passion. She had been married. She had borne a child. But she was passive and emotionally asleep. The spring came. She felt it in her skin and in her spirit. She became suddenly aware of her husband. She thought of the dark night and the warm bed and the man, and on that night she saw him caress another woman. There the story ends. The story itself is the awakening woman as she walks home in the sunlight, as she prepares for a dinner-party

that night, as she looks at her flowers, as she talks with her
guests and as she watches her husband expectantly. A spring
that came too late. A woman who woke in time to see her new
feeling frustrated.

In another story, *The Garden Party,* a young girl is busy with
the preparations for a lawn fête. Everything is in a bustle. The
men have come to put up the marquee. The sandwiches are
piling up, and a man is killed in one of the cottages nearby.
But the party must go on. The band has been hired. The
marquee is up. The sandwiches are ready. The hostesses are
dressed and the people are arriving. After it is all over the
girl is sent by her mother with a basket of delicacies for the
widow. She goes in her party dress, carrying the basket and
her floppy garden hat. She sees the man lying quietly in
death. She sees the tears of the widow and the women gathered around. But what she really saw for the first time, and
with all the force of first sight, was the shifting movement of
life, the shadow meeting sunlight on the lawn, the wind disturbing the grain, the change as sand silted down into sand,
and death beside a garden party.

Mansfield achieved her effects by the drawing out of an idea
very faintly from another idea, and by deftly superimposing
a feeling upon the narration of a set of circumstances. It was
all done with the utmost delicacy, and the emotional impact
upon the reader is produced often through the use of just one
phrase set in the context. The stories usually hinge upon this
key phrase. The note-book of the author, published in part
by Middleton Murry in the introductory note to the volume
called *The Dove's Nest,* shows how in many cases the key phrase
was the contact the author herself used to start the composition
of her story. In *The Doll's House* the Burnell children have
been given a big house for their dolls. It is like a grown·up
house, and even has a lamp in it. The children boast about it
at school, and they are allowed to bring certain chosen children
home after school to see the house. Little Kezia, who is probably Katherine Mansfield's portrait of herself as a child, brings

home the two forlorn and ostracized children of the village charwoman. She cannot bear them to be left out. They are sent away by the young aunt of the Burnell children, and as they leave the younger of them says to the older, "I seen the little lamp." Then the story ends. The note-book contains the sentence, "I seen the little lamp," set down by itself, and it was evidently the start of the story in the author's mind. As the story evolved it became in itself a masterpiece of child portraiture such as has not been painted by any other woman, not even by George Eliot in Maggie Tulliver. It contains all the unconscious imitative cruelty of children one to the other. Through the Burnell sequence of stories, and here and there throughout all the volumes, there are portraits of children which consistently sustain the talent shown so immortally in *The Doll's House.* Her success with children came out of the childlike mind of Mansfield herself. She retained into adulthood that peculiar lilting childish response to life, and combined it in her writing with a slightly ironic sophistication. The result was a charm of expression which was innately engaging. It made comments both sweet and not sweet. It made them whimsical and literal, varying between the two in a surprising way all her own, and producing a peculiar kind of sophisticated guilelessness. It is this quality in Mansfield as much as anything else which has given her a following of enthusiastic literary worshipers. It is a native part of the charm that was her own personal charm. It shows as much, and possibly a little more, in her letters and in her journal, as in her stories.

Because of the posthumous care of her literary reputation in the publication of her letters and her journal by John Middleton Murry, the story of Mansfield stands out with unusual clarity. She was a girl of acute sensitiveness, in a furor of rebellion because she could not fit into the established and expected order. She was a highly individualized person, with an unusual amount of artistic resentment against the ordinary and the drab. This was very marked in her early years. It made her actively rebellious against society and its conventions. She wrote stories

about stuffy people because she hated them. But in her later
years she mellowed. She had had a great love, life's greatest
mellower. She had known pain and weakness, and it taught her
the weakness of the human spirit and how easy it is to go with
no resistance along with the current. Gradually all aspects of
the ordinary and the drab changed in her consciousness, and
she began to see the ordinary and the drab as a furtive symbol
of something else. A new feeling came into her writing.

Hers was a nature which had thought it did not belong to the
orbit in which it was, that yearned for the unbearable beauty
and for the high lift of sheer enjoyment. It was a nature which
came to realize as the years passed and suffering went deeper and
deeper into it that what she needed most was not the sustained
high note of life, but just love and understanding. It made her
feel that need in others, and she wrote as if trying to give to
the people on her pages what she needed so badly for herself.

The letters of Murry belong with the great collections of love
letters from women. They are letters written by a woman with
an art at her finger-tips—the perfect art the possession of
which is supposed to make everything else unnecessary to a
woman—writing—the one thing in which a woman may lose
herself and her pain and her need of all else. But it was not
so with her. Maybe it is not so with any woman. Love was
life to Mansfield. Through the most of her illness she was separated from the man she loved so much. The letters she wrote
to him are heart-breaking both in their sorrow and in the beauty
of their phrasing. Little things meant so much to her, a letter
from him, a little pot of tea, a cigarette, the warmth of the
sun on her skin, the color of the wall-paper in the procession
of bedrooms in the procession of hotels, the ways of her little
cat. The letters are not all cries of pain. There are gurgles of
laughter. There are astute comments upon books, authors and
events. There are flickers of moods, and there are sedate notices about the price of fruit and milk and butter. All of her
remarks are touched with the creative lovely spirit of the writer.
She lets herself go down on paper, and the reader may feel her

and enjoy the society of a very engaging woman. The letters are spontaneous outbursts of herself, some of them torn from the woman who cried for her man, and others of them put down in delight because he had written her a letter or sent her a telegram, or maybe just because she thought he needed to know that she was managing to extract some amusement from having tuberculosis. They are brave and tender. They are broken and frightened. Some of them are gay and exciting. Some of them are forlorn. But all of them are thoughtful. A collection of letters which sing many different little songs about herself, a woman of amazing volatility and amazing variety. Alone most of her time, and facing death by herself, she made her love for Murry immortal in her letters to him, and her name immortal by the stories by means of which she said to death that it could not take all of her. Her letters, her journal and her stories she would leave behind her as Katherine Mansfield. Thus would she survive.

That the survival might be in its most perfect form she disciplined herself as a worker, with the result that in no other woman's writing, with the exception of Jane Austen and Virginia Woolf, is there such sheer style in composition. Nowhere is there a line that is sloppy. Nowhere is there a phrase that is unfinished. All through there is a depth of humanity and understanding of the human heart which has only one other peer among woman writers, in Willa Cather, and it is the more remarkable in that it came from a woman who spent most of her most creative years in a sick-room. Her feeling for humanity stretches out over all races and over all classes and over all ages and over the two sexes. Old men and faltering old women, frustrated spinsters, and married women full of emotional longing, small children puzzled at the ways of adults, wistful servant girls, pathetic little governesses, clerks, fading actresses, restless society women and the young things responding to the first glow of romance. Germans under the necessity of being dignified, French having to be astute, British trying to be nonchalant. Mothers feeling themselves not quite strong enough for their racial task; fathers feeling themselves not quite fit for their economic burden. Mansfield, lying desperately ill, writing about what she had seen and what she knew in between sessions with new doctors and new climates, always aware of her own need of love, and never resenting it, and coming as the years passed and the loneliness increased to love life for its own dear self with a passionate clinging love. She refused during the war to allow her German stories to be republished. She would allow no stories of hers to be used as propaganda against a people who were not enemies when she wrote the stories, but only people who happened to amuse her by their efforts to conduct themselves adequately as Germans. Mansfield at this time needed money. The stories would have sold well. She refused because it would not have been ethical. This gesture makes her one of the international heroines, a dying woman who would allow no work of hers to be used to increase hatred and thus promote death in the world. There was enough death. She was dying, and she knew how hard it was to die.

Though she felt the war acutely, and though she felt it personally through the death in military service of her brother, she wrote nothing that can be classed as war literature. The great heroism of men at war, and of women left alone through war, she left untouched. She held herself down to the little moments coming into ordinary lives, and to the little glimpses coming to children and people who would never have very much from life. "I seen the little lamp," and so she died in her early thirties.

WILLA CATHER

The story of Katherine Mansfield should be written by Willa Cather. Nobody else could write it so well. It is the story of "a bird shot down in its first flight," as is her own story, *Lucy Gayheart,* using her own phrase. No other woman writes tragedy so superbly as Cather. It is tragedy from which something survives which is not tragedy.

It is the work of a woman of utter sincerity towards the art of her work, and also towards the people about whom she writes, and the country in which they live. It is quiet work, giving the impression of spiritual stillness. It is the supreme example of the artist quality peculiar to women, a remnant saved out of the life she has seen. It is in its way also the supreme example of the spiritual artistry of the new world. Underneath its great stillness there lies the faith of the pioneer in the something in life making struggle worthy. It is free from the nervousness and the speed and the staccato sound of the surface life of America, the sound which gets into most of the contemporary writing of America. She has gone back to the spiritual beginnings of the new world for her spiritual contact and for the literal theme of some of her stories. And it is just possible that she is prophetic, and going beyond the present to the future, and underneath the present to the spiritual truth of the people who make up the new world. It is work that is in the ordinary sense unemotional. Its emotion is implied rather than presented.

It links with the work of Mansfield in that it is free from the sexual resentment of most of the women writers, if not all the rest of them. This is interesting inasmuch as they are both women of new worlds. It indicates the effect of environment upon the young writer. Mansfield, though she spent most of her adult years in England, grew up in the new world of New Zealand. Cather grew up in the middle-west of the United States. Women in countries still in the relatively pioneer state have a high value. It goes back to the early psychology of the pioneer towards women. There were never enough women to go around. So men in new countries value women as men in old countries do not. The colonial man lets his women do much as she pleases. He gives her as much as he can give her. Women, therefore, in new countries have no shadow of a subjected past. If she remembers hardship it was a hardship shared with men, and she has no hang-over of resentment against sexual injustice in her mentality. It is good to be a woman in a new country. Relatively free from big organized wars, the women in new countries are not told to produce more and more children, and they have accordingly an intellectual conception of themselves as something else besides racial vessels. They have not in the main had to fight for their rights as European women have had to fight for theirs. They have not in the main a problem of surplus women as there is in England, for example. In America women got their citizenship when they asked for it, and without on the whole any bitter fight. They got education when they asked for it. They got their chances in commerce when they showed inclination towards commerce. So such writing as Cather does can come from a woman in America totally free from the abiding sense of injustice that is in most of the writing by English women. It is free from a depressing sense of its limitation as feminine writing, and is also free from a subconscious effort to be masculine. It is the work of a woman sure of herself as a woman in a land in which it is not difficult to be a woman. This same freedom to be feminine shows also in Mansfield. It is truer of Cather than it is of any other of the American women writers because of her spiritual authenticity. She is the great artist American women writers have produced, and she has nurtured herself upon the spiritual realities of America, so the little efforts showing in other American women writers to strut because of their equality with men does not show in her. She passes it by as a bit of natural exuberance in the young. It does not touch her because she has gone beyond that exuberance back and forward and underneath to the spiritual realities. Both in Mansfield and Cather, women are not creatures to be studied as new creatures just emerging from subjection. They are ordinary human beings linked with men through the need of men and women for each other for the making of the race. Neither of them tells a sexual story. Both of them take sex for granted, and go on to the real story of life, the struggle of the spirit in its earth environment. In this respect they belong together. And as artistes they belong together, both of them superb tellers of stories. Both of them using the relatively short form of the story as being native to women. Cather's stories are much longer than the stories of Mansfield, but they are still short, measuring them by the standard length of most novels. If she had been ill as Mansfield was, she might have used the very short form used by Mansfield. If Mansfield had been well, it is likely she would have been able to sustain, and would have chosen to sustain her little glimpses out to the length used by Cather.

There is, however, a great difference between the work of the two women in its content. Mansfield was interested in the little story which disclosed character and its frustration. She was a realist. Cather is interested in the story which shows the character of a human being as it comes under the influence of a great idea, a great emotion, or a great realization of life. She is a romantic.

Her people are people who touch greatness. She takes them from varying times, but she sets them down in the country she knows. So that while the characters themselves are romantic figures belonging to any time, she sets them in a background which is accurately local. She gives them roots. They belong to a place. But not in a narrow sense. The American who goes down to the spiritual reality of America cannot be narrow. The immense spaces have entered into the human composition.

The art of Cather is an effect produced upon the senses and the spirit by means of a story told with what appears to be simplicity and is not simplicity. She looks with a fine long perspective at the material she is using, and presents the story as if it were a memory. It is the very art which in her latest story, *Lucy Gayheart*, she gives to Sebastian the singer. She makes no effort, as Sebastian made no effort, to get dramatically inside the story songs. She allows herself, as he allowed himself, no passionate absorption in them. The result of this is a certain emotional aloofness, which, however, does not translate itself into coldness of interpretation. The woman writing is a warm human woman, innately understanding her people. The perspective of memory brings a certain stillness to the narration of the story, but it also brings a rich sense of the meaning of it. There is evoked from the stately narration a simple faith in the spiritual permanence which underlies impermanence. This is the reason she handles tragedy in such a way as to render it not altogether tragedy. This is the reason she handles history in such a way as to render it not just history. She treats life as an experience which, while it varies infinitely in infinite details, is in the long view of it an experience in humanity changing very little. Everything evens out in the end to the story of human hearts and how they do for themselves and for one another in a few definitely given situations. Because any story is a generic experience it is not necessary to get impertinently close to the particular folk of it. There is no need to pin them down upon a fictional dissecting-table and take their emotional processes apart. Because there is generic unity between the writer and the reader and the people of the story, the story tells itself, as if it were a memory in the mind of the writer and of the reader.

It is a very fine art in story-telling.

Cather is concerned mostly with lives that are touched with romance, and have upon other lives a curious lifting effect. The magnetic inspirational people are the people about whom she centers her stories. They are not necessarily inspirational folk in the accepted general sense. She takes sometimes a life that looks to be an ordinary life among quiet people and in a quiet place, but through it is shot that strangely communicable essence, the shine of the spirit which binds other people to the individual either in love or in curiosity. It is always a human being tingling with life among a group of human beings afraid to let life flow swiftly through them that she takes for the focus of her narrative. It was the feel of life in their blood-stream and in their glands that sent the pioneers out over the plains and through the mountains and down the rivers of America. It was the call of life that sent the missionaries compassionately and heroically out to far places under the egis of the Church. It was the power of life in them that made certain women draw men to them. It was the coursing of life in them that made these men and women about whom she writes turn to religion, to art, and sometimes to love. They are all of them people of such intrinsic vitality that all they need to do is to appear on her pages and the pages take life from them as the ether takes life around them in the places in which they are living. It is these people who are the theme of Cather. She makes no effort to get at what made them able to feel life vividly. She never pokes into their forebears. She never probes into their souls. She simply tells the story of how they lived and of how they affected the people around them.

All her stories are told with an even and sustained narration. It can hardly be said that one story is better than the other stories. One story does not stand technically far above the others. In selecting one or two as her most interesting work it is only a matter of personal taste in the material used.

The Professor's House is possibly the most ambitious of her novels. It deals with the shine coming from a character who never appears actually in the story and yet dominates it completely, a man who is dead, but who left behind him a legacy of money, as well as of romance. The Professor's family have the benefit of his legacy of money and the Professor has the benefit of his legacy of spirit. The young man had come after a great adventure in the Southwest among the remaining signs of Indian civilization to be a student in the Professor's college. He had concentrated upon an invention, and then he went to war, leaving his whole estate to one of the daughters of the Professor. It turned out to be a very big estate. But it was not nearly so big as the estate left by him in the spirit of the Professor. He, sitting alone in his study, thought of the young man and of his family gorged with the wealth of the young man's labors, and also of the record he had left of a lost people. It makes a fine mellow tale. It is full of the golden sunshine of the Southwest and its stillness and its vastness. The deep tones of the colors seep through the senses, the sky that is very blue, the sand that is very red, the ether that seems to be golden. The contours of the country stamp themselves into the imagination, huge and sharp and imposing. Rocks that are mountains, mountains that are worlds set aside by themselves. Stretches of earth. And an old man lonely amid wealth, hungering for the bigness and the golden shine of a young man's spirit.

Death Comes to the Archbishop is also set in the Southwest. It has to do with a French missionary of the early times and the remnant of a strange people. To these people and to the world that was a new world to the white people the Archbishop came, bringing his consciousness of God and his faith in the manifestations of the Church. He moves through the magnificent scenery of the country and in and out among the Indians, the whites and his fellow missionaries, a figure of sweet and strong dignity. There is not much story in it to entertain the casual reader. It is too quiet and undramatic. Yet it remains one of the few outstanding stories of the great missionary priests of America. The Archbishop was one of the shining folk. The Indians felt a friend in him, and perhaps a little of a god. His associate, Father Joseph, left a comfortable parish to follow him into new territory and went at his bidding into still newer territory. Churchmen in Europe gave him what he wanted for his church in the New World. When he came to die the people gathered outside the place in grief. It is a beautiful story. A man's life shadowed on the lives of those around him, and throughout the country, human and at the same time a little more than human because so aloof from the motives of most lives. The translation of the Archbishop's spirit into the unknown at death is in some ways the finest piece of Cather's prose, held down as it is by reverent discipline to the story itself. It was a patient death, and showed the compassionate spirit of the man, as it also showed the patient compassionate understanding of the writer.

It is patience and compassion that are the predominating tones in the composition of Cather.

It is patience and compassion that provide the spiritual overtone of two studies of women, and they are entirely different studies, *A Lost Lady* and *Lucy Gayheart*.

A Lost Lady tells the story of a woman who had a big capacity for love in its physical aspect. She glowed with the vitality of sex. *Lucy Gayheart* is the story of a girl with a big capacity for love in its spiritual sense. She radiated the vitality of romance. Both stories are written with a maturity of art which sets them apart. Both are tragedies. *A Lost Lady* is the tragedy of a woman who has to find her outlet in somewhat tawdry men, though she was married to a man of heroic proportions. *Lucy Gayheart* is the tragedy of a young girl who could only find her romantic outlet in a man out of her reach. The Lady takes love where she can find it, and its very exuberance in herself makes her attractive to all the men who come near her. Lucy gives her feeling of romance to an artist who is tired spiritually and hungry for faith and young vitality. The feeling is all she may give him. He is drowned. The Lady is driven from experience to experience in search of satisfaction. Lucy is driven to death in search of fulfilment. Both stories are written with humanity and with profound understanding both of the normal and the fey woman. So deep is the humanity that the story of the Lady, which in other hands might have been sordid, has an immaculate dignity. So deep is the humanity that the story of Lucy, which in other hands might have been sentimental, has a pure reality. The Lady was a woman trapped by her own exuberance. Lucy was a girl led into tragedy by her romanticism. Both of them shone, the Lady with the sheer vigor of herself, and Lucy with the fey joy of herself. Both of them affected others out of ordinary proportion. The Lady was remembered, and Lucy was never forgotten by one man who had loved her in his own way that did not happen to be her way. So great was his remembrance of her that he treasured the marks of her footprints made in the half-dried asphalt outside her house, little feet running away in flight from him.

All the stories of Cather give the impression of having been written slowly. They have matured as human life matures beneath the surface. In the finished presentation there is nothing excitedly premature, nothing quickly snapped out for publication. They are conservatively thoughtful and reservedly emotional. There are no mannerisms of narration, no jerks of tempo, and no stamp of a marked and individual style artificially acquired. The material she uses is finely human, and her treatment of it is gentle. There is no satirical slant, and no sophisticated fatigue. Neither is there any twist into caricature, yet it is not matter-of-fact, and certainly not sentimental. Not one element of the sob-sister ever enters into her composition, and yet its overtone is definitely one of pity. The stories have a gravity and a dignity which in less artistic hands might have easily become didactic. The artistic touch of Cather is as deft as it is dignified. The portraits which accompany the central portraits are exact and true and filled in with enduring craftsmanship. They, like the central figures, are left with their reticences. They are also left with their dignities. They live in the pages as they lived their lives, true to their own integrities.

Cather's work has no peer among the women writers of her time. Along with Mansfield she has freedom from the prevailing resentment of women and from their enthusiasm over a new order of things for them in their worlds. Along with her she has a woman's peculiar insight into the meaning of little gestures and small phrases. Along with her she has an artistry that is instinctive, and a malleability of technique. Along with Dane she has a feeling for the heroic and the courage a woman needs when she writes about men on a heroic scale. Along with Woolf she has style in prose which makes one of her sentences like a piece of very fine old lace. But by herself she has all these qualities together with a brooding awareness of life. It is as if with her own heroine, Lucy Gayheart, Cather had realized sometime during her development that life itself is the sweetheart, and so she looks upon the life that she treats in fiction with the appreciation of a woman in love. But with none of the anxiety of the woman in love. She is more than all else the woman of wisdom. There is something of the same quality in her that there was in George Eliot when she wrote *Silas Marner*. The same benign restraint, the same artistic recording of a simple story, the same quiet passion for spiritual justice, and the same great kindness of judgment. But there is one difference. Eliot never, even at her simplest, altogether lost her obligation to justify something. It drove her to writing. It entered into all her composition. In all her stories there is one standing as the symbol of herself. In *Marner* it was the lonely weaver, misunderstood and maligned, weaving a fabric by himself. This is not true at all of Cather. If there is to be found in the work of Cather a woman called Willa Cather, it is to be found in an abstraction. It is to be found in the hunger of the spirit for the dynamic lift of itself above the mundane, either through its comprehension of life as the sweetheart, or through the magnetism of another. To this theme she returns again and again, and in her hands it becomes the ultimate romance, the search of the spirit for the shine of life. The effort of the spirit to hold within itself some fraction of that shine. Her great characters all have it in great part, and her people all have it in some part. To look for it is to see it. To want it is to have it. So her work is work endowed with spirituality, but not mysticism. It is the natural spirituality of the human being born in a country which still feels in its depths the optimism of a new world, and the vision of its explorers and the faith of its pioneers. She is in the sustained creative urge of the first discoverers of America—the second chance of mankind—the new world in which men and women did not need to be as they had been forced to be in the old world, cowardly and greedy and ugly. It is not the new world as it seems to be now in its transition. It is the new world in its spiritual reality, the shadow of which, seen in its incidental reality, does not quite measure up to the spiritual reality. It is this reality which she puts into her work, the romance of America and the ultimate romance of life —the shine of life.

CLEMENCE DANE

Clemence Dane is the writer who, among all the women writers, most completely represents the intellectual tone and emotional concept of the woman particular to this age. She is the zenith of the go-getter. She is the energetic, ambitious woman looking around her to see if she can do things as well as men can do them. But she is an artist because she subdues this energy and ambition with the artist's fidelity to form and content. She has the motivation of the woman we call modern. She grasps the particular effect of this age upon women. She sees the issues. But she is more interested in putting down what she grasps and what she sees in artistic form than she is in anything else.

Her book, *A Regiment of Women,* is a book which would only have been possible from a writer living in a country containing a surplus of women, and in which sex bitterness reached the peak it reached in the militant suffragette campaign. Her main character is the type of woman who entered vigorously into this campaign, though the story has nothing to do with suffrage and the general question of women's rights, but is simply the story of a woman of this type functioning as a teacher in a girls' school in England. Dane, however, it may be said in passing, is the one woman who should take the material offered by the suffragette campaign and set it down in a novel or a play. She understands the motivation of such women. It must not be gathered from this that there was an implication of Lesbianism in the suffragette campaign. That may or may not be so. But there was a bitterness, and a sense of sex bitterness has some relation to the possibility of the development of Lesbianism in women. The women who forced the attention of the world through an adaptation of the old feminine trick of nagging in a guerrilla campaign did so motivated by an intense resentment of the assumption by the male of an entirely suppositional superiority. Some of them undoubtedly were women of unusual intellectual capacity, who could find under the prevailing system no professional outlet for their intellectuality. Others of them were simple women who simply wanted representation in the government of the particular interest of women and children and the home, and took the stand that men did not always represent the interests of women fairly and adequately.

A Regiment of Women has a bearing upon the general question because it shows the dangers to the race of subjecting the intellectuality of women to only certain chosen professions supposedly suitable for them; it shows also the dangers to the race when hatred of men is allowed, or even fostered, in these women of intellect. It is a story of implied Lesbianism, and at least of intellectual Lesbianism in women who taught in a girls' school. It is a far more tragic story than is Radclyffe Hall's Lesbian story in its actual content, but in its implied teaching it is not nearly so tragic. For it treats the subject as a subject. It makes no appeal for understanding. Radclyffe Hall set out to make a persecuted figure of the Lesbian. She told a story of social crucifixion. She produced a feeling of a great sexual, and therefore racial, mystery. She wrote about the inverted Lesbian. Dane set out to make a pathological figure of the Lesbian. She told a story of social functioning. She produced a feeling of a sad but not incurable situation among women. She wrote about the Lesbian extravert. Hall's story is plaintive. Dane's story is scientifically cool.

The leading character of the novel is a highly cultivated young woman teaching in a girls' school. Secondary to her is another young woman, somewhat younger, not so cultivated, and completely innocent of perverted emotionalism until she falls under the sway of her associate. There is a third leading character, a small girl who comes into the school with an already damaged nervous system. She attracts the attention of the two teachers, and becomes the victim of the drama. There is one man. He comes into the story to explain the implications of the situation to the younger teacher, and in time to save her, but not in time to save the little girl.

The older of the two teachers is a woman just entering her thirties. She is attractive. She is brilliant. She focuses the attention of the school upon herself. She is its first person. Beside her the principal is a shadow. She is an enigma and a magnetic force. The students hang upon her words. The other teachers stand in awe of her, some of them hating her, consciously for her superiority, and subconsciously for the danger innate in her personality. Others admire her to the point of worship. But nobody can overlook her. She rides her small world supreme. She is a woman who hates men, and loves power over other women. She has to have the devoted love of women. She has to be a dictator to women. She chooses the girls she wants. She goes after them as she would have gone after men. When searching for her prey and stalking it she points all her charm. She bridles her caustic tongue, and she pulls in all her selfishness. She surrounds her victims with irresistible attentions. She turns their heads. She seduces them intellectually. In this mood she is a woman of very winning ways, and an adept at covering her tracks. It all appears like the interest of a kind-hearted intellectual woman in the development of a younger woman or a student. It all appears quite impersonal, as consciously it is, for the woman is an undoubted intellectual, having in addition much personal charm. She has a lot to give. She is a great teacher. She could fire the ambitions of those associated with her. She could wind her personality so completely around them that they would make themselves over to suit the plan with which she presented them. Then the damage sets in, and the associate finds herself so under the control of another woman that she can have neither day nor night nor a thought nor a feeling of her own.

It is a familiar story. There are plenty of women of this type, hanging upon young girls who work under them, and convincing themselves as well as the young girls that it is all a professional interest, which it is in part and until it becomes a personal interest, compensating the women for men, and as they get older, for children of their own.

The first part of the story is given to the winning of the younger teacher by the heroine. Under the impression that she is improving herself and her professional chances, the younger girl comes step by step to utter servitude towards the older woman. The second part shows the heroine feeling herself tentatively secure in the affections of the girl, and demanding more and more of her time and her affection. The peak of the story is reached when the heroine begins to play upon the affections of her victim, and trying to torment her with jealousy draws the little girl into the story. The culmination of her effort lies in the suicide of the little girl, whose emotions cannot stand any playful use of them by others. She is at first spurred on to work that is beyond her capacity, and then she is thrown back hard upon herself when she fails in her work and in her emotional appeal to the older teacher. The child is merely seeking the mother she needs. She thinks at first that she has found it. When it is taken from her she cannot face life and throws herself out of the attic window of the school because the beloved teacher has spoken sharply to her. The third part of the story goes on into the awakening of the younger teacher through her reaction to the death of the child, and her suspicion of its cause. She breaks down nervously, and becomes the victim of hallucinations regarding the tortured spirit of the child. She thinks she sees her following her. During a holiday which she is forced to take to straighten out her nerves, she meets a man who is able to explain to her what it has all been, to free her from the hallucinations, and in the end to free her from the domination of the older woman. The break comes through the jealousy of the older woman. The threat of a man on her horizon pulls out all her carefully guarded secrets. She turns angrily upon the girl, and the girl in her horror rushes to the man.

The story is handled as drama in prose fiction. It falls naturally into three acts. Each part is built up as an act, with the center of the story coming in the second-act part, and winding up in the third. It is a story of magnificent power, gauntly set down, and yet with human warmth and with fine psychological understanding. The heroine is not treated as a melodramatic vixen, but as a woman in the grip of a complex psychiatric ailment, and the little girl who died, as well as the young teacher

who suffered, are characters who happened to lie in the path of
the heroine's need. Yet the study is not that of a psychiatric
ailment, but of its effect in a social group of women. The
study, therefore, relates itself to the history of women, and
particularly to an age in which through war there are many
women left without men of their own and children of their
own, and faced with the dangers of their own suppressed inclinations. It relates itself to an age when there is accomplished
a partial intellectual freedom for women, and when there are
tentative opportunities for their intellectuality, and it features,
therefore, an intellectual sadism which is far more dangerous
in women than the purely emotional sadism in a relatively
similar situation drawn by Charlotte Brontë in *Jane Eyre*.
With artistic fidelity Dane treats the story intellectually, and
presents it as a situation arising from causes which we all understand more or less clearly. She makes no treatise of it, however. She leaves it to tell its own story.

It is in *Broome Stages* that the full power of Dane in fiction
is felt. It is a story prolonged through generations, including a
gallery of individual portraits, but it winds out at the end into
a single portrait of a family, and a single portrait of a man,
the Broome man. It is also a study of motivation and the
character of the acting genus, particularly as it manifests itself
in the male.

The Broomes hailed from Richard Broome, who had commerce in his childhood with a witch. She had given him a motto
which, taken into the mind, acted like an occult mandate upon
the life. Through it Richard Broome learned to "beckon" his
audiences, and became the greatest actor of his time. The one
prohibition connected with the famous motto was that it must
be handed down from father to daughter and from mother to
son. The early Broomes heeded the law, and each of them became in his time the great actor of the period. The family
branched into the nobility, but always came back to the theater.
They produced dramatists and managers as well as actors, and
established a great theatrical tradition. But one of them, Harry

Broome, broke the law of the motto, and gave it to his son instead of to his daughter, and from that day fate began to take unpleasant ways with the Broomes.

Dane builds up the story with a dramatist's sense of approach and climax. Each section of the novel is a play in itself, following the laws of a play. Each of the Broomes approaches his destiny, enters into it, reaches his fulfilment, and attempts to make the fulfilment last. And each of them is carried along by the power of that destiny, forced to surrender at the last to his children and their part in the Broome destiny. It was the fate of all of the Broomes except one to consider himself the destiny of the clan. They could not individually, except in one case, stand back when the time came to stand back individually and allow the family destiny to proceed on to the next generation. This makes their story one of feud and struggle. It is the same feud and the same struggle played out in different generations over and over again, and Dane takes it over and over again throughout the saga with increasing mysterious power. It is a story which, in less dramatic hands, would have become monotonous, for it is a convolution and a series of convolutions taken with gently increasing tempo and accent. It reaches one great climax in the life of Harry Broome, and from him it proceeds on to build up into another climax with a subtly altered accent, and this climax is a doom. The witch's motto has been broken, and the broken law twists the story, though carrying on its original rhythm. The change does not show at first. The reader feels only slightly the altered accent, but as the years pass the accent becomes more and more marked. Deterioration has set in, and degeneracy has touched the Broome tradition and finally masters it. The feud between father and son, elementally heroic in the beginning, matter-of-fact towards the center, becomes at the end sophisticatedly amusing.

Behind this one absorbing drama between the old and the young are lesser dramas. Women straining to understand their men, humoring them, loving them, occasionally opposing them. We see women in every generation of the story drawn to the Broome men and held to them through the occult beckoning power. And we see women providing small audiences for the try-out of the Broome male. Then, as the doom settles slowly upon the story, the accent changes here too, and we see women using the Broome men, playing them for careers, and going their own way to what they want for themselves.

Dane is the most masculine of all the women writing in the School of Femininity. Yet *Broome Stages* remains in spite of this an essentially feminine story. On the outside it appears to be what is perhaps the most ambitious attempt ever made by a woman to write on the scale men use in their writing. It seems to be a woman saying to herself, "I will write as a man would write, sweeping down through the ages as men sweep with their writing, drawing men, drawing women, in variety, in depth and breadth." All of these things Dane has done. It is a book which can stand side by side with the family stories written by men. It dares the critic with its virility and its sustained sense of climax to say it is less than the work of a man. Its history is immaculate. It presents in its flow an amazingly intimate and comprehensive picture of the social feeling of the periods through which it takes its course. It presents through the Broomes a history of the theater in England. It combines a story and a text. The reader has a fine narrative and a fine history. And with these there is also a cool insight into the workings of both the masculine and the feminine mind that makes the critic stop to ponder the accepted idea of the inability of a woman to portray a man. Before us lies a picture of the force of dynasty in Victorian and pre-Victorian England, focused in the story of a theatrical dynasty, playing against the background of aristocratic and industrial England. Before us lies a picture of the peculiar force of the family cell transmitted man by man through generation to generation. Before us lies a picture of a slightly occult destiny taking its hold of one man and through him gathering hold of a whole family, and through the family spreading itself out into the culture of a people. It is, taken all in all, a story such as no other woman has written or attempted to write. But there is this to remember: It is the story of one man—the Broome man. He lived for the theater. He beckoned to women and to audiences. He tried hard to hold himself supreme in the center of destiny. He was carried in spite of himself into the next generation, and on until he became part of the cultural heritage of England. But he remains one man. In one part of the story he was a woman and his name was Domina Broome, the only one of the Broomes who could stand back when the time came to stand back and let the next generation take the stage. But for all of that he remains one man. Domina, daughter of Harry Broome, is the center of the story. It reaches up to her and her feud with her father and her love affair with her cousin. Through her the force of the broken motto acts. She serves the next generation by bearing a son who is the son of her cousin, and from then on the family degenerates until it reaches her grandsons, one of whom is homosexual, and another of whom is troubled with too premature a development of talent.

It is a woman's story because Domina is its center. Domina expressed in her time the rebellion of the woman against the domination of the man. She had in her a man's energy. But she was in skirts. Her father broke the law of the motto, and she broke the biological law. The children of cousins were not quite as the original Broomes were, and the power to beckon was not quite as it had been in the earlier Broomes, though the technique was there. And the Broome man comes out in the closing sections of the saga a broken man. Yet he still engages the attention of the woman writing.

He is composed of two elements. In one part he is, for all his variations and for all his ups and downs of character development, the portrait of the man the woman writing wanted to be. In his other part he is the portrait of the woman's concentration upon the man of her family—the son. All women have, even if pressed far down in the subconscious, the wish to have been a man. And a woman writing is influenced by that wish when she comes to writing about men. All women down through the

ages have thought when they have thought of children born
to them, of men children. For the men constitute the family.
The girls are born to their mothers, sometimes willingly enough,
and more willingly as time has introduced the feminist doctrine,
but subconsciously it is the son who dominates the subconscious imagination of the mother, even if not the conscious
imagination. It is a force carried over from the tribal sense,
which even the most modern woman cannot control within herself. For girls in their time enter into other families as vessels
of its destiny, but the boy remains—and constitutes in his turn
the family into which he is born. So we have this story, which
in its way has attempted and fulfilled more than any other story
written by a woman, and which is on first appearance a story
a man might have written, turning upon other than first study
to be very much a woman's work, by the very reason of its
utter concentration upon the man of the story. It is probably
the first time in the writing of women that a woman has struck
down deep enough into the layers of her own consciousness to
bring out the racial and personal concentration of womanhood
upon men. Dane in *Broome Stages* has gone far beyond the
romance-image man drawn by women in search of emotional
relief. She has gone far beyond the image of women more or
less related to her idea of herself. She has gone even beyond
the portraiture of women diversified into individuals, remaining
in spite of that general portraiture of the race woman. She
has got down to something that lies very far down in every
woman—to her sense of the man she herself could have been
had the cells altered just a little, blending this with her abiding
sense of her son, and balancing both these, because she is an
aloof intellectual as well as an emotional creator, with her
observation of what men actually are. And so it remains in its
being very much a woman's story.

VIRGINIA WOOLF

One puts down *Broome Stages* and takes up *Orlando*. It is
another story carried down through many generations. But the

one is a story seen upon a stage, and the other is a story seen in the mind of a woman who sits by herself thinking, putting down a phrase here and a phrase there as she thinks, saying the phrases over to herself for the feel of them and sliding them along one after another until there is a rope of matched and matchless prose.

Virginia Woolf has written prose the equal of which there is none among all the contemporary women writers using English, and perhaps not in the past among women. She is the supreme stylist in language. Writing prose concerning which one uses the adjective perfect, she has produced a number of books, all of which are enduringly beautiful and femininely tender, and two books which are outstanding contributions to the thinking of women about themselves, *Orlando* and *A Room of One's Own.*

In *Orlando* she took a life and stretched it out to enter into many generations of life in England, and in the course of that stretch she altered its sex and linked it symbolically to the history of letters in England, thus satisfying the purely literary thinker as well as the feminist.

The medium of Woolf is neither verse nor prose. It is neither absolute fiction nor absolute essay. It is language. There are behind the woman writing generations of culture. The daughter of Sir Leslie Stephen, she comes from people who have used the English language as language rather than speech for a long time. She belongs to the aristocracy of culture. Thinking and writing in the medium of good and beautiful language are as natural to her as breathing.

It sets her apart from other women writing. For they have come either from the leisured social classes, to whom reserve in the expression of feeling is ingrained, or from the middle and working classes, to whom the expression of thought is a process of hard determination or a triumphant lift above the round of the usual. These other writers use speech rather than language because there are behind them generations of people using speech either sparingly or volubly rather than language. The difference is unmistakable. In one paragraph of Woolf there are a sound and a grace that have no peer at least among the women. Not one flurry of commercial haste disturbs the cadence. Not the least interest in the limelight for her ideas, not the least attention to what an editor may or may not want, not the least calculation of the selling value coming out of writing down to an average level of intelligence, influences her. She thinks because her people have been thinking for generations. She writes because her people have been expressing themselves easily for generations. More than this, with the natural exclusiveness of the cultivated mind she does not expect her work to be interesting to those who are not in her class. It is work written for people of culture. It belongs particularly to those who have a taste for fine language set into imaginative prose. To those who have no feeling for fine prose it may seem to be the slightly elevated experimental effort of a bluestocking woman to be different in her writing from every other woman in her time and before it. It presents nothing into which the average reader who likes thought made easy can crunch satisfyingly. It gives no violent kick to the reader who needs to be prodded into mental activity. It hardly gives anything to the modern mind, all excited and almost intoxicated as it is by the noise of the modern scene. It is quiet against the row of the age.

Orlando is the story of a young man born into the aristocracy at the time of Elizabeth. He lived on into the reign of James, and still on, becoming a woman long before Victoria's time, and mixed with the lords and ladies, the writers and the bums, the governors and the molls, and wrote some verse. This is all, apart from its style, that there is to the story. It is remote from the life of the day, as all art is remote, and particularly the art of verse, and it seems to have little to offer us in the din and confusion of the age of machinery except the peace to our spirits of rest in fine thinking and fine writing. What else did Ecclesiastes have to offer? Except the peace in its utterances for all its spiritual weariness that caused it to survive when all the racket of its day had died down and was drowned out by other and still other rackets.

Into the story the writer has set down with the utmost delicacy the first tentative question of women. What happens when the intellectuality generally prescribed for men only does occur in a woman? Orlando woke one morning after a long sleep and found that he was a woman. He lives for awhile with gypsies away from the world, needing to get used to the idea. He finds that being a woman has not changed his tastes. He still wants to write poetry when the mood comes over him to write. The question becomes more pressing, though still delicately pressing, when Orlando sells one of the pearls and provides herself with the wardrobe of a lady of caste and takes passage to England. For all this change has taken place in Turkey, where Orlando had been English ambassador. The question is never answered. As Orlando moves down through the centuries the story presents a picture of life as it was in the class of Orlando in each age. Gently time rolls over into other times, customs change, England drinks tea instead of wine, the houses cover themselves with ivy, dampness hangs over the land, and men take to writing prose instead of verse. Men still think highly of themselves and less highly of women, and nothing really changes for women. Orlando is a woman and she wants to write. But it is hard as a woman to get the experience and the stimulus necessary to writing. A woman has to sit at home and wait for a wedding-ring. She may go and call upon other women. If she has the money and the social background she may have the *literati* in to tea in the afternoon, or to dinner at night. She may listen to their conversation. She may say the odd word herself. But when she goes out in search of experience she has to put on the clothes of a man and pretend she is a man for the time being. A woman comes to the throne. Women begin to think. They begin to make curious demands. But nothing much changes. Orlando finds she must have a wedding-ring before she can produce her book. It is ages before she finds the wedding-ring and ages pass before her book is written. When it is written her life as a woman must go on. There is her estate to manage, and shopping to do, and many, many details to look after. Though she has written a book, and though critics have praised it, she is still a woman.

It is a story told with such winning artistry that its meaning matters hardly at all. It may be the story of how letters developed in England. It may be the story of how women got into letters in England. It may just be the story of England. For certainly it has all the fragrance of history. In the long progress through the years little images remain, the visit of Elizabeth to Orlando's home, the ways of Elizabeth with her court, the skating on the Thames one winter when it turned to ice, the visit to England of a voluptuous Russian lady with the embassy from Russia, the visit made to Orlando of the most eminent litterateur of his time, and the ink-spots he left in the place. All these are etched into the narrative with gracious lines. Whatever it means, it does leave literature at the end in the hands of a woman, and she is not very sure what to do with it. Before it comes to its end the writer touches upon many philosophical ideas, the influence of the skirt upon thinking, the influence of the machine upon thinking, the influence of biology upon thinking. Nothing is set down didactically. Nothing is put down vehemently. All that she says that has philosophy in it is carried along in the movement of the story, and everything comes out in the end to a feeling that the way of the artist in the phrasing of words and the setting of thought into sentences is a lonely way, and when the artist and the philosopher are a woman it is a way of peculiar uncertainty.

Virginia Woolf is a philosopher rather than a story-teller. She is intellectual rather than emotional so far as the content of her material is concerned, but part of the charm of her style lies in the emotional quality of her phrasing. There is feeling in and underneath the placing of her words together, but it is an esthetic emotionalism. She has tone and color, and they come over the senses of the reader as music comes. No matter to what subject she gives her attention and her expression, it comes out into prose a finished and lovely thing. She has that breathless something which holds the esthetic emotions in thrall, whether she writes about waves, or about people going to a Light House, or about people walking down the street in the morning, or about Mrs. Browning's little dog, Flush, or about an abstrusely intellectual concept. It is a rich prose, carefully matured in the mind before it is written down, and bringing with it the undertone of all the feeling associated with it, and producing an overtone of atmosphere peculiar to her. It strikes upon the spirit like music. It remains in the mind like a song, and it leaves behind it an effect all its own, something like the effect of silence following after music, and something like sound made after silence.

A Room of One's Own is a long essay put into a little book by itself, dealing with the idea that women, in order to achieve what men have achieved in letters, must have solitude and the freedom which leisure gives and money provides. She traces the comparative silence of women to their economic dependence. She takes up the wild rebellious cry of Mary Wollstonecraft, and with her own scholarly artistry makes it far more effective. Women, she says, have not done much for learning, for art or for government, because they have had no money of their own, and very little leisure and almost no solitude. She tells the story of women in England, and notices while she tells it how little there is to tell. For as men wrote history, there was nothing to write about women. They did nothing except get themselves husbands and provide those husbands with children. When some of the women began to write, they began with a lack of self-confidence, and she traces this lack back to poverty. For a woman, even if she married a man with money, did not necessarily have the right to any of that money, and not having any that was her own, she felt apologetic about herself and everything she did. She relates lack of self-confidence to nervousness, and nervousness to imitativeness. She considers the pioneer feminists striving to get education for girls upon some comparatively equal basis with boys. She considers the early novelists, and points out that very often women wrote novels who far better would have written something else, because it was only novels from women that would sell. She tells us that in all things relating to women and their mental development there is the restriction of not quite enough money and not quite enough of the assurance and the graciousness that enough money brings.

It is the old, old story. It strikes the reader with conviction and at the same time with astonishment. Mary Wollstonecraft, at the end of the eighteenth century, protesting the entire lack of intellectual and economic opportunity for women. Virginia Woolf, well on into the twentieth century, deploring the lack of a financial estate for the development of women. Women have colleges, but these colleges are not endowed as the colleges of men are. She takes us into the libraries, into the dining-rooms, and we find a great difference. She picks up the picture of the mother of a young woman scholar. She thinks of how that mother and her mother might have concentrated their energies upon the founding of an estate and upon the endowment of places of learning for their daughters. She remembers that had they done so there might presumably have been no daughters, scholarly or otherwise, not to mention the sons. Thus she touches upon the biological doom of women which has held them even as their economic doom has held them handicapped in the development of their own individuality. She suggests, without unduly stressing it, that if women are to make of themselves what they want to be—the equals of men in all things—and still to remember the race, there must be superwomen, able by some miracle to hold their own with men in intellectual and industrial competition, and at the same time to continue the race. It is the great question of women. There is now no real argument about the right of a woman to intellectual achievement if she can achieve it. There is now no real argument about her right to her share of industrial labor. There is not much argument left about her right to declare her opinion in the affairs of the state. There is only the question of how she can do it. There is only the question of adapting industry and scholarship and government to the functioning of women for the race. There is only the question of allowing those women who have neither the inclination nor the chance as things are to be completely racial, an outlet for their energies and ambitions with no restrictions put upon them because of sex. There is only the question of allowing a woman to choose which way she shall go, and to try if she so wishes to be both racial and individual. It is enough of a question. With patient irony Woolf mentions the amount of opinions men have set down in writing about women. In the libraries a list of books, very long and very varied, about women by men. In the libraries hardly any books at all about women by women. And none at all about men by women. The twentieth century, and still no philosophy written by women for women, except the grains of it that are to be found in fiction. The twentieth century, and still no solution to the great question raised by the feminists. What is a woman to do when she finds in herself the brain capacity of a man and the biological capacity of a woman? Which capacity must she starve, and what happens to the one if she starves the other, and what happens if she starves neither? Can she muster the strength in one short life with even fewer years in it of bloom for a woman than for a man to take to herself love and bear children, and at the same time hold a job and make money and progress intellectually? And can she in one short life create both with her body and with her mind? And further, if she can manage in some way to do this, what are its possible effects upon her nervous system, and its probable effects upon the nerves of her children? The baby and the book. The care a baby needs. The care a book needs, taking the book as the symbol of intellectual achievement.

So Woolf leaves the question. She has put it down with a profound and weary skepticism. It is old-world writing. It is old-world thinking. It is like Ecclesiastes. It is a mind that deals with a comparatively recent new question which knows

in itself that there is nothing really new. It is a mind that is
aware of the eternal changelessness of a matter relating far more
to biology than it relates to intellectuality. It is a big, fine,
cultivated mind that realizes that all things go back in the end,
and must go back, to the species, and that the story of the
species is a story that for its long, involved and varied history
changes very little or not at all. It is thought set down in
English that only could have come from an Englishwoman of
old culture, that accepts things as they happen to be biologically for women, and yet is aware of mind as something perhaps not quite so attached to biology as recent findings might
have us believe, and as the old beliefs accepted implicitly. So
she is interested in turning over in her mind the facts about
women, and what they may do, or may not do, with a situation
intellectually a little different from any situation of history so
far as the records show. She holds no brief one way or another,
except that, being a woman, she feels the weight of the biological law concerning women, and being an intellectual, she
wonders to what lengths the intellect of women may go given
a full chance. But, being more than a woman, and more than
an intellectual, an artiste, she puts down her thoughts in prose
that is tinged with the same sad glory that went into the prose
of Ecclesiastes. It is prose that comes out in its finish to be the
beginning of a philosophy written for women by women. Mary
Wollstonecraft ushered it in with all the vehement conviction
of the publicity agent, in a long book and long loud sentences,
elbowing the idea out to her time and the time ahead of her.
Virginia Woolf carries it forward with the quiet hesitancy of
the scholar and the exquisite fidelity of the artiste, in a short
book and beautifully measured phrases, turning the idea over
and over in her mind for her time and the time ahead of her.

It is a stopping-point in the School of Femininity, with one
thing definitely gained. Many women writing novels about
themselves. Many women thinking about womanhood. A few
women writing with artistry to place against the artistry of men,
and one woman writing with superb style about something not

altogether decided either in her own mind or in the minds of such women as remain normal and racial. It marks the beginning perhaps of a new stage in the story of women, with women putting their resentment behind them, yet remembering their subjection and feeling that because they are women they have something to say about themselves and about the race which is valuable because it is feminine. Thinking that it should be put beside what men say about themselves and the race, and wanting above everything else that the writing of women should come from women whose lives are relatively normal and full, and knowing the difficulty of that. For women know the capacity of women for concentration, and how concentration upon one aspect tends to wipe out all other aspects for them, and their intense fidelity to what they have undertaken. The more so if it be the racial duty. Women of the twentieth century with two things before them, and a decision to be made which perhaps can never be altogether decided. The baby. And the book.

THE END